Capital, the State and Labour

UNU World Institute for Development Economics Research (UNU/WIDER) was established by the United Nations University as its first research and training centre and started work in Helsinki, Finland in 1985. The principal purpose of the Institute is policy-oriented research on the main strategic issues of development and international cooperation, as well as on the interaction between domestic and global changes.

UNU World Institute for Development Economics Research (UNU/WIDER)
Katajanokanlaituri 6 B
FIN-00160 Helsinki, Finland

Capital, the State and Labour

A Global Perspective

Edited by

Juliet Schor

Director of Studies, Committee on Degrees in Women's Studies, Harvard University, US

Jong-Il You

Assistant Professor of Economics, University of Notre Dame, US Associate Professor of Economics, Ritsumeikan University, Kyoto, Japan

Edward Elgar
Aldershot, UK • Brookfield, US
United Nations University Press

Published jointly by
Edward Elgar Publishing Limited
Gower House
Croft Road
Aldershot
Hants GU11 3HR
UK

Edward Elgar Publishing Company
Old Post Road
Brookfield
Vermont 05036
US

United Nations University Press
5-53-70 Jingumae
Shibuya-ku, Tokyo 150
Japan

British Library Cataloguing in Publication Data
Capital, the State and Labour: Global
Perspective
    I. Schor, Juliet B. II. You, Jong-Il
    331

Library of Congress Cataloguing in Publication Data
Capital, the state, and labour : a global perspective / edited by
    Juliet Schor, Jong-Il You.
        p.   cm.
    Includes bibliographical references and index.
    1. Comparative industrial relations—Congresses. 2. Labor policy—
Congresses. 3. Capitalism—Congresses. 4. Labor economics—
Congresses. 5. Industrial policy—Congresses. 6. Economic policy—
Congresses. I. Schor, Juliet. II. You, Jong-Il, 1958–
HD6959.C37   1995
331—dc20   95–15673
                                                                        CIP

ISBN 1 85898 295 2

Available exclusively in Japan from United Nations University Press
UNU Press ISBN 92-808-0900-8

Printed and bound in Great Britain by
Biddles Ltd, Guildford and King's Lynn

Contents

List of illustrations		vii
List of contributors		xi
Acknowledgements		xii
Preface		xiii

1   Introduction: after the Golden Age   1
Juliet B. Schor and Jong-Il You

2   Capital–labour relations in OECD countries: from the Fordist
Golden Age to contrasted national trajectories   18
Robert Boyer

3   Cooperative employment relations and Japanese economic growth   70
William Lazonick

4   Changing capital–labour relations in South Korea   111
Jong-Il You

5   'New unionism' and the relations among capital, labour and
the state in Brazil   152
Edward J. Amadeo and José Márcio Camargo

6   Capital, the state and labour in Malaysia   185
K.S. Jomo

7   Capital, labour and the Indian state   238
J. Mohan Rao

8   After a dark Golden Age – Eastern Europe   282
Janos Köllö

9   Reform and system change in China   319
Carl Riskin

10   Capital–labour relations at the dawn of the twenty-first century   345
Alain Lipietz

Index   373

Illustrations

TABLES

2.1	The four pillars of the Fordist capital–labour relation	24
2.2	The national variants of Fordist compromise: a tentative typology for the Golden Age	30
2.3	Two strategies for adapting the capital–labour relation	35
2.4	Changing pattern in FCLR	36
2.5	Changing nominal wage formation: some stability tests for the period 1972–88	41
2.6	Economic trends affecting the Fordist capital–labour relation	45
2.7	The factors affecting workers' bargaining power	49
2.8	Changes in labour contracts and categories of workers involved	52
2.9	A taxonomy for alternative capital–labour relations	54
2.10	How is training organized?	56
2.11	Outline of a typology: four trajectories	61
4.1	Indicators of export-led growth	113
4.2	Transformation of employment structure, 1963–88	114
4.3	Employment structure by class of workers, 1963–88	115
4.4	Employment share of the formal sector, 1960–86	116
4.5	Capital intensity and labour-market characteristics, 1985	116
4.6	Percentage of social expenditure in central government expenditure	120
4.7	International comparison of work week and accident rate, 1985	121
4.8	System of remuneration for production workers, 1979	122
4.9	Index of productivity and wages in manufacturing, 1963–88	127
4.10	Indices of manufacturing industries	128
4.11	Employment adjustment during recession by size of firm	130
4.12	Capital–output ratio and capital–labour ratio in manufacturing, Korea and Japan, 1964–85	131
4.13	Union membership and unionization rate	132
4.14	Number of labour disputes, 1975–89	134
4.15	International comparison of stoppage incidence	135
4.16	Change in sexual/industrial composition of union membership	136

4.17 Structure of manufacturing industry by employment 137
4.18 *Chaebols'* shares in manufacturing, 1977–83 139
4.19 Agricultural terms of trade, 1976–86 139
4.20 Rates of unemployment and underemployment, 1963–86 140
4.21 Educational composition among entrants in manufacturing 141
4.22 Wage bargaining settlements by size of employer 144
4.23 Decomposition of real GDP growth rates 144
5.1 Composition of the labour force by sector in Brazil, 1986 155
5.2 Composition of the labour force by sector in São Paulo, 1986 155
5.3 Composition of the labour force by sector in the northeast, 1986 156
5.4 Distribution of employed workers by occupations in non-agricultural activities, Brazil, 1979–84 156
5.5 Average rates of growth of industrial output by sectors in Brazil, 1955–85 161
5.6 Labour turnover in the automotive industry, January–June 1977 163
5.7 On-the-job accidents in Brazil, 1969–74 165
5.8 Personal distribution of income in Brazil, 1960–76 167
5.9 Social security and health expenditures as percentage of GDP in Brazil, 1970–75 167
5.10 Number of strikes in Brazil, 1978–86 172
5.11 Relative wages in Brazil, 1980–86 178
5.12 Relative prices in Brazil, CPI components/WPI 180
6.1 Employment status by ethnic group and gender, 1947, 1957, 1970 and 1980 194
6.2 Peninsular Malaysia: employment status by ethnicity, 1947 and 1980 196
6.3 Peninsular Malaysia: percentage distribution of employment status by gender, 1947 and 1980 197
6.4 Peninsular Malaysia: employment by sector and ethnicity, 1970 and 1985 198
6.5 Peninsular Malaysia: labour force by ethnic group and activity, 1957, 1970 and 1984 200
6.6 Peninsular Malaysia: labour force by ethnic group and work category, 1957, 1970 and 1993 202
6.7 Peninsular Malaysia: trade union membership by ethnicity, 1949–86 210
6.8 Peninsular Malaysia: trade union membership by gender, 1952–88 211
6.9 Peninsular Malaysia: trade union membership by union size, 1962–88 213
6.10 Peninsular Malaysia: total trade union membership by union size, 1962–88 214

6.11 Peninsular Malaysia: trade unions by union size, 1962–88 215
6.12 Peninsular Malaysia: number of strikes, workers involved,
     working days lost, total union membership, percentage involved,
     1947–88 216
6.13 Peninsular Malaysia: percentage of strikes by industry,
     1947–88 218
6.14 Peninsular Malaysia: percentage of strikes by dispute issues,
     1953–88 220
6.15 Peninsular Malaysia: percentage of strikes by outcome when
     strike ended, 1953–88 222
7.1 Non-household manufacturing employment 242
7.2 Ownership structure of factories, 1978–79 243
7.3 Manufacturing employment growth, 1961–81 256
7.4 Real wages, salaries and workforce composition, 1960–82 257
7.5 The product wage in manufacturing, 1961–87 259
8.1 Work time, paid holidays and overtime rates, 1985 293
8.2 The composition of an average day of the year of adult men in
     selected countries 295
8.3 Selected indicators of East European countries 303
9.1 Comparison of characteristics of countries with per capita
     incomes of less than 150 yuan and more than 500 yuan 333

FIGURES

2.1 The Fordist hypothesis – summary 23
2.2 Two configurations for capital–labour restructuring 47
2.3 From Fordism to alternative capital–labour relations 57
5.1 Monthly rate of inflation 174
5.2 Data for the industrial sector in Brazil: productivity, real
     wage and product wage 175
5.3 Data for the industrial sector in Brazil: wage share and real
     wage/productivity 176
5.4 Data for the industrial sector in São Paulo: productivity, real
     wage and product wage 177
5.5 Data for the industrial sector in São Paulo: wage share and real
     wage/productivity 177
5.6 Relationship between the average wage and minimum wage in
     São Paulo 179
5.7 Coefficient of variation of wages in São Paulo 180
10.1 After-Fordist professional relations 352
10.2 Around Fordism 357

GRAPHS

2.1   Greater stability of the wage share after the Second World War   26
2.2   A general deindexing of nominal wage with respect to
       consumer price   39
2.3   An ambiguous evolution of the impact of unemployment on
       wages   42

Contributors

Edward J. Amadeo   Pontifícia Universidade Católica, Rio de Janeiro, Brazil

Robert Boyer   Centre d'Etudes Prospectives d'Economie Mathéma-tique Appliquées à la Planification (CEPREMAP), Paris, France

José Márcio Camargo   Pontifícia Universidade Católica, Rio de Janeiro, Brazil

K.S. Jomo   University of Malaya, Kuala Lumpur, Malaya

Janos Köllö   Hungarian Academy of Science, Budapest, Hungary

William Lazonick   University of Massachussetts, Lowell, US

Alain Lipietz   Centre d'Etudes Prospectives d'Economie Mathéma-tique Appliquees a la Planification (CEPREMAP), Paris, France

J. Mohan Rao   University of Massachussetts, Amherst, US

Carl Riskin   Queens College and Columbia University, New York, US

Juliet B. Schor   Harvard University, Cambridge, Massachusetts, US

Jong-Il You   University of Notre Dame, Indiana, US and Ritsumeikan University, Kyoto, Japan

Acknowledgements

Many people contributed to this volume. Our greatest debt is to Steve Marglin who was instrumental in both formulating the project and giving advice and comments throughout. We would also like to thank the following people for their advice and comments on earlier drafts of these papers or their participation in the conference at which these papers were originally presented: Alice Amsden, Tariq Banuri, Sanjay Baru, Sukhamoy Chakravarty, Susan Collins, Ronald Dore, Andrew Glyn, Steve Herzenberg, Jukka Pekkarinen, Michael Piore, Terry Sicular and Ajit Singh. The authors would also like to thank the following people for help in arranging research trips or other research assistance: Y.K. Alagh, Neil Blackadder, John Boi, Nicole Fratellini, Janet Gonzalez, Thomas Lowitt, Vadim Radaiev, Sandor Richter and N.R. Sheth.

Preface

Throughout the twentieth century, relations between capital, state and labour have been considered as vitally important issues. They have had a significant influence on economic development and political stability. At the end of the century, these relations are changing again. The dismantling of the welfare state, the economic difficulties, the technological progress, the new industrial and occupational patterns influence all countries. These developments in different regions and industries also have specific patterns. A fundamental question of the future is: Can capital–labour relations be better harmonized? Can the state play a useful role in this process?

The development of capital–labour relations studied in this book points strongly towards a kind of 'discontinuity' which has become apparent mainly during the past ten to fifteen years or so and coincided – interestingly, but perhaps accidentally – with the end of the Cold War period. In fact, one of the main messages of this book is that, even in capital–labour relations, the world has arrived at a turning point where old practices and approaches have lost much of their appeal and potential for success.

As explained in the introductory chapter by Professor Juliet B. Schor and Dr Jong-Il You, this book is the result of a research effort started at UNU/WIDER in 1985 by a group of economists with the aim to develop an alternative macroeconomic view of the development processes. In earlier publications resulting from this research, the UNU/WIDER macroeconomic group dealt with the rise and fall of the Golden Age, as it was called by the authors. The Golden Age was the successful period of continued growth and high employment covering the two decades after the Second World War.[1] The second book focused on the policies that followed this Golden Age period.[2]

The authors have concluded that the period of Taylorism (based on the detailed division of work) together with Fordism (separation of the planning and designing of the work from its actual performance) has now lost much of its dynamism and capacity to enhance productivity. Various innovative ways to organize production are emerging but no obvious common alternatives have been discovered yet. The Japanese model has been studied as one of the successful alternatives on which future developments could be based. But even this is still uncertain, since it will require new attitudes, as is argued by William Lazonick who writes in this volume about the Japanese relations (Chapter 3).

xiii

Indeed, one of the main conclusions of this book is that predictions regarding the future development of capital–labour relations are veiled by uncertainty. Capital–labour relations are one of the fundamental issues in the economy, and the development of these relations is of great interest not only to managers and workers but also to policy makers. The future development of labour relations deserves further research which would take into account the experiences of the different countries and regions and which would also combine the socio-economic, technological, institutional and policy dimensions of the changes.

Mihály Simai
Director
UNU/WIDER

NOTES

1   *The Golden Age of Capitalism: Reinterpreting the Postwar Experience*, edited by Stephen Marglin and Juliet Schor, Oxford University Press, 1990.
2   *Economic Liberalization No Panacea: The Experiences of Latin America and Asia*, edited by Tariq Banuri, Oxford University Press, 1991.

1. Introduction: after the Golden Age

Juliet B. Schor and Jong-Il You

I A BIT OF HISTORY – THE WIDER MACROECONOMICS POLICY PROJECT AND THE ORIGINS OF THIS VOLUME

In the summer of 1985, a group of about fifteen economists gathered in Helsinki at the newly established World Institute for Development Economics Research (WIDER) to begin a research project on alternative macroeconomic policy. Its members were from a variety of analytic traditions (Keynesian, Marxist, regulationist, development) and a variety of countries (the United States, the UK, France, India, Brazil, Chile, Japan). We were working to create a synthesis of alternative traditions (especially Marx and Keynes). We hoped to become a new voice in the global policy debate, articulating a more democratic, more humane, and more successful approach than the standard prescriptions of the World Bank and the IMF.

The first round of research was presented at a conference in the summer of 1986 and ultimately led to two volumes, *The Golden Age of Capitalism: Reinterpreting the Postwar Experience*,[1] *Economic Liberalization No Panacea: The Experiences of Latin America and Asia*.[2] The research had been motivated in large part by the belief that after the war, the world economy had experienced a 'Golden Age' of high growth rates, low unemployment and rapid growth in consumption per head, but that the conditions underlying that Golden Age had broken down in the 1970s. We were interested in understanding why the breakdown had occurred and in identifying the conditions for a resumption of growth, albeit with a new institutional structure.

The research yielded a rich historical and theoretical analysis in which the role of relations between employers and workers (or 'capital' and 'labour') turned out to be pivotal for the success and then decline of the Golden Age. In particular, the analysis highlighted relations *in the production process*. During the Golden Age, 'Taylorization' proceeded rapidly, in the USA as a continuation of prewar trends, and elsewhere due to the adoption of the successful American methods. By Taylorization, we mean the separation of conception (i.e. design and engineering) and execution of work; a highly fragmented division of labour;

uniformity in production methods (the so-called 'one best way'); and the dominance of machine-pacing and rule-directed bureaucratic systems, in contrast to the knowledge and authority of production workers themselves.[3]

Our use of the term Taylorization (or Taylorism) is not meant to imply that we believe the *particular* project of Frederick Winslow Taylor succeeded. That project was far more ambitious and politically complex than what we have described as Taylorism, and we do not believe that it did achieve its aims of eliminating conflict between worker and employer, or 'scientifically' determining production methods. Rather, we mean to suggest that the essential spirit of Taylor survived, especially in the breakdown of production into small tasks and the separation of conception and execution. Taylorism was exported first from America to Europe, just after the war, and subsequently to much of the rest of the world. As the papers in this volume suggest, Taylorism was perhaps the one part of the postwar institutional structure which was common to industrialized and industrializing countries and to socialist and capitalist countries.[4]

In any case, developments within the production process were at the core of the decline of the Golden Age. Our research identified two main changes in the advanced capitalist countries. First, the possibilities for continued Taylorization were exhausted, through both 'extensive' (bringing additional people into wage labour) and 'intensive' Taylorization (alterations in existing production processes). This showed up in productivity slowdowns in various countries. Second, in the late 1960s, worker resistance developed, particularly in Western Europe. By the early 1980s, the search for alternatives to Taylorism was well underway in North America and Western Europe. This led to the period of great enthusiasm for Japanese management.

Once the WIDER group had completed its initial research, it was clear that a more detailed look at capital–labour relations was needed. In the advanced capitalist countries (ACCs), we wanted to investigate the experimentation and diversity in capital–labour relations which were occurring. We also wanted to take another look at the Japanese case, given its centrality in current thinking. And in the rest of the world, large-scale changes were underway. The first round of research[5] had argued for the importance of labour market institutions and the production process in understanding the relative performances of Latin American and Asian NICs (newly industrializing countries). These factors had been neglected in the macro-development literature on comparative performance (which placed such heavy emphasis on exchange rates, tariff policies, the degree of government intervention, and the like). The next step was to look in detail at how capital–labour relations had functioned in these countries through the Golden Age period and its decline.

The 1980s was also a fascinating period for another reason: capital–labour relations were in flux almost everywhere. The turmoil in North America and Western Europe was well known. But South Korea and Brazil were also in a period of rapid change in production relations. So too were Eastern Europe and China, as were countries in South and Southeast Asia. The great exception was Japan, to whom many others were looking for an answer.

These then were the questions which motivated the current volume. What were the histories of capital–labour relations in the newly industrializing countries which had led to the current turmoil? Where were Western Europe and North America headed? Why was the socialist bloc, where economic dynamics were so different, undergoing a common experience? How was Japan managing to avoid the pressures faced elsewhere? Were capital–labour relations converging around the world? Or was the simultaneous eruption of change merely coincidental?

II ORIGINS OF THE TURMOIL IN CAPITAL–LABOUR RELATIONS

The natural explanation for the simultaneity of change is global economic factors. Not only is there turmoil in capital–labour relations but also in other important aspects of the institutional environment, such as the role of the state in economic management, the extent and nature of international competition and international monetary and financial relations. This suggests that the simultaneous changes in capital–labour relations are but a part of the general institutional turmoil in the global economic order. The origins of this turmoil lie in the 1970s, and the end of the Golden Age.

During the Golden Age, the memory of the Great Depression receded as the advanced capitalist countries were able to achieve macroeconomic stability, near-full employment and high rates of growth. One would be mistaken to consider this remarkable achievement as the miracle of free markets. Rather, it was a result of a set of institutional (as opposed to market) mechanisms which made up a coherent regime of accumulation which we shall call 'Fordist'. At the core of the Fordist regime are the Fordist capital–labour relations which struck a deal between employers and workers in terms of how to organize production and how the fruits of production were to be distributed. Fordist production methods refer to the deepening of the Taylorist separation of conception from execution and the detailed division of labour achieved through the use of machine-paced control and special-purpose machines. Under the Fordist compromise workers accepted Taylorization and the authority of management in exchange for a certain degree of job security (seniority provisions) and increases in real wages commensurate with productivity gains (productivity sharing) institutionalized by collective bargaining. The coherence of this model lies in the fact that it realized productivity gains based on increasing returns to scale and that the productivity sharing ensured steady growth in consumption of standardized products which was necessary to realize the productivity potential. The robustness of the Fordist capital–labour relations was bolstered by an activist state committed to providing a social safety net and maintaining high levels of employment and capacity utilization through Keynesian demand-management policies. These domestic institutional arrangements functioned well within the stable international order based on American hegemony which permitted relatively expansionary Keynesian policies everywhere.

The Golden Age also saw a significant drive towards industrialization in many developing countries, especially the NICs, as they embraced the ideals of the Fordist production–consumption pattern in the name of modernization and national economic independence. Prosperity in the ACCs and the concomitant growth in world trade provided an auspicious ground on which the developing world could pursue industrialization to break away from its colonial past. In important respects the developing countries were following the cues from the ACCs. Not only did they try to copy the ACCs' production methods, with Taylorization of the labour process and all. They also wholeheartedly accepted that the state was to play a leading role in economic development, although they differed on precisely what role the state should play. However, capital–labour relations in the developing countries were a far cry from the full-fledged Fordism of the ACCs, reflecting vastly different economic and political contexts in which elements of Fordism were introduced. In most of the developing world the modern industrial sector that was built on imported (semi-) Fordist technologies employed only a small fraction of the workforce with a preponderant share of employment in the traditional rural sector and the urban informal sector. Moreover, the Fordist social compromise in terms of productivity sharing, job security and other social provisions was largely absent. Therefore, even in the most advanced of the developing countries (i.e. NICs) capital–labour relations represented at best a highly incomplete Fordism. However, the South is not a homogeneous entity and in this region capital–labour relations exhibited great diversity.

This is not the place to engage in an extended debate on why the Golden Age ended. Suffice it to note that the Fordist regime of accumulation entered a crisis in the late 1960s on the domestic front and that attempts to boost economic growth through Keynesian policies were running into deep trouble in the 1970s. The onset of the crisis of Fordism in the ACCs was marked by the social unrest in the late 1960s. Near-full employment and the extensive social safety net reduced the cost of job loss and therefore workers became more militant. They were able to secure real wage increases above productivity gains, while exerting less effort. The result was a decline in the profit share and a slowdown of productivity growth. These problems were not cured by subsequent increases in unemployment, however. The pressures on the profit share intensified with increasingly fierce international competition and rising raw material prices, and the slowdown in productivity growth continued as Taylorist methods ran into their limits.

In the production process, workers were resisting Taylorism, which itself was not suitable for rapidly responding to the increasing volatility of international markets and the growing appetite of consumers for differentiated products. Nor was Taylorism well disposed to exploit the possibilities of the new information technologies which have much greater potential when utilized by highly skilled and cooperative workers. These limitations manifested themselves more and more acutely in a changing competitive environment as the other elements of the Golden Age institutional arrangements unravelled.

The initial response of the ACCs to the crisis of Fordism was the Keynesian expansionary policy, with the United States in the lead. However, due to the breakdown of the Bretton-Woods system in the early 1970s, and the two OPEC oil shocks, inflation accelerated even as economic growth was slowing and unemployment rising. Beginning with the appointment of Paul Volcker at the Federal Reserve Board in 1979, disinflation became the paramount policy objective and macroeconomic policies in the ACCs turned largely restrictive.

International trade was no longer a positive-sum game in this environment: it became a battlefield in which one country fought another for a greater share of the markets, which were growing all too inadequately to employ willing hands. The situation was further complicated by the rise of the NICs and the bloated Japanese trade surplus. Moreover, huge speculative movements of capital led to wild swings in exchange rates. Instead of equilibrating current balances and thereby permitting national policy autonomy, these gyrations only added uncertainty and volatility to international markets. It was in these circumstances that all the basic Fordist institutions came under attack in the name of 'supply-side' economics: the Keynesian principle of demand management first, the welfare state next and, inevitably, the Fordist capital–labour relations.

In the South the end of the Golden Age came in the early 1980s with the onset of the debt crisis, which was triggered by a huge increase in the interest rate and the world recession following the turn to monetary restrictiveness mentioned above. The troubles of the 1970s in the ACCs had not had much impact on the South due to global Keynesian policies and the recycling of the oil dollar. To be sure, there had been growing disenchantment with the nature of economic growth in the South, as income distribution deteriorated and poverty and unemployment continued amidst growth in most of the developing countries. (East Asian NICs were the well-publicized exception.) The benefits of growth were not widely shared, in part due to the highly incomplete nature of the Fordism introduced in these countries. Nonetheless, the 1970s were a decade of ascendancy rather than setback as far as the South was concerned: economic growth continued, Vietnam defeated the United States, OPEC successfully raised oil prices, and the New International Economic Order was on the agenda. With the onset of the debt crisis these trends were dramatically reversed. Most of the economies in Africa and Latin America collapsed. US military might was reimposed on 'aberrant' Southern countries. Oil and other raw materials prices declined precipitously. The very countries which had been calling for the New International Economic Order now were forced to implement IMF–World Bank-sponsored adjustment programmes. In the name of monetary stabilization, liberalization and privatization these programmes sought to roll back the interventionist state and impose free-market ideology. Public spending was cut, often with tragic consequences, and resources were redeployed to export activities.

Pressures on capital–labour relations in the South came mainly from two contradictory forces. The first was the equity-orientated critique of development which was taken up by organized labour in the developing countries. As industrialization progressed in the South, wage–labour relations spread and the industrial working class grew in numbers and became an increasingly important potential social actor. A social crisis was thus developing in countries where the fruits of economic growth escaped the wage labourers who had also been deprived of their traditional economic protection in the villages. Even in countries such as South Korea and Taiwan, where trickle-down worked fairly well because of the earlier land reforms, a political crisis was developing as workers began to challenge their political disempowerment and lack of social protection. The equity-orientated critique of development corresponded to the need to develop a broad-based domestic market (except of course in highly open and small trading-post economies) for sustained growth. This force tended to push capital–labour relations in the direction of a more complete Fordism – the original dream of modernization, no doubt with big regional variations. A smooth gradual progress towards Fordism, however, was not in store for most of the South. The debt crisis-induced imposition of the free-market ideology and the roll-back of the state created a contradictory second force in the 1980s and precipitated turmoil in capital–labour relations. Indeed, the Golden Age was over. The necessity to enlarge export earnings, the race to attract more foreign capital, the cuts in social spending and the swelling ranks of the openly unemployed on top of the large 'disguised' unemployment, all exerted huge pressures on what little institutional protection workers had enjoyed. The social crisis deepened and, in many countries, exploded.

III   OVERVIEW OF THE VOLUME

The volume opens with a paper by Robert Boyer on the state of capital–labour relations in the OECD – the breakdown of the Fordist capital–labour relations and the search for new models. Boyer identifies 'four pillars of the Fordist capital–labour relation' – the intensification of Taylorism; productivity sharing; interrelative or connective bargaining and stable wage differentials; and a Keynesian and social welfarist state. In an advance over the existing literature on Fordism, he rejects the idea of a homogeneous Fordist model, proposing instead a typology of what he terms 'one model, many national brands'. For example, the United States and France are found to be more Taylorist with respect to the firm-level division of labour, while Sweden, Germany and Japan have stronger craft traditions. Similarly, the extent of inflation protection and productivity sharing varies by country, as does the degree to which labour-market conditions (especially the rate of unemployment) affect wage determination. Other dimensions of difference are the extent and type of labour mobility, the mix of private and public consumption, the degree of state involvement in economic development and the degree of labour-market centralization. Boyer identifies typical Fordism (United States, France); flawed Fordism (United Kingdom); flexible Fordism (Germany, Japan); mismatched Fordism (Italy); and corporatist or social democratic Fordism (Sweden, Austria).

The unravelling of the Fordist system entailed the beginning of major changes in capital–labour relations. Central to this unravelling was a drop in the rate of growth of productivity across the OECD quite generally. The productivity slowdown in turn put pressure on other aspects of capital–labour relations, such as wage formation, the degree of centralization, and the extent of welfare state spending. In Europe and the United States, the belief that market 'rigidities', (especially in labour) were the cause of the decline in productivity growth and profitability became widespread. In the 1980s, countries increasingly retreated from the 'four pillars' and the environment shifted dramatically in favour of business and against labour. At first, two clear patterns emerged – a more adversarial one in countries such as the United States and France; and a corporatist response in Sweden and Austria, where the state initially managed to preserve employment.[6]

During the 1980s, the search for new models of labour relations was carried out in earnest throughout the OECD. While a return to the *status quo ante* still had some advocates, the far more common view was that the world had changed fundamentally, and that history was not reversible. Any successful new model would have to deal with the more internationally competitive environment facing even large countries, the declining importance of manufacturing, and the growth of 'flexible specialization', i.e. customization in consumer demand, as well as 'flex spec' in workers – the increase in the number of women workers, demands for more varied work schedules, and so on. This was the context in which interest in Japanese management flourished, and the debate on 'flexibility' in Europe took place.

The area of skill formation and workplace control has been at the centre of these debates. Boyer puts the matter starkly: is the direction of change for machines to gain control over workers or for workers to gain control over machines? That is, an intensification of Taylorism or a rejection of it? Using productivity growth as the measure, the most successful of the OECD countries were those least closely associated with classic Taylorism and most willing to train workers and foster skill levels. Second, there are the issues of job security, collective representation and remuneration. Here again we find a spectrum, from competitive environments with low unionization, no job tenure or explicit productivity sharing, to the Social Democratic models (Kalmarian, Uddavallian models) which combine high levels of training and skill development with employment security, rent sharing and collective representation. Boyer identifies cases in all the cells of the skills/remuneration matrix and ends with a certain amount of agnosticism about what the future holds. This issue is visited again in the concluding paper by Lipietz (Chapter 10).

In Boyer's typology Japan is seen as a hybrid case, which bypassed Taylorism in favour of high levels of skill formation and training. Other dimensions of the Japanese case deviate from classic Taylorism, such as employment security, a productivity-based bonus system, and a limited welfare state. Lazonick extends this analysis. A central question is how Japan has been able to combine the permanent employment system with such high productivity growth. In the cases of Eastern Europe, China, India and also parts of the OECD, job security had a strong negative impact on labour effort and productivity performance. By contrast, in Japan, employment security has been an integral part of the system of labour relations. Japan is also anomalous in that full employment did not result in exploding wage demands and high strike activity, as in other places.

Lazonick characterizes the Japanese system as 'cooperative'. Cooperation was reproduced by high productivity growth and the sharing of gains by employers. Japanese unions were able to assess corporations' financial ability, thereby reducing suspicions and strife over the extent of gain sharing. Productivity performance was maintained by a process of continual upgrading of skills and employer willingness to allow workers to learn many aspects of production, as well as by extremely long working hours and a high pace of work. In the United States, management ultimately 'took skills off the shop floor' because they were unable to create cooperative employment relations in which they could trust production workers. In Britain, management had to 'leave skills on the shop floor' because they were unable to break the knowledge monopolies of craft workers; this resulted in a stalemate and deteriorating productivity performance. In Japan, by contrast, management 'put skills on the shop floor', and thereby achieved phenomenal productivity performance.

Lazonick likens the Japanese situation to that of the United States in the early twentieth century: an ascending country undergoing rapid technological and organizational change in which employers buy labour peace with rising real wages. This is a key point, suggesting that the Japanese model is difficult if not impossible to replicate in declining nations.

This characterization of the Japanese situation is not without its critics. It has been argued that the much vaunted skills of the Japanese production worker are more illusory than real, and that the Japanese workplace is not significantly less Taylorized than US or European workplaces. It is argued that job rotation moves workers through a series of jobs which involve only very simple and menial tasks. Furthermore, some critics see Japanese cooperation as cooptation, arguing that Japanese workers are unable to exercise significant resistance to exploitative conditions such as long working hours and a high pace of work, which has been dubbed 'management by stress'.[7] While the critics sound a useful cautionary note to Western enthusiasm for the Japanese model, their story also leaves some important questions unanswered. If Japanese workers are really so powerless, why has management granted such large real wage increases? And why does full employment not have the adverse effects on productivity and profitability that we see in the West?

The second section of the volume contains three papers on NICs – South Korea, Brazil and Malaysia. (India is sometimes considered a NIC, but the capital–labour relations in the core industries are more like the quasi-socialist model of Eastern Europe and China.) Although the history of industrialization in these countries dates back to around the turn of the century, the rapid industrialization that earned them the title of 'NIC' began in the 1960s in South Korea and Brazil and in the 1970s in Malaysia. Jong-Il You, Edward Amadeo and José Camargo, and Jomo all emphasize the fact that industrialization in these countries proceeded with Taylorization of the production processes, but the Fordist social compromise was conspicuous by its absence.

The lack of the Fordist social compromise in the NICs is not hard to explain. They lacked strong independent labour unions and powerful working-class politics that could obtain such a social compromise. In all three countries the state suppressed independent unionism. The right to strike was severely curtailed and the dissident labour leaders were routinely persecuted by the state. In both South Korea and Malaysia labour repression has a long history dating back to the Japanese and the British colonial rules. In the post-independence period labour repression continued as the governments of South Korea and Malaysia regarded organized labour as a threat to both the political stability and the investment climate. The Brazilian case is somewhat different. During the period of 'state corporatism' based on the Vargas labour legislation (from the 1940s until the military coup in 1964) organized labour was not repressed but coopted and made dependent on the state. The military government then undermined the paternalistic measures, reinforced authoritarian features of labour laws and embarked on a ruthless suppression of organized labour.

The broadly similar pattern of capital–labour relations in the NICs should not blind us to the significant differences reflecting different historical, political and economic–structural conditions among these countries. South Korea consciously emulated the Japanese model of economic development in its quest to catch up with the former colonial master. The Japanese influence in Korean capital–labour relations is seen in enterprise unionism and attempts to involve the workers in the industrial learning process in some core industries, although the job security inherent in the Japanese 'permanent employment' system was distinctively lacking. Another important feature which sets South Korea apart from Brazil and Malaysia is the extraordinary growth in real wages and the increase in the wage share of income over time. Unlike in most developing countries rapid industrial growth quickly translated into a tightening labour market, since land reform in the 1950s reduced the pool of 'unlimited labour supplies' and rural incomes were rising steadily on account of agricultural productivity growth and the state's price-support programme for rice. The Brazilian case exhibits a contrasting picture. Collective bargaining took place at the regional and occupational level with no union representation at the enterprise level. The principle of Taylorism was implemented without modification. And the military government took away wage-bargaining rights from the unions and pursued a policy of wage repression, causing a sharp decline in the wage share and a tremendous concentration of the distribution of income. Malaysia presents yet another story. Malaysia seems to have developed rather confrontational industrial relations early on and a wage-bargaining system at the national or regional level in some industries. With a succession of anti-labour policies, however, the unions became more and more docile. The spurt of export-orientated industrialization since the 1970s led to Taylorization of workplaces. While the plantation sector is still very important and there are ethnic divisions within the working class, Malaysia does not have a large 'reserve army' as Brazil does. Therefore, rapid industrial growth tightened the labour market and real wages grew in industry (but not in plantations) despite the large inflow of immigrant labour. But the wage share of income has actually declined.

The South Korean and the Brazilian papers argue that fundamental changes in capital–labour relations are occurring. Malaysian capital–labour relations, while not exactly in turmoil, are by no means tranquil. Following the democratic opening in the political system in 1987, South Korean workers rose up and engulfed the nation in an unprecedented strike wave. Since then organized labour has gained a measure of independence and strength, with union membership increasing rapidly. The labour mobilization forced the South Korean government to re-examine not only its labour policies but its priorities in economic policy in general. However tentatively, it has been implementing many elements of the Fordist compromise such as softening its anti-labour stance and instituting minimum wage law, a national pension system and national health insurance.

The government plans to introduce unemployment insurance in the near future. Furthermore, as the unions gained large wage increases, domestic consumption replaced exports as the principal engine of growth.

The democratic opening in Brazil came much earlier, in 1975, but the transition to democracy was gradual and prolonged. As in South Korea democratization led to reactivation of the labour movement and a sharp increase in strike activity, and the draconian labour laws of the military government became unenforceable. Thus an institutional vacuum reigned in industrial relations until the adoption of the new Constitution in 1988, in which the reactivated labour movement was able to bring about important changes in the character of capital–labour relations in the formal sector. The 'new unionism' broke with the 'state corporatist' legacies by creating national union centres and the Party of the Workers (PT), to strengthen itself as an independent organizational and political force on the one hand, and by creating workers' councils at the plant level and decentralizing wage bargaining to strengthen its ties with the rank and file on the other. Organized labour, thus invigorated, was able to secure basic labour rights as well as to protect the real incomes of its members in a hyper-inflationary environment set off by the debt crisis. However, a large proportion of the workers remained in the informal sector and they bore the brunt of the structural adjustments. Brazil has yet to stabilize its distributional struggles and the hyperinflation they generate, and yet to forge a consensus on the developmental strategy.

In both South Korea and Brazil, therefore, the political changes have triggered labour activism and subsequent changes in capital–labour relations. Ultimately, there was a contradiction in the model of 'Taylorization without the Fordist compromise' in the sense that it created a growing industrial working class with increasing resources (education as well as incomes) and aspirations while subjecting them to oppressive working conditions and leaving them politically disenfranchised and economically insecure. Industrial conflict was bound to arise, therefore, as soon as the lid was lifted. In South Korea, You argues, the political changes that led to weakening of labour repression were themselves caused in part by increasing labour unrest. In Brazil, where organized labour and the working-class politics are much stronger, Amadeo and Camargo argue, they have played an important role in shaping the course of democratization.

The big difference between South Korea and Brazil is in the economic conditions of the 1980s. Although both countries were hit by the debt crisis, South Korea was able to come out of it sooner and to maintain higher rates of growth during the decade than Brazil. Therefore, the rise in social conflict under the weight of the debt crisis was relatively short-lived in South Korea whereas it is still afflicting Brazil. With the easy availability of surplus, the South Korean economy has accommodated a turn towards a more complete Fordism, with a touch of the Japanese model. However, in Brazil, as economic difficulties continue, the future direction of capital–labour relations remains clouded.

Malaysia has maintained political stability since 1971. Accordingly, there has not been a drastic change in capital–labour relations, as in South Korea and Brazil. Even though the success of export-orientated industrialization expanded the ranks of the industrial workers and tightened up the labour market by the late 1970s, the unions became more docile, with few exceptions, as they became more fragmented and were unable to cope with increasing restrictions on union organizing and other anti-labour government policies. In the 1980s this trend continued with a new twist. Jomo argues that the labour policy component of the 'Look East' policy adopted by the Mahathir Mohamad government, whose ostensible objective was to promote Japanese-style cooperative capital–labour relations, mainly served to weaken organized labour by encouraging the formation of in-house unions to replace troublesome unions already in existence. No genuine effort was made to imitate the full scope of the Japanese model. The emphasis on the work ethic and loyalty to the company without job security is reminiscent of the Factory Saemaul Movement in South Korea (You, this volume p. 122). Jomo notes that job security and income security decreased in the 1980s. He further argues that greater flexibility in the labour market, including the casualization of employment, is linked to the broader industrial restructuring in East Asia in which Malaysia has become an important recipient of foreign investment by the more advanced East Asian countries. If the South Korean and Brazilian experiences are any guide, however, the high rates of growth in Malaysia will eventually translate into a resurgence of labour activism.

The final three papers in the volume look at the cases of India, Eastern Europe and China. The NICs have been described as having adopted Taylorism without the Fordist compromise. This also characterizes the industrial sectors in Eastern Europe, India and China. One difference is that it was the Soviet Union which played a large role in the export of Taylorist methods, rather than the 'productivity missions' of the United States. And Taylorism was considerably more 'incomplete' in these areas than in the OECD and the NICs. In Eastern Europe, for example, Janos Köllö explains that production technologies never had the opportunity to perform as expected, on account of widespread input shortages, shortages of spare parts, inferiority of inputs and the like. The result was that workers had to exercise high levels of ingenuity and creativity to keep these production processes going, so that the separation of conception and execution was continuously eroded, as was the minute division of labour. In Köllö's words, 'the East-Taylorian factory shows distinctive features. The special kind of "job enrichment" … eroded formal rules, made the use of scientific management almost completely irrelevant and [gave] bargaining power to large groups of workers' (Köllö, this volume, p. 290).

In the Chinese case, Taylorist methods encountered a more direct resistance. As Carl Riskin describes, Taylorism was introduced by the Soviets in the 1950s, in the heavy-industry sector. It replaced the immediate postwar 'East China system' of collective management by committee, rank and file participation, and minimal wage differentials. By international standards, Taylorism was fairly widely adopted in China – at the peak in 1956, 42 per cent of industrial workers were on piece rates. By the late 1950s, the rank and file had been effectively disenfranchised in production, in return for economic benefits and security. But Mao was always opposed to Taylorist production methods, and the Cultural Revolution was in large part an attempt to change the political nature of the factory. Although the Cultural Revolution ultimately failed to sustain a permanent change in production relations, pure Taylorism never triumphed.

Mohan Rao argues that the Indian industrial sector is also basically Taylorist, characterized by 'hierarchy, minimal worker participation and separation of knowledge from execution'. However, he argues that 'managerial control of the work process has rested on insecure foundations'. (Rao, this volume, p. 244). It has foundered on employee resistance and a measure of autonomy. Köllö, and to a lesser extent Riskin, have identified a similar situation. Köllö uses the term 'everyday power' to describe the ways in which workers have been able to retain 'small freedoms' from managerial control. Everyday power is 'hidden, informal and possessed by small groups or individuals' (Köllö, this volume, p. 284). As he explains, it is not based on law, but custom. Everyday power is something which workers in all economies have, but its extent has been notable in these three countries.

Everyday power can be understood as a product of another feature of these production systems – job security. In Eastern Europe, chronic labour shortages made management reluctant to dismiss unproductive or disobedient workers, because their ability to replace them was not assured. Disincentives against workers' quitting were small, as the labour market was systematically biased towards the employee. In India and China there was no situation of economy-wide labour shortage. Rather, job security was particular to industrial sector workers. It resulted more from workers' ability to protect their privileged positions and led to labour immobility in the industrial sector. In the large-firm sector in India, for example, job security resulted from a combination of union power and legislative protection. Dismissing permanent employees for disciplinary or economic reasons was either impossible or prohibitively expensive. Firms frequently operated with excess labour. In China, urban industrial workers were basically given jobs for life – the so-called 'iron rice bowl' policy. In return for this lifetime job security, they forfeited the right to change jobs and locations. Finally, in all three cases systems of remuneration evolved to divorce pay from performance. In China, the counterpart of the iron rice bowl was egalitarian pay ('everyone eating from the same big pot'). In India, incentive-based wages were eroded in favour of cost-of-living adjustments and in the public sector there was ongoing pressure for wage uniformity irrespective of performance. Similarly, in Eastern Europe, pay was not incentive-based.

The basic configuration in Eastern Europe, India and China then was this: Taylorism plus job security plus the independence of performance from remuneration. As Köllö, Rao and Riskin recount, this combination proved disastrous. Workers had no income-based incentives to spur their performance. They exercised everyday power against management in order to further their own ends. For example, Eastern Europe workers would deliberately slow down production during regular shifts in order to get more highly paid overtime hours. Taylorist technologies spawned alienation which, in combination with everyday power, led to serious problems of low productivity and indiscipline. Eventually, this system of capital–labour relations failed dramatically, contributing to stagnation. Recent developments can be seen as a reaction to this failure. In thinking about why India, Eastern Europe and China were unable to incorporate job security and relatively egalitarian wage structures into a successful production system, one is inevitably led to the Japanese case, where job security has been compatible with outstanding productivity growth. Lazonick and Boyer's analyses suggest that the combination of skill enhancement and gain sharing are the keys to the Japanese success.

IV   THE CURRENT ENVIRONMENT

The final chapter of the volume is a synthetic and visionary piece by Alain Lipietz, 'Capital–labour relations at the dawn of the twenty-first century'. Lipietz sees the current environment as essentially a choice between two paths – the neo-Taylorist/liberal-flexibility model and a paradigm of negotiated involvement represented in its fullest form by Kalmarianism. Although he does not engage in a strictly predictive exercise, Lipietz does discuss the 'menu of possibilities' among the components of a mode of regulation, ruling out infeasible combinations and unlikely trajectories. In broad outline, he argues that liberal flexibility/neo-Taylorism in one incarnation or another now appears likely for most of the cases analysed in the volume. Writing in 1990, he predicted that Eastern Europe is the area most likely to go in a fully neo-Taylorist direction, which to date has certainly been borne out. This direction is also most probable for industrializing countries, notably China and India, where Soviet-style development is now dead forever, and liberalization is the order of the day. Lipietz sees a process of what he has elsewhere called primitive (or 'bloody') Taylorization,[8] that is, targeted export-orientated industrialization with extremely high rates of exploitation of labour and low technological sophistication.

Malaysia is the purest case of primitive Taylorization in this volume. Primitive Taylorization is also well entrenched in China and India, and likely to continue. Brazil and Korea, the highly successful NICs, are the possible exceptions. In Brazil, primitive Taylorization has been transcended, largely on the strength of the domestic market. At present the situation has not resolved itself between a full-fledged move to classical Fordism and the alternative, neo-Taylorist/liberal flexibility. A backsliding into primitive Taylorization also remains a possibility. South Korea, on the other hand, seems to be evolving toward some variant of the Japanese model. Democratization plus the absence of a debt constraint make this likely.

V A FINAL NOTE ON DEVELOPMENTS SINCE THE COMPLETION OF THE PROJECT

The papers in this volume were written between 1989 and 1991. Since then the world has changed a great deal. But we do not believe it has vitiated the analyses contained here. To the contrary. The papers shed a great deal of light on the developments since then. And some of them seem quite prescient. Köllö's paper in particular reads as a brilliant exposé of why the system of Eastern Europe was bound to collapse. And he does correctly predict 'unpredictable' political developments.

The concluding analysis of Lipietz raises the prospect of proliferating neo-Taylorist paradigms. This has occurred with a speed and force which we did not expect. The spectacular backdrop has been the collapse of socialism virtually everywhere. The more everyday events have been the US recession beginning in 1990, the bursting of the Japanese bubble, the stalling of the drive towards European unity and the eventual descent of Western Europe into recession. The effect of these developments has been to plunge much of the world into a kind of 'economic pessimism'. Pessimism is now very prevalent in Europe, Japan and the United States. The spectre of a globalized economy and the 'hyperspeed' of technological change have accelerated the momentum of the neo-Taylorist/liberal-flexibility paradigm. This is occurring even in Northern Europe: Germany recently cut welfare benefits for the first time. And in Sweden, the collapse of confidence in the social democratic model has been dramatic.

But is liberal flexibility the last word? Or, to use the catchword of the day, have we reached 'the end of the history' of labour relations and macroeconomic management? We think not. The current enthusiasm for these post or 'after' Fordisms fails to recognize their drawbacks and inconsistencies. What firms gain in the short term, they may lose in the long. Perhaps most obvious is the dilemma of training and skill enhancement in a liberal-flexible environment.

It is widely recognized that new technologies require higher levels of computer literacy and worker discretion than the mass production, dedicated machinery of the earlier era. But the incentive structure makes skilling problematic. The growth of a competitive market in labour and the decline of long-term employment relations which are occurring in the United States, for example, means that companies can no longer count on workers remaining with them once they have been trained. The erosion of employer loyalty is creating a similar trend on the employee's side. Among professional and technical employees, high levels of mobility raises the ante with respect to theft of proprietary technical and commercial information. Similarly, with competitive pricing of labour, rather than the Fordist compromise of gain sharing, can workers be trusted to actually use their skills cooperatively? In a liberal-flexible environment fear of job loss and wage decline is a prime motivator. But how well will negative incentives operate in a world of expensive, high-technology equipment and processes? Will the adversarial, low-involvement paradigm ultimately be compatible with new production methods? At the moment, employers think they can have it both ways – high effort and motivation (through negative incentives) without compromises to labour (e.g. gain sharing, employment security, negotiated involvement). It is very unlikely they are correct. To get full benefit from the varied skills needed with the new technologies, employers must be able to rely on workers' goodwill and motivation. Reliance on intensive supervision and high unemployment is costly and ultimately less effective than genuine cooperation, as the Japanese case shows.

The competitive model also fails to solve the Keynesian problems of unemployment and inadequate aggregate demand. In the Fordist era, high employment was ensured through productivity sharing and government expenditures. With the globalization of the economy, the abandonment of the productivity formulae and the reduction of the welfare state, the maintenance of domestic demand in any one country is very problematic. The current economic discourse is almost wholly microeconomic – oriented to the problem of raising productivity and profitability at the firm level; there is real amnesia about aggregated demand. On the employment front, there is at least one obvious accommodation for the OECD, and that is to use productivity gains to reduce worktime, thereby spreading the work. But despite extremely long working hours in the United States and Japan, this option is not yet being seriously discussed. In Europe, the German government is even trying to raise working hours, and appears oblivious to the connection between unemployment and worktime. Economy-wide reductions in worktime appear unlikely in the short term. Therefore, it seems probable that labour-saving technical change in the context of increasingly open economies without government-sponsored demand stimulus will yield substantial unemployment.

Nor does liberal flexibility admit of an easy answer to the growing environmental dangers of the productivist model (see Lipietz). At this point, a sustainable world economy will certainly require a great deal of coordinated global activity and negotiation. But the rush toward marketization and privatization is not at all conducive to such coordination. Nor does it address the growth imperative which underlies the market economy. The more probably outcome is minor environmental regulation with a continuing deterioration of the world's ecosystems.[9]

The problems of skill development, motivation, excessive mobility, aggregate demand and unemployment, and environmental degradation will create pressure for change. They will propel local, individualized solutions. For example, in the United States, although large firms are still rejecting worker involvement, there is a rapidly growing, highly successful type of small and medium sized company which is adopting employee involvement, profit sharing, and other innovations located primarily on the right side of Boyer's taxonomy. Experimentation remains vital. It is our belief that by the time we actually reach the twenty-first century, these innovations will be very much on the global capital–labour agenda.

NOTES

1. *The Golden Age of Capitalism: Reinterpreting the Postwar Experience*, edited by Stephen A. Marglin and Juliet B. Schor, Oxford: Clarendon Press, 1990.
2. *Economic Liberalization No Panacea: The Experiences of Latin America*, edited by Tariq Banuri, Oxford University Press, 1991.
3. For more on Taylorization, see Marglin and Schor, note 1, Chapters 1 and 2. Also Richard Edwards, *Contested Terrain*, London: Heinemann, 1979.
4. The possible exception is Japan, although this is a controversial question. Our own view is that Japan did adopt some aspects of Taylorism, but that it represents a mixed case. We shall return to this issue below.
5. See Banuri, note 2.
6. See *Social Corporatism: a Superior Economic System?* edited by J. Perkarinen, M. Pohjola and R. Rowthorn, Oxford University Press, 1992.
7. See K. Dohse et al. 'From "Fordism" to "Toyotism"? The Social Organization of the Labour Process in the Japanese Automobile Industry', *Politics and Society*, vol. 14, no. 2, 1985.
8. See his *Mirages et Miracles: Problèmes de l'Industrialisation dans le Tiers-Monde*, London: Verso, 1987.
9. For more on this see *The North, the South and the Environment*, edited by V. Bhaskar and Andrew Glyn, London: Earthscan, 1995.

2. Capital–labour relations in OECD countries: from the Fordist Golden Age to contrasted national trajectories

Robert Boyer

I A CRUCIAL ISSUE FOR THE 1990s

During the 1980s, many observers became convinced that an exceptional era was over and that firms, unions and governments were groping for new organizational forms. Previous research by the World Institute for Development Economics Research (WIDER) (Marglin and Schor, 1990) has convincingly argued that the arrangements built after the Second World War are now challenged, due to a converging series of pressures originating from the international system, the impact of product and process innovations, sharpening competition, and a shift in economic policies.

More precisely, it has turned out that post-Second World War capital–labour relations had generated increasing difficulties in attaining productivity increases, and that near-full employment had strengthened the bargaining power of unions, both at the level of the firm and of government economic policies. A macro-economic-oriented analysis has shown the likelihood of a structural crisis in the very accumulation regime built on these specific capital–labour relations, labelled as Fordist. The present paper follows up these results and investigates more closely the main features of these original institutional arrangements; tries to characterize the basic transformations occurring during the last fifteen years; and finally delineates not one but several alternatives to post-Second World War capital–labour relations.

This is a necessary, if difficult task. Previous long-run historical studies have shown that the capital–labour relation is a basic institutional form within capitalist economies. It integrates workers within society, whereas it brings constraints, incentives, and therefore regularities into firms' strategies. Consequently, the capital–labour relation links decisions at the micro-level with key features of the accumulation regime at the aggregate (or macro-) level. Each era of capitalist history has relied upon a specific configuration of the productive process and lifestyle of workers. If such a statement still holds for modern economies, then investigating post-Fordist labour institutions constitutes an essential part of any prospective view. A previous international comparison tried such an exercise for EEC countries and developed some prospective scenarios (Boyer, 1988b).

Can such an analysis be carried out meaningfully at the level of OECD countries? On the one hand, this geographical area is congenial to the surge and demise of Fordism: it was invented and has been progressively implemented – not without contradictions and major imbalances – in the United States since the First World War. After 1945, quite consciously in most cases, the Fordist model was exported to Europe and Japan, and spread throughout OECD countries. Consequently, a rather significant homogeneity was created by the adoption of the same production and consumption norms and adherence to the international order created under *Pax Americana*. Seen from outside, for instance from Latin America, South Asia or Africa, striking similarities emerge among large or medium sized OECD countries. This legitimates the writing of a paper covering at least eight advanced economies: Austria, France, Italy, Japan, Sweden, the United Kingdom, the United States and West Germany.

On the other hand, seen from within advanced capitalist countries, many important differences and possibly diverging patterns emerge within the OECD. Given the rising number of comparative case studies, the unity of Fordist capital–labour relations can no longer be maintained. Clearly, work organization and collective bargaining are not at all the same in the United States and Japan: the discoverer of Fordism has been imitated by a brilliant follower who seems to have superseded American standards and invented a new configuration for scientific management. This helps explain why Japan is analysed in more detail in a separate chapter (Chapter 3). In the same way, German and French trajectories, which used to look so similar during the Golden Age, now appear as rather contrasted, as far as capital–labour organization is concerned. A comparison of Italy with the UK suggests that beneath rather close macroeconomic achievements, quite different industrial and labour organizations are operating. Finally, even within the so-called social democratic countries, Sweden and Austria exhibit rather distinctive features in industrial restructuring and labour–market functioning and policies. According to this kind of evidence, dealing with OECD countries as a whole is basically erroneous.

This paper attempts a very uncertain compromise between these two conflicting views. Instead of aggregating the OECD within the group of advanced capitalist countries, it provides an analysis of eight significant national examples, according to a common set of questions, hypotheses and methods. The variety of national strategies reveals the diversity of new capital–labour configurations which could replace the Fordist compromise. Simultaneously, the analysis will run from understanding the past towards enlightening some possible future recompositions.

In a first step, the typical Fordist compromise and its four major components are presented, but the existence of various national arrangements will be stressed (Section II). Then it is argued that these institutional arrangements have been challenged, circumvented, destroyed, or significantly altered during the last two decades. These changes are more structural and far-reaching than short-run and transitory: an impressive series of pressures are reshaping all the components of the Fordist capital–labour nexus (Section III). Contrary to what many best-sellers in the management literature suggest, these transformations do not take place along a broad and clearly designed avenue. The very succession of managerial fads, and the alternation of opposite strategies from firms to governments, suggest that this process is multiform, difficult to grasp, contradictory and uncertain. Consequently, any relevant analysis has to carefully sort out basic and far-reaching innovations, backward-looking and archaic strategies and finally continuities and hysteresis phenomena. In fact, combining these contradictory factors delivers a series of major configurations for present and probably future capital–labour relations (Section IV). Investigation of the factors shaping contrasted national trajectories is a challenging task for further research (Section V).

II   CAPITAL–LABOUR RELATIONS AND THE GOLDEN AGE IN RETROSPECT

Why begin with familiar ground? Going back to the foundation of the Golden Age helps to understand the originality of the 1980s and 1990s, while it also introduces a very important notion, that of national trajectories along the same basic Fordist model. Because it is out of the scope of the present paper to study all OECD countries, we have, for all empirical purposes, selected eight for their diversity: four EEC countries (Italy, France, Germany and the UK), Japan, the US and two social democratic countries (Austria and Sweden).

The Fordist Compromise in Historical Perspective

Of course long-run trends seem to rule the capital–labour relation (CLR). First, wage-earners tend to comprise a larger and larger share of the working population. Nevertheless, during structural crises, for example the interwar period, self-employment appears again as an alternative to dependent labour. Second, the struggle for control over the labour process and the stimulus of competition leads capitalists to mechanize and replace individual know-how by machinery or control procedures within the firm. But there are exceptions, for example in Japan and West Germany, which will play a role in the discussion of post-Fordist trajectories. Third, and recurrently, workers and their collective organizations are fighting for better wages and working conditions. Therefore, for each epoch, there prevails one form or another of tacit or explicit compromises about the rules governing the CLR. For some authors (e.g. Brenner, 1988; Bernstein, 1988) such a steady evolution in technologies and institutions itself would induce a continuous economic dynamic.

The 'regulation' approach has challenged this conception, since long-run economic laws are far from evident and still more because even apparently slow alterations might finally induce big changes in the accumulation regime or regulation mode. For example, catastrophe theory and non-linear dynamic systems convincingly argue that small changes in initial conditions can lead to diverging dynamic patterns. The argument is reinforced for social and economic systems in which innovations and conscious or unintended institution building induce new collective and individual behaviours as well as macroeconomic regularities. This seems to have been the case after the Second World War: major transformations in the world system, monetary and state management, and changes in the forms of competition and the CLR have launched a new avenue for advanced capitalist countries (Aglietta, 1982; Boyer and Mistral, 1978; Lipietz, 1983).

The catastrophic evolutions of the 1930s, distrust of pure *laissez-faire* strategies, the large-scale transformations of technology, social organizations and state interventions occurring during the war put the design and implementation of a genuine CLR at the top of the postwar agenda. An unprecedented conjunction of political and social forces led to this new order. In spite of inescapable and sometimes violent conflicts, all political parties and social groups did accept the rebuilding or modernizing of national economies. New managers replaced old Malthusian entrepreneurs, more open to social and technological innovations. In some key sectors, nationalized firms have been playing an important role in this paradigm shift. From the side of labour, the *aggiornamento* is impressive too: *de facto* if not *de jure*, the unions and their constituents accepted scientific management methods, which they previously opposed. In exchange, they demanded and won the principle that wage-earners would benefit from such a new productive deal, via direct wage increases. In this process the state took a significant place in fostering these Fordist agreements, in that it helped in capital accumulation via adequate public infrastructure spending, a permissive credit and monetary policy and of course a new countercyclical economic policy, legitimized by Keynesian theory (Boyer, 1990b). Finally, the collective side of labour force reproduction in the fully developed capitalist environment was recognized by a kind of Beveridge welfare state (André and Delorme, 1983).

The CLR was an essential part, but a part only, of this Fordist Beveridge–Keynes compromise. Basically the bargain could be presented as follows: on one side, managers and stockholders were recognized as having the leading role and initiative in organizing the production process and making strategic choices about markets and investments. On the other side, the unions were struggling for the major share of productivity increases, associated with the diffusion and maturation of Fordist production methods and consumption and lifestyles (Figure 2.1). It can be shown that a rather coherent accumulation regime has been built upon this genuine social compromise (Aglietta, 1982; Bertrand, 1983; Boyer, 1988a).

The general acceptance of scientific management, associated with the backlog due to the Second World War generally resulted in a tremendous increase in labour productivity. Collective agreements usually set wage increases according to expected productivity achievements, whereas labour conflicts focused on wage demands. Consequently, the real wage would rise and allow typical wage-earners to buy and benefit from mass-produced goods (cars, home appliances, homes and so on). In turn this spurred the production of consumption goods, which called for new and modern equipment. A virtuous spiral of cumulative growth began and was perpetuated, provided that the indexing of wages with respect to productivity was neither too low nor too high (Boyer, 1988b). The implicit compromise of income sharing allowed stable and high profits – a basic condition, along with buoyant demand, for accumulation to be sustained.

The Four Pillars of the Capital–Labour Nexus

In retrospect, the main features of the Fordist capital–labour relation (FCLR) are clear. By contrast with the 1980s, the 1960s were built upon four major founding principles (Table 2.1).

A deepening in labour division has been a distinctive feature of the post-Second World War era. On one side, there has been a clear distinction between conception and execution, production and sales, marketing and finance and so on. This allows an unprecedented technical and social division of tasks, within the original terrain of Fordism, i.e. the manufacturing sector, but also in all the related tertiary sectors. Within the plant, specialized equipment is designed to embody the greater technical knowledge; the assembly tasks require a very low grade of education and skill. The Fordist principle of mass production of very standardized goods sets the pace in industrial organization.

This is the modern method for reaping increasing returns to scale in the Adam Smith tradition, given the technical opportunities and the social compromise of the post-war era. Therefore, there was an unprecedented rate of growth in labour productivity in most OECD countries, with the exception of the United States, where growth has remained static for over a century (Maddison, 1982). During the last Fordist boom in 1969–73, even the United Kingdom exhibited very high productivity growth rates (Table 2.1, item 1). But this achievement

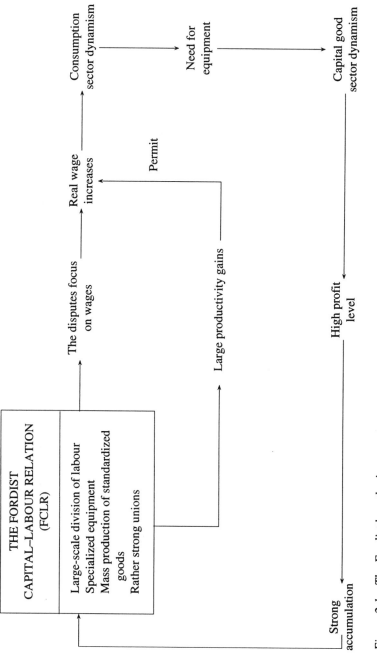

Figure 2.1 *The Fordist hypothesis – summary*

Table 2.1 The four pillars of the Fordist capital–labour relation (FCLR)

	Austria	France	Italy	Japan	Sweden	United Kingdom	United States	West Germany
1. Mechanization of manufacturing, 1969–73								
(i) Labour productivity per hour (variation in %)	–	6.1	4.0	6.8	–	4.0	3.3	4.0
(ii) Output capital ratio (variation in %)	–	0.3	–2.0	–3.8	–	–0.6	1.0	–2.0
2. The dividend of progress for labour								
Wage elasticity								
(i) Price	0.97	0.94	0.96	0.93	n.a.	0.99	1.01	0.99
(ii) Productivity	n.a.	0.4	0.33	0.25	n.a.	0.1	0.30	1.20
		(1.2)	(3.5)	(1.2)		(1.5)	(3.8)	(6.2)
3. Connective bargaining								
Wage rate dispersion (coefficient of variation in %)	21.0	12.0	8.0	29.0	8.0	17.0	22.0	12.0
4. The welfare and Keynesian state								
Share of collective redistribution in GNP (%) in 1973	41.3	38.3	37.8	22.4	44.7	40.6	30.6	41.5

Sources:
Item 1 – Glyn (1988), Tables A2 to A7.
Item 2 – (i) OECD (1986), p. 17. (ii) Le Dem (1987), p. 16 bis; Poret (1986), p. 24, Artus (1983); Juillard (1990); Kremp and Mistral (1988).
Item 3 – Rowthorn (1990), Table 1.
Item 4 – OECD (1988), 'Economic Outlook', December, Statistical Appendix, Table R14, p. 193.

had a cost in most countries, namely that capital deepening propelled a decline in the output–capital ratio (Glyn, 1988).

A compromise on productivity sharing guided wage formation, in contrast to previous competitive mechanisms according to which labour scarcity was the major factor in real wage dynamics. First, there was successful pressure by unions and workers to get indexation with respect to consumer prices, either by explicit clauses within collective agreements, or by the formation of inflation expectations which became a permanent feature of Fordist growth (Benassy, Boyer and Gelpi, 1979). Conceptually, after the Second World War the wage was no longer a pure market variable since it took into account a minimum standard of living. Second, this wage was then raised according to the general advances in productivity. During the Golden Age, most government officials – even the most conservative – promoted what they called 'sharing the dividend of progress'.

The surprise is precisely that this broad vision of the world did inspire actual wage policies by firms (Table 2.1, item 2). With uneven lags, all countries exhibited a perfect indexation with respect to consumer prices, and this was far from a fact of nature – in the nineteenth century the corresponding elasticity was about 0.1–0.2 (Boyer, 1979).

Productivity sharing is a little more complex to prove. The best evidence rests on the noticeable constancy of distributive shares (corrected for the shift towards salaried activities) in the medium term. The changes occurring after the Second World War clearly point towards this rough stability for France, the United States and the United Kingdom, and possibly Germany (Graph 2.1). Nevertheless, significant fluctuations in income shares still exist in Japan, which might imply a unique form of wage formation. Long-run econometric studies for wage formation in the United States seem to confirm these transformations towards more sluggish adjustments and a declining impact of unemployment fluctuations (Sachs, 1978). This is a typical pattern for most OECD countries (Schor, 1985). For the contemporary period, other econometric studies seem to confirm productivity sharing, either instantaneously (Germany, Japan) or over a multi-period labour contract (US, probably France) – see Mimosa (1990) and Boyer (1990a).

Connective bargaining created strong complementarities in wage increases which started from the leading highly unionized sectors and progressively spread to the secondary sectors and finally to public civil servants (Piore, 1986; Coriat, 1985,1990). The innovation with respect to the previous century or even the interwar period was far-reaching: labour struggles used to create wage differentials across skill levels, sectors or regions; within the FCLR, successful wage demands set the pace for average nominal wage increases. At least three mechanisms contributed to this spreading – the rather extensive centralization of collective bargaining usually negotiated at the sector or even the national

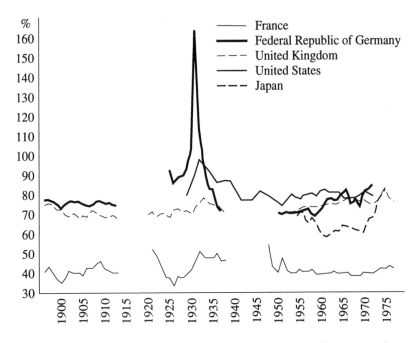

%
160
150
140
130
120
110
100
90
80
70
60
50
40
30

———— France
———— Federal Republic of Germany
– – – United Kingdom
———— United States
– – – Japan

1900 1905 1910 1915 1920 1925 1930 1935 1940 1945 1950 1955 1960 1965 1970 1975

Note: Share of wage in value added, after correction for the increasing share of wage-earners in total working population

Source: Basle, Mazier and Vidal (1984), p. 105.

Graph 2.1   Greater stability of the wage share after the Second World War

economy level, the mobility of workers moving towards the best paid job, and finally government minimum wage policy (where it existed).

Most indexes for wage dispersion confirm an increase in stability of wage differentials under Fordism (Table 2.1, item 3), a feature which partially changes in the contemporary crisis (OECD, 1985, Chapter 5). Nevertheless, within this new historical configuration, some national specificities are observed in the conventional opposition between primary and secondary jobs (Doeringer and Piore, 1971), and a remaining competitive wage formation legacy, which explains why in the United States wage differentials still play a role after the Second World War. Similarly, wage dispersion seems to be the highest in Japan, which suggests again a unique and decentralized process in industrial relations. On the contrary, most European countries experience a low dispersion in the sectoral wage. A more egalitarian configuration is observed in Sweden, probably due to solidaristic wage policies, and in Italy, where complete indexing with respect to prices seems to have significantly reduced wage differentials (Rowthorn, 1990).

The fourth pillar of the FCLR, the basic social compromise and new conception of the role of the state induced and legitimated an impressive redistribution of income via the Keynesian and welfare state. Interpersonal and intergenerational solidarities which used to operate through family ties were fulfilled by more collective and horizontal institutions. The welfare system was therefore a key component of this new deal between citizens and the state. The recognition of the social wage – general access to health, basic education, the provision of pension funds for poorer citizens and unemployment benefits – explain the surge of redistribution mechanisms by the state or by collective agreements.

Again, this introduced a far-reaching innovation in the CLR and consequently affected wage and productivity dynamics. On one side, the disciplinary role of firings and unemployment became less evident (with a possible adverse impact upon productivity), whereas real wage increases were more stable, thereby smoothing the cycle. On the other side, the variety of public entitlements were built-in stabilizers, given the tax and welfare financing systems. Nevertheless, this Keynesian–Beveridge state is unequally developed among advanced capitalist countries (Table 2.1, item 4). Just before the 1973 oil shock, the share of collective redistribution was higher in social democratic countries such as Sweden and Austria. EEC countries were experiencing a similar redistribution, albeit generally lower in Italy. The lowest size for welfare is observed in the United States and still more Japan, where family solidarity and private pension funds constituted an alternative to public welfare. Clearly, for most components of the CLR, Japan is exceptional (Lazonick, Chapter 3, this volume).

To summarize, Fordism manifested itself through common features across advanced capitalist countries. Nevertheless, the previous description suggests that the precise configuration of this model may vary from country to country.

One Model, many National Brands

Let us now adopt a more qualitative and institutional view about these cross-country differences. Each of the components of the CLR exhibits clear national specificities (Table 2.2).

The work process is typically Fordist in the US, which is not at all surprising, and in France too. Deep divisions between blue and white collar workers, or engineers and the rank and file is common, whereas managers rely on mechanization for solving technical and even social problems (Noble, 1984; Brie, 1987). But in other countries, a craftsmanship tradition and an explicit organization of professional markets (Marsden, 1988) moderate the Fordist principle of maximum division of labour and blue collar deskilling. Germany, Japan and Sweden belong to this mitigated or hybrid Fordism. Contrary to genuine scientific management, which constantly seeks to take the skills off the shop floor, in these countries 'the employers have put the skills on the shop floor and invested in the capabilities of shop-floor workers' (Lazonick, Chapter 3, this volume). The British CLR is another enlightening case: the very constitution of the bargaining power of workers has relied on very precise craft boundaries and work rules, which might operate as barriers to the continuous rationalization process intrinsic to the Taylorist principle. Somewhat loosely, these contrasted configurations can help explain productivity differentials (Table 2.1).

Labour mobility is necessary for coping with the permanent changes brought about by capital accumulation, competition, the search for innovation and the inescapable decline of some obsolete industries. Again, each economy seems to have built its own mobility itinerary. In the United States, workers move from firm to firm, and region to region. In France, regional mobility is usually lower, whereas most of the adjustments have taken place in small or medium sized firms. In Italy, disequilibrium between the South and the North explains most of the features of workers' behaviour and expectations. In Germany, active local or regional markets allow the movement of skilled workers from firm to firm. In Japan, on the contrary, quasi-permanent employment in large firms is not necessarily counterbalanced by higher mobility within the subcontractors (Koike, 1987). The contemporary strategy of the Japanese large firms is not so different from the American mass producers in the 1900s and 1920s (Lazonick, Chapter 3, this volume), but might have been implemented more systematically (Boyer and Orléan, 1990). Finally, in social democratic countries (Sweden and Austria), adaptation to the changing economic outlook seems largely centralized and operating via public organization, regional or national (Strah, 1988; Andersson, and Mjoset, 1987; Standing, 1988).

The wage compromise is more or less formalized into collective agreements and labour contracts. For indexing with respect to prices, the spectrum ranges from a complete, quasi-instantaneous and contractual clause (Italian *scala mobile*) to a legal interdiction (Germany and France). These configurations seem to affect mainly short-run adjustments, since in the long run indexing is complete (Table 2.1). The same observation can be made for indexing with respect to productivity: quasi-explicit in Japan, via the high variability of bonuses, implicit but strong in Germany, operating in the medium run in the US and France, integrated in the official wage policy in Scandinavian countries. Nevertheless, most of the research on wage formation does not focus on the core of Fordist mechanisms (roughly speaking, wage growth = consumer price inflation + productivity growth), but on the small residual part of competitive mechanisms, as conventional Phillips curves do. For the whole sample of OECD countries (Thouluc, 1988), the moderating impact of unemployment on wages comes out as modest since the corresponding elasticity is estimated at around 0.4. But the mechanism is somehow unstable in the short run and it is difficult to relate the various elasticities to national specificities. For example, given the statistical methods for measuring unemployment in Japan, the labour market seems extremely competitive (Le Dem, 1987; Chan-Lee et al., 1987).

Wage earners lifestyles exhibit a large variety of lags with respect to the 'American way of life', another image for Fordist consumption norms. The gap has been vanishing quite quickly in France and Italy, along with the decline of the agricultural sector. In the United Kingdom, Sweden and Austria, collective consumption has played a significant role in shaping consumption patterns and habits. At one extreme, the United States, Fordism has been synonymous with commoditization of private consumption and lifestyle; at another (Sweden), it has been associated with quite a-Fordist uses, generally collectively organized (health, education, training and retraining). In finalizing the macro model representative of post-Second World War growth, this is a feature to be included: the coherence between the spreading of Fordist production and the transformations in consumption helped to stabilize the growth pattern. On the other hand, any divergence between them may trigger a structural crisis. For example, the 1981 French reflation was rapidly blocked by large increases in imports of modern equipment and consumer goods (Boyer, 1987). In the United States too, the demise of the FCLR is related to the preference of American consumers for foreign durable goods.

Even if the characterization is somewhat impressionistic, a national flavour for each of the OECD countries can be determined. The United States and France seem to embody *typical Fordism*, since they make a clear distinction between engineers and technicians on one side, and blue collar and low skilled workers on the other. Nevertheless, genuine US Fordism is market-driven, whereas in France the state has played a prominent role in promoting and implementing it via labour laws, nationalized industries and numerous incentives of economic policy. At the opposite extreme, the British case shows that Fordism is not always an inevitability which imposes itself due to its superior economic efficiency. A strong labour movement, defending precise skills, tasks and job rules, can block most of the productive potential associated with modern management methods. This can be called *flawed Fordism*. Similarly, Italy provides a suggestive example of possible discrepancies between Fordism as production techniques and as a principle of work organization. When the struggles of the hot autumn of 1969 led to new labour laws, they simultaneously recognized the principle of productivity sharing and the control by workers of plant organization at the shop-floor level. The system was potentially explosive and did break down at the end of the 1970s (Wolleb, 1988; Maruani et al., 1989). In this

Table 2.2   The national variants of Fordist compromise: a tentative typology for the Golden Age

	Austria	France	Italy
1. Organization of the work process	Not very Taylorist	Taylorist Large gap between conception and execution	Highly Taylorist in large firms
2. Stratification of skills	Average	Large and institutionalized	Large
3. Labour mobility	High	Low	Regional (from South to North) Average
4. Wage formation			
(i) Indexing with respect to			
• Price	Almost complete	Complete if not permitted	Fully institu-tionalized
• Productivity	Not clear	Implicit	Not explicit
(ii) Influence of unemployment	Significant	Moderate	Quite high
(iii) Indirect wage and welfare (as proportion of direct wage)	High	High	High
5. Lifestyle and consumption norms	Initially lagging	Closing gap	Initially lagging
Global features of Fordism	Corporatist Fordism	State-led	Lagging and im-perfectly institu-tionalized

Sources:
Items 1 and 2 – Mainly Campinos-Dubernet and Grando (1988), Aoki (1988), Strath (1987), OECD (1988d).
Item 3 – OECD (1986), p. 63, Table II.3 for 1971, or p. 66, Table II.4.
Item 4 – OECD (1986), p. 17, Table I.2.
(i) and (ii) For the indexing with respect to productivity see Poret (1986), Table 7, p. 24.

Japan	Sweden	United Kingdom	United States	West Germany
Teamwork of polyvalent workers more than Taylorist	Early attempts to replace Taylorism	Balkani-zed via multiple crafts & work rules	Typically Taylorist and Fordist	Professional & craft markets more than Taylorist
Moderate	Moderate	Precise boundaries	High	Moderate
Average	Average/ high	Average	High	Average
Complete	World more than consumer prices	Slow but complete	Partial and/or slow	Slow and partial (forbid-den)
Explicit via bonuses	In the export sector	Not clear	Implicit but existing	Quite strong
High	Significant	Low	Average	Apparently low
Very low	High	Low(welfare tax-based)	Low	Average
Fast closing gap	Modern with large welfare	Modern with welfare	Largely 'commodi-tized'	Rapid moderni-zation
Hybrid Fordism	Democratic Fordism	Flawed Fordism	Genuine Fordism	Flex-Fordism

mismatched Fordism, political and social struggles contradict the maturation of mass production.

A quite different configuration prevails in Germany; there the manufacturing industries as well as the educational and vocational systems have never tried to implement completely the Fordist logic. Managers encouraged high skill levels and workers' involvement, whereas final products were more differentiated than standardized (Streeck, 1989a,b). Similarly, collective agreements and bargaining within firms partially integrated new technologies and work organization. Finally, wage formation has been much more linked to actual performance than in most other countries. One might label this configuration as *flex-Fordism*. Japan is still another case, since high skills and a significant polyvalence allow rapid shifting from one production to another; products can both be mass produced and somewhat differentiated. This is a *hybrid Fordism*, which may represent an alternative to genuine Fordism both in work organization (Jacot, 1990), and management (Aoki, 1990).

Clearly the degree of centralization/decentralization is an open variable in the Fordist model (Rowthorn, 1990; Calmfors and Driffill, 1988; Bowles and Boyer, 1990). The Scandinavian countries and Austria provide a striking example of an industrial modernization which largely takes place in a small open economy and nevertheless allows a very centralized capital–labour compromise, emerging from the interactions between firms, a strong union and state civil servants (Bosworth and Rivlin, 1987). Interestingly enough, even within a corporatist or Social Democratic Fordism, macroeconomic performance might be rather different; Austria and Sweden do not exactly follow the same trajectory, as far as macroeconomic outcomes are concerned (see Table 2.7).

III   BREAKDOWN IN THE 1970s: EVIDENCE AND INTERPRETATIONS

This genuine and symbiotic interaction between industrial relations and macrodynamics seemed to deliver an infinite prosperity (Lutz, 1990) at least according to most contemporary views. Since then, various social crises, two oil shocks, globalization of competition at the world level, a wave of technological innovations and of course a drastic revision in economic policies have induced a significant alteration in the Fordist capital–labour relation. After a short chronology, the main institutional changes will be investigated. It will be argued that the Fordist capital–labour relation is experiencing a large-scale transition towards various alternatives.

A Brief History: a Drama in Four Acts

To understand how such a happy Fordist regime has ended in a sharp critique of the rigidities and inner limits of Fordist industrial relations, a short retrospective will be enlightening. Basically, this begins as a comedy, passes through a dramatic episode and might end like a tragi-comedy!

Act I starts at the end of the 1960s and stops before the second oil shock of 1979. The social unrest associated with the hot May of 1968 or the Italian autumn of 1969 challenged the Fordist division of labour and excessive deskilling and mechanization. But unions, business associations and governments usually interpreted this episode as an inducement to complete the Fordist agenda. The minimum wage was generally significantly increased and the welfare state extended to new areas such as training. A second major challenge was associated with the first oil shock; it was interpreted as a benchmark, but then only for energy management and finance. Consequently, all the governments, including the most conservative, have been extending unemployment benefits and training, and giving subsidies to firms in order to curb the job reductions which took place within the manufacturing sector. In France, for example, the Chirac government extended severance payments and instituted control over dismissal by the Ministry of Labour. Similarly, Keynesian countercyclical measures helped in limiting the rise of unemployment. By symmetry with respect to the statement by President Nixon: 'Now we are all Keynesians!', everyone was Fordist but some were ignoring it. The FCLR was so pervasive that it was considered as natural, i.e. part of the social compromise between citizens and the state, wage-earners and business. OPEC's monopoly had created energy scarcity and major international financial imbalance and was the culprit, not the Fordist capital–labour relation.

Act II begins after 1979 and lasts approximately until the mid-1980s. In fact the previous strategy had led to persistent inflation even during recessions, and a worsening of public deficits, while the trend in unemployment was upward. Similarly, Keynesian therapies, when applied at the national or even international level, did not provide their expected results. Then came the monetarist and conservative backlash. On one side, monetary stability had to be maintained at any cost in terms of unemployment. Most of the central banks followed the Federal Reserve Board, and adopted rather restrictive monetary policies. The related increases in real interest rates led to a levelling in firms' profits, and pushed them either into bankruptcy, or massive lay-offs and concession bargaining. The idea emerged that labour–market institutions were restricting mobility, employment and wage adjustments. If such large unemployment rates persisted over a decade, clearly the monopolistic or oligopolistic character of labour markets was to be blamed. In France, for example, after 1976, Prime

Minister Raymond Barre set up a new economic policy, based upon both price and wage freezes, the search for a better match of vacancies and unemployed workers, and a restrictive money supply. During this period, most governments tried to promote deindexing of the nominal wage with respect to past consumer prices. More and more, the FCLR was, first implicitly and then explicitly, questioned. Of course, the conservative counter-revolution is clearer in the United Kingdom and the United States than in West Germany or France, but similar conceptions and strategies were spreading across all OECD countries. Nevertheless, social democratic countries remain largely exceptional.

Act III puts forward an ideal for the capital–labour relation, at odds with the Fordist one. First, European governments realize that the cost of the smoothing of unemployment has been a steep decline in profit margins and therefore sluggish investment. Here comes the famous Helmut Schmidt's theorem: 'Today's wage austerity provides tomorrow's profit, i.e. the day after tomorrow's investment and consequently future job creation.' This macroeconomic vision is quite opposite to the Fordist virtuous circle (see Figure 2.1). Second, pre-Keynesian conceptions concerning the self-adjustment of pure and perfect labour markets challenge the Fordist institutions and compromises. Consequently, by reducing the legal power of unions (especially in the UK), by decreasing unemployment benefits, by legalizing atypical labour contracts and of course promoting the transparency of employment offers and demands, most governments have been dreaming of implementing a competitive capital–labour relation. Third, the Keynesian principles are strongly under attack because they overemphasize demand factors and frequently forget the supply side of the economy. Both the so-called and mysterious Laffer curve and the impressive comeback of neo-Schumpeterian ideas about the role of entrepreneurs and innovation in the process of capitalist development challenge the Fordist–Beveridge and Keynesian model. During the mid-1980s, few governments dared to stick to the old capital–labour compromise, with the possible exception of the social democratic countries. During the same period, many official reports called for a drastic increase in flexibility of labour contracts, wages, and a scaling down of the welfare state (OECD, 1986). As far as the ideas are concerned, Fordism was actually dead!

Act IV begins at the end of the 1980s, after a surprisingly long recovery starting after 1983 in the United States and diffusing into Japan and Europe. A partial restoration of profit shares, a slackening of monetary policy in order to prevent recurring financial crises from causing a cumulative depression, opportunities opened up by innovation in finance as well as information technologies – all these factors promote more optimistic long-run views, which generate a boom in productive investment and even public infrastructures, especially in Europe (Economie Européenne, 1989). The rigidities of the labour markets become less evident in this context of renewed job creation. Labour mobility and especially leaving rates vary procyclically and therefore increase endogenously with the boom (Boyer, 1990c). Similarly, the consequences of previous conservative strategies can be assessed and compared with more cooperative social democratic alternatives (Leborgne and Lipietz, 1989). Therefore, the objective of adapting to international competition and new technological opportunities has been looked at by contrasting and somewhat conflicting strategies. For simplicity's sake, two diverging transformations can be identified (Table 2.3).

Table 2.3   Two strategies for adapting the capital–labour relation

	Defensive strategy	Offensive strategy
1. Work organization	• Exporting old Fordist methods • Reinforcing controls via new technologies • Marginally improving Fordism	• Modernizing even mature industries • Enhance workers' commitment • Use information technologies to find alternative to Fordism
2. Wage formation	• Two-tier contracts • Deindexing of wages • Weakening of unions	• Homogeneous labour contract • Genuine wage formula (e.g. profit sharing) • Joint bargaining of wage, employment and welfare by firms or national unions
3. Connective bargaining	• Decentralization of bargaining • Make wages more sensitive to individual financial situation • Relative wages become adjustment variables	• Possible centralization • Solidaristic wage policies • Rather stable wage hierarchy
4. Welfare and Keynesian state	• Reduction in unemployment benefit • Budget cuts • Goal of private insurance	• Intensive training programmes • Investment in infrastructure (education, transportation, communication) • Rationalization of welfare state

Defensive strategies combine a kind of Fordist nostalgia with the belief that market mechanisms should take charge of the whole process of CLR restructuring. Work organization should be only marginally transformed; for example information technologies should be used to reinforce controls over blue collar workers. Wage formation should be separate from any collective agreement and left to market adjustment or micro-bargaining at the more decentralized level.

Capital, the state and labour

Table 2.4   Changing pattern in FCLR

	Austria	France	Italy
1. Fordism becomes less productive Productivity rate (%) per year			
(i) Before 1973	5.4	4.4	5.0
(ii) After 1973	2.1	2.3	1.7
2. Breakdown of the Fordist wage formula			
(i) Institutional pressures	Existing	State-driven	Strong at the firms' level
(ii) Significance of a shift into the wage equation	Yes	Yes	Uncertain
3. More atomistic bargaining			
(i) Institutional evidence	Pressures for decen-tralization	Yes	Yes, 'Economia sommersa'
(ii) Evolution in wage rate dispersion	Slight rise	Decline and then rise	Decline
4. Rationalization of the Keynesian welfare state			
(i) Actual level of its share in GNP (1986)	51.9	51.8	50.5
(ii) Break in previous upward trend	Not clear	Slowing down	Slowing down

Sources:
Items 1 (i) and (ii) – Computed from OECD, (1988d), p. 195.
Item 2 – (ii) Chan–Lee et al., (1987), Table 8, p. 157; Tsuru (1988); Kremp and Mistral (1988), pp. 110–111.
Items 2 (i) and 3 (i) – OECD (1987) Chapter 3; ETUI (1988), ILO (1987).
Item 3 (ii) – Klau and Mittelstadt (1986), p. 46, item 5; Dell'Aringa and Lodovici (1989), p. 54.
Item 4 – OECD (1988d), Table R14, p. 193.

Japan	Sweden	United Kingdom	United States	West Germany
8.2	2.8	3.3	0.9	4.4
2.9	1.0	1.5	0.4	2.1
Some but mitigated via bonuses	Some but genuine productivity sharing	Strong at the political level	Less cost of living adjustment new collective agreements	Not very strong (Flex-Fordism!)
Yes	No	Likely	Yes	Possibly
Not clear	Some pressures for decentralization	Already quite decentralized	Yes	Not clear
Rise	Decline	Decline and then rise	Rise	Quite stable
33.1	63.5	46.2	36.9	46.6
Decrease since '83 (–1.0)	Decrease since '82 (–3.1)	Decrease since '84 (–1.8)	Yes, quasi-constant since '82	Decrease since '82 (–2.8)

Consequently, connective bargaining would break down and the relative wage would become an important variable in labour–market adjustments. Finally, the Beveridge and Keynesian welfare state should be reduced and replaced by private insurance, whereas conventional public expenditures should be kept to a minimum. The United States and the United Kingdom provide good examples for this vision.

Offensive strategies are built upon a long-term view: some short-run imbalances are to be accepted in order to invest in training and retraining workers, to elaborate sophisticated wage systems to ensure workers' consent and commitment, and finally to preserve some solidaristic mechanisms which enhance the acceptance of restructuring, and therefore help in achieving long-run efficiency. According to this second vision, Fordist hierarchical controls have to be replaced by more subtle incentives to obtain workers' commitment. A compromise about the sharing of the dividends of progress is still necessary, even if possibly quite different from the Fordist one. In turn, this compromise enhances product and process innovations and provides long-run competitiveness for the firm or the nation. Public policies should precisely provide the collective ingredients of such a strategy: good infrastructure, an efficient educational system, incentives for innovations and so on. Sweden, Germany and Japan provide good examples of these strategies, although they are quite different in many other respects (degree of centralization, importance of unions, and size of the welfare state).

During the mid-1980s, the defensive strategies were generally considered as necessary and efficient. Now, after a decade, the offensive strategies seem to be as good as, or even better than the former. Significantly enough, influential OECD reports have changed their emphasis from defensive to offensive flexibility (OECD, 1986, 1988c). This is not necessarily a happy end for the Fordist legacy. On the contrary, all these episodes have significantly altered most of the features inherited from the Second World War.

Changes in the Components of the FCLR

Has this paradigmatic shift in the realm of ideas implied equivalent transformations in the Fordist labour regime? Much international comparative research allows a provisional description of the main changes actually observed within the management of firms (OECD, 1985, 1988a, 1988c; Boyer, 1988b, 1990a; Rowthorn, 1990, Brunetta and Dell'Aringa, 1990). The four basic features of Fordism have significantly changed.

As a productive device, Fordism loses some, if not all, of its efficiency. After 1973, labour productivity significantly slowed down for all OECD countries (Table 2.4, item 1). Capital productivity too continued to decline, which explains why total factor productivity has decelerated in comparison with the 1960s. Such a decline still represents a puzzle, even for the most sophisticated statistical and

Parameter a of the equation $\dot{W}N = a \cdot \dot{p}_c + b \cdot \log U + c \cdot \dot{p}_r + d$

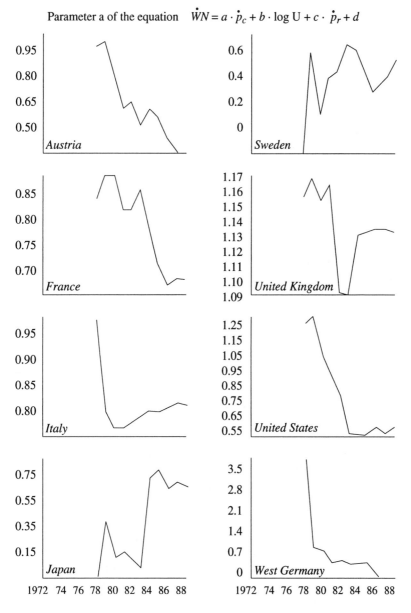

Graph 2.2 A general deindexing of nominal wage with respect to consumer price (evolution of elasticities derived from recursive estimates from 1978 to 1988)

econometric studies (OECD, 1989). Clearly the old methods for reaping increasing returns to scale by standardizing products and mechanizing are no longer efficient. Many managerial and economic studies overwhelmingly confirm that quality and differentiation of consumer and equipment goods are crucial in the new climate of international competition (Porter, 1990; Krugman, 1990). If, under Fordism, 'big was beautiful', it has been argued that smaller plants and runs for each product will prevail in the future (Piore and Sabel, 1984). But this view can be mitigated: scope and scale economies do not exclude one another (Chandler, 1990) and mass production in modern information technologies is not over. Nevertheless, the correlation between productivity increases and demand growth has steadily declined through the 1970s (Boyer and Petit, 1989). In other words, both quantitatively and qualitatively, one of the basic pillars of the Fordist regime is challenged. Consequently, this relative productive failure has challenged the viability of the capital–labour compromise.

The Fordist collective agreements no longer rule wage formation. An impressive amount of evidence suggests that in many OECD countries, two of the basic Fordist indexing mechanisms have been challenged, and consequently transformed (Table 2.4, item 2).

First, many governments have promoted the breaking down of any explicit indexing mechanism of nominal wages with respect to past consumer prices. For example, in France and Italy, the Ministry of Finance or/and the central bank have played a decisive role in implementing such a strategy. In other countries, the weakening of unions and the rise in unemployment have indirectly allowed such a deindexing. Some econometric studies confirm that such a shift has affected the dynamics of average nominal wages in all OECD countries (Table 2.5). More precisely, during the 1980s, the elasticity of wages with respect to consumer prices has been reduced in Austria, France, Italy, the United Kingdom, the United States and Germany (Graph 2.2). More sophisticated investigation confirms this deindexing process, especially for France: the process is more sluggish and the medium run elasticity is no longer equal to unity (Ralle et al., 1989).

Second, managers and governments have searched for more competitive mechanisms for wage formation. Either they have been promoting more decentralized wage bargaining, or they have implemented wage norms or guidelines which implied a quasi-constancy of the average real wage (ILO, 1984). The impact of these strategies should be captured by a decline in the parameter which measures the influence of unemployment on wage evolution. The related estimates confirm such a mechanism for Italy and Germany, but the evidence is opposite or mixed for most other OECD countries (Graph 2.3). Indeed, estimates over a longer period seem to confirm a stronger unemployment impact for the United States (Kremp and Mistral, 1988) and for Japan (Tsuru, 1988). Nevertheless, the shifts in estimated parameters are smaller than would be expected simply by taking for granted all the statements from firms, experts

Table 2.5   *Changing nominal wage formation: some stability tests for the period 1972–88*

Estimated equation: $\dot{W}N = a \cdot \dot{p}_c + a_{-1} \cdot \dot{p}_{c-1} + b \log U + c \cdot \dot{p}_r + d$

	Austria	France	Italy	Japan	Sweden	United Kingdom	United States	West Germany
• Price $\dot{p}_c$	0.35	0.68	0.80	0.64	0.47	1.13	0.55	0.04
	(1.6)	(5.7)	(4.9)	(2.2)	(1.2)	(3.4)	(3.5)	(0.15)
• Price (–1) $\dot{p}_{c-1}$	0.28	0.32	-0.09	0.04	0.30	-0.21	0.36	0.35
	(1.4)	(2.8)	(0.55)	(0.3)	(0.68)	(0.8)	(2.3)	(1.60)
• Log unemployment U	-4.02	-3.66	-8.12	-13.6	-9.5	-1.75	-4.14	-2.92
	(4.1)	(5.1)	(3.5)	(2.5)	(2.9)	(0.9)	(2.7)	(5.8)
• Productivity $\dot{p}_r$	-0.04	-0.14	-0.09	0.02	0.34	0.39	0.42	0.21
	(0.2)	(0.38)	(0.39)	(0.03)	(0.52)	(0.7)	(2.2)	(1.3)
• Constant	7.35	9.3	23.9	14.9	10.7	6.0	8.8	8.0
	(4.0)	(2.6)	(4.0)	(2.3)	(2.8)	(1.0)	(3.0)	(6.1)
SER	1.3	1.0	1.6	1.8	2.8	2.8	0.8	0.9
DW	0.99	1.00	2.96	0.90	1.67	2.67	1.98	2.03
R²	0.85	0.96	0.92	0.93	0.42	0.80	0.87	0.90
Stability tests								
CUSUM								
CUSUM²						X		X
Chow's test	X(77,78, 79,80)	X(77,78, 79)		X(77,78, 79)			X(79)	

Note: The figures within brackets give the estimates for the t-student statistics.
Source: Computed from: OECD statistics databank, normalized unemployment rates – least squares estimates.

41

Parameter b of the equation $\dot{W}N = a \cdot \dot{p}_c + b \cdot \log U + c \cdot \dot{p}_r + d$

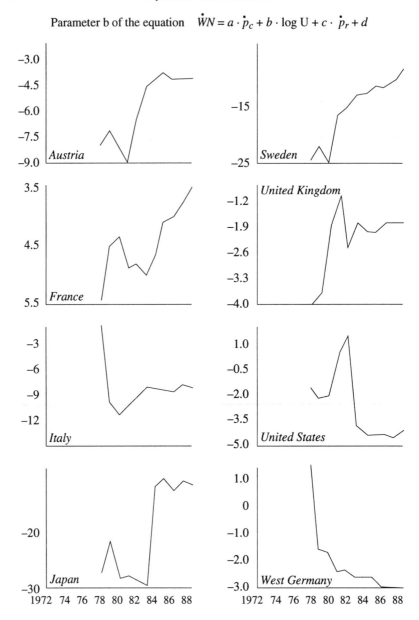

Graph 2.3   An ambiguous evolution of the impact of unemployment on wages
(evolution of the semi-elasticity derived from recursive estimates
from 1978 to 1988)

and ministers about the need for flexibility. In fact, a large degree of inertia characterizes even the transition periods from one growth regime to another. This is an important finding for any prospective assessment.

Decentralization of bargaining and resegmentation of labour markets have altered the stability of the wage hierarchy. Under Fordism, nationwide or sectoral key collective agreements used to set the pace and norm for wage formation in other sectors. Strong unions using parity and equity arguments and quasi-full employment were two efficient ways to gain a noticeable stability in the wage hierarchy. Most of these conditions vanished during the 1970s. With the exception of Sweden and Austria (See Table 2.7, item 1), union density and initiatives steadily declined, whereas large-scale job destruction in the manufacturing sectors, the rise of smaller firms with fewer union opportunities and persistent long-run unemployment, have made wage formation more dependent on competition (Table 2.3, item 3). Since job losses and creations are highly sensitive to the sector and the product, to management style and regional localization, and to the intensity of foreign competition, connective bargaining has broken down. According to a trickle-down strategy, the widening of income differentials has frequently been assumed as a condition for job creation, especially in the United States (Bowles et al., 1983) and the United Kingdom. Wage dispersion has indeed increased, between sectors, regions and nations, and widened the distance between the well paid and the poorer, at least in decentralized industrial systems (Rowthorn, 1990). No country more than the United States exhibits such a breakdown of the ideal of general increases in the standard of living (Juillard, 1990). In the long run, this is the evidence for the dismantling of the Fordist growth regime: a cumulative differentiation of lifestyles between the 'yuppies' and the poorest minorities would induce a dualistic society, and has indeed done so (Steinberg, 1985) putting new demands upon governments (Piore, 1989). France is not exceptional – even under a mild socialist government, income inequalities have slightly increased since the mid-1980s (CERC, 1989). Thus, a third pillar of the FCLR is slowly decaying.

The welfare and Keynesian state is itself under pressure from business associations and conservative governments. During the first phase of the Fordist crisis (Acts I and II), state interventions and welfare entitlements cushioned adverse effects for households (unemployment benefit, health care, retraining) and firms (subsidies and tax credits). Consequently, persistent public deficits have been observed for almost a decade, whereas the share of public spending and welfare transfers rose continuously until the end of the 1970s. But after 1979, governments have been constantly concerned to reduce total public interventions. Cutting public expenditures and reducing taxes have not been as easy as was contemplated by free marketeers. Nevertheless the previous surge in deficits has been stopped in every country, including social democratic ones such as Sweden (Table 2.4, item 4). As far as capital–labour relations are concerned, the minimum wage has been moved much more carefully and often implicitly reduced in order to promote young workers' employment. Unemployment benefits, when they were generous, have occasionally been reduced, but the global budget for unemployment relief has generally increased. Similarly, many specific measures have been designed in order to curb long term unemployment: special subsidies, tax cuts, public retraining and so on. Therefore, the management by the state of the FCLR has been amended at the margin and somewhat rationalized, rather than revolutionized. For example, private insurance schemes have not really developed outside the promising, but limited market of yuppies and the upper middle classes. Nevertheless, the breakdown of the Fordist engine has made the welfare state's financial problems more acute, and consequently exacerbated the previous problems.

Clearly, the FCLR has been under numerous and severe pressures during the last two decades. The issue is now the following: are these changes purely transitory or do they delineate a long-run structural alteration in the capital–labour relation? Even if such a prognosis is difficult, let us risk some prospective views.

The Consequence of Adverse and Converging Pressures

The first hypothesis to be contemplated is simple enough: the FCLR must have been more severely challenged in countries where the adverse trends have been more acute. During the 1970s, three major reversals have been observed.

Expansionary Keynesian policies have been replaced by restrictive and conservative strategies in most OECD countries. The main objective has been to stop any danger of accelerating inflation, via binding monetary norms imposed by the central banks. Actually, the first part of the 1980s has exhibited an impressive and rather unexpected decline in the inflation rate (Table 2.6, item 1). Even the surge of inflation during the last few years of the 1980s has been rather moderate by comparison with the 1970s. Even after the stock market crashes, most monetary policies have been careful enough in that respect. An unprecedented level of real interest rates has actually checked credit and monetary supply (Table 2.6, item 2). Still more, the rise in interest rate payments by non-financial sectors has exerted strong distributive pressures. It has been convincingly argued that the central banks have themselves reacted not only to inflation and external deficits but to social unrest (Epstein and Schor, 1988). Conversely, the surge in the real interest rate has been used by firms to curb wage demands and more generally to question the viability of the past Fordist compromise. Note that in Italy the shift in monetary policy has been the premise for revising downwards the indexing mechanisms (Wolleb, 1988). Similarly, in the United Kingdom, monetarist management has not been without influence on the weakening of unions and workers (Glyn, 1988).

Table 2.6   Economic trends affecting the Fordist capital–labour relation

	Austria	France	Italy	Japan	Sweden	United Kingdom	United States	West Germany
1. The shift towards price stability								
• Peak inflation rate (%) (1980 or 1981)	6.8	13.6	21.1	8.0	13.7	18.0	13.5	6.3
• 1987 minus peak rate (%)	–5.4	–10.5	–16.5	–8.2	–9.5	–13.8	–9.8	–6.1
2. Rise of real interest rates								
• Trough	n.a.	–1.0	–3.0	–2.9	–2.5	–4.8	–0.7	1.1
(date)		(76–80)	(71–75)	(71–75)	(71–75)	(71–75)	(76–80)	(61–65)
• Peak	n.a.	4.3	5.6	4.5	3.9	4.5	6.8	4.7
(date)		(81–84)	(81–84)	(81–84)	(81–84)	(81–84)	(81–84)	(81–84)
3. Adverse evolution of profit rate								
• Peak	n.a.	10.8	–	39.5	8.2	7.6	14.0	14.2
(date)		(73)		(70)	(74)	(64)	(65)	(66)
• Trough	n.a.	4.9	–	18.5	–2.9	1.5	6.1	5.6
(date)		(82)		(75)	(77)	(74)	(74)	(75)
4. Internationalization of trade import penetration for manufacturing								
• 1970	27.5	16.2	16.3	4.7	28.3	14.2	5.5	19.5
• 1979	34.1	22.1	28.7	5.6	36.6	24.8	9.0	29.4
• 1985	36.4	27.4	31.3	5.3	41.4	33.2	12.9	35.8
5. Quality of international specialization								
• Employment in low-growth sectors (share in %)	n.a.	43.9	48.4	35.6	46.3	38.2	30.4	38.2
• Sensitivity to foreign competition	Average	High, mainly price taker	Average	Low	Average	Average, partially price maker	Average	Low, largely price maker

Sources:
Item 1 – OECD (1988d), p. 190.
Item 2 – Atkinson and Chouraqui (1985), p. 6.
Item 3 – Chan-Lee et al., (1987), p. 11.
Item 4 – Berthet-Bondet and Blades (1988), p. 11.
Item 5 – Meyer-zu-Schlochtern (1988), pp. 12–14.

The credit crunch has been more challenging, the lower the profit rate. In the 1960s, non-financial firms benefited from a leverage effect: a slightly negative real interest rate added to the rate of return to invested capital. Through the 1980s, the same leverage effect vanished or reversed, because monetary policy and the profit squeeze generated by the 1968–73 boom worked in the opposite direction. According to X-efficiency theory, firms should have been induced to revise their labour contracts in order to scale down unit costs. Consequently the breakdown of the Fordist compromise should be more severe, with a larger profit rate decline (Table 2.6, Item 3). But this does not seem to have been a purely cyclical phenomenon, since the two recessions generated by the oil shocks did not trigger an endogenous recovery of the profit share. The case has been well documented for the US: the non-reproductive cycles of the 1970s probably delineate a downward Kondratieff depression (Bowles et al., 1983), i.e. a structural crisis, due to the fact that institutions did not deliver an endogenous recovery.

The slowing down and uncertainties of the world economy destabilize the previous configuration for competition and they break open the Fordist national virtuous circle. This has a direct impact on the previous links between productivity–real wage–consumption and investment. First, national manufacturing sectors become price takers rather than price makers. Consequently, conflict over income distribution becomes more acute. If wage increases can no longer be passed into nominal prices, they directly reduce the profit rate, i.e. capital accumulation, and finally either job creation or standards of living. Therefore, the wage becomes a cost which is detrimental to external competitiveness, and not as much a component in aggregate demand as it was in the Fordist regulation mode. Such pressures upon the FCLR should be the more acute, the more open the national economy is or has become. As it happens, contrary to the interwar period, a creeping protectionism has not prevented external trade from representing an increasing share of national production (Table 2.6, item 4). *A priori* the challenge would be more important for the larger economies, which were not so accustomed to maintaining long-run structural competitiveness. Perhaps French and US industrial relations are more challenged by this continuing internationalization. Incidentally, labour-intensive industries, often price takers, suffer a great deal from such world competition (Table 2.6, item 5). Of course, organizational and technological innovations can compensate, by shifting employment from low value-added sectors and firms to more efficient ones. Sweden is a good example of such an offensive strategy. Clearly, in the long run, any advanced capital–labour relation can only be sustained via a continuous inducement to innovation.

Corporatisms Fare Better than other Industrial Relations

The Swedish evolution puts at the forefront the issue of workers' bargaining power and their relations with political strategies and reforms. In the 1960s, the unions and grass-roots workers generally took the initiative in labour conflicts. Most managers were ready for significant concessions in order to buy social peace. In other words, labour used to have a large or significant bargaining power over wages, labour organization and welfare, even under rather conservative governments. But the last two decades have sharpened some major differences between two broad configurations (Figure 2.2).

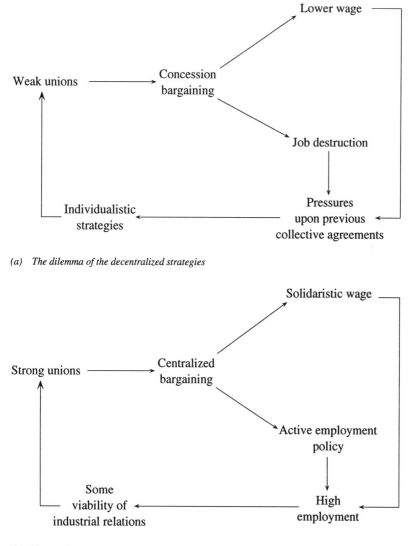

(a)   The dilemma of the decentralized strategies

(b)   The persisting virtuous circle of Social Democratic systems

Figure 2.2   Two configurations for capital–labour restructuring

In highly decentralized and adversarial systems, the initiative and bargaining power have drastically shifted to business. The surge of unemployment has disciplined workers (Table 2.7, item 3). On one side, segmented and dualistic labour markets have implied wage moderation, at least in the secondary sectors. On the other side, job preservation has been considered as important, along with wage increases; consequently unions have frequently been constrained to concession bargaining. The United States is a clear example of such a reversal (Rehmus, 1986; Rosenberg, 1988). Once initiated, this process has been cumulative (Figure 2.2(a)): the threat of job delocalization or bankruptcy has weakened unions' position, and ultimately the attractiveness of membership. Union density has continuously declined, thus reducing the union impact on wage differentials (Table 2.7, item 1). Worker militancy has itself been severely disciplined by unemployment and uncertain prospects. In these countries, strike activity has been drastically reduced through the 1980s (Table 2.7, item 2). In some respects, most European countries share these general trends. The only difference is that the unemployment crisis first stimulated union membership and strike activity, but the persistence of long-run unemployment and the failure of divided unions to find a viable new strategy has led to the same vicious circle.

Corporatist industrial relations suggest that this is not a unique path for restructuring the FCLR and facing international competition. In social democratic countries, such as Sweden and Austria, this perverse spiral was stopped at the very beginning. A clear commitment of governments to maintain quasi-full employment was part of the founding compromise (Therborn, 1986). In this model, job opportunities are more important than wage increases, since strong unions can accept a short-run decline in workers' income, provided that new jobs are created and intensive retraining policies are pursued (Rowthorn, 1990; Calmfors and Driffill, 1988; Bruno and Sachs, 1985). A very deep and long-lasting entry into the political élites and even managerial decisions has given a prominent role to a unified union, which can bargain at the macroeconomic level and take into account possible feedback effects on external competitiveness and job creation (Bowles and Boyer, 1990). Given this favourable context, strikes exploded during the 1980s, some of them challenging the official union's strategies. Nevertheless, the contrast with decentralized and adversarial industrial relations is striking (items 1, 2 and 3, Table 2.7 for Austria and Sweden). Consequently, given the same international uncertainties, high interest rates, and sluggish markets, these societies have found in their institutional forms tools for sustaining the previous social democratic compromise (Figure 2.2(b)).

The international crisis makes apparent major differences which were partially hidden when growth was stable and fast. In retrospect, the capital–labour compromise is different between the two industrial systems – more than a simple prefix should be added to the FCLR. Such a diverging path might delineate different models, even in the very long run. This is evidence for the

Table 2.7   The factors affecting workers' bargaining power

	Austria	France	Italy	Japan	Sweden	United Kingdom	United States	West Germany
1. Union density (%)								
1970	64	22	39	35	79	51	31	37
1979	59	28	51	32	89	58	25	42
1984/5	61	28	45	29	95	52	18	42
Pattern of evolution	Slight decline	Rise, stagnation and decline	Rise and decline	Steady decline	Clear rise	Rise and decline	Steady and strong decline	Rise and stagnation
2. Days of strike (evolution %)								
From 1970 to 1979	−66	182	151	237	−82	268	−70	−79
From 1979 to 1985	250	−77	−86	−72	1762	−78	−65	−93
Pattern of evolution	Decline and surge	Surge and decline	Surge and decline	Surge and decline	Decline and surge	Surge and decline	Steady decline	Steady decline
3. Unemployment rates (%)								
1970	1.1	2.5	5.0	1.2	1.2	2.4	5.0	0.6
1979	1.7	6.0	7.2	2.1	1.7	4.5	5.8	3.3
1989	3.4	9.5	12.1	2.3	1.4	6.2	5.3	5.5
Pattern of evolution	Slow rise	Continuous rise and slow decline	Continuous rise	Slow rise and decline	Slow rise and decline	Fast rise slow decline	Strong cyclical component	Continuous rise and recent decline

Sources:
Item 1 – National sources for France imply a strong decline of union density during the 1980s. For comparative purposes, Freeman figures have been kept (Freeman 1988, p. 69).
Item 2 – Annual Statisitcs BIT various years: 1972, 1982, 1986. If the corresponding year was exceptional the variation rate has been computed with the average around the corresponding year.
Item 3 – OECD (1990a), p. 212.

structural character of the transformations of the capital–labour relations inherited from the Second World War.

Slow but Far-Reaching Structural Changes

The future of industrial relations is nowadays characterized by the opposition of two conflicting hypotheses. For many North American scholars, concession bargaining, resegmentation of labour markets, wage flexibility and welfare rationalization were only the consequence of the most severe recession of the post-Second World War era (Rehmus, 1986). If economic trends were reversed, then most of the capital relation would turn back to the previous configuration, perhaps with alterations at the margin. In other words, changes in capital–labour relations would be totally reversible. Most macroeconometric models share the same hypothesis.

For others, the innovations linked to information technology, as well as new trends in lifestyles and international competition, would definitely rule out any capital–labour compromise as implying too many rigidities in a world of fierce competition where flexibility is decisive in survival. Still more, archaic unions would slowly decay in their inability to cope with the individualistic expectations of new generations. The two decades would be the starting point of an irreversible process. One finds for example such a vision in the 'New Industrial Divide' – both unions and the Keynesian state would undergo an irreversible decay (Piore and Sabel, 1984).

A third vision is adopted here. After the destruction or reform of most of the components of the FCLR, every nation would grope in the search for a new capital–labour relation which would make national political and cultural heritage coherent with the new trends in lifestyle, technology and finance. Two symmetrical types of evidence can be given against these two overly simplistic views. The reversibility hypothesis is first contradicted by the very observation of American industrial relations. Concession bargaining and innovations to find new labour contracts are still frequent even after the seventh year of the longest boom in American history (ETUI, 1990). Clearly, the economic recovery has not been sufficient to curb the previous transformations in the FCLR. Similarly, in Europe at the end of the 1980s, atypical labour contracts still continue to be the major component of job creation; the conventional Fordist agreements are exceptional (OECD, 1990). But the complete breakdown of labour legislation and collective agreements do not necessarily define an irreversible and inescapable scenario. The social democratic nations do prove the resilience of a capital–labour compromise, if it is coherent with innovation and long-run competitiveness. But paradoxically, the Social Democratic model is challenged in the early 1990s. Perhaps the Swedish wildcat strikes and wage explosions are expressing the very success of this model in maintaining full employment. Still more, decentralized industrial systems, such as the United States and the United Kingdom, experience too much wage drift and consequently inflationary pressures, fuelled by easy monetary policy (OECD, 1990).

All the previous arguments in favour of the transition towards a new CLR can be complemented by more structural factors (Table 2.8).

Internationalization now concerns trade and finance, but also production and even innovation. Consequently, any CLR mode has to build into its inner organizational forms the competitiveness objective. Very small open economies have been accustomed to such a challenge for half a century at least. For larger countries, belonging to the EC or even the United States, not to speak of Eastern Europe, a significant redesign of their capital–labour compromise is inevitable.

New and more demanding generations call for more autonomy in the workplace and more freedom in choice of lifestyle. In this respect the feminization of the labour force definitely introduces a great deal of novelty in conventional industrial relations (Table 2.8, item 1). At least two sources of income are now needed to sustain a standard of living which used to be provided by only one male worker. The genuine ideal of Henry Ford (1930), according to which women should be kept home, is now dead, and women seem to have definitely gained new status in the workplace and within society.

New productive principles and tertiarization challenge the old vision of labour, which was centred on manufacturing processes requiring muscle more than cleverness and commitment. Information technologies will probably have some role in completely redesigning the role of human labour, not only in the manufacturing sectors but in services too. The deepening of the division of labour, growth in the tasks of management, conception, marketing, insurance, finance, and concern for health, education and training will ultimately redefine the boundaries between the various jobs. Remember that all through the crisis, the global trend toward tertiarization has not altered; quite to the contrary (Table 2.8, item 2).

The trend towards differentiation of lifestyles reinforces the previous factors. On one side, customizing mass produced goods is a permanent feature in the history of the so-called American system (Hounshell, 1984; Chandler, 1990). From Ford T to Ford A, from the annual model change launched by General Motors to Toyotism (Jacot, 1990), the same strategies are implemented in order to capture market shares and oligopolistic power. This might challenge the precise and paralysing job rules inherited from Fordism. Similarly, wage earners might want to play with a whole spectrum of labour contracts. Under Fordism full-time jobs and labour contracts with indefinite duration used to be the rule. Nowadays, part-time jobs comprise most employment growth (Table 2.8, item 3), and this is only a small piece of evidence of the numerous innovations which have taken place during the last two decades. Finally, even if financial concentration again increases (Harrison, 1989), at the plant level average size has

Table 2.8 Changes in labour contracts and categories of workers involved

	Austria	France	Italy	Japan	Sweden	United Kingdom	United States	West Germany
1. Feminization of labour force Variation of activity rate 1979–87 (1973–79)								
• Male	-0.3 (-1.4)	-7.1 (-2.6)	-3.6 (-2.5)	-1.8 (-0.8)	-3.8 (-0.2)	-2.9 (-2.5)	-0.3 (-0.5)	-4.7 (-4.6)
• Female	+3.8 (+0.6)	+1.6 (+4.1)	+4.5 (+5.0)	+3.1 (+0.7)	+6.7 (+10.2)	+4.0 (+4.8)	+7.2 (+7.8)	+2.2 (0.0)
2. Tertiarization of employment Decline in manufacturing employment share, 1979–85 (%)	n.a.	-3.1	-3.6	+0.8	n.a.	-5.6	-3.2	-2.5
Employment share of services in 1985 (variation, 1973–85) (%)	54 (+11)	60 (+11)	55 (+13)	56 (+9)	65 (+12)	65 (+12)	69 (+16)	54 (+10)
3. Part-time jobs Increase in shares (1979–88)	-0.1	+3.7	+0.5	+1.2	+0.2	+4.0	+0.3	+1.2
4. Distribution to employment according to plant size (1980–86)								
• Less than 10 employed	n.a.	+2.9	n.a.	+0.3	n.a.	+2.0	+0.4	+0.8
• More than 500 employed (change in share, total = 100)	n.a.	-3.2	n.a.	-0.4	n.a.	-2.2	-0.3	-0.5

Sources:
Item 1 – OECD (1988d), September, p. 218, Table H.
Item 2 – Bertrand (1989), p. 10; Broclawski et al. (1988) p. 15.
Item 3 – OECD (1990b), pp. 12–13.
Item 4 – Bertrand (1989), p. 23, for France; Sengenberger and Loveman (1987), pp. 115–19.

declined both in manufacturing and in services (Sengenberger and Loveman, 1987). Perhaps the shift of employment towards small size firms will delineate more than a mere transition from one industrial regime to another (Table 2.8, item 4).

To conclude, all these factors support the basic hypothesis of this paper: the 1980s have experienced a significant or complete redesign of capital–labour relations. These changes are likely to be structural and far-reaching, and not at all transitory and reversible. Given the previous analyses, can any scenarios be proposed?

IV NEW CONFIGURATIONS FOR THE 1990s

As a way of anticipating this volume's concluding chapter by Alain Lipietz, it is necessary to derive some scenarios for the future CLR in the next century, however difficult such an exercise might be.

A Typology for Alternative Capital–Labour Relations

Any configuration for the CLR can be captured by the description of work organization on one side and the institutional setting for wage formation on the other. Consequently, most past and contemporary capital–labour relations can be illustrated by combining alternative work organizations and wage formation principles (Table 2.9).

Across the table, the unfolding of *scientific management* can be followed. Initially, the rationalization of work aims at dividing complex tasks into simpler ones, via a measure of operating time: this is the Taylorism stage. Once decomposed, these tasks can be mechanized and combined along the assembly line, at least for mass produced goods: Fordism deepens the Taylorism breakthrough. If typical Fordism used to mass produce standardized goods, this system has exhibited strong rigidities and an intrinsic inability to cope with fast changes in demand and consumers' expectations. Therefore, the annual model change introduced by General Motors during the 1920s already aimed at making mass production flexible. This general trend was still being reinforced during the 1970s and 1980s, due to the numerous innovations by Japanese firms such as Toyota. At the extreme, mass production would vanish and would be reproduced by flexible production of customized goods, by polyvalent workers using computerized equipment.

Down the table is displayed the *capital–labour compromise* about rent or productivity sharing. The upper part emphasizes the role of market adjustments: in competitive 'regulation', labour mobility is supposed to provide both wage and employment flexibility. But the history of industrial relations shows that

Table 2.9 *A taxonomy for alternative capital–labour relations*

Labour contract	Large-scale and rigid division of labour a	Large-scale and rigid division of labour + automation b	Flexible automation + flexible organization c	Flexible automation + learning by doing + training d
Wage and employment flexibility (1)	Taylorist	Fordist 'T'	Californian	Flexible specialization
Contractual wage, flexible employment (2)	Neo-Taylorist	Fordist 'A'	General Motors	Cooperatist
Three components wage formula with job tenure (3) = (1) + (2)	Rejuvenated Neo-Taylorist	Corporatist–Fordist	Saturnian	Toyotist–Sonyist
Three components wage formula + meso/macro-tuning (Job duration, wage funds, employment banks, training and retraining)	Social-Democratic Taylorist	Social-Democratic Fordist	Kalmarist	Uddevallist

the very technical centralization has enhanced the formation of unions and workers' demands for higher wages and more generally collective agreements codifying some institutional mechanisms for wage formation, for example cost of living adjustments. A flexible employment contract, implying lay-offs, is used to cope with uncertainty and economic fluctuations. Another avenue for capital–labour compromise starts with job security. At the beginning of this century, this was the initial strategy of large American corporations, such as Ford, but this tenure was mainly implemented by large contemporary Japanese firms. In that case, wage flexibility was the necessary complement for this implicit employment stability. Finally, the contractualization of the CLR might concern the very reproduction, of skill and investment decisions, i.e. the conditions of long-run competitiveness. The social democratic compromise gives a good example of such a highly institutionalized CLR.

According to this broad historical retrospective, capital–labour relations have evolved from elementary forms of scientific management and competitive wage formation to a high level of mechanization, associated with collective agreements codifying an explicit capital–labour compromise. For convenience, these stages have been labelled respectively Taylorist and Fordist. The distinction between Fordist T and Fordist A refers to the shift from totally standardized products to annual model changes, following Hounshell (1984) and Chandler (1990). The Taylorist CLR refers to purely atomistic industrial relations, whereas a neo-Taylorist CLR implies rather strong unions and wage contracts.

Let us explain briefly the labelling of the other cells. A Californian CLR combines flexible automation and organization with atomistic competition in labour markets. The General Motors CLR is a variant of Fordist A, pushing organizational flexibility. A Saturnian CLR borrows its name from the Saturn experiment by General Motors: basically it combines sophisticated flexible automatization with an agreement about job tenure. The Toyotist or Sonyist CLR follows the same logic but mechanization is not used as a form of control, since the ensuring of workers' commitment allows large learning-by-doing effects and internal flexibility to product and process changes. A further implication of this model concerns the global institutions associated with training, solidaristic wage policies and wage funds. A social democratic compromise can be associated with various work organizations: Fordist, flexible automation, based on continuous learning by doing and retraining. These give respectively a Social Democratic Fordist CLR, a Kalmarist configuration (taking the name of a pioneering experiment in work in organization in a Volvo plant during the 1970s), and finally the Uddevallist CLR, which corresponds to the most advanced experiment away from Fordist principles. Finally, at the other extreme, a totally decentralized industrial system can be associated with the same organizational principle and delineate a flexible specialization case. *A priori*, technology is far from implying any definite organization (Peitchinis, 1985; d'Iribarne, 1989a).

In the new productive model, the commitment and the skills of workers are crucial for innovation, competitiveness and adaptation to changing markets and tastes. This introduces a discontinuity with respect to one century of scientific management: skills are no longer removed from blue collar workers; on the contrary managers try to enhance them. In a sense, however paradoxical it might sound, workplace democracy is at the top of the agenda for the next century (Coriat, 1990). In this new era, the method for upgrading skills has a large impact upon the viability of any CLR. But again, a variety of compromises and organizations can cope with such a challenge (Table 2.10). Under Toyotism, skills formation and retraining are internalized within large firms, whereas the capital–labour compromise, often implicit, is specific to each firm; it reinforces corporatist or paternalist strategies. At the other extreme, Kalmarism combines nationwide capital–labour compromise with a public external organization for skills formation. In the Uddevallist model, given the same national setting, more training will be done internally in each firm. Finally, the Saturnian model is more decentralized for wage formation, employment and skills enhancement. These configurations may have very different impacts on performance (Streeck, 1988a; Campinos-Dubernet et al., 1988).

Table 2.10   How is training organized?

	Training and skills	
	Internalized	Externalized
Decentralized	Toyotism	Saturnian
Centralized	Uddevallist	Kalmarist

Note: Tables 2.9 and 2.10 are adapted from joint research with Benjamin Coriat (1989).

Given this typology, what could be the future of the capital–labour relations in advanced capitalist countries? The present analyses suggest that Taylorism and Fordism definitely belong to the past, and are now ruled out by more efficient and possibly more promising organizations. Furthermore, the eight countries under review do not belong to the same CLR, and therefore could experience different trajectories.

Two Strategic Choices

Thus, the demise of Fordist capital–labour relations is largely recognized, but various alternative restructurings are competing with each other. How should we proceed? Firms, governments and unions are facing two important issues, to which contradictory responses can emerge according to the basic specificities of each national economy and political process (Figure 2.3).

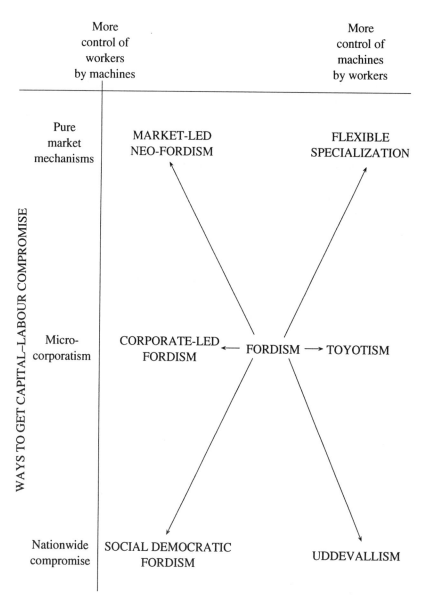

Figure 2.3   From Fordism to alternative capital–labour relations

How should the advances in information technology be used in restructuring work organization? This is no longer an issue restricted to the manufacturing sector, since these technologies permeate the whole economic system, especially the banks and insurance companies, engineering, marketing, and public and private management. Overwhelming evidence suggests that the same technological device can be given different roles in capital–labour management.

If conventional scientific management principles are still dominant, then 'electronized equipment goods' (robots as well as computers) will be used by managers to restore control over blue- and white-collar workers. For example, new flexible automated equipment could be designed to maintain a clear separation between conception and execution tasks (Noble, 1984). Consequently, a neo-Fordist work organization would deepen previous trends in scientific management. Many examples of such a strategy can be seen among American (Adler, 1990) and French manufacturers (d'Iribarne, 1989b). In most cases – but of course there are exceptions – the name of the game is simple: 'Remove the skills from the grass-roots workers!'

But the same equipment or small adaptations of them can support an alternative strategy, the motto of which would be quite different: 'Give as many skills as possible to workers.' Then due to the workers' commitment, firms can simultaneously achieve quality of product, high productivity and market versatility. Indeed, information technologies would help, but not necessarily imply, more control of machines by workers (Shaiken, 1984). This Toyotist or flexible specialization strategy is at odds with the neo-Fordist one which aims to control workers by machines. This restructuring seems common to very different national economies: Japanese, as well as Swedish and German firms seem to share this concern.

Recent detailed investigations and international comparative studies suggest that the second strategy gives better results than the first one. For example, in the car industry, the new conceptions provide simultaneously higher productivity and better quality, lower unit costs and larger flexibility to demand variations (Roos, 1989). For the most advanced flexible manufacturing systems, i.e. computer integrated manufacturing, comparative analyses show convincingly that the performance of any given plant is highly correlated with the skills involved. Given numerous breakdowns and the progressive learning about how to repair and prevent them, only well trained workers can maintain decent capacity utilization rates (Ayres, 1990; Badham, 1990). Similarly, in the service sector, the efficiency of computer networks is closely associated with the quality of data, i.e. the concern of white-collar workers for their jobs. If not, 'garbage in, garbage out!' Consequently, in Figure 2.3, the most promising strategies are related to the enhancement of skills and organizational flexibility. But now a second major issue has to be addressed.

How should the dividends of this new configuration be distributed? Again, the previous international comparison suggests that there is not necessarily one best way: alternative strategies might cope with the same restructuring of work organization. How and at what level should the sharing of the related rents be negotiated? Three major strategies are available.

First, *market mechanisms* can be considered the more efficient tool to guide such a restructuring process. Labour mobility from obsolete firms to promising ones, as well as efficient labour markets would provide incentives for such a diffusion of the new productive organization. According to a *laissez-faire* strategy, the past Fordist collective agreements should vanish and be replaced by purely individual strategies.

Micro-corporatism is an alternative arrangement. On one side, workers, managers and stock-holders would negotiate a long-run compromise about rent sharing, at least for large conglomerates (Aoki, 1988, 1990). On the other side, labour mobility would provide a diffusion of these capital–labour relations to the rest of the economy. State intervention would be moderate as within the purely decentralized case.

Social democratic compromise extends this configuration to the whole economy via centralization of wage bargaining, subsidies to industrial restructuring, retraining, and via macroeconomic policy to sustain this basic capital–labour relation. Consequently, state interventions are numerous and imply many genuine institutions as well as large social transfers.

During the 1960s and 1970s, economists used to think that market mechanisms generally provided an optimum outcome, superior to micro- or social democratic corporatism. Modern micro-theories emphasize the externalities associated with network information technologies (Arthur, 1988) and the spillovers from one innovation to another (Romer, 1986). Consequently, pure market competition might lock economies into an inferior state and conversely some coordination rules could provide better outcomes. This is a first reason for the possible superiority of corporatist institutions. Another one is still more important for the CLR: the apparent inability of pure and perfect competition to provide the adequate skills. Firms would underinvest in training, since it raises a public good dilemma: why train if skilled workers can be poached from other firms? The more decentralized industrial systems (US and UK) exhibit poor vocational training. The problem is especially acute in the United States (Dertouzos et al., 1989; *Business Week*, 1988). On the other hand, some international comparative studies suggest the superiority of meso- or micro-corporatist training institutions (Streeck, 1989a,b). Therefore, each economy manifests some institutional and technological inertia, more or less related to the form of labour division and ways of obtaining social and political compromises about the CLR. Consequently, each economy does not have the same opportunity to follow a given strategy: some are more likely than others.

Four National Trajectories

The choice among alternative strategies is always, at least partially, the consequence of the regulatory schemes of the various countries. A substantial amount of comparative research (including Flanagan et al., 1983; Boyer, 1986; Lawrence and Schultze, 1988; Sarfati and Kobrin, 1987; ILO, 1987; OECD, 1988a, 1989; Schmitter and Streeck, 1988; Brunhes, 1989), points to four major trajectories regarding the wage–labour relationship (Table 2.11). The following analysis confines itself to advanced capitalist countries, leaving aside the newly industrialized countries, despite their growing importance in the international division of labour.

A decentralized and adversarial trajectory rests, in general, on a broad decentralization of wage bargaining; it favours recourse to external mobility and relies on the market, rather than on trade union efforts, to adjust employment to technical innovations, to the pressures of competition and to the frequent disruptions which have characterized the international economy in the past two decades. In theory, mobility of employment and the corresponding flexibility of wages constitute the key variables in the adjustment to changing circumstances. This model offers a definite advantage during recessionary periods or with respect to the decline of aging sectors. Yet it has a number of defects. The extreme flexibility of wages, the heterogeneity of legislation concerning trade union rights and the modest levels of the minimum wage may inhibit labour-saving technical change. Why chance expensive and risky innovations to obtain results that can be achieved through a defensive flexibility? As several econometric studies have shown (e.g. Dumenil and Levy, 1989), in the long run the sluggishness of real wages slows overall productivity. The reader will have recognized this as a description of the American and Canadian economies. This would propel these economies towards a market-led neo-Fordism (Figure 2.3).

A microcorporatist model, on the contrary, seems to characterize Japan. A compromise concerning the sharing of surpluses resulting from quick reactions to market opportunities and from productivity gains made possible by the effects of experience is evident in its large enterprises. Obviously the subcontracting network helps to soften the impact of economic fluctuations, but it also plays a role in the ongoing modernization strategy. The versatility of labour and product innovation are the key factors in long-term adjustment, while flexibility and large bonuses facilitate short-term adjustment. This model is therefore effective in both respects, in as much as the compromise within large enterprises does not hinder short-term adjustments, and yet stimulates technical change. Nevertheless, there is no denying the disadvantages of this system. Long-term prospects hinge on favourable global economic conditions and the financial system's willingness to gamble on a bright future. In addition, this model cannot be applied in traditional or labour-intensive industries, unless the

Table 2.11 Outline of a typology: four trajectories

Trajectories	Decentralized and adversarial	Micro-corporatism	Social Democratic	Hybrid
Institutional characteristics	– Decentralization – External mobility – Market forces – Little trade union involvement	– Compromise within the firm – Internal mobility – Weak trade union involvement	– High degree of centralization – Region- and state-sponsored mobility – Much involvement of strong trade unions	– Relative centralization – Weak internal mobility/ enforced external mobility – Trade union tradition
Adjustment variables	– Lay-offs – Variation of average wage – Variability of wage dispersion – Regional mobility	– Internal transfers from job to job – Pressure for product innovation – Multiple skills – Reliance on bonuses	– Industrial redeployment – Possibility of wage flexibility – Flat wage structure – Training	– Staff cutbacks – Rigidity of real wages – Weak variation of wage dispersion – Unemployment among the young
Advantages	– Quick response to recessions – Adjustment to structural changes	– Short-term response: bonuses – Long-term response: productivity and product innovation	– Maintenance of wage uniformity – Affirmation of the principle of full employment	– Maintenance of the welfare state – Stimulation of productivity
Drawbacks	– Inadequate training – Little long-term investment – Possible inhibition of technical change	– Build-up of labour – *De facto* segmentation of the labour force (large enterprises/ subcontractors) – Limitations in labour-intensive industries	– Strain on the capital– labour compromise – Strain on public finances – Adverse effects of flat wage structure on incentives	– Arbitration in favour of jobholders – Erosion of the wage–labour relationship – Youth unemployment – Forced reduction of activity rates
Examples	United States	Japan	Sweden, Austria, West Germany	France, Italy, UK

corresponding enterprises are part of large conglomerates that can guarantee a high level of internal mobility. In Japan's case, this decentralized offensive flexibility is therefore accompanied by some segmentation and inequality among wage-earners. This second trajectory is the example of a Toyotist capital–labour relation (Figure 2.3).

The model of offensive flexibility in the social democratic mould constitutes a third configuration which is of interest because it stands in sharp contrast to the previous two models. The strength and solidarity of the workers' movement, and its close ties to the Social Democratic Party, have led to a unique institutional configuration, characterized by a multiplicity of collective mechanisms which ensure the mobility of wage-earners and adaptation to technical change. The advantages of this system are to be found in the assistance made available for industrial reconversion, the possibility of timely wage flexibility and the priority accorded to full employment. Contrary to the European model, preference is given to training and active employment creation measures over traditional unemployment benefits (OECD, 1989). Nevertheless, if we are to judge by its sociopolitical track record in the 1980s, this system also exhibits certain tensions: the temptation of enterprises to question the compromise of the 1980s, persistent public deficits, and the counterproductive effects of an overly flat wage structure. And yet, the return to nearly full employment is proof that this model has coped successfully with the structural changes of the 1970s and 1980s. The 1990s, however, are again challenging the compromise, especially as regards earlier wage restraint. But this model, far from representing a transitory exception to defensive flexibility strategies, seems to be blessed with a gift for regulation which, barring major transformations, may keep it viable for quite some time. This third trajectory corresponds to the Uddevallism model, shown in Figure 2.3.

Lastly, a hybrid model seems to characterize the general situation in the EC, allowing for occasionally significant differences between individual countries. The system is characterized by the interplay of market forces and institutionalized compromises in which the trade unions have traditionally played an important role. Branch level collective agreements typify this approach to wage setting. In the 1970s, given the initial rigidity of real wages, enterprises relied on adjustments in staff levels. As a result, unemployment in Europe is distributed very unequally among the various occupational groups, with the young bearing a disproportionate share of the burden. This is not to imply that the European model is without merit: indeed, the maintenance of social transfers and public interventions has enabled individual countries to tolerate levels of unemployment higher than any experienced since the 1930s. Moreover, despite the stability of real wages, incentives for productivity have never totally vanished, and there is, therefore, cause for optimism as regards long-term competitiveness and continued improvement in the standard of living. This trajectory is hard to locate on Figure 2.3 since it combines Toyotism, Uddevallism and corporate or market-led Fordism, in various proportions in the different countries or regions within the same countries.

The position of the EC calls forth two comments, one retrospective and the other prospective (Emerson, 1988). In the 1980s Europe showed the poorest results as regards unemployment and, to an extent, inflation. Arguments in support of this contention exceed the scope of this article, but the area is the subject of much active research which is expanding the frontiers of macroeconomics and labour economics (e.g. Boyer, 1988b; Feeman, 1988; Brunetta and Dell'Aringa, 1990; OECD, 1988d; Calmfors and Driffill, 1988). Briefly, it can be argued that the Community has yet to make a choice. It benefits from neither the defensive flexibility of the American continent, nor from the advantages of a social democratic global compromise. This intermediate position between purely centralized and decentralized models, between Fordist inertia and promising work experiments and between systems of industrial relations with either strong or very weak trade unions, is qualified as 'hybrid', since it combines features of both the market-oriented and social democratic strategies.

V CONVERGENCE THEORY REVISITED

Finally, this chapter proposes an unconventional view of the transformations which will shape the twenty-first century. The falling of the Berlin wall and the total collapse of Eastern Europe, as well as the faddism concerning the Japanese model, that every firm or nation should adopt and import, have given a new appeal to convergence theory: in the 1960s, it was fairly common to think that all economic systems would evolve towards a unique configuration. In the 1990s, this vision is recurring. Furthermore, the breakdown of the so-called communist regimes has sometimes been interpreted as the end of history: is not democratic capitalism the only viable form of organization? So, Schumpeter and Hayek will finally have defeated Marx and Keynes.

Of course, capitalism has overcome the challenge of the communist regimes but it has itself evolved far away from its early configuration and taken contrasted national forms. Consequently, the same constraints and opportunities may generate quite contrasted institutional forms. This sketchy, but we hope suggestive analysis of the capital–labour relation hints that many paths are open to capitalist dynamics, and that history is neither totally reversible nor absolutely irreversible. Still more, in the long run, strategic political choices during structural crises might exert a determinant role in shaping new social relations and correlatively economic regulation modes. The contrast between the Swedish social democratic compromise and Japanese micro-corporatism or the distance between the American highly decentralized system and the European hybrid configuration is sharp enough to show that it is not a purely cosmetic choice, but a true and challenging one.

REFERENCES

Adler, P. (1990) 'Capitalizing on new product and process technologies: current problems and emergent trends in US industry', mimeograph prepared for the International OECD Conference 'Technological Change as a Social Process: Society, Enterprises and the Individual', Helsinki, 11–13 December 1989, Paris: OECD.

Aglietta, M. (1982) *Regulation and Crisis of Capitalism*, New York: Monthly Review Press.

Andersson, J.A. and L. Mjoset (1987) 'The transformation of the Nordic models', forthcoming in *Cooperation and Conflict.*

André, C. and R. Delorme (1983) *L'Etat et l'economie*, Paris: Seuil.

Aoki, M. (1988) *Information, Incentives, and Bargaining in the Japanese Economy*, New York: Cambridge University Press.

Aoki, M. (1990) 'Toward an Economic Model of the Japanese Firm', *Journal of Economic Literature*, vol. XXVIII, March, pp. 1–27.

Arthur, B. (1988) 'Competing Technologies: an overview', in G. Dosi et al. (eds) *Technical change and Economic Theory*, London: Pinter.

Artus, P. (1983) 'Formation conjointe des prix et des salaires dans cinq grands pays industriels: Peuton comprendre les écarts entre les taux d'inflation?' *Annales de l'INSEE*, no. 49, January–March, pp. 5–52.

Atkinson, P. and J.C. Chouraqui (1985) 'Taux d'intérêt réels et perspectives de croissance durable', *Document de Travail OCDE*, no. 21, Department of Economics and Statistics, May.

Ayres, R.U., E. Dobrinsky, W. Haywood, K. Uno and E. Zuscovitch (eds) (1990) *CIM: Economic and Social Impacts*, Laxenburg: IIASA.

Badham, R.J. (1990) 'Socio-technical CIM trajectories in national systems of innovation: The need for an interdisciplinary approach', mimeograph prepared for the 'CIM: Revolution in Progress' Conference, Laxenburg: IIASA, 1–4 July.

Basle, M., J. Mazier and J.F. Vidal (1984) *Quand les crises durent...*, Paris: Economica.

Benassy, J.P., R. Boyer, and R.M. Gelpi (1979) 'Régulation des économies capitalistes et inflation', *Revue Economique*, vol. 30, no. 3, May.

Bernstein, M. (1988) 'The great depression and regulation theory: A North American perspective', mimeograph, International Colloquium on the Regulation Theory, Barcelona, 16–18 June.

Berthet-Bondet, C., D. Blades and A. Pin (1988) 'The OECD compatible trade and production data base 1970–1985', *Working Paper* no. 60 *OECD*, Department of Economics and Statistics, November.

Bertrand, H. (1983) 'Accumulation, régulation, crise: un modèle sectionnel théorique et appliqué', *Revue Economique*, vol. 34, no. 6, March.

Bertrand, H. (1989) 'Modèle d'emploi européens: convergence ou divergence?' Mimeograph INNOVENCE, November, research conducted for the Commission of European Communities.

Bosworth, B. and A. Rivlin (eds) (1987) *The Swedish Economy*, Washington D.C: The Brookings Institution.

Bowles, S. and R. Boyer (1990) 'Labour market flexibility and decentralisation as barriers to high employment? Notes on employer collusion, centralised wage bargaining and aggregate employment', in R. Brunetta and C. Dell'Aringa (eds), *Labour Relations and Economic Performance*, Basingstoke: Macmillan, pp. 325–52.

Bowles, S., D. Gordon and T. Weisskopf (1983) *Beyond the Waste Land*, New York: Basic Books.

Boyer, R. (1979) 'Wage formation in historical perspective: the French Experience', *Cambridge Journal of Economics*, no. 3, March, pp. 99–118.

Boyer, R. (ed.) (1986) *La Flexibilité du travail en Europe*, Paris: La Découverte.

Boyer, R. (1987) 'The current economic crisis', in S. Hoffmann and G. Ross (eds) *The MITTERRAND Experiment*, Cambridge: Basil Blackwell, pp. 33–53.

Boyer, R. (1988a) 'Formalizing growth regime', in G. Dosi et al. (eds) *Technical change and Economic Theory*, London: Pinter pp. 608–30.

Boyer, R. (ed.) (1988b) *The Search for Labour Market Flexibility*, Oxford: Clarendon Press.

Boyer, R. (1990a) 'The transformations of the capital labour relation and wage formation in eight OECD countries during the Eighties', in Mizoguhi (ed.) *Making Economies more Efficient and Equitable, Factors determining Income Distribution*, Tokyo, 27–29 November, 1989, Oxford University Press.

Boyer, R. (1990b) 'The forms of organisation implicit in the General Theory: an interpretation of the success and crisis of Keynesian economic policies', in A. Barrere (ed.) *Keynesian Economic Policies*, London: Macmillan, pp. 117–39.

Boyer, R. (1990c) 'The Economics of Job Protection and Emerging Capital Labour Relations: From the Perspective of "Regulation Theory"', mimeograph CEPREMAP, May, prepared for the International Conference on 'Workers' protection and Labour Market Dynamics', Berlin, 16–18 May.

Boyer, R. (1990d) 'New Directions in Management Practices and Work Organisation', mimeograph CEPREMAP, November, prepared for the OECD Conference on 'Technical Change as a Social Process: Society, Enterprises and Individual', Helsinki, 11–13 December, 1989, Paris: OECD.

Boyer, R. and B. Coriat (1989) 'La démocratie salariale', mimeograph CEPREMAP.

Boyer, R. and J. Mistral (1978) *Accumulation, Inflation, Crises*, Paris: Presses Universitaires de France, 2nd edition (1982).

Boyer, R. and A. Orléan (1990) 'Convention salariale: du local au global, l'exemple fordien', mimeograph CEPREMAP, April.

Boyer, R. and P. Petit (1989) 'Technical change, cumulative causation and growth: an exploration of some post Keynesian theories, mimeograph CEPREMAP, May, prepared for the International OECD Seminar on 'Science, Technology and Growth', 5–8 June.

Brenner, R. (1988) 'The Regulation Approach to the History of Capitalism', mimeograph, International Colloquium on the Regulation Theory, Barcelona, 16–18 June.

BRIE (Berkeley Roundtable on Industrial Economics) (1987) *Round Table on Production Reorganization in a Changing World Economy*, Berkeley: Actes du Colloque, 10–12 September.

Broclawski, J.P., J. Dessaint, F. Ecalle and C. Mazas (1988) 'L'emploi dans les services. Comparaisons internationales', *Document de travail Direction de la Prévision*, no. 88–8.

Brunetta, R. and C. Dell'Aringa (eds) (1990) *Labour Relations and Economic Performance*, Basingstoke: Macmillan.

Brunhes, B. (1989) 'La flexibilité du travail: réflexions sur les modèles européens', *Droit Social*, March, reprinted in *Problèmes Economiques*, no. 2.125,17 May, pp. 23–7.

Bruno, M. and J. Sachs (1985) *Economics of Worldwide Stagflation*, Oxford: Basil Blackwell.

Business Week (1988) 'Human Capital, The Decline of America's Work Force', 19 September, pp. 44–72.

Calmfors, L. and J. Driffill (1988) 'Centralization of Wage Bargaining', *Economic Policy*, no. 6, April, pp. 13–61.

Campinos-Dubernet, M., J.M. Grando and G. Margirier (1988) 'Comparaison internationale des modes de gestion de la main d'oeuvre dans le secteur du BTP. L'effet du rapport monopoliste', mimeograph, International Colloquium on the Regulation Theory, Barcelona, 16–18 June.

CERC (1989) *Le Revenu des Français*, Paris: La Documentation Française.

Chandler, A. (1990) *Scale and Scope: The Dynamics of Industrial Capitalism*, Cambridge Mass.: Belknap Press.

Chan-Lee, J.H., D.T. Coe and M. Prywes (1987) 'Mutations micro-économiques et désinflation salariale macroéconomiques dans les années 80', *Revue Economique de l'OCDE*, no. 8, Spring.

Coriat, B. (1985) 'L'emploi dans les stratégies d'automatisation: le modèle automobile américain', mimeograph, January, Paris.

Coriat, B. (1989) 'Mutations technologies et Democratie salariale', in *La Nouvelle Revue socialiste*, No. 5, May, reprinted in *Problèmes Économiques*, no. 2.138, 30 August 1989, pp. 14–21.

Coriat, B. (1990) *L'atelier et le robot*, Paris: Christian Bourgois.

Dell'Aringa, C. and S. Lodovici (1989) 'Industrial relations and economic performance', Universita Cattolica del Sacro Cuore, D.P. no. 16, September.

Dell'Aringa, C. (1990) 'Industrial Relations and the Role of the State in EEC Countries', mimeograph, presented for the EEC working group on 'Wages in Europe', 18–19 June.

d'Iribarne, P. (1989a) *La logique de l'honneur*, Paris: Seuil.

d'Iribarne, P. (1989b) 'Nouvelles technologies et nouveaux modes d'organisation: le cas français', ronéotypé CEREBE, prepared for the OECD Conference 'Technological Change as a Social Process: Society, Enterprises and the Individual', Helsinki,11–13 December.

Dertouzos, M.L., R.K. Lester and R.M. Solow (1989) *Made in America*, Cambridge Mass.: MIT Press.

Doeringer, P. and M. Piore (1971) *Internal Labor Markets and Manpower Analysis*, Lexington, Mass.: D.C. Heath

Dumenil, G. and D. Levy (1989) 'Micro adjustment behavior and macro stability', mimeograph CEPREMAP, no. 8915, June.

Economie Européenne (1989) 'Relever les défis du debut des années 90', no. 42, November.

Emerson, M. (1988) *Why Model for Europe?*, Cambridge Mass.: MIT Press.

Epstein, G. and J. Schor (1988) 'Macropolicy in the Rise and Fall of the Golden Age', *Working Paper WIDER*, no. 38, February.

ETUI (1988) Les négociations collectives en Europe Occidentale en 1987 et les perspectives pour 1988', Bruxelles, June.

ETUI (1990) 'Les négociations collectives en Europe occidentale en 1989 et les perspectives pour 1990', Bruxelles.

Flanagan, R.J., D.W. Soskice and L. Ulman (1983) *Unionism, Economic Stabilization, and Incomes Policies*, Washington DC.: The Brookings Institution.

Ford, H. (1930) *Ma vie et mon oeuvre*, Paris: Payot.

Freeman, R.B. (1988) 'Contraction and Expansion: The Divergence of Private Sector and Public Sector Unionism in the United States', *The Journal of Economic Perspectives*, vol. 2, no. 2, Spring, pp. 63–88.

Glyn, A. (1988) 'Productivity and the Crisis of Fordism', mimeograph, International Colloquium on the Regulation Theory, Barcelona, 16–18 June.

Harrison, B. (1989) 'Concentration without centralization: The changing morphology of the small firm industrial districts of the third Italy', mimeograph, International Symposium on Local Employment, National Institute of Employment and Vocational Research, Tokyo, 12–14 September.

Hounshell, D.A. (1984) *From the American system to mass production, 1800–1932*, Baltimore, Md: Johns Hopkins University Press.

ILO (1984) *Collective Bargaining and Recession in Industrial Market Economies*, Geneva.

ILO (1987) *Labor in the World*, Geneva.

Jacot, J. H. (1990) 'Du fordisme au toyotisme? Les voies de la modernisation du système automobile en France et au Japon', *Etudes et Recherches*, Commissariat Général du Plan, no. 7–8, February, La Documentatin Française.

Juillard, M. (1990) *La fin du modèle americain?* Paris: Editions Economica.

Klau, F. and A. Mittelstadt (1986) 'Flexibilité du Marché du Travail', *Revue Economique de l'OCDE*, no. 6, Spring, pp. 8–51.

Koike, K. (1987) 'Human Resource Development and Labour–Management Relations', in *The Political Economy of Japan*, vol. 1, *The Domestic Transformation*, Stanford Ca. Stanford University Press, pp. 289–330.

Kremp, E. and J. Mistral (1988) 'Flexibilité des salaires: l'impact des années Reagan', *Economie Prospective Internationale*, no. Special 36, Paris: La Documentation Française.

Krugman, P. (1990) *Rethinking International Trade*, Cambridge Mass.: MIT Press.

Lawrence, R.Z. and C. Schultze (eds) (1988) *Barriers to European Growth: A Transatlantic View*, Washington, DC: The Brookings Institute.

Leborgne, D. and A. Lipietz (1989) 'Pour éviter l'Europe à deux vitesses', EALE Conference, Turin, September.

Le Dem, J. (1987) 'Les salaires dans le modèle MIMOSA', mimeograph, CEPII-OFCE, no. 87–04, June.

Levi-Garboua, V. (1982) 'Les modes de consommation dans quelques pays occidentaux. Comparaison et lois d'évolution (1960–1980)', *Rapport CREDOC*, June.

Lipietz, A. (1983) *Le monde enchanté. De la valeur à l'envol inflationniste*, Paris: La Découverte.

Lutz, B. (1990) *Le mirage de la croissance marchande*, Paris: Editions de la Maison des Sciences de l'Homme.

Maddison, A. (1982) *Les phases du developpement capitaliste*, Paris: Economica.

Marsden, D. (1988) *The End of Economic Man?*, Brighton: Wheatsheaf.

Marglin, S. and J. Schor (eds) (1990) *The Golden Age of Capitalism*, Oxford: Clarendon Press.

Maruani, M., E. Reynaud and C. Romani (eds) (1989) *La flexibilité en Italie*, Paris: Syros Alternatives.

Meyer-Zu-Schlochtern, F.J.M. (1988) 'An international sectoral data base for thirteen OECD Countries, *OECD Working Paper*, no. 57, Department of Economics and Statistics, November.

Mimosa (Equipe) (1990) 'Mimosa, une modélisation de l'économie mondiale', *Observations et Diagnostics Economiques, Revue de l'OFCE*, no. 30, January.

Noble, D. (1984) *Forces of production*, New York: Knopf.

OECD (1983) 'Comité de la Main-d'oeuvre et des affaires sociales', mimeograph MAS/WP3(83)3, Groupe de travail sur les relations professionnelles, négociations collectives et politiques économiques, November.

OECD (1985) *Perspectives de l'Emploi*, September.

OECD (1986) *Flexibility and labour markets*, Paris: OECD.

OECD (1987) *Structural Adjustment and Economic Performance*, Paris: OECD.

OECD (1988a) 'Performances économiques et ajustement structurel, le marché du travail et les relations profesionnelles', mimeograph, MAS/WP3(88)2, Groupe de travail sur les relations professionnelles changements en cours dans les relations professionnelles, February.

OECD Working party on Industrial Relations (1988b) 'Industrial Relations: Agenda for Change', mimeograph, MAS/WP3(88)1, February.

OECD (1988c) 'New Technologies in the 1990s. A Socio-economic Strategy', Report of a Group of Experts on the Social Aspects of New Technologies.

OECD (1988d) *Structural Adjustments and Economic Performance*, Paris.

OECD (1989) 'Science, Technology and Growth', International Seminar, Paris, 4–7 June.

OECD (1990) *Employment Outlook*, Paris: OECD.

OECD (1990b) 'OECD figures', *OECD Observer*, no. 164, Supplement.

Peitchinis, S. G. (1985) *Issues in Management–Labour Relations in the 1990s*, London: Macmillan.

Piore, M. (1986) 'Perspectives on Labor Market Flexibility', Mimeograph MIT, 9 January, in a special issue *Industrial Relations*, edited by C. Brown and B. Harrison.

Piore, M. (1989) 'Post-Reagonomics: The Resurgence of the Social Sphere in Economic and Political Life?' Mimeograph MIT, November, revised January 1989.

Piore, M. and C. Sabel (1984) *The Second Industrial Divide: Possibilities of Prosperity*, New York: Basic Books.

Poret, P. (1986) 'La formation sectorielle des salaires dans cinq économies européennes: premiers résultats d'une etude statistique', *Document de travail*, no. 86–7, Direction de la Prévision.

Porter, M. (1990) *The Competitive Advantage of Nations*, London: Macmillan.

Ralle, P. and J. Toujas-Bernate (1989) 'Les salaires desindexés depuis 1983', mimeograph INSEE, Département des Etudes Economiques d'Ensemble, Division des Etudes Economiques, no. 39/G231, November.

Rehmus, C. (1986) 'L'avenir des relations de travail aux Etats-Unis', *Travail et Société*, vol. 11, no. 2, May, pp. 151–62.

Romer, P. (1986) 'Increasing Returns and Long-run Growth', *Journal of Political Economy*, vol. 94, October, pp. 1002–1038.

Roos, D. (1989) 'The Importance of Organisational Structure and Production System Design in Deployment of New Technology', OECD, DSTI, International Seminar on Science, Technology and Economic Growth, Paris, 6 June.

Rosenberg, S. (1988) 'The Restructuring of the Labor Market, the Labor Force and the Nature of Employment Relations in the United States in the 1980s', mimeograph, prepared for the International Conference on 'Economic Development and Labor Market Segmentation', University of Notre Dame, 17–20 April.

Rosenberg, S. (1989) 'De la segmentation à la flexibilité', *Travail et Société*, vol. 14, no. 4, October, pp. 387–438.

Rowthorn, R. (1990) 'Wage Dispersion and Employment in OECD Countries', prepared for the International Symposium on 'Making Economies more Efficient and Equitable, Factors determining Income Distribution', Tokyo, 27–29 November, 1989. Oxford University Press, forthcoming.

Sachs, J. (1978) 'The changing cyclical behavior of wages and prices: 1890–1976', Working Paper no. 304, National Bureau of Economic Research.

Sarfati, H. and C. Kobrin (eds) (1987) *La flexibilité du marché de l'emploi: un enjeu économique et social*, Geneva: ILO.

Schmitter, P. and W. Streeck (eds) (1989) *Comparative Governance of Economic Sectors*.

Schor, J. (1985) 'Changes in the Cyclical Pattern of Real Wages: Evidence from Nine Countries, 1955–80', *The Economic Journal*, vol. 95, no. 378, June, pp. 452–68.

Sengenberger, W. and G. Loveman (1987) 'Smaller Units of Employment: A synthesis Report on Industrial Reorganisation in Industrialised Countries', mimeograph, IILS, New Industrial Organisation Programme DP/3/1987.

Shaiken, H. (1984) *Work Transformed: Automation and Labor in the Computer Age*, Lexington Mass.: Lexington Books.

Standing, G. (1988) *Unemployment and Labour Market Flexibility: Sweden*, Geneva: ILO.

Steinberg, B. (1985) 'Le Reaganisme et l'économie américaine dans les années 1980, *Critiques de l'Economie Politique*, no. 31, April–June, pp. 5–24.

Strath, B. (1987) *The Politics of De-industrialisation*, London: Croom Helm.

Streeck, W. (1989a) 'On the Social and Political Conditions of Diversified Quality Production', mimeograph, LME's International OECD Conference 'No way to full employment?', Berlin, 7 July.

Streeck, W. (1989b) 'The social dimension of the European Firm', mimeograph prepared for the 1989 meeting of the Andrew Shonfield Association, Florence, 14–15 September.

Therborn, G. (1986) *Why Some People Are More Unemployed than Others*, London: Verso.

Thouluc, H. (1988) 'La détermination de l'emploi et la formation des salaires dans sept grands pays de l'OCDE. Une étude sur données empilées', mimeograph, Ministère de l'Economie, des Finances et de la Privatisation, D.P., G.P.E.M., January.

Tsuru, T. (1988) 'Change in the Wage–Unemployment Relation: The Reserve Army Effect in the Postwar Japanese Economy', mimeograph, The Institute of Economic Research, Hitotsubashi University, 7 April.

Wolleb, E. (1988) 'Mutamenti nei rapporti di produzione nella crisi: Ascesa e tracollo del fordismo in Italia', in R. Boyer and E. Wolleb (eds) *La flessibilita del Lavorno in Europa*, Milan: Franco Angeli.

3. Cooperative employment relations and Japanese economic growth

William Lazonick

I INTRODUCTION

There is widespread agreement that cooperative employment relations have played an important role in the phenomenal success of the Japanese economy over the past four decades. Japanese workers have been, and remain, willing to work long hours at a steady pace. In return they have seen their incomes rise dramatically. But these rising incomes have not been a burden on Japanese economic performance. Japanese workers have limited their wage demands to levels that reflect the current ability of their companies to pay without jeopardizing long-term corporate goals. Employers, in turn, have been willing to share the benefits of corporate prosperity with workers, thus ensuring that workers would continue to identify with the goals of the corporation.

The characteristic features of the Japanese employment environment might lead a 'Western' economist to expect to find low levels of productivity and high levels of labour–management conflict in Japanese industry rather than the high productivity and cooperative relations that in fact prevail. Many, if not most, Western economists (whether neoclassical, neo-Keynesian, or neo-Marxian) expect that when the threat of job loss is low workers will supply less effort and produce less output. Yet three major features of the employment environment in Japan all serve to reduce the threat of job loss facing Japanese workers.

First, a substantial proportion of male blue-collar workers have access to 'permanent employment' – the assurance of a continuous relation with a particular organization over the course of their working lives. Especially in the highly productive dominant enterprises (Toyota, Hitachi, Sony, Fujitsu, Matsushita, Canon, NEC, Nissan, etc.) that have been the driving forces in Japan's economic growth over the past four decades, male blue-collar workers have virtually no fear of dismissal. Second, the Japanese labour force lacks large numbers of ethnic minorities who can serve as a labour supply for low-paid, insecure jobs or who can compete with Japanese-born workers for better paid, blue-collar jobs. Third, the occupational structure and sustained growth of the

Japanese economy have generated full employment, and, at times, acute labour shortages. Even in companies where the institution of permanent employment is not entrenched, replacement workers are hard to find.

By lessening the competition for jobs, and hence the threat of job loss, therefore, the Japanese employment environment should give workers the power to reduce their work effort and raise their wage demands, thus contributing to the inflationary tendencies and labour–management conflicts that have occurred in the advanced capitalist economies of the West. According to a 'Western' perspective, that is, employment security, ethnic homogeneity and full employment should have impeded Japan's economic performance. By all accounts, they have not. Indeed, it can be argued that, by promoting cooperative employment relations, these features of the Japanese employment environment have helped to generate the nation's sustained economic growth. The purpose of this essay is to explain how and why the Japanese employment environment has benefited the Japanese economy, and in the process to consider whether and to what extent the Japanese model of employment relations can be (or already has been) diffused to the advanced capitalist economies of the West. Throughout this essay I shall compare Japanese employment relations primarily with those that have prevailed in the United States, and to a lesser extent with those that have prevailed in the United Kingdom (for an elaboration of this three-nation comparison, see Lazonick, 1990). In the conclusion, I shall explore briefly the implications of my analysis of employment relations and economic growth in Japan for the future of employment relations in the world economy more generally.

II   THE JAPANESE EMPLOYMENT ENVIRONMENT

Hours, Earnings, and Income Distribution

Japan entered the 1960s as a low-wage economy, especially compared with the United States. But by 1970 Japan's hourly wage rate in manufacturing had surpassed that of France and by 1975 that of the UK. Depending on the prevailing exchange rate, during the 1980s hourly wages in Japan were at times higher than those in Germany and the United States (Shirai, 1983, p. 131; Abegglen and Stalk, 1985, p. 194; *Year Book of Labour Statistics [YBLS]*, 1987, p. 317). By advanced capitalist country (ACC) standards, in the 1950s Japanese manufacturing workers laboured long hours for low pay; in the 1980s they laboured long hours for high pay.

In Japanese manufacturing, the average working hours per employed person peaked at 207 per month in 1960. From 1984 until 1988 working hours averaged about 180 hours per month (about 184 for men and about 168 for women). Despite a reduction in hours worked per year of about 13 per cent between 1960 and the mid-1980s, average Japanese working hours remained substantially above those in the other ACCs. For example, the work year of the average Japanese employee exceeded that of the average US employee by 517 hours. About 47 per cent of the differential was because of more hours worked per day and about 53 per cent because of more days worked per year (Maddison, 1987, p. 687). Compared with Germany (where the hours of work per year were just slightly more than in the United States), in Japan virtually all of the extra hours worked were because of more working days. Compared with all the ACCs, the most important difference in days worked derives from the retention of the six-day work week in Japan (see Maddison, 1987, p. 687; Koshiro, 1983, p. 243; Japan Economic Institute, 1990).

In 1987 the average monthly remuneration for Japanese male manufacturing workers was ¥381,000, about $26,000 per year at the prevailing exchange rate (*YBLS*, 1987, p. 105). For women in manufacturing, the average annual pay was just over $11,000 – about 42 per cent of the average for men. Indeed, Japan has one of the most unequal gender-based distributions of income in the world. In 1980 the female–male hourly wage ratio in Japan was 0.54, compared with 0.66 in the United States, 0.72 in Germany, and 0.79 in the UK (Mincer, 1985, p. 56). At the same time, Japan's household distribution of income is one of the most equal in the world, with lower-income Japanese households being particularly favoured. In part, Japan's relatively equal distribution of income derives from hierarchical pay differentials within enterprises that are much more compressed than in most, if not all, of the other ACCs. But in large part, the relative equality derives from government policies to maintain the economic viability of small-scale enterprise in agriculture, retailing and manufacturing. Particularly in agriculture, these policies are integral to Japan's social welfare system, and the success of these policies explains why Japan has not relied as heavily as the ACCs of the West on government transfer payments to ensure social welfare (see Vogel, 1980, ch. 8; Koike, 1988, pp. 47–53).

In 1980 12 per cent of the Japanese labour force were still engaged in agriculture, as compared with 6 per cent in the ACCs in general. Most Japanese agricultural workers grow rice on small family farms. Aided by advanced growing techniques (acquired with government assistance), Japan's rice yields per acre are among the highest in the world (Reich et al., 1986, p. 162; Vogel, 1980, pp. 80–81; see also Sawada, 1970; Tsuchiya, 1970). So too are the prices that farmers receive; during the 1960s and 1970s the government purchase price of rice was as much as four times the world price. These agricultural policies have kept the incomes of full-time farm households close to the level of urban wage-earning households.

These agricultural policies carry both costs and benefits to blue-collar workers. On the cost side, they have to spend a higher proportion of their incomes on food than do workers in other ACCs. In 1979 food represented 35 per cent of the expenditures of Japanese consumers, well over twice the proportion in the United States and perhaps as much as one-third higher than in the ACCs in general (Reich et al., 1986, p. 163). On the benefit side, however, is the availability of farming as an extra, or even an alternative, source of income for wage-earners who do not have 'regular employee' status (see below) or for full-time wage-earners who have had regular employee status but have reached the mandatory corporate 'retirement' age (usually between 55 and 60). In 1984 farm households with primarily non-agricultural earnings represented 71 per cent of all farm households, up from 65 per cent in 1980, and 51 per cent in 1970 (Reich et al., 1986, p. 163). According to an authoritative survey of Japanese agricultural policy written in the mid-1980s:

> Since 1981, the number of people abandoning other occupations to enter agriculture as the main job has actually exceeded the number leaving agriculture for other occupations. In 1983, moreover, 96 per cent of males going into farming as the main job were over fifty, and most of them had worked previously as part-time farmers. Innovative mechanization that facilitated small-scale part-time farming makes this trend possible, and may thereby serve as an obstacle to the consolidation of farmland and the formation of cooperative units. (Reich et al., 1986, p. 197)

Given the social welfare functions of the agricultural sector, however, the net social and economic impacts of the consolidation of Japanese farmland would not necessarily be positive. By permitting older workers to remain productive and independent after their retirement from corporate employment, the organization of Japanese agriculture functions as an effective and humane old-age security system. By facilitating the early retirement of older corporate employees, the system of small family farms increases the demand for younger workers – the potentially most productive members of the labour force – to fill the positions that the older workers have vacated. In short, Japan's agricultural policies have been the key to keeping the labour force fully employed, the household distribution of income relatively equal, and state welfare expenditures low.

The Japanese government has also helped to sustain small-scale enterprise in manufacturing and retailing. In manufacturing, dominant firms make extensive use of small-sized and medium-sized enterprises as subcontractors (see Odaka et al., 1988). Especially during the 1950s and 1960s, the government has aided the start-up and survival of smaller scale firms by making inexpensive finance available to them. This support has also helped the small supplier to strengthen its hand in dealing with the dominant enterprise, thus increasing the pressure toward more equality in the distribution of income (Friedman, 1988, pp. 167–8).

In retailing, the role of the state has been more far-reaching. During the 1970s, the Japanese government passed laws to limit the growth of retail chains by making it difficult to secure the right to open stores of any substantial size. By a 1973 law, government permission was required to open a store with more than 1500 square metres of floor space. In 1978 these strictures were also applied to stores with more than 500 square metres of floor space. Government approval for larger stores was rarely forthcoming, and over time applications for new stores over 500 square metres simply declined (McCraw and O'Brien, 1986).

Employment Opportunities

The policies to support small enterprise have helped not only to equalize the distribution of household income but also to create independent employment opportunities for those among the Japanese labour force who because of individual preference will not, or because of lack of educational credentials cannot, gain access to positions of regular employment with a corporation. In 1987 25 per cent of the entire Japanese labour force and 19 per cent of the non-agricultural labour force were classified as self-employed or as persons employed by family members. Among the male labour force, these figures were 20 per cent and 16 per cent respectively.

While the number of self-employed and family workers in agriculture has declined over the past few decades, in non-agricultural industries the number of self-employed persons increased by 31 per cent between 1960 and 1987 and the number of family workers by 12 per cent. The increase in self-employed was particularly rapid in manufacturing, where the number of self-employed grew by 62 per cent, slightly faster than the growth of the manufacturing labour force as a whole. In 1987 in non-agricultural industries, 65 per cent of the self-employed but only 18 per cent of the family workers were men. In manufacturing these figures were 60 per cent and 16 per cent respectively (*YBLS*, 1987, p. 8).

The persistent viability of small enterprise has occurred in Japan alongside, and indeed because of, the growth of the dominant enterprises that have been central to Japan's rise to international industrial leadership. The largest corporate employers in Japan are not large by US standards. In 1989 the ten largest industrial companies in Japan had an average of 114,000 employees; the average for the ten largest US industrials was 301,000 (*Fortune*, 1989, p. 291; *Dun's*, 1990, p. 345). Many large Japanese employers keep the number of their employees down through the practice of subcontracting work to smaller firms. For example, in 1989 Toyota's sales were 75 per cent greater than Nissan's, and its assets were 11 per cent greater. Yet Toyota employed 21 per cent fewer people because of its more extensive use of subcontracting.

In some cases, the core company subcontracts with firms that simply supply labourers to work at the core company's facilities. More often the core company purchases inputs from satellite firms with which it has developed long-term relations, and hence from which it can expect the timely delivery of the quality and quantity of specialized inputs that it needs (see Watanabe, 1971; Sheard, 1983; Shimokawa, 1985; Asanuma, 1989; Dore, 1986, Part III; Odaka et al., 1988; Chalmers, 1989; Helper, 1990; Smitka, 1990). Historically, the widespread use of subcontractors in Japan appears to have stemmed from the slow growth and weak financial condition of firms that ultimately emerged as dominant (Helper, 1990). It also appears that in the 1950s, as enterprise unionism diffused across dominant firms, these major employers chose to subcontract rather than produce in-house to avoid taking on more permanent employees.

Nevertheless, once begun, many subcontracting arrangements tend to be long-lived because of the importance of organization-specific investments to ensure prompt delivery of inputs of the requisite quality. The core companies typically fund a portion of these investments, and the subcontractor is not easily replaceable. In terms of both pay and employment security, the employees of such 'first-tier' contractors benefit from the growth of the core company. It is the secure product-market positions of the dominant enterprises in Japanese manufacturing that gives stability to the subcontracting arrangements with suppliers and distributors, which in turn enables these small-sized and medium-sized firms to provide stable and remunerative employment to their own workers.

Labour–Management Relations

Those blue-collar workers with the most employment stability and the best long-run prospects for pay increases are, however, men who work as 'regular' employees for the core companies. Within these enterprises, shop-floor workers have been able to lay claim to a share of the rapid productivity growth on which the Japanese 'miracle' has been based. In part, the bargaining power of shop-floor workers derives from the generally high levels of employment and conditions of labour shortage that have resulted from the combination of rapid economic growth and government employment policies. But these workers have rarely used this power to disrupt production; prolonged work stoppages have played only a minor role in enabling Japanese workers to secure higher incomes.

Of the main ACCs, only Germany and Sweden have experienced greater industrial peace than Japan since the 1960s (Shirai, 1983, p. 137; *YBLS*, 1987, pp. 318–9). Even then, in both 1978 and 1984 work stoppages in Germany escalated enormously, while the Japanese experience since 1974 has been a general decline in labour strife. For the periods 1980–83 and 1984–87 respectively, on an average per annum basis, the number of labour disputes lasting more than half a day were 897 compared with 440; the number of workers involved in disputes was 312,000 compared with 124,000; and the number of days of work lost in disputes was 650,000 compared with 282,000 (*YBLS*, 1987, p. 319). The

low levels of work stoppage in the mid-1980s are particularly revealing of the
stability of cooperation in Japanese employment relations because these were
years of persistent labour shortage. A more truculent and adversarial labour force
might have sought to take advantage of the labour shortage to shift more income
their way and secure more leisure.

Key to labour peace has been not only the ability of Japanese corporations
to meet workers' demands but also the ability of Japanese unions to assess the
corporations' ability to pay. Enterprise unions enforce workers' claims on
enterprise earnings, taking into account the financial needs of the firm in the
light of changing product-market conditions and desirable investment strategies.
Through industry and national coordinating committees, the bargaining of
enterprise unions, characterized by strategic strikes of 12 to 49 hours in duration,
becomes part of a public debate over the general ability of the Japanese economy
to pay wage increases. For the workers, their contribution to this debate
culminates in the Spring Offensive – the labour movement's concerted effort
to influence the setting of the levels of wage increases that occurs in enterprises
throughout the country simultaneously on 1 April of every year.

Enterprise-level bargaining means that percentage pay increases vary across
companies, even within the same industry. But through the public debate over
the economy's ability to pay and the coordinated efforts of the enterprise unions
to influence the share that goes to workers' incomes, the increases in any
particular firm become part of a national pattern. Hence, although enterprise
unions bargain at the company level, they support a broader social movement
that creates considerable coherence in levels of remuneration across the Japanese
economy as a whole (see Shimada, 1970; Koshiro, 1983; Dore, 1987, pp. 70–73).

Standards of Living

On the basis of long-term employment relations and collective bargaining, the
long and hard work of Japanese blue-collar men has been rewarded with higher
pay. For many Japanese workers who live in the crowded Tokyo–Osaka
industrial district, nominal income gains were severely eroded in the 1980s by
the rapid rise in the cost of housing. With food prices also high by international
comparison, it might be difficult to argue that Japanese blue-collar workers have
a higher standard of living than their fully employed counterparts in the West.
What they do have, however, is long-term employment stability and (save for
another round of land and housing speculation) the prospects of sharing in the
growing wealth of the nation.

What Japanese workers also have are longer lives and safer work conditions
(notwithstanding reports of employees, typically managers, who have literally
worked themselves to death – Sanger, 1990; for another account that portrays
'salarymen', as distinct from blue-collar workers, as bearing the brunt of the

Japanese commitment to work, see Woronoff, 1983). The post-Second World War growth of Japanese wealth does not appear to have been at the expense of shop-floor workers' health. In 1955, on the eve of the Japanese 'miracle', the average life expectancy at birth was 64 years for a Japanese man and 68 years for a Japanese woman. In 1975 these figures were 72 years for men and 77 years for women, and by 1987 76 years for men and 81 years for women – the highest average life expectancies in the world (*Japanese Statistical Yearbook [JSY]*, 1989, p. 55). As for safety in the workplace, data on the frequency and severity of industrial injuries show continuous and dramatic declines from the 1960s into the late 1980s (*JSY*, 1989, p. 745; see also Koshiro, 1983, p. 73). Notwithstanding the high costs of food and housing, when all the relevant factors are taken into consideration, the standard of living of Japanese workers has risen immensely over the past four decades.

Segmentation of the Labour Force

Beginning with the rise of the cotton textile industry a century ago, the cheap labour of young women has been central to Japanese industrialization (on the early textile mills, see Saxonhouse, 1976; Kidd, 1978; Tsurumi, 1984; Hunter, 1984). But the use of women to occupy low-wage jobs that offer limited employment security and upward mobility is by no means unique to Japan. What is unique about the Japanese labour force is the relative absence of ethnic minorities, alongside women in general, as a supply of low-paid labour. Registered aliens make up well under 1 per cent of the Japanese population. The vast majority (over 90 per cent between 1960 and 1980) of registered aliens are Koreans and Chinese. During the 1980s the proportion of registered aliens began moving up perceptibly, largely because of a greater number of Chinese and Filipinos (who represented 48 per cent and 17 per cent of the net increase in registered aliens between 1980 and 1988 – *JSY*, 1989, p. 45). In the face of acute labour shortages, there has also been a significant increase in illegal unskilled male labour into Japan, mainly from China, the Philippines and Bangladesh. In 1989 official sources estimated that there were 100,000 illegal immigrants in the country, but others have put the number as high as 400,000 (*New York Times*, 29 October 1989, p. E3).

The increased reliance of the Japanese economy on foreign labour is, however, very recent and still relatively small. In the absence of a large reserve army of underprivileged ethnic minorities, the Japanese have relied on tradition to locate within the Japanese population itself a 'secondary' labour force of low-paid workers. Besides women, who constitute the vast majority of the secondary labour force, there is a small group of Japanese men and women who, although ethnically indistinguishable from other Japanese, have been branded since the Tokugawa period as outcasts by birth because of the odious jobs (such as leather tanning and grave digging) that their ancestors had. They are the Burakumin – their numbers estimated at between 1 and 3 per cent of the Japanese population – and to this day they have no choice but to fill the lowest paying, least desirable jobs in Japanese society (Cornell, 1967; Wagatsuma and de Vos, 1967). A 1965 government report showed the Burakumin to have inferior living conditions, limited educational attainment, and lack of access to the secure jobs for which the Japanese economy is so well known (Upham, 1987, pp. 79, 85). Commercially published books that list the place names of Buraku ghettos are purchased by companies to help to ensure that they do not mistakenly hire Burakumin as permanent employees. Despite governmental concern with the social welfare of the Burakumin, there is, according to Frank Upham (1987, p. 123), 'little evidence to suggest that the government's agenda will ever include aggressive measures to ensure Burakumin access to permanent employment in large firms, which leaves them, whatever their individual educational attainment or employment qualifications, as a pool of low-wage temporary workers.'

The relatively small numbers of workers from poorer Asian nations and of Buraku descent aside, historically the Japanese economy has relied on girls and women to provide it with supplies of cheap labour. During the post-Second World War decades women have consistently accounted for 40 per cent of the total labour force, and, as a proportion of the manufacturing labour force, have increased from about one-third in the 1950s to 40 per cent in the 1980s (*JSY*, 1989, p. 71). During the 1980s in establishments employing 30 or more workers, among 'regular' workers the average monthly cash earnings of women were just over 50 per cent of those of men; in manufacturing the female–male proportion was only 42 per cent (*JSY*, 1989, p. 94).

Male–female income inequality is inherent in women's lack of access to permanent employment, the seniority wage system, and membership of enterprise unions. These are the three features of Japanese employment relations that make the Japanese system unique – an OECD report of 1977 called them the 'three pillars' of Japanese industrial relations (OECD, 1977). The pillars support the house of male labour only.

Employment Classifications

The official government classifications of workers are not very helpful for understanding the very different labour markets into which men and women enter in the Japanese economy. The government classifies those participants in the labour force who do not fall into the categories of 'self-employed' and 'family workers' as 'employees', who are then subdivided according to the duration of their employment contracts into 'regular', 'temporary', and 'daily' workers. Regular workers have contracts of indefinite duration, temporary workers have contracts for one month to one year, and daily workers have contracts for less than one month. Many companies employ temporary workers to expand their labour forces in periods of abnormal demand and to avoid overcommitting themselves to the long-term employment of these recruits. Not surprisingly, temporary workers find their conditions of work much less satisfactory than regular workers (see, for example, the critical account of work life as a temporary worker in Kamata, 1982). On the basis of performance, however, it is possible for temporary workers to be promoted to regular employee status.

Over 70 per cent of all Japanese workers, and 90 per cent of all employees, are classified as regular workers. About two-thirds of all regular employees are men and about 95 per cent are regular workers. About four-fifths of all female employees also have regular-worker status, although this proportion has fallen by about 5 per cent since the 1960s and 1970s while the proportion of female employees who are temporary workers has risen by a similar amount (*YBLS*, 1960, p. 16; *YBLS*, 1965, p. 12; *JSY*, 1989, pp. 72–3).

Permanent Employment

Most men, but very few women, who are classified as regular workers have permanent employment status. Permanent employment is found especially in companies that have attained large and entrenched, if not dominant, market shares in their industries, and which are hence both willing and able to offer workers the prospect of long-term attachment to their particular companies. By ensuring the long-run attachment of the employee to the firm, permanent employment enables employers to develop the skills of employees and makes it less necessary for employees to place the attainment of their short-run individual interests ahead of the longer-run goals of the enterprise as a collectivity. Given permanent employment, during the first decade of an employee's career, promotion and pay increases can occur without reference to an employee's productive contributions. During this developmental stage, job rotation into different technical specialities and different workplaces is the rule. In contrast to the American practice of applying the terms unskilled, semi-skilled, and skilled to different types of jobs to be filled by different types of blue-collar workers, the Japanese have used these terms to apply to the stages through which a blue-collar worker passes during the first ten years of employment. When qualitatively new investment strategies require qualitatively new skills, the permanent employment system gives employers the incentive to invest in the retraining of blue-collar workers who are in mid-career.

The existence of permanent employment and the emphasis on seniority in promotion and rewards encourages workers to identify with the goals of the company and to cooperate with each other in contributing to the fulfilment of these goals (see Aoki, 1988, chs 1 and 2). These collective efforts are rewarded by semi-annual bonuses that can amount to one-third of an individual's annual earnings but that are adjusted according to the current profitability of the firm and the financial requirements of long-term investments (see Freeman, 1989, ch. 12, who, however, overemphasizes the importance of bonuses as the foundations of Japanese employment relations). It is only in mid-career that promotion on the basis of individual performance becomes important, although even then seniority continues to have some influence on promotion decisions and remains the main determinant of wage increases.

In terms of the promise of long-term attachment, Japanese 'white-collar' positions are similar to junior management positions in well-managed corporations in the United States. Indeed, the burgeoning research into the history of US managerial enterprise in the United States suggests that the extension of 'permanent employment' to managerial personnel dates back as much as a century in the United States (see Chandler, 1977 and 1990 for long-run historical perspectives and abundant references). But, with a few exceptions, such as IBM and Kodak, these same US corporations will not countenance the notion that blue-collar workers are permanent members of the enterprise. Seniority provisions of US collective bargaining agreements do, it is true, often ensure that the most experienced workers have long-term attachments to particular workplaces. But, as evidenced for example by corporate resistance to laws that would require that affected workers receive advance notice of plant closure, the ideology of American management has been that the company should be able to hire and fire blue-collar workers at will.

Enterprise Unions

In Japan, enterprise unions are the prime institutions for protecting the integrity of permanent employment and the seniority-wage system. Despite the widespread recognition that permanent employment is a characteristic feature of Japanese employment relations, the employment security inherent in it does not have clearcut legal status. According to one authority, 'no reference to [permanent employment] is found in any collective bargaining agreement or the Rules of Employment [under the Labour Standards Law]' (Gould, 1984, p. 11). The Labour Standards Law, passed after the Second World War, states that any employer has the right to dismiss an employee but must give 30-day prior notice or else 30 days' severance pay. Under the doctrine of 'abuse of the right to dismiss', however, the courts have circumscribed the ease with which employers can terminate employment by demanding that the employer justify a dismissal on grounds that the court deems to be legitimate (Koshiro, 1983, p. 245; Gould, 1984, pp. 11, 70, 109). Given the nebulous legal status of the workers' right to long-term employment security, the union movement, dominated by enterprise unions, has been a critical institution for protecting the permanent employment status of its members.

Indeed, the percentage of the Japanese labour force that is unionized is usually put forward as the estimate of the proportion of the labour force that possesses permanent employment status (see, for example, Abegglen and Stalk, 1985, p. 201). In 1970 35 per cent of employees in the Japanese labour force were union members, in 1980 31 per cent, and in 1988 27 per cent (*JSY*, 1989, p. 114). But not all union members are in enterprise unions, and not all employers who offer long-term employment security deal with unions. Enterprise unions, moreover, organize both white-collar and blue-collar employees together. College-educated male employees who enter the firm as white-collar workers are generally on career tracks that will take them out of the ranks of unionized employees into managerial positions with the same company. They continue to enjoy permanent employment status, but they are no longer counted as union members.

If one assumes that all men who work for public and private corporations that employ 100 or more people have permanent employment status, then the proportion of the Japanese labour force permanently employed at the end of 1987 was 25 per cent – a figure just a few percentage points less than the proportion of the Japanese labour force in unions at that time. Only a portion of the male regular workers are blue-collar workers. At the end of 1987, regular male production workers in manufacturing establishments with 30 or more employees represented 59 per cent of male regular workers in these establishments, and only 9 per cent of all males in the entire Japanese labour force (*YBLS*, 1987, pp. 8, 14).

But just because a male worker is not counted as a permanent employee does not mean that he is a member of what US economists have called the secondary labour force. As already indicated, the long-term character of relations between core companies and their satellite firms has a stabilizing impact on the employment and earnings of workers in smaller (although to a much lesser extent in the smallest) enterprises which do not have enterprise unions (on the 'peripheral' labour force in firms that are subcontractors, see Chalmers, 1989). The success of the core companies in capturing large shares of international markets – a success that is in part attributable to the cooperative employment relations that have permanent employment as their foundation – has increased the economic viability and strengthened the permanency of these interfirm relations. The permanent employment status of regular male workers in core companies reflects, therefore, just part of a broader structure of the long-term employment relations that characterize Japanese industry and that have been integral elements of the dynamics of Japanese economic growth.

Women in the Labour Force

The employment experiences of male regular workers who can harbour expectations of permanent employment must also be distinguished from those of women who generally cannot. At the end of 1987 women represented 31 per cent of all regular workers in Japanese manufacturing and 36 per cent of all regular production workers in manufacturing establishments with 30 or more employees (*YBLS*, 1987, pp. 8, 14). Although the employment tenure of these women is of unspecified duration, the prevailing expectation is that they will drop out of the labour force after marriage. In the United States, the labour force partici-pation of women remains stable between the ages of 20 and 45 at about 70 per cent (Edwards, 1988, p. 245n). But in Japan the labour force participation of women is significantly lower for those aged 25–34 (54.5 per cent in 1988) than for those aged 20–24 (73.7 per cent), 35–44 (64.5 per cent), and 45–54 (66.4 per cent) (*JSY*, 1989, p. 71). As these figures indicate, many women re-enter the labour force when their children are grown. But they do not retain the right to reinstatement with a particular employer. The traditional gender-based division of labour in the society is reinforced by statistical discrimination – the assumption by employers that the women whom they currently employ will sooner or later drop out of the paid labour force to become home makers. As a result of this assumption, even those women who intend to remain in the paid labour force are denied the opportunities for skill development and earnings growth that firms offer to male regular employees as a matter of course.

The traditional gender-based division of labour also makes it possible to employ women as 'part-time' workers. In Japan, a 'part-time' worker is one who is employed for less than 35 hours per week, and is therefore not entitled to all the pay and welfare benefits of 'full-time' workers.

About 70 per cent of part-time workers are women. About 17 per cent of female part-timers were in manufacturing, representing 14 per cent of the female man-ufacturing labour force. They were fairly evenly distributed across small, medium, and large manufacturing enterprises (*JSY*, 1989, p. 103; *YBLS*, 1986, p. 9).

Part-timers are not necessarily temporary workers. Of workers who made up the non-agricultural labour force in 1986, part-time employees represented 12 per cent of the total and 23 per cent of women, whereas temporary employees were only 6 per cent of the total and 15 per cent of women (*Japan Labor Bulletin*, 1 November 1987, p. 5).

The proportion of the non-agricultural labour force in part-time employment has been rising steadily from the 1960s when just over 6 per cent of all workers and 8–12 per cent of women were part-timers. A 1984 survey found that 86 per cent of female part-timers were married and 78 per cent were aged 35 or over. In response to the query of why they had taken up part-time work, 54 per cent answered to earn supplementary household income, 15 per cent to improve their standard of living, 11 per cent as a main source of income, and 10 per cent to earn income for leisure (Japan Institute of Labour, 1986, p. 14).

Responses to Labour Shortages

In sharp contrast to the movement of women into part-time employment, some more highly educated women have managed recently to gain permanent employment status. The continued growth of the Japanese economy and the expansion of its overseas business activities in the 1980s created severe shortages of highly educated personnel. In 1984 women represented over 23 per cent of enrolments at Japanese universities. But Japanese employers had been reluctant to hire female university graduates (as distinct from junior college graduates) on the grounds that they were likely to drop out of the labour force in their mid-20s. While the traditional gender-based division of labour has always provided the rationale for denying permanent employment to women in general, highly educated women have been particularly subjected to statistical discrimination. The productive potential of university-educated women could be greatly increased through in-house training programmes. But the company would not benefit from its investment in these human resources if (as was expected) these women chose not to pursue their careers.

From 1986 the impetus that the labour shortages gave to hiring female university graduates to be trained as technical specialists was reinforced by the implementation of the Equal Employment Opportunity Law (EEOL). This law did not compel employers to grant permanent employment status to women. But, through what the Japanese call 'administrative guidance', the state in effect legitimized employers' desire to develop long-term employment relations with women whose capabilities could be enhanced by costly in-house training and who could thereby alleviate the shortage of technical specialists. The EEOL also encouraged female university graduates to pursue careers by making it socially acceptable for them to refuse to be home makers in the traditional gender-based division of labour (see Cannings and Lazonick, 1994).

The proportion of women among new university graduates entering employment had been increasing steadily throughout the 1960s and 1970s, but then levelled off in the early 1980s. These women were regular employees but were not considered to be permanent employees. The EEOL appears to have had an impact on the quantity of female university graduates employed as well as on the quality of their employment. Between 1986 and 1987, for the first time in Japanese history, the number of female university graduates who entered employment increased while, simultaneously, the number of male university graduates who entered employment decreased. During the remainder of the 1980s, as acute labour shortages for educated personnel persisted, women continued to account for almost all of the annual increases in the number of university-educated recruits (*JSY*, 1985, p. 90; *JSY*, 1989, p. 90; see also Cannings and Lazonick, 1994).

Since the passage of the EEOL, university-educated women have, by virtue of the in-house training required to enable them to fill the shortage of technical specialists, been granted permanent employment status. But, in general, they have not been granted this status on the same terms as men. Under the traditional system, when virtually all permanent employees were men, all university graduates would enter the company as white-collar employees to be groomed for promotion into the managerial ranks after a decade of service. With the implementation of the EEOL, alongside this traditional 'managerial employee track' has arisen a 'clerical employee track'. In some firms, lying between these two tracks, is another one for 'specialized employees' in jobs requiring high levels of skill and knowledge, so that there is now a 'multiple-track employment system' for university-educated white-collar employees. Among other things, the lower tracks do not require their occupants to move to different localities over the course of their careers, and promotion ladders run only up to lower-level or local management positions. The evidence thus far is that these tracks have been filled almost entirely by women (Sugeno, 1987). Of particular importance for the shop-floor focus of this essay, moreover, the extension of (Japanese-style) 'equal employment opportunity' for women has been confined to the 'white-collar' ranks. If anything, through the use of 'part-timers', the tendency during the 1980s was to make employment for 'blue-collar' women more insecure.

Although the shortages of highly trained technical specialists posed the most acute labour supply problems for Japanese companies during the 1980s, the expansion of Japanese business at home and abroad has created labour shortages of blue-collar workers as well. There have been at least four different types of employer responses to these shop-floor labour shortages. One response (or more accurately non-response) has been to resist pressures (largely emanating it seems from Japan's international competitors) to reduce Japan's long work week. With labour in short supply, employers would not easily be able to secure the person-hours of labour required to meet their output targets by hiring more workers for fewer hours each. In addition to the quantitative problem of scarce labour, the extent to which companies invest in the capabilities of specific workers also encourages employers to insist on using these human assets more intensively. Moreover, the existence of permanent employment leads employers to want to minimize the number of workers to whom they are committed. In any case, Japanese enterprise unions have not demanded a short work week for their members, most likely because of the ability of workers to share in the gains that derive from high levels of output per worker (see Japan Economic Institute, 1990, where it is also argued that workers prefer long hours because of the expense and inaccessibility of leisure in Japan).

A second response has been to seek out new sources of temporary labour. In recent years, there has been a small but visible influx of foreign workers, some of them illegal, into the Japanese labour force (see for example *Japan Labour Bulletin*, 1 November 1988, p. 8). Of much more importance has been the shift of manufacturing operations overseas, in part to the United States and Europe (Kenney and Florida, 1991; Oliver and Wilkinson, 1988, ch. 5), but increasingly also to Asian countries such as Malaysia and Thailand (see *New York Times*, 8 May 1990, pp. A1, D18). In 1990 Japanese companies already employed 10 per cent of the Thai manufacturing labour force, with a predicted rise to 15 per cent by 1992 (*New York Times*, 10 May 1990, pp. D1, D9).

Meanwhile, at home, labour shortages have eased the social problems of structural adjustment in heavy industry. Because of worldwide excess capacity, the steel and shipbuilding industries have had to cut back their labour forces dramatically since the mid-1970s, and these cutbacks have continued in the 1980s. At the end of 1982 the iron and steel industry employed 268,000 regular workers, down by 100,000 from 1975, while the shipbuilding industry employed 156,000 regular workers, down from 255,000 in 1975. At the end of 1987 iron and steel employed 223,000 regular workers and shipbuilding 89,000 (*YBLS*, 1975, p. 15; *YBLS*, 1982, p. 19; *YBLS*, 1987, p. 15; the figures cited are for employees in establishments with 30 or more workers). The labour shortages, combined with the high level of general education of Japanese blue-collar workers, have facilitated the reallocation of the displaced workers to new employments.

Moreover, rather than, in the face of excess capacity, letting these 'mature' industries simply run down (which would only ensure that another round of employee cutbacks would have to come later), the Japanese steel and shipbuilding companies have continued their former policies of scrapping existing but serviceable plant and equipment and making massive investments in state-of-the art technologies to ensure that they will have long-run international competitive advantage (see McCraw and O'Brien, 1986). As one report has put it:

A few years ago the belching smokestacks [of Kimitsu works, Japan's largest steel plant] were a symbol of the kind of inefficient heavy industry that the [Japanese] Government was committed to paring down in the face of heavy competition from South Korea. But today, after hundreds of millions of dollars of investment and a program to retire or retrain excess workers the Nippon Steel Corporation's giant Kimitsu Works has caught up with its lower-cost Korean competition, and 13,000 workers keep Kimitsu running at closer to capacity. (*New York Times*, 11 April 1990, pp. A1, D7)

As even this example of a so-called 'mature' industry shows, labour shortages as well as Japan's relatively low cost of capital have encouraged investments in shop-floor technology that replace labour with machines. In 1980 Japanese industry already had installed about 20,000 robots at a time when US industry had only installed a few thousand. By 1989 the number of robots in Japan was over 200,000 while the number in the United States was less than 40,000. Indeed, in 1989 the number of robots installed in Japanese industry was greater than the entire stock of robots in the United States in that year (Tanzer and Simon, 1990).

The low cost of capital, a factor that is often cited as the prime reason for Japan's competitive success (see for example Iacocca, 1990) is not unrelated to the labour shortages. Inexpensive finance as well as scarce labour are both cause and effect of a cumulative process of economic growth. Capital has been inexpensive in Japan because the financial system has been structured to make financial resources available to industrial enterprises for economic development (see Suzuki, 1980; Ballon and Tomita, 1988). Inexpensive finance makes it easier for industrial enterprises to make long-run commitments to workers, while labour shortages encourage firms to do so. These employment commitments in turn help to ensure the cooperation of workers in developing and utilizing the productive resources in which these enterprises have invested. The superior development and utilization of productive resources in turn enable firms simultaneously to pay higher wages to workers, charge lower prices to consumers (thus increasing the market shares of these firms), and reap higher profits as a residual (see Lazonick, 1990, Appendix). The results of this cumulative process of growth are increases in the supply of finance available to industry as well as the demand for labour, not only in manufacturing industry itself but also (in part because of the augmented incomes of employees as consumers) in services. These conditions of cheap capital and scarce, but still cooperative, labour in turn encourage new rounds of investments in effort-saving technological change which again open up the possibility for the generation of value gains that can be shared among employers, workers, consumers and (even) shareholders.

In historical perspective, this dynamic process of economic growth is not unique to Japan. As I have argued elsewhere (Lazonick, 1990), on the basis of highly integrated managerial structures but less cooperative employment relations with blue-collar workers, such a cumulative process of value creation characterized the rise of US industry to international dominance in the first half of this century. Indeed, in the United States this dynamic process of economic growth was most evident in the high fixed-cost consumer goods industries such as automobile and electrical appliance manufacture – the very industries in which, beginning in the 1960s, leadership passed to Japan. The next section of this essay will explain why Japanese industry came to possess the cooperative employment relations that I have thus far only described. Then section IV will outline how these cooperative employment relations have contributed to the superior productive capabilities that Japanese industry brings to international competition.

III EMPLOYMENT RELATIONS AND TECHNOLOGICAL CHANGE

Effort-Saving Technology

Cooperative employment relations in Japan are both cause and effect of what I call 'effort-saving' technological change – technological change that increases the amount of output that can be produced from a given input of effort (see Lazonick, 1990, Appendix). Attempts to create value – high-quality products at low unit cost – by increasing the supply of effort on a given technology are limited by the physical capabilities of workers or, even before the limits of these physical capabilities are reached, by their refusal to work longer and harder. Attempts to create value by investing in effort-saving technologies can overcome these physical and social limitations. An effort-saving technology permits the same amount of effort to produce more output per unit of time than is possible using the old technology, thus creating the possibility for making managers and workers better off without necessarily requiring the expenditure of more effort by workers.

The extent to which an investment in an effort-saving technology in fact creates this 'positive-sum' situation depends on the costs of introducing the new technology. Because investment in effort-saving technologies generally increases the company's fixed costs, the value gains (if any) on the new technology compared with the old technology are greater at high levels of effort than at low levels of effort. But, as long as the level of effort supplied by workers before the technological change is high enough to offset the higher fixed costs of the new technology once it has been put in place, then the effort-saving impact of the technological change can increase the amount of surplus value and workers' wages without requiring workers to supply more effort than before.

Mainstream economic theory has a limited understanding of the interaction of employment relations and technological change in the process of economic growth. In neoclassical economic theory, the choice of process technology is simply a managerial response to relative factor prices. The elasticity of substitution of labour for capital determines shares of capital and labour in the value of the output produced. A neoclassical economist might allow that, by raising wages and hence by altering relative factor process, employment relations – specifically, the collective bargaining power of labour – can affect the choice of technology. But neoclassical theory has viewed the productivity of any particular technology (a particular combination of capital and labour inputs) as exogenous to the firm and hence as independent of the structure of employment within the firm.

Such a view ignores the role of employment relations in determining productivity. As efficiency-wage theorists have recognized, a critical dimension of the employment relation is not only the level of wages but also the level of effort supplied by workers (see Akerlof and Yellen, 1986; Katz, 1986). Indeed, a central assumption of efficiency-wage theory is that, because of the nature of firm-specific employment relations (in particular, the tendency of workers to 'shirk' in the absence of positive wage incentives), high wages are offset by high levels of effort in the determination of unit labour costs. But efficiency-wage theory has not developed the implications of its focus on the 'effort bargain' for the firm's choice of technology among readily available alternatives or for the firm's decision to invest in the development of new technologies, including the in-house development of workers' skills. Efficiency-wage theory does not analyse the possibility that, through its effort-saving impact, technological change can make it possible for the incomes of both capitalists and workers to increase without workers necessarily supplying higher levels of effort.

Marxian economic theory (at least as put forth by Marx himself) recognizes that technological change is *potentially* effort-saving – it can permit workers to supply less effort to the production process without reducing labour productivity. The orthodox Marxist view is, however, that, alongside its effort-saving character, technology is also *skill-displacing* – it deskills shop-floor workers. Indeed, a basic tenet of Marxian theory is that, by deskilling shop-floor workers, technological change increases the power of capitalists to extract more effort from workers for less pay, and that indeed, in terms of employment relations, deskilling of shop-floor labour and the extraction of unremunerated effort are characteristic features of *successful* capitalist development (see Marx, 1977, ch. 15; Braverman, 1974).

These Marxian conclusions distort the historical experience of successful capitalist development. At any point in time, there are groups of workers in even the most successful capitalist economies who are subject to persistent exploitation – they are compelled by the force of the circumstances under which they sell their labour-power to provide high levels of effort for low levels of pay. The tendency toward exploitation increases, moreover, when firms, industries, and national economies that have been successful in the past enter into periods of relative decline. But when a capitalist economy is ascendant, the long-run tendency has been for workers to share in the benefits of effort-saving technological change. Indeed, workers' expectations of such benefits have resulted in their cooperation in the development and utilization of the new technologies that are the foundations of long-term economic growth (see Lazonick, 1990, chs. 6–10).

Shop-Floor Skills and Industrial Leadership

With cross-national shifts in international industrial leadership, the shop-floor characteristics of this dynamic interaction of employment relations and technological change have been transformed dramatically. When, in the last half of the nineteenth century, UK industry held a dominant position in the international economy, capitalist employers remained heavily dependent on experienced shop-floor workers to keep imperfect machinery in motion, to coordinate the flow of work through the production process, and to train the next generation of workers. Employers also paid these experienced workers relatively high and stable wages to ensure that these workers would supply high levels of effort.

The prime reason for the persistence of craft control in UK industry well into the twentieth century, when the UK was no longer the 'workshop of the world', was that capitalist employers had relied so heavily on the skills and efforts of shop-floor workers throughout the nineteenth century when UK industry was predominant. In the process, capitalists had not developed the managerial structures and related employment relations that, as the cases of the United States and Japan, among others, would show, were to become increasingly critical to the development and utilization of effort-saving technology in the twentieth century (Lazonick, 1990, ch. 6).

In the first half of the twentieth century, when US industry rose to a position of international dominance, employers did design process technologies to reduce their reliance on shop-floor skills. To develop and utilize these new technologies, however, employers had to make substantial investments in the skills of managerial employees, many of whom were skilled workers elevated from their prior shop-floor positions. At the same time, the very extent of the fixed costs incurred by these investments in both machines and managers made it imperative for employers to pay their shop-floor workers relatively high and stable wages to ensure the high levels of shop-floor effort required to get the volume of production per unit of time that could drive down not only unit labour costs but also unit capital costs (Lazonick, 1990, chs. 7–9).

Hence, in the context of successful capitalist development in the United States, the Marxian notion of the deskilling of shop-floor workers is relevant, but only when it is recognized that this deskilling could only be accomplished by creating a hierarchy of highly skilled employees within the managerial structure. Moreover, the high fixed costs of the deskilling strategy gave machine operatives (generally classified as 'semi-skilled') considerable power to inflict damage on their employers, and hence made it imperative for employers to try to win the 'good will' of these workers through the offer of higher pay, more employment stability, and better work conditions. Despite the deskilling of shop-floor labour and virtual absence of collective bargaining in the oligopolistic industries, during the 1920s blue-collar workers were still able to reap some of the benefits of effort-saving technological change (Lazonick, 1990, ch. 7).

In terms of the skill content of shop-floor work, the Japanese case of successful capitalist development over the past four decades contrasts sharply with both the UK model of the nineteenth century and the American model of the first half of the twentieth century. Whereas UK employers simply *left skills on* the shop floor and American employers sought to *take skills off* the shop floor, Japanese employers have *put skills on* the shop floor by investing in the development of the capabilities of their shop-floor workers.

It might appear at first sight that the Japanese model stands in sharper contrast to the American than to the UK model because in both the UK and Japanese cases skills remained in the possession of workers on the shop floor. But seen from the perspective of the development of the skills of *all* employees – both those who occupy 'white-collar' positions in the managerial structure and those who do 'blue-collar' work on the shop floor – the Japanese model is much more an extension of the US model than the UK model. For what the Japanese have done is to extend the organization-specific investments in human resources, which have long been critical to the success of US managerial structures, to male shop-floor workers as well as to managerial men. In the UK case, in contrast, until quite recently even larger companies made little in the way of organization-specific investments in human resources, whether at the managerial or shop-floor level.

What remains to be explained, therefore, is why employers in Japanese industry have been willing to develop the cognitive capabilities of their shop-floor workers, whereas US industrial employers have, since the late nineteenth century, been obsessed with taking skills off the shop floor. After answering this question, I shall then be able to explain how the development of the skills of blue-collar workers has enabled Japanese employers to take the lead in the introduction of effort-saving technology in the last half of the twentieth century. For these investments in workers' skills and effort-saving technology have been central to the cooperative employment relations that are both cause and effect of Japan's economic success.

IV   THE EVOLUTION OF JAPANESE EMPLOYMENT RELATIONS

Pre-Second World War Origins

Why have Japanese managers been willing to develop the skills of their shop-floor workers? In many respects, the evolution of organizational structure in dominant Japanese industrial enterprises from the late nineteenth century into the 1930s resembles what Alfred Chandler (1977) has called the 'managerial revolution' in American business. As successful enterprises expanded the scale and scope of their activities, there was an increased separation of asset ownership from managerial control and the replacement of owner-entrepreneurs by pro-fessional managers promoted from the ranks. Just as the first two decades of the twentieth century saw a radical transformation of the US system of higher education to serve the technical and organizational requirements of big business, so too in Japan the larger firms in industries such as textiles, shipbuilding, machine making, electrical manufacture and oil refining were recruiting large numbers of college graduates by offering them careers within their organizations. During the 1920s in both the United States and Japan dominant industrial enterprises established systematic internal career structures for the purpose of developing managerial skills and forming the next generation of top executives (compare Daito, 1986 and Lazonick, 1986; see also Hirschmeier and Yui, 1981, pp. 205–7; Yonekawa, 1984; Morikawa, 1989).

As the managerial hierarchies evolved during the interwar period, foremen became the lowest-ranking salaried employees. As in the United States, in Japan foremen tended to be promoted from the shop floor, and occupied the highest position to which blue-collar workers could normally aspire (Daito, 1986, p. 174; Koike, 1988, ch. 4). In both countries, male blue-collar employees of dominant firms had by the 1920s received implicit promises of employment security that were broken in periods of depressed trade. In both countries, through the interwar decades, shop-floor workers failed to get *formal* employment security, and the organized labour movements, although often militant, remained weak (Gordon, 1985, Parts II and III; Garon, 1987; Levine, 1958, ch. 3; Evans, 1970; Okayama, 1983).

In the late nineteenth century, Japan, like the United States, had skilled workers, often employed as internal subcontractors, who exercised consider-able control over hiring, firing, and the organization of work on the shop floor. But there was one critical difference between US and Japanese shop-floor relations in this era. Japan's skilled workers did not form collective organiza-tions that succeeded in exercising craft control on the shop floor. In the United States, the American Federation of Labour (AFL) was formed in 1886 to increase the bargaining power of craft workers as industrial enterprises themselves expanded in size and became more powerful, and as the combination of mech-anization and the influx of immigrant labour threatened the craft workers' jobs. A victory such as that of the Amalgamated Association of Iron and Steel Workers over Carnegie Steel in 1889 revealed the considerable power that an AFL union could wield. Then again, the stunning and irreparable defeat that the very same union suffered at Carnegie Steel's Homestead works in 1892 showed how a powerful mass producer could ultimately get the upper hand.

The struggle over the 'right to manage' that US corporate management took up when it confronted the craft unions and created the non-union era profoundly influenced the evolution of US labour–management relations during the first half of the twentieth century and beyond (see Lazonick, 1990, chs 7 and 8). First,

US management determined that skills had to be taken off the shop floor, in the hopes of making any particular worker easily replaceable and of depriving current workers of the power to control the flow of work. Then, when the crisis of the Great Depression precipitated the rise of mass production unionism, US management insisted on its 'right to manage' even as union members were establishing seniority rights to employment and indeed often to particular jobs.

Rather than recognize that, *de facto*, these shop-floor workers had become 'permanent employees' of the firm who, as in the case of salaried personnel in the US and all regular male workers in Japan, should be rewarded as such, US management continued to tie rewards to a structure of hourly-rated jobs as if it made no difference which 'hourly' workers flowed in and out of them. The unions then, quite naturally, linked seniority to these job structures, so that, ironically, US management ended up making the long-term commitments to specific workers that, in their insistence on 'the right to manage', they had been so eager to avoid. At the same time, US management gave up considerable control over the organization of work and the allocation of workers. Rather than maintaining flexible control over the development and utilization of productive resources that had become attached to the enterprise, US management became entrapped in the elaboration of a structure of job classifications and work rules that became increasingly difficult to change.

The craft traditions that engendered these managerial strategies and responses in the United States did not exist in Japan in the late nineteenth century (Gordon, 1985, p. 24). Many of the US craft traditions as well as skills had been imported into the United States during the nineteenth century by skilled West European workers (primarily from the UK and Germany). Japan had no such influx of skills and traditions. Although the Japanese labour force was highly literate at the onset of industrialization, it lacked industrial skills, let alone well defined craft skills. Without the possibility of a highly specialized division of craft labour, workers with a broad array of skills were most useful to Japanese employers, particularly in the as yet unmechanized metalworking and shipbuilding industries. The institutional means for developing such workers was reliance on the *oyakata*, skilled workers who, as internal subcontractors, took on from 60 to 300 apprentices, and trained them on the job.

The trainees did not necessarily remain committed to one *oyakata*, but would often change 'masters' in order to develop their skills and enjoy better pay and work conditions. The absence of craft unions meant that there were no institutional barriers to the movement of workers or the development of broad-based skills. Because of the slow mechanization of Japanese industry as well as the absence of masses of immigrants competing for existing jobs, skilled Japanese workers felt much less pressure than Americans to create craft organizations. Rather both the *oyakata* and their trainees relied on the power of exit. In the words of Andrew Gordon (1985, p. 25; see also pp. 33–5), 'They set the tone of worker behavior in heavy industry with frequent job changes, movement from small shop to large factories and back, disregard for effective craft restrictions, and the desire for independence.'

Nevertheless, in 1897 unions arose throughout heavy industry under the leadership of some workers who, while in the United States, had developed connections with the American Federation of Labour and had brought back Samuel Gompers's philosophy of cooperation with employers. But these unions were soon repressed out of existence by the Public Peace Act of 1900. Union leaders abandoned the ideology of Gompersism for that of socialism (Okayama, 1983, pp. 162–3; Okuda, 1972). Although the union movement re-emerged in Japan in 1912, again influenced by AFL-inspired notions of labour–management cooperation, by the 1920s a variety of ideological orientations, most of them leftist, sought to exert their influence (Garon, 1987, chs 2–4).

Meanwhile, in the first two decades of this century, the larger employers, particularly in heavy industry, were pursuing policies to integrate skilled or 'key' workers into their organizations, in part to reduce labour mobility and in part to fend off union organizers. From 1900 (when independent trade unionism was repressed), the larger firms replaced the *oyakata* with, or transformed existing *oyakata* into, first-line supervisors who, through the offer of salaries and regular employment, were integrated into the emerging managerial hierarchies (Evans, 1970, pp. 116–18; Okayama, 1983, pp. 160–61; Gordon, 1985, pp. 36–59). These 'key' workers did not necessarily enjoy 'lifetime employment' – they could be, and were, laid off during periods of depressed trade (Okayama, 1983, p. 169).

The transition from labour contractor to salaried supervisor did not, however, put an end to one of the prime functions of the *oyakata* – the training (as well as recruiting) of skilled labour. Severe shortages of skilled labour plagued employers during periods of prosperity throughout the first four decades of this century. But labour shortage did not lead Japanese management to pursue strategies to take skills off the shop floor, as was the case in the United States. Rather the more dominant enterprises that could count on retaining the workers whom they trained set up in-house schools that admitted boys between the ages of 14 and 17 (Okayama, 1983, p. 164; for a case study of shipbuilding, see Fukasaku, 1992). The role of the first-line supervisor was not simply to drive workers in the manner of the US foreman, but also to transform unskilled workers into skilled workers. However much the Japanese foreman sought to extract more effort from his subordinates, his task was made easier by the fact that he was the one who provided these workers with the skills that would enable them to earn a living.

'There was no real shortage of recruits into industry', Ronald Dore (1973, p. 387) has written. 'The problem was to train them, and having trained them, to keep them.' To do so, Japanese management applied, in a piecemeal, selective, but still reversible fashion, the inducements that have become identified with the 'Japanese employment system', and in particular the promise of employment security and pay increases based on seniority (Gordon, 1985, Part II). Again, on the surface, these attempts to reduce labour mobility were not very different from the employment strategies pursued by the most progressive US mass producers in the 1910s and 1920s. But because Japanese employers were not engaged in a battle to obliterate craft control and, what is the other side of the same relationship, because they were willing to develop the skills of their shop-floor workers in whatever manner could best serve the needs of production, they tied pay increases *directly* to length of service with the company as well as life-cycle needs and individual merit. Japanese management did not insist, as was the case in the United States both during and after the non-union era, on paying for the job rather than for the worker.

Developments after the Second World War

Andrew Gordon (1985, p. 350) has argued that, in the aftermath of the Second World War, with the aid of pro-union legislation promoted by the Supreme Commander of the Allied Powers (SCAP), 'Japanese workers very nearly established a labour version of the Japanese employment system: guaranteed job security, an explicitly need-based seniority wage, and a significant labour voice in the management of factory affairs.' The most radical shop-floor action of the new unions was not to control the allocation and demarcation of jobs as was the case with both the AFL and CIO unions in the United States, but to exercise 'production control': the taking over of idle factories by the workers so that they could be put into operation, create value, and enable workers to earn a living (Gordon, 1985, p. 343; see also Moore, 1983). As far as workers were concerned, it was management that was guilty of the 'restriction of output' that was keeping them unemployed.

Through SCAP containment of the union movement, including a Red Purge of 12,000 unionists (that mimicked the ouster of 900,000 alleged communists from the American CIO in 1949) and the promotion by the companies of enterprise unions that organized blue-collar workers with white-collar workers, the 'labour version' of the Japanese employment system was defeated (Gordon, 1985, ch. 10; Cusumano, 1985, ch. 3; Halberstam, 1986, Part III). Japanese management moved forward under the slogan 'recovery of management authority'. Yet, unlike the 'right to manage' movement in the United States in the 1940s (see Harris, 1982), the importance of creating a structure of labour relations that permitted the skills of the Japanese worker to be developed and utilized was never an issue.

Indeed, by forcing reluctant Japanese management to recognize enterprise unions as an alternative to independent industrial unions, Japanese workers helped to create a system that would ensure them a share in the value gains of the enterprises for which they worked. As we have seen, only 25 to 30 per cent of the Japanese labour force have permanent employment. But virtually all the male employees of the dominant mass producers – the companies primarily responsible for Japan's penetration of world markets – have this status. Since the late 1950s the enterprise unions that represent these workers in bargaining with their particular employers have been able to capture shares of the value gains that, by adjusting variations in the companies' economic performances, reflect the abilities of their companies to pay. The union may take up any particular worker's grievances concerning promotion and transfer. But the bargaining process that resolves these grievances has not imposed the rigid work rules and job classifications that became characteristic of unionized workplaces in the United States. Hence, in contrast to their US counterparts, Japanese employers do not face worker-imposed barriers to the development of workers' skills by means of job rotation and the retraining of workers to meet the labour requirements of technological change.

Although disciplined by the presence of the enterprise union (as well as evolving labour law – Gould, 1984) to keep their promises of employment security, Japanese management remains both willing and able to place skills and authority with workers on the shop floor (Koike, 1988, ch. 4; Aoki, 1988, ch. 2). With the cooperation of the enterprise union and the collective skills of its shop-floor labour, Japanese management has also been both willing and able to remain in the forefront of changes in process technology.

V   ORGANIZATION AND TECHNOLOGY ON THE JAPANESE SHOP FLOOR

During the 1980s the search for new structures of cooperative industrial relations took on fresh urgency in the United States as formerly dominant mass producers realized that they were rapidly, and perhaps irreversibly, losing their market shares to foreign competitors, and in particular to the Japanese. At the beginning of the 1980s – after a decade in which the Japanese share of the US automobile market had increased from 4.2 per cent (less than half the European share) to 22.8 per cent (well over five times the European share – Altshuler et al., 1986, p. 24), prominent US government and corporate officials still took the position that lower wages accounted for Japanese competitive advantage (see the discussion in Abernathy et al., 1983, pp. 58–9). Remuneration to Japanese automobile workers at the beginning of the 1980s was on the order of only half that paid to their US counterparts (see Abernathy et al., 1983, p. 60; Cole and Yakushiji, 1984, pp. 124–6).

Closer scrutiny revealed, however, that Japanese competitive advantage was driven by more than lower wages. Productivity estimates showed the Japanese advantage in terms of small cars produced per unit of labour to be anywhere from 1.2:1 to 2.4:1. According to the Abernathy, Clark, and Kantrow estimates (rounded off for ease of exposition), the total Japanese labour-cost advantage was about $670 in purchased components and materials (which constituted about 55 per cent of the total unit costs in the US and about 57 per cent in Japan), and another $340 in other manufacturing costs. That is, lower wages represented only about 30 per cent of Japan's unit manufacturing cost advantages. Of the $2110 in higher unit manufacturing costs, US companies recouped about $810 because of lower shipping, sales and administration costs (Abernathy et al., 1983, p. 61; Cole and Yakushiji, 1984, pp. 124–6). But the salient point is that, whatever the wage advantages of the Japanese automobile producers, they were clearly superior to their US competitors in the creation of value on the shop floor.

The argument that Japan's prime competitive advantage was lower wages justified the adaptive (as distinct from innovative) response of US producers to the competitive challenge by relocating in areas where they would have access to cheaper, non-union labour. But, as the Japanese continued to make inroads into the US market, despite 'voluntary export restraints' that began in 1981 – and as more and more observers from U.S. industry and academia trooped over to Japan to see just what the 'miracle' was all about – Americans began to recognize Japanese manufacturing superiority, not only in automobiles, but also in consumer electronics, electrical machinery, semiconductors and steel. It became clear, moreover, that Japanese value-creating capabilities derived not only from the possession of superior product design and process technology, but also, and perhaps even more fundamentally, from the ways in which dominant Japanese manufacturing enterprises organized their productive activities and, in particular, developed and utilized skills on the shop floor.

Visitors to Japanese factories observed, and began to write about, Japan's use of just-in-time inventory systems (JIT), shop-floor quality control (QC), and flexible manufacturing systems (FMS). In these workplaces, the creation of value requires that shop-floor workers not only have more and better skills than has been traditional in the United States but also that they have degrees of authority and responsibility to plan and coordinate the flow of work that, since the late nineteenth century, have been denied to most US workers. Japanese shop-floor workers have responsibility, and the necessary skills, for ensuring the quality as well as the quantity of the manufactured goods that they produce (see Cusumano, 1985; Jacobson and Hillkirk, 1986, ch. 7; see also Ohno, 1982).

Flexible manufacturing systems permit frequent variations in the character-istics of products manufactured in a given workplace. In contrast to the traditional mode of transforming high fixed costs into low unit costs by manufacturing large volumes of a standardized product, with FMS high levels of capacity utilization, and hence economies of 'scope', can be achieved by serving various smaller segments of a product market during a given time period. Critical to the success of FMS are rapid set-up times in changing equipment from one relatively short production run to the next. In Japan, the term 'single set-up' means making the necessary changes in under ten minutes. In other countries these set-ups take several hours (Cusumano, 1985, pp. 285–7). Dramatically reduced set-up times have been achieved in Japan in part through mechanization, but also by training workers to coordinate the set-up process, including the performance of preparatory tasks while machines are still producing the previous job lot.

The success of FMS requires that workers possess the skills necessary to coordinate the changes and that they supply their effort to set up the new run as quickly as possible. The history of Toyota indicates that in Japan flexible mass production originated before the advent of numerically controlled machine tools, computers, and other high-technology components of modern FMS. The prior development of shop-floor skills and the delegation of authority to workers created the human-resource basis for the introduction of flexible technologies, which in turn have enabled Japanese manufacturing companies to transform the high fixed costs of these investments in FMS into low unit costs.

The more skill that workers possess and the more effort that they supply, the greater the reduction in unit costs as the fixed costs of plant and equipment are spread over the output produced for a variety of market segments. In effect, such 'flexible mass production' lowers unit costs by means of 'shop-floor economies of scope' (for the importance and meaning of economies of scope, see Chandler, 1990, ch. 1; Lazonick, 1991, ch. 3). The use of just-in-time inventory systems is particularly cost-effective in flexible mass production. With input requirements changing from one product run to the next, long runs of 'product-specific' intermediate inputs cannot be transformed into final output as quickly, and hence the use of JIT avoids the stockpiling of many different types of supplies.

JIT originated at Toyota in 1948 not only as a cost-cutting measure but also because, facing a total market demand for all types of transportation vehicles that was a tiny fraction of the US market (one and a half day's production in 1950), a large variety of small runs was required to spread out fixed costs (Cusumano, 1985, pp. 265–6). Developed at Toyota in the 1950s and 1960s and then diffused to other Japanese mass producers in the 1970s and 1980s, JIT requires workers to coordinate the flow of work across vertically related activities, using the kanban system of worker-generated orders and withdrawals to 'pull' the necessary intermediate products where and when they are needed.

By relying on blue-collar workers to coordinate and implement JIT, management has left considerable initiative and decision-making power on the shop floor. The failure to order and deliver inventories 'just in time' can bring the whole set of downstream activities to a halt. As practised in Japan, the success of JIT assumes that management can rely on workers to cooperate in supplying effort to facilitate the smooth and speedy flow of work. In addition, the success of JIT requires that Japanese shop-floor workers possess broad-based skills, developed through systematic job rotation, that enable them to participate in the prevention of machine breakdowns, the minimization of downtime, and the repair of defective work-in-progress whenever and wherever they are needed. Japanese workers involved in JIT also have the authority to stop the flow of work if and when bottlenecks occur (Cusumano, 1985, pp. 276, 305–7, 327–8).

Japanese management would not, therefore, be able to make use of JIT if it did not trust workers' abilities to make the right decisions or if it thought that workers would use their positions of shop-floor control to delay the flow of work for the sake of on-the-job leisure. In his account of the development of JIT at Toyota in the 1950s, Cusumano (1985, p. 265) related how the 'workers checked for mistakes as they took the parts they needed, eliminating large numbers of inspectors, and corrected defectives in process, eliminating large rework or reject piles'.

In contrast, employment relations on the US model have not permitted shop-floor participation in ensuring the quantity and quality of work. Struggling as they were with unionized workers over the 'right to manage' in the decades after the Second World War, US management had little reason to believe that, if the necessary skill and authority were vested in shop-floor workers, the rejects would not pile up. Given the history of labour–management conflict in US manufacturing, US managers had good reason to believe that workers would make use of such control to restrict output, and thereby decrease the amount of effort that they had to expend to earn a given wage (see Lazonick, 1990, chs 7–9). In any case, the detailed internal job structures and promotion policies that had become basic to plant-level collective bargaining in the United States by the 1950s made it impossible for workers to develop the broad-based skills necessary to contribute to JIT.

At the same time, however, the experience of Japanese transplants abroad suggests that, given the appropriate employment environment, many of the basic features of the Japanese model of employment relations can be adopted with success outside Japan (for Japanese transplants in the United States, see Fucini and Fucini, 1990; Florida and Kenney, 1991; in the UK, see Oliver and Wilkinson, 1988). The appropriate employment environment is one in which, first and foremost, a company is able and willing to make realistic promises to its shop-floor employees that they are permanent members of the organization. To provide such realistic promises, the company must already be dominant in its industry and must have demonstrated that it has been willing and able to make the commitment of permanent employment to its shop-floor employees in the past. In the ACCs of the West, there are many companies that have sufficient market dominance to make permanent employment a realistic possibility for shop-floor workers. Indeed, as an essential element of their rise to dominance, these companies have invariably offered something akin to permanent employment to their managerial employees. But, especially in the UK and the United States, these long-term commitments have generally not been extended to 'hourly-rated' workers on the shop floor. Once entrenched, such a legacy of exclusion is difficult to overcome. Shop-floor workers are suspicious of the promises of management and hence are prone to use whatever power they have to reduce the amount of effort they expend for a given wage. In turn, management is reluctant to make significant investments in the skills of workers for fear that the possession of such capabilities will increase the power of workers to control the relation between effort and pay.

Enhanced capabilities by shop-floor workers are critical for the successful use of not only JIT but also QC. When defective inputs appear using JIT, throughput cannot be maintained by drawing replacements from a buffer stock; there is none. But the very involvement of shop-floor workers in the coordination of JIT puts them in the position to engage in quality control. They can inspect work-in-progress while they coordinate the flow of work. Quality control can be made a line rather than a staff function. As operated in Japan, QC does not require a large quality-control bureaucracy within the managerial structure (Cusumano, 1985, pp. 265, 293, 328; see also Hayashi, 1983). For QC to occur on the shop floor requires, however, that workers have the skills to determine when an intermediate product is defective. The Japanese have developed relatively simple statistical control techniques that can be used and applied by shop-floor workers in contrast to the much more complicated techniques generally used in the United States that can only be understood and applied by highly trained engineers (Cusumano, 1985, pp. 320–21). In 1962 Japanese mass producers began to establish QC circles – groups of workers meeting together to discuss quality control problems – to promote, in Michael Cusumano's words, 'the shift of QC and inspection responsibilities to the shop floor and the improvement of company methods for personnel administration and worker training' (Cusumano 1985, p. 333).

The basic QC concepts originated in the United States, dating back some sixty years to a book written by a Bell Laboratories engineer, W.A. Shewhart (1931). In the 1950s, a small number of Americans, most notably Armand V. Feigenbaum, W. Edwards Deming, and J.M. Juran, brought the QC concepts to Japan. In 1956 Feigenbaum wrote in a *Harvard Business Review* article entitled 'Total Quality Control' that 'in organizing a modern quality control function the first principle to recognize is that quality control is everybody's job'. From his perspective as head of quality control at General Electric, Feigenbaum went on to say:

The simple fact of the matter is that the marketing man is in the best position to evaluate adequately customer's quality preferences; the design engineer is the only man who can effectively establish specification quality levels; the shop supervisor is *the individual who can best concentrate on the building of quality* [my emphasis]. Total quality control programs therefore require as a first step, top management's re-emphasis on the responsibility and accountability of *all* [his emphasis] company employees in new design control, incoming material control, product control, and special process studies. (Feigenbaum, 1956, p. 98; see also Cusumano, 1985, pp. 324–5)

For Feigenbaum, as for most other managers of US mass-production enterprises in the decades after the Second World War, 'all company employees' did *not* include shop-floor workers. Whatever the seniority rights that the unions had foisted on management, US managers did not consider hourly-rated shop-floor workers to be members of the corporation. Hence for purposes of making 'quality control everybody's job' (as well as for virtually all other activities requiring the integration of conception and execution), 'everybody' went no further down the organizational hierarchy than the first-line supervisor – that is, those employees who were part of the managerial structure. As in the case of JIT, so too with QC: US management was not about to grant workers skills and authority that they might use to exercise control over the flow of work.

In 1981 Kaoru Ishikawa, a leader of the QC movement in Japan, explained why firms in his country had been successful in introducing QC on the shop floor whereas US firms had made QC a managerial function. As described by Cusumano, every reason that Ishikawa gave pointed to an organizational segmentation between management and the blue-collar workforce in the United States that did not exist in Japan.

Most important, he believed, was Japan's weak tradition of specialization in industry. Japanese companies never felt comfortable with the Taylor system of creating a rigid set of rules for job routines to distinguish responsibilities among workers and between labor and management. The absence in Japan, after the mid-1950s, of powerful industrial unions, which enforced job classifications in the United States, also allowed managers to rotate employees freely and to assign them multiple tasks. Furthermore, the 'vertical' character of personal relationships in Japanese society, reproduced in companies, made it seem natural for managers to make QC primarily a 'line' rather than a 'staff' function, and to extend the responsibility to maintain quality to the factory level while reducing the roles of staff specialists. (Cusumano, 1985)

Ishikawa went on to add that Japan's superior educational system made it possible to teach statistical control methods to workers, and that the practice of lifetime employment gave the firm an interest in investing in the worker, while secure employment and the Japanese seniority-based pay system made it easier for the worker to identify with the goals of the enterprise (Cusumano, 1985, p. 331).

In sum, like FMS and JIT, QC as applied in Japan requires that shop-floor workers possess a high degree of skill and puts them in positions of considerable authority and responsibility to coordinate the flow of work. Why have Japanese manufacturers been more successful in developing and utilizing these work innovations than their American competitors? It may well be that Japanese workers have different 'utility functions' than their American counterparts, and hence are willing to supply more effort for a given amount of pay, even though their skill endowments and their related responsibilities in the production process provide them with more power than workers in the US to control the pace of work. If so, I would argue that these effort–pay preferences are not simply or even primarily the products of a distinctive Japanese culture but have been greatly influenced by the social relations of the workplace that have evolved in Japan over the past century. The history of particular employment environments matters because the evolution of social relations of production plays a role in shaping the behaviour – or culture – that workers manifest at a point in time. In turn, the existence of a culture that has evolved on the basis of a particular employment environment makes it difficult, if not impossible, to alter the social relations of production that have characterized the past – even when what worked in the past is no longer suitable for creating value in the present (see Lazonick, 1990, chs 6–10, and 1991, chs 1–3).

In participating in the value-creation process, Japanese workers are involved in structures of social relations that provide them with incentives to cooperate in achieving high rates of throughput without sacrificing quality (see Aoki, 1988). It is indeed the expectation of such cooperation that gives Japanese management the incentive to invest in both human skills and effort-saving machines as well as to delegate considerable authority and responsibility for the coordination of work to employees on the shop floor.

As I have already argued, since the late nineteenth century, the managers of US companies engaged in mass production have been concerned with taking skills and authority *off* the shop floor to deprive workers of the power to control the pace of work. It would require a dramatic restructuring of labour relations in the US to give US managers the confidence that shop-floor workers would use their skills and authority inherent in Japanese practices to augment the managerial surplus rather than restrict output.

Shop-floor skills and worker attitudes required to create value using flexible mass production do not appear just because a company has invested in flexible machine technologies (see Shaiken et al., 1986; see also Shaiken, 1984). US companies that invest in FMS do not take advantage of the potential complementarity between programmable technology and shop-floor skills. On the contrary, management tries to use the new technologies in ways that increase its control over the flow of work (see Noble, 1979 and 1984). The transformation of labour–management relations so that shop-floor workers have an interest in using their skills to enhance productivity rather than restrict output constitutes a precondition for the effective utilization of these technologies in today's international competition.

VI COOPERATION AND ECONOMIC GROWTH

The rise of Japanese industry to international dominance has rendered obsolete the structure of shop-floor employment relations that characterized US industry during its era of hegemony. Unlike Japanese enterprises (although with a few exceptions already noted), US industrial enterprises had never made long-term employment *commitments* (as distinct from implicit promises) to their shop-floor workers. Inherent in the insistence by US managers of their 'right to manage' the shop floor was the ideology that, at any time and for any job, any individual shop-floor worker was dispensable – paid by the 'hour' for the job at hand and no more. In terms of workers' skills, this managerial ideology could claim some relevance. Intent on taking skills off the shop floor where workers might use them to control the pace of work, US managerial enterprises had not made significant investments in the skills of shop-floor workers, thus making it unnecessary for management to look on any particular shop-floor worker as one of the company's valued assets. But in terms of workers' *efforts*, managerial ideology was much less well founded. In practice, to gain the cooperation of shop-floor workers in maintaining the rapid and steady flow of work so essential to achieving low unit costs, management had to offer them a measure of employment security and a share (however indirect) in the prosperity of the enterprise (see Lazonick, 1990).

Before the Great Depression, some of the more farsighted industrial managers had systematized their personnel policies to provide hard-working shop-floor workers with realistic promises of economic security. When, during the Great Depression, the promises were not kept, workers took the matter of economic security into their own hands. Once the major industrial corporations had recognized the new mass-production unions, it was not managerial personnel policy but workers' own collective organizations, emphasizing as they did seniority rights, that would provide workers with the employment security and economic gains critical for eliciting their cooperation in the workplace. In effect, managers of most of the great US industrial corporations came to rely on independent union organizations to ensure the long-term relation between these workers and the company.

This institutional arrangement remained viable as long as the US industrial corporations continued to dominate their markets. But when, in the 1960s and 1970s, the corporations stumbled in the face of international competition, and sought to roll back the bargaining gains that workers had made over the previous decades, the adversarial character of US labour–management relations broke through the corporate veneer. In industries such as steel and automobiles that were dominated by adaptive (as distinct from innovative) oligopolists, the costs of the accord with labour that had been struck in the 1940s began to outstrip productivity gains. As long as there were no serious foreign competitors and no significant domestic price competition, US corporations were able to pass off higher labour costs to consumers in the form of higher prices. By the late 1960s, however, the limits of the adaptive strategy had been reached. With powerful international competitors on the scene, domestic inflation only served to erode US international competitive advantage.

The US competitiveness problem was not only higher wages but also lagging productivity growth. High wages, tight labour markets, and the availability of unemployment benefits – not to mention the restiveness of younger blue-collar workers, both black and white, in the wake of the civil rights and antiwar movements – had weakened managerial control over shop-floor workers. Alienated in any case by the routine nature of their work and without any formal power to influence the nature of the work environment, blue-collar workers sought to control their expenditure of effort by unauthorized work stoppages, work to rule and absenteeism, all of which had adverse consequences for productivity.

In the 1970s many observers of US industry pointed to the alienated shop-floor worker, confined to routine and repetitive tasks requiring little skill development, as an explanation of the slowdown in the growth of labour productivity in US manufacturing that had begun in the mid-1960s. In many plants around the country, companies initiated experiments in job enlargement and job enrichment to try to enhance 'the quality of work life' (as it was called) in order to elicit more effort from workers. Although the initial impacts of these programmes were generally positive, many of the experiments in the early 1970s were cut short when the workers whose jobs had been enriched and enlarged began questioning traditional managerial prerogatives. In the long run, attempts such as these at piecemeal transformation of the organizational structure may well have reduced rather than enhanced organizational capability by creating expectations for more meaningful work which in the end were not fulfilled (Marglin, 1979; Walton, 1985).

As stated earlier, in the 1980s Japanese success in taking market share away from once-dominant US mass producers made it clear that the prime source of Japanese competitive advantage was not low wages (as many Americans had chosen to believe in the 1970s) but superior organizational capabilities. As a result, many US industrial managers also came to recognize that the major difference between the internal organization of US and Japanese enterprises was the extent to which Japanese managers *developed* skills on the shop floor and delegated authority to blue-collar workers to use those skills to ensure a rapid flow of high-quality work. As a result of the Japanese challenge, US industrial managers began to realize that enhancing 'the quality of work life' was not just a means of eliciting effort from workers (as had been the case in the failed experiments of the 1970s); rather industrial managers came to recognize that upgrading the skills of the shop-floor labour force was an end in itself because it augmented the human resource assets that the company 'possessed'. To maintain the rapid flow of high-quality work using new automated manufacturing technologies requires shop-floor workers with the cognitive capabilities to ensure that the machines work properly with a minimum of downtime. US mass-production industries could no longer compete using workers whose own mechanical motions merely complemented those of the machine, as had previously been the case. The effective use of the new technologies requires shop-floor workers who can ensure the quality, as well as the quantity, of work.

As a precondition for technology-specific training for workers under the auspices of the employing enterprise itself, the large-scale adoption of new 'flexible' technologies requires a supply of more highly educated shop-floor workers than US industry has used or has had available in the past. To generate a large supply of workers capable of acquiring the requisite training both within and outside the manufacturing enterprise, institutional rigidities in the US educational system must be confronted. When, in the early twentieth century, vocational schooling entered US secondary education to track youths away from college and into the blue-collar labour force, the resultant segmentation of the labour force was consistent with the social division of labour between managers and workers in the world of work (see Bowles and Gintis, 1976). But in recent decades the same educational system has lost touch with the changing human-resource needs of an industrial era in which the potential for automation has created a new role for shop-floor workers in monitoring the quality, as well as ensuring the quantity, of work.

What is now needed is an educational system that rejects the conception of the worker as a mere appendage of the machine, and prepares future workers for active involvement in speeding the flow of work while maintaining its quality in the 'flexible' factory. There is no point, however, in building new organizational structures and educational systems if those who run the largest industrial corporations eschew innovative investment strategies that can make use of skilled workers who are encouraged to exercise initiative on the shop floor. Yet prevailing organizational structures may be inhibiting the adoption of innovative investment strategies. Existing organizational structures within the US manufacturing enterprises reflect a century-long managerial obsession with taking skills off the shop floor. It would appear that even as we enter the 1990s many if not most US managers are reluctant to develop skills on the shop floor for fear of losing control over the flow of work to an adversarial labour force.

There is no doubt that the dramatic rise of Japanese industry has rendered obsolete the sharp gulf between shop-floor workers and management that characterized leading capitalist competitors in the past (for the transformation of employment relations in different national contexts, see Boyer, Chapter 1, this volume). During the twentieth century, the organization of industry in the most successful capitalist economy has become increasingly collective, requiring planned coordination and cooperative relations among individuals, enterprises and states involved in the development and utilization of productive resources (see Lazonick, 1991). More than any other capitalist economy in history, the Japanese have elaborated the model of collective capitalism, in large part by constructing cooperative employment relations that include workers on the shop floor. Japanese employers have invested in shop-floor productive capabilities, including the skills of shop-floor workers. In turn, Japanese shop-floor workers have provided the high levels of effort that are required to transform these investments into high-quality products at low unit costs. As a result, both employers and employees have reaped the material benefits of capitalist economic growth.

Once the dynamic between cooperation and growth has been set in motion, success has bred success. Cooperative employment relations have contributed to the growth of the Japanese economy, and the growth of the Japanese economy has sustained the viability of cooperative employment relations. For those business organizations and national economies that want to meet the Japanese challenge, the task will not be easy but the message is clear. Cooperative employment relations must replace the conflictual relations of the past.

REFERENCES

Abegglen, James C. and George Stalk, Jr (1985) *Kaisha: The Japanese Corporation*, New York: Basic Books.

Abernathy, William J., Kim B. Clark and Alan M. Kantrow (1983) *Industrial Renaissance: Producing a Competitive Future for America*, New York: Basic Books.

Akerlof, George A. and Janet L. Yellen (eds) (1986) *Efficiency Wage Models of the Labor Market*, New York: Cambridge University Press.

Altshuler, Alan, Martin Anderson, Daniel Jones, Daniel Roos and James Womack (1986) *The Future of the Automobile*, Cambridge, Mass.: MIT Press.

Aoki, Masahiko (1988) *Information, Incentives, and Bargaining in the Japanese Economy*, Cambridge: Cambridge University Press.

Asanuma, Banri (1989) 'Manufacturer–Supplier Relationships in Japan and the Concept of Relation-Specific Skill', *Journal of the Japanese and International Economies*, vol. 3, no. 1.

Ballon, Robert J. and Iwao Tomita (1988) *The Financial Behavior of Japanese Corporations*, New York: Kodansha International.

Bowles, Samuel and Herbert Gintis (1976) *Schooling in Capitalist America*, New York: Basic Books.

Braverman, Harry (1974) *Labor and Monopoly Capital*, New York: Monthly Review Press.

Cannings, Kathleen and William Lazonick (1994) 'Equal Employment Opportunity and the "Managerial Woman" in Japan', *Industrial Relations*.

Chalmers, Norma (1989) *Industrial Relations in Japan: The Peripheral Workforce*, London: Routledge.

Chandler, Jr, Alfred D. (1962) *Strategy and Structure: Chapters in the History of American Enterprise*, Cambridge, Mass.: MIT Press.

Chandler, Jr, Alfred D. (1977) *The Visible Hand: The Managerial Revolution in American Business*, Cambridge, Mass.: Harvard University Press.

Chandler, Jr, Alfred D. (1990) *Scale and Scope: The Dynamics of Industrial Capitalism*, Cambridge, Mass.: Harvard University Press.

Clark, Kim B., Robert H. Hayes and Christopher Lorenz (eds) (1985), *The Uneasy Alliance: Managing the Productivity–Technology Dilemma*, Boston: Harvard Business School Press.

Cole, Robert E. and Tazio Yakushiji (eds) (1984), *The American and Japanese Auto Industries in Transition*, Ann Arbor: Center for Japanese Studies, University of Michigan.

Cornell, John B. (1967) 'Individual Mobility and Group Membership: The Case of the *Burakumin*', in R.P. Dore (ed.) *Aspects of Social Change In Modern Japan*, Princeton: Princeton University Press.

Cusumano, Michael (1985) *The Japanese Automobile Industry*, Cambridge, Mass.: Harvard University Press.

Daito, E. (1986) 'Recruitment and Training of Middle Managers in Japan, 1900–1930', in Kesaji Kobayashi and Hidemasa Morikawa (eds) *Development of Managerial Enterprise*, Tokyo: University of Tokyo Press.

Dore, Ronald (1973) *British Factory – Japanese Factory*, Berkeley: University of California Press.

Dore, Ronald (1986) *Flexible Rigidities*, Stanford: Stanford University Press.

Dore, Ronald (1987) *Taking Japan Seriously*, Stanford: Stanford University Press.

Dun's Census of American Business (1990) New York: Dun and Bradstreet.

Edwards, Linda N. (1988) 'Equal Employment Opportunity in Japan: A view from the West', *Industrial and Labor Relations Review*, vol. 41, no. 1.

Evans, Jr, Robert (1970), 'Evolution of the Japanese System of Employer–Employee Relations, 1868–1945', *Business History Review*, vol. 44, no. 1.

Feigenbaum, Armand V. (1956) 'Total Quality Control', *Harvard Business Review*, vol. 34, no. 6.

Fortune (1989), 'The International 500: The Biggest Industrial Corporations Outside the US', 31 July.

Freeman, Richard B. (1989) *Labor Markets in Action,* Cambridge, Mass.: Harvard University Press.

Friedman, David (1988) *The Misunderstood Miracle: Industrial Development and Political Change in Japan*, Ithaca: Cornell University Press.

Fucini, Joseph J. and Suzy Fucini (1990) *Working for the Japanese: Inside Mazda's Auto Plant*, New York: Free Press.

Fukasaku, Yukio (1991) 'In-Firm Training at Mitsubishi Nagasaki Shipyard, 1884–1934', in Howard F. Gospel (ed.) *Industrial Training and Technological Innovation*, London: Routledge, 1991.

Fukasaku, Yukio (1992) *Technology and Industrial Development in Pre-war Japan*, London: Routledge.

Garon, Sheldon (1987) *The State and Labor in Modern Japan*, Berkeley: University of California Press.

Gordon, Andrew (1985) *The Evolution of Labour Relations in Japan: Heavy Industry, 1853–1955*, Cambridge, Mass.: Harvard University Press.

Gould IV, William B. (1984) *Japan's Reshaping of American Labor Law*, Cambridge, Mass.: MIT Press.

Halberstam, Michael (1986) *The Reckoning*, New York: Morrow.

Harris, Howell John (1982) *The Right to Manage: Industrial Relations Policies of American Business in the 1940s*, Madison: University of Wisconsin Press.

Hayashi, Masaki (1983) 'The Japanese Style of Small-Group QC-Circle Activity', The Institute of Business Research, Chuo University, October, Research Paper no. 2.

Helper, Susan (1990) 'Comparative Supplier Relations in the US and Japanese Auto Industries: An Exit/Voice Approach', *Business and Economic History*, second series, vol. 19.

Hirschmeier, J. and T. Yui (1981) *The Development of Japanese Business*, second edition, London: Allen & Unwin.

Hunter, Janet (1984) 'Recruitment in the Japanese Silk Reeling & Cotton Spinning Industries, 1870s–1930s', *Proceedings of the British Association for Japanese Studies*, vol. 9.

Iacocca, Lee (1990) 'Let's End the "Poltoonery"', *Newsweek*, 16 April, p. 10.

Jacobson, Gary and John Hillkirk (1986) *Xerox: American Samurai*, New York: Collins.

Japan Economic Institute (1990) 'The Long Workweek in Japan: Difficult to Reduce', *JEI Report*, 11A, 16 March.

Japan Institute of Labour (1986) *Problems of Working Women*, Japanese Industrial Relations Series no. 8, Tokyo: Japan Institute of Labour.

Japan Statistical Yearbook (*JSY*) (1981) Tokyo: Statistics Bureau, Management and Coordination Agency.

Japan Statistical Yearbook (*JSY*) (1985) Tokyo: Statistics Bureau, Management and Coordination Agency.

Japan Statistical Yearbook (*JSY*) (1989) Tokyo: Statistics Bureau, Management and Coordination Agency.

Kamata, Satoshi (1982) *Japan in the Passing Lane: An Insider's Account of Life in a Japanese Auto Factory*, New York: Pantheon.

Katz, Lawrence (1986) 'Efficiency Wage Theories: A Partial Evaluation', in Stanley Fischer (ed.) *NBER Macroeconomics Annual 1986*, Cambridge, Mass.: MIT Press.

Kenney, Martin and Richard Florida (1991) 'How Japanese Industry is Rebuilding the Rustbelt', *Technology Review*, February–March, pp. 24–33.

Kidd, Y.A. (1978) 'Women Workers in the Japanese Cotton Mills: 1880–1920', Cornell University East Asia Papers, no. 20.

Koike, Kazuo (1988) *Understanding Industrial Relations in Modern Japan*, New York: St Martin's.

Koshiro, Kazutoshi (1983) 'Development of Collective Bargaining in Postwar Japan', in Taishiro Shirai (ed.) *Contemporary Industrial Relations in Japan*, Madison: University of Wisconsin Press.

Lazonick, William (1986) 'Strategy, Structure, and Management Development in the United States and Britain', in Kobayashi, K. and H. Morikawa (eds) *Development of Managerial Enterprise*, Tokyo: University of Tokyo Press.

Lazonick, William (1990) *Competitive Advantage on the Shop Floor*, Cambridge, Mass.: Harvard University Press.

Lazonick, William (1991) *Business Organization and the Myth of the Market Economy,* Cambridge: Cambridge University Press.

Levine, Solomon (1958) *Industrial Relations in Postwar Japan*, Urbana: University of Illinois Press.

Maddison, Angus (1987) 'Growth and Slowdown in Advanced Capitalist Economies: Techniques of Quantitative Assessment', *Journal of Economic Literature*, vol. 25, no. 2.

Marglin, Stephen A. (1979) 'Catching Flies with Honey: An Inquiry into Management Initiatives to Humanize Work', *Economic Analysis and Workers' Management*, vol. 13.

Marx, Karl (1977) *Capital*, vol. 1, New York: Vintage.

McCraw, Thomas K. and Patricia O'Brien (1986) 'Production and Distribution: Competition Policy and Industry Structure', in Thomas K. McCraw (ed.) *America versus Japan*, Boston: Harvard Business School Press.

Mincer, Jacob (1985) 'Intercountry Comparisons of Labor Force Trends and of Related Developments: An Overview', *Journal of Labor Economics*, vol. 3, 3.1.

Moore, Joe (1983) *Japanese Workers and the Struggle for Power, 1945–1947*, Madison: University of Wisconsin Press.

Morikawa, Hidemasa (1989) 'The Increasing Power of Salaried Managers in Japan's Large Corporations', in William D. Wray (ed.) *Managing Industrial Enterprise: Cases from Japan's Prewar Experience*, Cambridge, Mass.: Harvard University Press.

Noble, David (1979) 'Social Choice in Machine Design: The Case of Automatically Controlled Machine Tools', in Andrew S. Zimbalist (ed.) *Case Studies on the Labor Process*, New York: Monthly Review Press.

Noble, David (1984) *The Forces of Production*, New York: Knopf.

Odaka, Konosuke, Keinosuke Ono and Fumihiko Adachi (1988) *The Automobile Industry in Japan: A Study of Ancillary Development*, Tokyo: Kinokuniya.

Ohno, Taiichi (1982) 'How the Toyota Production System was Created', *Japanese Economic Studies*, vol. 10, no. 4.

Okayama, Reiko (1983) 'Japanese Employer Policy: The Heavy Engineering Industry, 1900–1930', in Howard Gospel and Craig Littler (eds) *Managerial Strategies and Industrial Relations*, London: Heinemann.

Okuda, Kenji (1972) 'Managerial Evolution in Japan', *Management Japan*, vol. 6, no. 1.

Oliver, Nick, and Barry Wilkinson (1988) *The Japanization of British Industry*, Oxford: Basil Blackwell.

OECD (1977) *The Development of Industrial Relations Systems: Some Implications of the Japanese Experience*, Paris: OECD.

Piore, Michael J. and Charles F. Sabel (1984) *The Second Industrial Divide,* New York: Basic Books.

Reich, Michael R., Yasuo Endo and C. Peter Timmer (1986) 'Agriculture: The Political Economy of Structural Change', in Thomas K. McCraw (ed.) *America versus Japan*, Boston: Harvard Business School Press.

Reich, Robert B. (1990) 'Who is Us?', *Harvard Business Review*, vol. 86, no. 1.

Sanger, David E. (1990) 'Tokyo Tries to Find Out if "Salarymen" Are Working Themselves to Death', *New York Times*, 19 March, p. A8.

Sawada, Shujiro (1970) 'Technological Change in Japanese Agriculture: A Long-Term Analysis', in Kazushi Ohkawa, Bruce F. Johnston and Horomitsu Kaneda (eds) *Agriculture and Economic Growth: Japan's Experience,* Tokyo: University of Tokyo Press.

Sawyer, Malcolm (1976) 'Income Distribution in OECD Countries', *OECD Outlook*, July.

Saxonhouse, Gary R. (1976) 'Country Girls and Communication among Competitors in the Japanese Cotton-Spinning Industry', in H. Patrick (ed.) *Japanese Industrialization and Its Social Consequences*, Berkeley: University of California Press.

Shaiken, Harley (1984) *Work Transformed*, New York: Holt, Rinehart and Winston.

Shaiken, Harley, Stephen Herzenberg and Sarah Kuhn (1986) 'The Work Process Under More Flexible Production', *Industrial Relations*, vol. 25, no. 2.

Sheard, P. (1983) 'Auto Production Systems in Japan', Papers of the Japan Study Centre, Monash University, vol. 8.

Shewhart, W.A. (1931) *Economic Control of Quality of Manufactured Product*, New York: Van Nostrand.

Shimada, Haruo (1970) 'Japan Labour's Spring Wage Offensive and Wage Spillover', *Keio Economic Studies*, vol. 7, no. 2.

Shimokawa, Koichi (1985) 'Japan's Keiretsu System: The Case of the Automobile Industry', *Japanese Economic Studies*, vol. 13, no. 4.

Shirai, Taishiro (1983) 'A Theory of Enterprise Unionism', in Shirai (ed.) *Contemporary Industrial Relations in Japan*, Madison: University of Wisconsin Press.

Smitka, Michael (1990) 'The Invisible Handshake: The Historical Development of the Japanese Automotive Parts Industry', *Business and Economic History*, second series, vol. 19.

Sugeno, Kazuo (1987) 'The Impact of the Equal Employment Opportunity Law at Its First Stage of Enforcement', *Japan Labor Bulletin*, vol. 26, no. 10.

Suzuki, Yoshio (1980) *Money and Banking in Contemporary Japan*, New Haven: Yale University Press.

Tanzer, Andrew, and Ruth Simon (1990) 'Why Japan Loves Robots and We Don't', *Forbes*, 16 April.

Tsuchiya, Keizo (1970) 'Economics of Mechanization in Small-Scale Agriculture', in Kazushi Ohkawa, Bruce F. Johnston and Horomitsu Kaneda (eds) *Agriculture and Economic Growth: Japan's Experience,* Tokyo: University of Tokyo Press.

Tsurumi, E. (1984) 'Female Textile Workers and the Failure of Early Trade Unionism in Japan', *History Workshop*, vol. 18.

Upham, Frank (1987) *Law and Social Change in Postwar Japan*, Cambridge, Mass.: Harvard University Press.

Vogel, Ezra (1980) *Japan as Number One*, New York: Harper Colophon Books.

Wagatsuma, Hiroshi and George A. de Vos (1967) 'The Outcast Tradition in Modern Japan: A Problem in Social Self-Identity', in R.P. Dore (ed.) *Aspects of Social Change in Modern Japan*, Princeton: Princeton University Press.

Walton, Richard E. (1985) 'From Control to Commitment: Transforming Work Force Management in the United States', in Clark, Hayes and Lorenz (1985).

Watanabe, Susumi (1971) 'Subcontracting, Industrialisation, and Employment Creation', *International Labour Review*, vol. 104, nos. 1–2.

Woronoff, Jon (1983) *Japan's Wasted Workers*, Totowa, NJ: Allanheld, Osmun.

Year Book of Labour Statistics (YBLS), 13 (1960) Tokyo: Division of Statistics and Research, Ministry of Labor, Japan.

Year Book of Labour Statistics (YBLS), 18 (1965) Tokyo: Division of Statistics and Research, Ministry of Labor, Japan.

Year Book of Labour Statistics (*YBLS*), 28 (1975) Tokyo: Statistics and Information Department. Minister's Secretariat, Ministry of Labour.

Year Book of Labour Statistics (*YBLS*), 35 (1982) Tokyo: Statistics and Information Department. Minister's Secretariat, Ministry of Labour.

Year Book of Labour Statistics (*YBLS*), 39 (1986) Tokyo: Statistics and Information Department. Minister's Secretariat, Ministry of Labour.

Year Book of Labour Statistics (*YBLS*), 40 (1987) Tokyo: Statistics and Information Department. Minister's Secretariat, Ministry of Labour.

Yonekawa, Shin'ichi (1984) 'University Graduates in Japanese Enterprises before the Second World War', *Business History*, vol. 26, no. 3.

4. Changing capital–labour relations in South Korea

Jong-Il You

I INTRODUCTION

This paper analyses the historical roots and the economic logic of the authoritarian capital–labour relations which provided an institutional basis for the hyper-growth during the last three decades in South Korea. It will also throw light on the causes and the nature of the massive wave of capital–labour confrontations since the partial 'democratization' in 1987.

The conventional wisdom of the Korean labour market has focused exclusively on the role of market forces in wage determination. According to this view, Korea was able to achieve high growth and low unemployment because wages were set around the market-clearing level; and, as a result, not only did the economic pie grow fast but it was equitably shared among the working population (Fields, 1984; World Bank, 1987; Krueger, 1988; Fields and Wan, 1989). While there is an element of truth in this view, its greatest weakness is its total neglect of the institutional setting upon which market forces operate. One consequence of this is its inability to answer the question why so many of the Korean workers are revolting against a system which obviously 'delivered the goods' in an, allegedly, equitable manner.

While all markets operate in a particular institutional setting (Hodgson, 1988; North, 1990), it is especially important to understand the institutional underpinnings in the case of the labour market. First, the peculiar nature of labour as a commodity – the inalienability of commodity labour from its owner – renders the definition of property rights, which in this case include the rights of the workers (labour rights) and the rights of the employers (management rights), intensely political and prone to conflict. Before the demand–supply analysis, therefore, it is important to understand what system of rights underpins the labour market and how that is legitimated or otherwise maintained. Second, unlike other commodities, the actual consummation of the labour exchange does not take place in the market but in the production process organized within the firm. If one wants to understand how labour resources are utilized, therefore, it is necessary

to go beyond demand and supply in the labour market and analyse the organization of work within the firm and its linkages with the technology of production,
or the system of production (see, e.g., Leibenstein, 1987). The system of rights
and the system of production provide the basis upon which capital–labour
relations are formed. The basic premise of this paper is that the institutional forces
of capital–labour relations are as relevant as the market forces to the regulation
of how productivity gains are generated and shared.

The historical/institutional analysis of this paper is guided by the hypothesis
that a successful model of capitalist development requires compatibility of the
capital–labour relations with other elements of the model. One dimension of
such compatibility is that the pattern of income distribution must remain
conducive to capital accumulation under the existing macroeconomic structure.
For example, sustained economic development is impossible if productivity gains
are appropriated mostly by capitalists (workers) in a wage-led (profit-led)
growth structure (see Bowles and Boyer, 1988). The gain sharing between
wages and profits has been emphasized by the neo-institutionalist analysts as
one of the reasons for the postwar boom in the advanced capitalist countries
(Bowles et al., 1986; Marglin and Schor, 1990). Another dimension of the required
compatibility, which takes on particular significance in the case of Korea, is
that between capital–labour relations and the political structure and, more
generally, the social order. Lack of this compatibility causes instability in
capital–labour relations.

Indeed, the persistence of the authoritarian capital–labour relations in Korea
until the current crisis was due to their compatibility with the prevailing sociopolitical order and macroeconomic structure. The dominance of the developmentalist
state *vis-à-vis* social classes was critical to maintaining the authoritarian
capital–labour relations. Also, the macroeconomic structure was such that the
authoritarian capital–labour relations helped sustain rapid economic growth, which
in turn helped legitimate the dominance of the state. From this perspective, the
unravelling of the model is also explained by the compatibility argument. The
very success of the model resulted in a strengthening of the social classes, including
the working class, slowly undermining the structural basis of the authoritarian
political system and capital–labour relations.

In the following pages the arguments presented above are developed in
detail. Section II starts out with some basic facts regarding the growth and the
segmentation of the labour market. Section III examines key aspects of the authoritarian capital–labour relations and their economic implications. The linkages
between the authoritarian capital–labour relations and the macroeconomic
structure of export-led industrialization are discussed next (Section IV). Section
V recounts the developments that led to the breakdown of the authoritarian
capital–labour relations. Section VI presents an analysis of the causes and consequences of the breakdown, and is followed by a brief conclusion.

II INDUSTRIALIZATION AND THE GROWTH OF WAGE LABOUR

Export-Led Industrialization and Wage Labour

Korea has undergone modern industrialization at a breakneck pace since the early 1960s. During the period 1962–85 GNP growth rate averaged 8.4 per cent, while manufacturing GDP grew at a compound annual rate of 15.0 per cent. The rapid economic growth in this period was led by exports as export growth consistently outstripped output growth; total exports grew at 24.5 per cent and manufacturing exports at 31.5 per cent. As a result, the ratio of total exports to GNP rose from 5.0 per cent in 1962 to 37.5 per cent in 1985, and the ratio of exports to output in manufacturing rose from 1.2 per cent to 27.9 per cent during the same period (Table 4.1).

Table 4.1 Indicators of export-led growth

	1962	1973	1978	1985
Total exports/GNP	5.0	29.9	30.6	37.5
Manufactures in merchandise exports	27.0	88.2	89.9	95.4
Manufacturing output exported (%, in current prices)	1.2	24.4	26.5	27.9
Compound annual growth rate of				
Total exports	39.3	18.3	8.1	
GNP	9.5	10.1	5.7	
Manufacturing exports	55.1	18.8	9.1	
Manufacturing GDP (%, in 1980 constant prices)	19.3[a]	17.8	7.4	

Note: [a] 1963–73

Sources: Bank of Korea (BOK); Economic Planning Board (EPB).

Table 4.1 shows also a considerable slowdown in export growth and narrowing of the gap between the export and GDP growth rates of the manufacturing sector over the years. During the first phase of export-led industrialization, 1962–73, manufacturing exports grew at an incredible 55 per cent annually, starting of course from a very low base. Industrial development in this period was concentrated in such labour-intensive export industries as textiles, clothing, plywood, electrical assembly, etc. The period 1974–78, the second phase, saw an accelerated growth of import-substitution capital-intensive industries under the policy of so-called 'big push' toward heavy and chemical industrialization. The third phase, 1979–85, is a crisis and restructuring period. A combination of internal problems and external shocks led to a significant fall in growth rates. But the basis for a renewed hyper-growth after 1986 was made during this period by industrial restructuring and stabilization of prices. Exports were no longer dominated by labour-intensive light manufacturing; its share in total manufacturing exports fell to 43.5 per cent in 1983 compared to 75.5 per cent in 1965. Instead, exports of transportation equipment, electrical equipment, office machines and petroleum products grew by leaps and bounds.

The rapid industrialization transformed a predominantly rural–agrarian economy into a predominantly urban–industrial economy. Table 4.2 documents this transformation in terms of employment structure; the share of agriculture and forestry in total employment was reduced from over 60 per cent in 1963 to less than 20 per cent in 1988, while that of manufacturing increased from a mere 7.9 per cent to 27.7 per cent during the same period. The urban-centred industrial growth created a huge flow of rural-to-urban migration.[1]

Table 4.2   Transformation of employment structure, 1963–88

Year	Total employment[a]	Agri. & mining	Manufac.	Social Overhead Capital & Services	Farm	Non-farm
1963	7,947	63.9	7.9	28.2	64.5	35.5
1973	11,139	50.4	15.9	33.7	50.5	49.5
1983	14,505	30.5	22.5	47.0	30.9	69.1
1988	16,870	21.4	27.7	50.9	24.1[b]	75.9[b]

Average Annual Growth Rate of Employment

1963–88	3.1	–1.5	8.3	5.5	–0.9[c]	6.2[c]

Notes:
[a] In thousands; the rest, in percentage.
[b] 1986.
[c] 1963–86.

Source: EPB, *Economically Active Population Survey*, various issues.

Due to this radical shift away from agricultural employment which is dominated by the self-employed and family workers toward urban–industrial employment, wage labour became the dominant mode of employment and capital–labour relations the dominant relations of production. Table 4.3 shows that the wage labour which comprised less than a third of the total employment in 1963 began to represent the majority of employment after 1983. In 1988 the share of regular employees, which was less than 20 per cent in 1963, reached almost 50 per cent.

Table 4.3   Employment structure by class of workers, 1963–88

Year	Whole country SE	FW	WL	(RE)	Farm households SE	FW	WL	Non-farm households SE	FW	WL	(RE)
1963	37.2	31.4	31.4	(18.8)	41.5	44.1	14.4	29.5	7.8	62.7	(41.1)
1973	34.5	27.7	37.8	(27.3)	41.3	46.4	12.3	27.6	8.5	63.8	(49.1)
1983	33.8	16.8	49.4	(41.4)	49.4	36.3	14.3	26.7	8.0	65.3	(55.9)
1988	30.2	12.8	57.0	(48.1)	*50.1	36.6	13.3	*25.5	7.1	67.4	(56.7)

Notes:
SE = Self-employed, FW = Family workers, WL = Wage labour, RE = Regular employees, WL = RE + daily workers.
*1986 figures.

Source: EPB.

Labour-Market Segmentation

The specific nature of capital–labour relations varies across different segments of the labour market. This paper does not attempt to analyse capital–labour relations in various segments of the labour market separately. However, the segmentation of the labour market itself is an important facet of capital–labour relations from a macroeconomic point of view, so a brief discussion is provided here. Also, the discussion on capital–labour relations will pay due attention to the variations across different labour-market segments.

One important demarcation is between the formal and the informal sector. In this paper, however, the informal sector is all but ignored, because, by definition, not much is known about it. Moreover, the rapid industrialization was accompanied by a continuous rise in the employment share of the formal sector. Table 4.4 reports this trend, using a somewhat arbitrary definition of the formal sector as comprising establishments with ten or more regular employees, following Bai (1982). Within the manufacturing sector, which is the focus of the present paper, about two-thirds of the employed have belonged to the formal sector since the late 1970s.

Within the formal manufacturing sector capital–labour relations vary according to such worker characteristics as education and sex as well as occupational characteristics. But the segmentation of overriding importance is between the capital-intensive sector and the labour-intensive sector. Table 4.5 shows that the higher the capital intensity, the higher the wages and the lower the turnover rates. The wage differential by capital intensity is much more pronounced than the differential by firm size in Korea.[2] In addition, the correlation coefficient between wages and firm size was only 0.15 in 1973 and 0.28 in 1983, while that between wages and the capital–labour ratio was 0.83 in 1973 and 0.62 in 1983 (H. Kim, 1988).

Table 4.4   Employment share of the formal sector, 1960–86

	1960	1970	1979	1983	1986
In the whole economy	7.1	15.3	27.5	29.9	33.3
In the manufacturing sector	46.9[a]	49.8	65.3	66.4[b]	68.9

Notes:
Bai (1982) divides the informal sector into the rural traditional and the urban traditional sector.
[a] Establishments with five or more employees, 1963.
[b] 1982.

Sources: Bai (1982); EPB; Ministry of Labour (MOL).

Table 4.5   Capital intensity and labour-market characteristics, 1985

	Highly K intensive industries	Moderately K intensive industries	Intermediate industries	Moderately L intensive industries	Highly L intensive industries
K–L ratio[a]	4.57	1.63	0.96	0.70	0.22
Wages[a]	1.56	1.32	1.06	0.81	0.72
Turnover[b]	3.5	4.7	5.4	5.7	6.9
% female	9.8	14.1	34.8	57.0	64.3

Notes:
High K intensity (HK) – industrial chemicals; petroleum refineries; iron and steel; MK – beverages; paper, glass, non-metal products; non-ferrous metals; transportation equipments; IK – food products; printing and publishing; petroleum, coal, plastic, metal products; machinery; electrical machinery; ML – textiles; wood products; furniture; pottery, china, etc.; professional goods; HL – apparel; leather products; footwear; rubber products; miscellaneous products.
[a] Ratio to the manufacturing average.
[b] Average monthly separation rate during 1970–71.

Sources: Pyo (1988) and MOL.

The importance of the segmentation between the capital-intensive and the labour-intensive sector lies in more than its quantitative significance. As Table 4.5 shows, it coincides with the gender-based segmentation. A sexual division of labour has developed such that young female workers are concentrated in labour-intensive export-oriented manufacturing, which is characterized by low skill requirement, low wages and sweatshop conditions.[3] The gender wage differential in Korea is among the highest in the world; the female average wage was 44 per cent of the male average wage in 1980. The segmentation between the capital-intensive and the labour-intensive sector, moreover, is systematically related to the macroeconomic structure of the dualistic growth (see Section IV).

III ASPECTS OF AUTHORITARIAN CAPITAL–LABOUR RELATIONS

This section describes the authoritarian capital–labour relations that existed until the recent breakdown. In doing so, it follows the approach developed by the 'regulation' school and conceptualizes capital–labour relations as consisting of two key components: regulation of the labour market and methods of organizing and controlling labour for production activities. The following four characteristics are found to have shaped the capital–labour relations: state repression of labour; weak unions and competitive wage formation; intra-firm labour controls based on authoritarian paternalism; and worker involvement in learning in the production system.

The Leading Role of the State and Labour Repression

The dominance of the state in guiding economic development in Korea is by now well documented. The state dictated the direction of production and investment activities with a variety of incentives and sanctions, thereby controlling and shaping the accumulation process (Barone, 1986).[4] The state played a hegemonic role in shaping the capital–labour relations, too. Concerned with creating a productive yet undemanding working class, the state developed a highly repressive system of labour controls, while promoting an ideology of cooperative capital–labour relations. The state repression of labour in Korea was instrumental in securing industrial peace and labour discipline (Deyo, 1989).

The hegemonic position of the state *vis-à-vis* both capital and labour draws from the distinct postwar historical conditions: the strong state and weak social classes. Capitalists were dependent on the state, with their meagre economic base having originated from the disposal of the industrial assets left by Japanese and the allocation of US aid in the 1950s under the Rhee government (1948–60). Landlords, badly discredited for their collaboration with the Japanese, were stripped of their political might and economic base through the land reform in the early 1950s. In addition, the American objective of building an anti-communist bulwark led to the repression of organized labour and other popular movements during the US military government (1945–48). The leftist labour union federation, *Chunpyong*, was quickly outlawed and overwhelmed by the Federation of Korean Trade Unions (FKTU) organized by rightist paramilitary groups. Under Rhee the FKTU became an official organ of the ruling party and hardly functioned as an independent labour union, with its corrupt leadership far removed from the rank and file (You, 1990).

On the other hand, state power was very strong due to the legacy from the colonial period of a strong military–administrative apparatus and a massive build-up of the military and the national police following the Second World War and the Korean War (Choi, 1983). During the 1950s, however, the strength of the state – both the relative *autonomy* in its ability to define goals and the *capacity* to mobilize resources and implement policies (Haggard and Moon, 1983) – was compromised by the close links between the ruling party, state bureaucracy and business élites through allocation of import licences and foreign exchange in return for kickbacks and political support. Through this process emerged a number of *chaebols*, whose profit making involved more arbitrage gains under overvalued currency and import protection than serious manufacturing activities (Jones and SaKong, 1980).

When the Rhee government was toppled by the student-led uprising in 1960 amidst economic difficulties caused by declining US aid, the military had a distinctive opportunity to assume power and impose its vision of how the country should proceed in the absence of powerful social classes. Since the military coup in 1961, through the successive governments of Park (1961–79) and Chun (1980–87),

> the military-dominated state has attempted to erase its essential illegitimacy ... by fostering rapid economic development. It has worked on a tacit social compact whereby citizens were expected to tolerate the banishing of their political rights in exchange for the regime's delivering prosperity. (Bello, 1990, p. 51)

Thus was born a strong developmentalist state. Immediately after the coup the military government took a few steps which made it clear that both business and labour interests would be subordinated to the state-directed economic development programme.

First, the legal punishment of business élites (*chaebols*) for their 'illicitly accumulated wealth' under the previous government of Rhee was minimized in return for their cooperation with the economic development programme (Haggard and Moon, 1983). The capacity of the state to discipline the business was greatly strengthened by the nationalization of the commercial banking system in 1961 and the control over the access to foreign loans.[5] Trade unionists and other radical reformist groups that emerged after the student uprising were again repressed in the name of national security. Upon reorganizing the FKTU under the direction of the Korean Central Intelligence Agency (KCIA) in 1963, Park imposed a strict ban on unions' political activities. The state controls over the formation, activities and dissolution of unions were also established by allowing only one union at an enterprise and by requiring all unions to affiliate with the FKTU.

The hegemonic role of the state, however, did not mean capital and labour were equal subordinates of the state. The policy of rapid industrialization dependent on penetration of foreign markets naturally favoured capital in its confrontation with labour.[6] Moreover, the state, rather than employers, has taken the leading role in labour control to the extent that they have developed a habit of delegating intra-firm labour relations to the government.

As rapid economic growth brought about a rapid accumulation and concentration of capital as well as a rapid growth of industrial wage labour, state power was confronted with the growing power of big business and the increasing capacity of the working class to defend its interests. Given the asymmetry of the power relations between capital and labour and of their relationship to the state, the outcome of this power dynamics was highly asymmetric, too. The relative autonomy of the state *vis-à-vis* big business has been increasingly compromised. But the fate of labour was less sanguine, as the state countered the growing resistance of labour with intensifying repression.

Amidst growing social unrest and labour protests the Park government banned all forms of collective action in 1971. It also developed an extensive KCIA-directed labour-control programme, ranging from intervention in the election of the FKTU officials to behind-the-scenes cooperation between management and the police. A brief period of reinvigorating the state-controlled FKTU to mobilize union support for industrial restructuring in the mid-1970s was followed by harsh repression in the late-1970s amidst growing labour protest and political unrest. Under the Chun government, labour unions were decimated as state repression intensified through both legal restrictions and the expanded labour-control programme coordinated by the National Security Commission (reorganized KCIA).

Labour-Market Institutions and Wage Formation

Due to the state repression of labour the labour unions remained weak during the export-led growth. The weakness of organized labour has several dimensions. First is a complete political exclusion of labour. Not only have the unions' political activities been prohibited, but no legitimate pro-labour or left-wing political parties have been allowed to exist. Organized labour, therefore, was not able to participate in the economic decision-making process: '[Labour unions] are so weak that not only do they not provide much opinion input, but their potential reaction is seldom considered as a constraint' (Jones and SaKong, 1980, p. 66).

Second, the labour unions are organized at the enterprise level and, therefore, rather fragmented. The FKTU, the single national union centre, and its constituent national industrial unions are little more than paper organizations and have functioned mainly to moderate union demands, implement government policy, and discipline recalcitrant locals (Deyo, 1987). Third, under the threat of repression by the state and the employers, most of the unions were company-dominated, unwilling or unable to truly represent workers' interests. Finally, the rate of unionization itself has been modest. Even at its peak, which obtained in 1977 as a result of strong union growth after the state began to promote corporate paternalism in response to the challenges posed by the first oil shock and the 'big push', only 24.3 per cent of the eligible workers were represented by labour unions (see Table 4.13 in Section V).

Complementing the weakness of organized labour was the weakness of the social welfare measures. In terms of the share of social expenditure in central government expenditure, Korea ranks among the lowest in the world (Table 4.6). There was no minimum-wage regulation until 1988, no unemployment insurance, no universal superannuation. Therefore, workers' welfare is highly dependent upon their employers. The favourable impact of this arrangement on worker discipline and corporate paternalism is obvious.[7]

Table 4.6   Percentage of social expenditure in central government expenditure

Year	LIE	LMIE	UMIE	IME	Korea
1972	10.3	17.9	30.8	46.6	7.0
1985	10.9	12.7	23.6	46.9	8.1

Notes: Social expenditure = expenditure on health, housing, social security and welfare; LE = low-income economies excluding China and India; LMIE = lower middle-income economies; UMIE = upper middle-income economies; IME = industrial market economies. Figures are weighted averages.

Source: World Bank (1987).

The weakness of organized labour and the social welfare system led to a rather unregulated wage formation. Although the annual collective bargaining during the Spring Wage Offensive spread rapidly, it was done in a very fragmented fashion, almost all at the enterprise level.[8] It is generally agreed that the unions had only a small, if any, impact on wage determination; by one estimate, the wage differential between the unionized and non-unionized workers in the textile and chemical industries was about 7 per cent in 1980 (Park and Park, 1984).

A chief consequence of the unregulated wage formation is the extreme flexibility of real wages (You, 1990). This, however, does not mean that some mythical competitive equilibrium wage rate obtained in the labour market. The abundance of surplus labour at least until the early 1970s and the pervasiveness of labour-market segmentation make the concept of equilibrium wage extremely fuzzy and unenlightening.[9] In fact, polarization between different segments of labour was another main consequence of unregulated wage formation.

It is important to note that competitive forces operate within the institutional and political context. First, wages are more flexible due to a high proportion of bonuses and overtime payment in the total compensation (about 30 per cent). When the total labour compensation is decomposed into bonuses, overtime pay and the base wage, the elasticities with respect to economic conditions are ranked in the same order (Ito and Kang, 1989).

Second, the lack of wage indexation led to severe downward adjustments of real wages during stagflationary periods caused by sharp increases in import prices or other supply-side shocks. Last, but not least, state repression was intensified during recessions, especially around 1971 and 1980, in part to restore growth by improving international competitiveness. As a result, real wage adjustments to recessions became more pronounced.

Intra-firm Control of Labour: Authoritarian Paternalism

Intra-firm control of the workforce is characterized by the managerial culture of authoritarian paternalism – authoritarian oppression for labour discipline and paternalistic cooptation for worker motivation – and the managerial practice of personalized hierarchical control.

Employers' authoritarian domination over workers is reflected in the arbitrary use of management authority, extreme abuse and social regimentation of workers, and their attempts, often in coordination with the police and the KCIA, to suppress independent unions at almost any cost.[10] Flexibility of real wages in the labour market was thus complemented by 'flexible exploitation' of labour power on the shop floor. Indications of flexible exploitation are found in the extremely long working hours and the high industrial accident rates – an indirect measure of work intensity and safety conditions. Table 4.7 shows that Korean workers work longer under more dangerous conditions than the workers in other developing countries as well as those of the advanced countries.

Table 4.7   International comparison of work week and accident rate, 1985

	Korea	Singapore	Hong Kong	Argentina	Mexico	US	Japan
WW	53.8	47.0	44.8	41.3	46.4	40.5	46.2
FIR	1.8	0.19	0.57	0.8	0.8	0.11	0.05

Notes:
WW = working hours per week in manufacturing. FIR = number of fatal injuries per 10,000 persons employed (10,000 workers exposed to risk, for Mexico); compensated accidents for Korea and Japan, reported accidents for the rest. Mexico for 1984.

Source: ILO Yearbook, 1987.

Even with the renowned discipline of Korean workers, however, authoritarian oppression alone has obvious limits in motivating workers and soliciting their involvement in the production process. Workers' resentment was expressed in high turnover rates as well as growing militancy. Employers sought to enhance worker loyalty by paternalistic arrangements, especially since the mid-1970s as the labour market began to tighten and technology upgrading became imperative in the aftermath of the first oil shock.[11] In addition to such gimmicks as company songs and company picnics, various company-sponsored welfare schemes such as provision of dormitories, transportation, mess halls and scholarships for the children of employees were developed. Tapping the well known educational zeal, many companies established secondary schools on the company premises to attract young workers from poor villages and reduce worker turnover (Amsden, 1989).

Leading the cultivation of corporate paternalism was, once again, the state. After the oil shock, the state launched a campaign known as the Factory Saemaul Movement (FSM) which had two components: to promote the idea of the enterprise family and capital–labour cooperation through the Labour Management Council and to create work team organizations such as quality control (QC) circles aimed at cost reduction, quality improvement and productivity increases. With its firm grip on the FKTU, the state was able to enlist the labour unions as instruments of FSM and, more generally, as partners of corporate paternalism with their own welfare schemes (Choi, 1983).

One aspect of corporate paternalism is that the wage structure reflects subsistence needs of workers more than productivity. Ono's analysis of the wage structure in Korea and Japan shows that the 'age' variable, which is presumably tied to 'life-security needs' (subsistence) of workers, performs better than the length of experience, internal and external to the current employer, in both countries (cited in Ito and Kang, 1989). The widespread seniority wage system and the practice of paying family allowances supports this finding. Korean firms usually determine starting wages according to who the person is (education and sex) rather than what task the person performs. Then an 'annual base-up' is added to the starting base wage as the length of service increases (Park, 1988).

Table 4.8   System of remuneration for production workers, 1979 (in percentages)

Main pay criterion	Large scale firm	Small and medium firm	Total
Seniority	53.9	46.1	50.8
Task	19.2	23.1	20.8
Performance	26.9	30.7	28.5

Source: Korea Employers' Association.

Table 4.8 shows that more than half of the large-scale firms use the seniority wage system, while less than half of the small-scale firms do so. Also, J.W. Lee (1983) finds that male workers get a much higher return for continued service to a firm than for relevant experience outside the firm, while the pattern is reversed for female workers. These facts suggest different degrees of corporate paternalism in various segments of the labour market. The following case studies convey the extent to which the mixture of paternalism and authoritarian oppression varies according to the segmentation between what Lipietz (1986) calls 'bloody Taylorism' and 'peripheral Fordism' based on sexual division of labour:[12]

1. A *male worker in heavy industry.* Kim Dae-dong, a high-school graduate, got his first job as a welder in a shipyard, Hyundai Heavy Industries Company, in 1973 and spent a year in training – six months of theory and basic exercises followed by six months on-the-job training. Kim's basic wage rose from the training wage of 4000 won per month to 120,000 won in 1977. In addition, he received a pre-fixed bonus and a variable production bonus, overtime pay (about 30 hrs/month), and an additional sum of money for his unbroken attendance record. All told, Kim's monthly wages were around 180,000 won, which looked good by the standards he had been accustomed to. His relationship with Hyundai went beyond a labour-for-wages deal. He lived in a company-owned apartment for 4000 won per month. The shipyard provided a free lunch, and a free dinner when overtime was worked. The company even paid for his marriage ceremony, which usually places a great financial burden on families in Korea. He was a non-unionized worker.

2. A *female worker in light manufacturing.* Lee Mi-hyun was seventeen years old when she came to Seoul to work in a wig factory. She lived in the company dormitory, where she would take her work after the official overtime work is over at 10 p.m. and work until after midnight in order to do as much work as possible, because she was paid on a piece-rate basis. Lee worked 16–18 hours a day, and she was allowed to take only two days off a month. She was very tired and she would skip lunch sometimes to take a nap. This enormous amount of work earned her 7400 won ($19) per month in 1974. She was once beaten by her supervisor so severely that her eardrum was broken.

Obviously, authoritarian oppression of workers is conditional on the weakness or absence of independent unions. But the managerial culture of authoritarian paternalism has deep roots in the patriarchal ideology strongly engraved in the traditional culture, so it is likely to be more enduring than the outright repression of labour. In particular, the gender-based segmentation of labour and the direct use of patriarchal authority in enforcing factory discipline may continue for a long time. In addition, even as the large firms have developed the mechanisms for 'bureaucratic control' (Edwards, 1979), labour management under authoritarian paternalism relies more on personal relationships or the 'politics of face' (Deyo, 1989) than on impersonal rules. For example, personal relationships are the most important employment channel: among the new entrants, 69 per cent in 1978 and 57 per cent in 1983 were employed through personal relationships (MOL, *Labor Statistics Yearbook*). Under the personalized hierarchical controls individual delinquencies and rebellions are more easily isolated.

System of Production and Taylorism

Built on imported Western technology, most modern industries in Korea have developed systems of production which closely resemble the Western counterparts. Technology transfers often lead to subsequent importation of 'advanced' (Taylorist) scientific management techniques and production control methods (Cha, 1985). Since the late 1960s, Korean firms have begun to introduce scientific management methods such as time and motion study, and industrial engineering (H. Kim, 1988). Also, the development of mass-production systems entailed fragmentation of work into simple and repetitive jobs and work intensification through removing slack in the work process. However, Taylorization of the labour process – separation of execution from conception – has been limited by the extent of managers' mastery over production processes and conditioned by the peculiarities of the Korean capital–labour relations.[13]

The massive challenge of learning to make whole new products and to develop whole new industries in a short time span led Korean managers to adopt a less Tayloristic approach towards labour-process management. In an enlightening study of technology learning in Korea, Amsden (1989) finds: 'managers could never hope to manage in a tight, "Taylorist", top-down fashion, at least not initially, *because no one at the top knew enough about the process to do so*' (p. 209; emphasis original). Taylorization, of course, has always been 'more of a capitalist project than an achievement' (Marglin, 1990a, p. 14). But Korean bosses, given the grave inadequacy of their knowledge, attempted to enlist production workers as partners of learning and chose a management method different from what a drive towards Taylorization would have entailed: Amsden finds that the number of layers of management has been kept quite small and engineers keep in close contact with the ranks.[14] A manager in the production engineering department of Hyundai Motor Co. explains:

> The engineering center is responsible for design. HMC gets its platform designs from Italian designers and designs the remainder of its cars. ... People from production departments and people from the engineering center meet everyday. They always have discussions. Designers come to the site because, Engineering Center has no experience, they are not experts. Even if designers are right, they have to meet the workers. When a new type of car (the Excel) got started, the engineering center worked especially close with production. This is easily done since they are stationed in the same plant. (Quoted in Amsden, 1989, pp. 178–9)

A substantial part of the workforce is formally involved in quality and process improvement through the QC movement. The QC movement began to spread widely from the mid-1970s, when the state began, through FSM, to promote and coordinate QC activities and, by the early 1980s, more than a third of all manufacturing workers were organized in QC circles (Kim, 1988). More often than not, QC circles were simply paper organizations with little worker involvement, especially in the sweatshops in labour-intensive industries. However, there are many cases that show substantial effects, especially among technologically dynamic firms in capital-intensive industries. For example, a large-scale firm in the heavy manufacturing sector estimates the savings resulting from the QC activities to be 5.5 billion won in 1983 (H. Kim, 1988). POSCO, the largest steel mill in the world, reported cost savings of 3.4 billion won from the 'self-management team' activities and 230 million won from individual suggestions in 1980 (Koo, 1982).

In addition to the challenge of rapid learning, several other features of Korean industrialization seem to have contributed to the emergence of a non-Tayloristic approach among Korean managers. First, compared with other NICs, Korea relied least on foreign direct investment and licensing, and most on turnkey plants and imports of capital equipment (L. Kim, 1987). In particular, the contribution of foreign direct investment to GNP growth during 1972–80 is estimated to be only 1.3 per cent. Thus, the mode of technology imports was such that technology-importing firms relied heavily on learning at the local level, which usually involves a good deal of so-called blue-collar R&D activities (Ranis, 1984). For example, in a comparative study of two otherwise similar electronics firms, Cha (1985) shows that a Korean company which had a long way to go to master the technology took QC activities and workers' suggestions very seriously, while a subsidiary of a Japanese firm showed no interest in them, because it was much more Taylorized, with all the instructions coming from the parent company. Second, the absence of craft union traditions meant control of production processes was not a serious point of contention between capital and labour. Minimizing worker discretion through Taylorization, therefore, was not a priority for Korean managers. Last, but not least important, is the strong Japanese influence in shaping management mentality and practices both through the lingering colonial legacy and a heavy dependence on Japanese technology.[15]

IV AUTHORITARIAN CAPITAL–LABOUR RELATIONS AND EXPORT-LED INDUSTRIALIZATION

This section examines the interconnections between the authoritarian capital–labour relations and the macroeconomic structure of export-led industrialization (ELI). It is argued that there was a mutual consistency, which helped sustain economic growth. The sustained growth, in turn, helped maintain the authoritarian political regime. In addition, the Korean model of capital–labour relations is compared with the Fordist model and the Japanese model.

The Macroeconomic Structure of ELI

As mentioned earlier, the rapid industrialization in Korea since the early 1960s has been fuelled by the growth of exports of manufactures. Export demand was critical to the growth of the manufacturing sector, since either the working-class consumption demand or the agricultural sector demand for manufactured goods was insufficient to provide a market for increasing industrial output in the early stages of industrialization. However, domestic demand became increasingly important and the gap between manufacturing export growth and manufacturing output growth narrowed (Table 4.1 in Section II). Rising incomes of households brought about changes in the consumption pattern, and the share of manufactures in household consumption expenditure increased; for instance, the share of the expenditure on household equipment rose from 2.7 per cent in 1970 to 5.6 per cent in 1979.

The changing pattern of demand growth is related to developments in income distribution. The unregulated wage formation under the authoritarian capital–labour relations did not entail a long-term wage squeeze. On the contrary, as shown in the last two columns of Table 4.9, the wage share of income – measured by the ratio of the nominal wage to the nominal value-added per worker or the ratio of the average real wage to the value-added productivity – in manufacturing increased considerably during the latter half of the 1970s, reflecting a tightening of the labour market. Although the recession and repression in the first half of the 1980s brought down the wage share from the late 1970s level, it was still much higher than the 1960s to the early 1970s level.

Academics from both the right and the left have sought a connection between labour repression as a means to ensure low labour costs and export-led growth (Kreye, 1980; Fields, 1984; Deyo, 1987). However, ELI in Korea was not based simply on continued exploitation of low-wage labour; in fact, the almost sevenfold increase in real wages during 1963–88, albeit from a very low base, is unprecedented in human history. That Korea did not rely on labour cost advantages alone to achieve competitiveness is clearly seen from the fact that hourly compensation costs for production workers in manufacturing rose from 6 per cent of the US level in 1975 to 18 per cent in 1988 (US Bureau of Labor Statistics, 1990).

Table 4.9   Index of productivity and wages in manufacturing, 1963–88

Year	Q/L	W	CP	MP	RW	WL/MPQ	RWL/Q
1963	34.0	2.2	8.9	10.3	24.5	62.9	72.1
1965	33.5	3.1	12.5	16.7	25.1	56.0	74.9
1968	38.8	5.7	17.0	19.3	33.7	76.1	87.0
1970	54.4	9.7	22.2	21.4	43.9	83.7	80.8
1973	69.0	15.2	29.0	27.0	52.5	81.9	76.1
1975	71.4	26.2	45.2	48.6	57.9	75.7	81.1
1977	80.7	47.2	57.4	55.8	82.2	105.1	102.0
1979	96.5	81.5	77.7	70.0	104.9	120.6	108.8
1980	100.0	100.0	100.0	100.0	100.0	100.0	100.0
1982	109.1	137.8	132.3	124.9	104.1	101.2	97.1
1984	127.4	167.2	137.6	125.3	121.5	104.8	95.4
1986	136.0	200.7	145.0	123.0	139.1	120.1	102.4
1987	137.0	224.1	149.4	124.0	150.6	131.9	109.9
1988	146.6	269.6	159.9	124.9	168.7	147.3	115.0

Compound annual rate of increase:

1963–73	7.1	21.3	12.5	10.1	7.9	2.7	0.5
1974–79	5.7	32.3	17.9	17.2	12.2	6.7	6.1
1980–86	5.0	13.7	9.3	8.4	4.1	–0.1	–0.9
1987–88	3.8	15.9	5.0	0.8	10.1	10.7	6.0
1963–88	6.0	21.2	12.2	10.5	8.0	3.5	1.9

Notes: Q = manufacturing GDP in 1980 constant prices (from National Income Accounts); L = manufacturing employment; W = nominal manufacturing wage index; CP = consumer price index; MP = manufacturing wholesale price index; RW = W/CP.

Sources: BOK; EPB.

In this context it is important to note that ELI in Korea did *not* entail increasing specialization in labour-intensive industries based on cheap labour. Rather, capital-intensive industries grew as fast as labour-intensive industries, as shown in Table 4.10, as import substitution was pursued with similar vigour as export promotion (Luedde-Neurath, 1986). Note that the capital-intensive industries coincide with the import-substitution industries.[16] What is interesting is that many import-substitution industries quickly moved on to export, as shown by the rising export share of capital-intensive industries. In Korea's dualistic growth of labour- and capital-intensive industries, import substitution and the domestic market provided a springboard in many industries. Therefore, an increasing wage share over the long term was compatible with the Korean model of ELI.

Table 4.10   Indices of manufacturing industries

	Import ratio 1966	Import ratio 1978	Export ratio 1966	Export ratio 1978	K/L[a] (average)	INT[a] (average)	GR[b] 1960–77
Capital-intensive intermediate goods	18.7	26.7	6.9	10.2	8.9	90.3	26.9
Capital-intensive final goods	14.6	12.3	3.4	12.9	4.9	17.8	15.5
Labour-intensive intermediate goods	13.6	12.9	8.8	25.4	2.1	77.1	22.4
Labour-intensive final goods	14.8	22.8	12.9	32.8	1.6	36.0	13.8

Notes:
[a] Capital–labour ratio (K/L) and intermediate output ratio (INT) are period averages during 1966–78.
[b] Average annual growth rate during 1960–77.

Source: Ohno and Imaoka (1987) pp. 312–13.

There is an important sense in which this dualistic growth was essentially export-led; the resources for the growth of capital-intensive/ import-substitution industries came in part from the surplus created by labour-intensive/export industries. In a demand-constrained economy, an expansion of exports, through the multiplier effect, increases national savings and thereby increases resources for investment. The importance of this mechanism increases when the import requirement of investment is high. The flow of surplus from the labour-intensive/export sector to capital-intensive/import-substitution sector was accomplished through the segmentation of both the labour market and the capital market. In the former the surplus was enlarged by using cheap labour, while this surplus was in part channelled to the latter which enjoyed disproportionate access to the preferential policy loans. That is, the surplus created by cheap labour in the labour-intensive sector provided cheap capital for the capital-intensive sector.[17]

The largely gender-based segmentation of labour and the polarization of wages, therefore, provides a key linkage between the authoritarian capital–labour relations and the macroeconomic structure of ELI in Korea. The higher wages and the higher degree of corporate paternalism and worker involvement in the capital-intensive/import-substitution industries also stimulated learning and productivity growth in those industries, which was important to the success of the dualistic growth (see Amsden, 1989).

Finally, another key linkage between the authoritarian capital–labour relations and the macroeconomic structure of ELI is the flexibility of real wages. Given the high dependence of the manufacturing sector on export demand, the flexibility of real wages smoothed the short-run macroeconomic adjustments.[18]

Moreover, the lack of real wage resistance to inflation helped sustain high rates of investment, a large part of which was financed by such inflationary measures as foreign borrowing and domestic credit expansion.

A Comparison with the Fordist Model

It is clear from the above that the capital–labour relations which prevailed during the ELI in Korea diverge from the Fordist model in significant ways. The Fordist model was based on a social compromise between capital and labour in which labour would get a fair share of productivity gains in exchange for submitting to capitalist control. But the Korean model was based on labour repression; an implicit social compact was made between the military-dominated state and the citizenry, in which the latter would be rewarded with rising income (but not income security) in exchange for tolerating curtailment of political and labour rights.

As a result, institutions that supported the Fordist compromise, such as labour unions, collective bargaining, provision for cost-of-living adjustments, minimum wage regulation and social welfare system, were either very weak or absent in the Korean model. Therefore, wage formation was unregulated, and a worker's welfare was more closely tied to the firm in which he or she was employed. The unregulated wage formation led to extreme flexibility of real wages in Korea, in contrast to the real-wage rigidity in the Fordist model. It also led to polarization of wage formation under severe labour-market segmentation.

There are differences in the system of production, too. The efficiency of the Fordist production system was compromised by Tayloristic work organization and rigid job rules. But in Korea the production management engaged workers in the industrial learning efforts and maintained close contacts between engineers and production workers. There was neither resistance to technical changes nor union-set job rules so that flexibility in labour usage was assured.

The differences in the capital–labour relations of the Fordist model and the Korean model are also reflected in the difference in the macroeconomic structure of the two models. Put simply, in the Fordist model growth of domestic consumption demand through roughly proportionate increases in purchasing power of all residents was the central force behind the rapid and stable growth. In Korea, flexibility and polarization in wage formation contributed to the success of export growth, which played a dynamic role in the rapid industrialization, and the dualistic growth of labour- and capital-intensive industries.

A Comparison with the Japanese Model

A comparison with the Japanese model illuminates the limits of the authoritarian paternalism that characterized Korean capital–labour relations. Given the historical entanglements between Korea and Japan, it is hardly surprising to find similarities in the capital–labour relations of Korea and Japan (Cummings, 1984). Corporate paternalism based on the enterprise union system and the flexible and involved work norms are the key elements of the Japanese model. Both elements were present in the Korean model. But they were much too limited because of employers' authoritarianism in enforcing labour discipline – a page from the book of the prewar Japan. Employers' authoritarian oppression became the deepest source of worker discontent and agitation and definitely weakened the effectiveness of paternalism as a managerial ideology. The ideology of 'enterprise-as-family' became hollow when workers found they were treated more like family servants than sons and daughters.

Table 4.11 Employment adjustment during recession by size of firm (in per cent)

| | Size (no. of employees) | | | |
	5–99	100–299	300 or more	total
1980	4.9	–5.9	–9.1	–3.8
1981	0.1	–1.9	–5.5	–2.5

Source: MOL, cited in Park (1986), p. 34.

In Japan employers buy the hearts and minds of the workers by job security, consensus building in decision making, and promotion opportunities to managerial positions (worker-manager).[19] In Korea employers retain a maximum amount of management prerogatives: firing is hardly contested, information on company matters hardly shared with workers, and worker-manager unheard of.[20] The fact that the paternalistic management practices do not include job security can be seen from Table 4.11. During the recession in the early 1980s, large-scale enterprises surpassed small- and medium-scale enterprises in laying off their workers – a far cry from the Japanese system of lifetime employment. Korean workers, on their part, responded with relatively high job mobility. The result was a high turnover rate – much higher than Japan and slightly higher than the US. During the 1970s the average separation rate was 5 per cent in Korea, while it was 1.5 per cent in Japan and a little over 4 per cent in the US (Ito and Kang, 1989).

Just as paternalism was limited by authoritarianism, so too was worker involvement in the production process. While workers were urged to place their knowledge of the production process in the service of rationalization, they were excluded from the decision-making processes. Thus, for instance, in a government-sponsored dialogue with the Korea Employers' Association (KEA), the FKTU complained about the lack of opportunities for union leaders at the enterprise level to participate in production planning and quality control (Choi, 1983). Employers would not let their prerogatives be compromised by involving workers in the decision-making process even if that could enhance workers' cooperation in the production process. The consequent limitation in worker involvement could be partly responsible for the rise in the capital–output ratio since the mid-1970s in Korea, while it fell in Japan (Table 4.12). Since the capital intensity increased much faster in Japan, Korean capitalists must have made poorer use of labour.

Table 4.12   Capital–output ratio and capital–labour ratio in manufacturing: Korea and Japan, 1964–85

| | Korea | | Japan | |
Year	K/Q	K/L	K/Qª	K/L
1964	2.18	4.96	2.24	2.27
1968	1.34	3.64	2.17	3.75
1970	1.31	4.68	2.08	4.77
1972	1.29	5.68	2.10	6.05
1974	1.21	5.67	1.76	7.27
1976	1.27	6.07	1.61	8.66
1978	1.45	7.74	1.47	9.67
1980	1.84	9.96	1.68	10.66
1982	1.98	11.41	1.45	11.76
1984	1.87	12.25	1.48	13.03
1985	2.04	12.99	1.57	13.89

Note: ª For the whole economy.

Source: Calculated from the data in Pyo (1988).

V   THE CRISIS AND THE BREAKDOWN OF THE AUTHORITARIAN CAPITAL–LABOUR RELATIONS

Apart from the problems of authoritarian paternalism, a number of economic problems confronted the Korean model of development. However, while economic problems such as foreign debt and inflation have not been fundamental obstacles to growth, the instability in the class relations that relied heavily on the coercive power of the state reflects a fundamental contradiction of the Korean model. The very success of the model contained the seeds of its own destruction; it would not be long before the rapidly growing working class would challenge the

oppressive system of control and the institutions that determined their economic
fortune at the discretion of employers and the vagaries of market forces.

Labour Protests in the 1970s

The first signs of workers' protest against the authoritarian labour regime
appeared in the early 1970s. In 1970, a garment worker, Chun Tai-il, set himself
alight to protest against the horrible working conditions which young female
workers were subjected to, after his efforts to form a labour union were frustrated.
Apart from making self-immolation a staple of labour and student protests in
the coming years, this incident was in many ways indicative of what was to follow
in the 1970s.

In the 1970s the independent (i.e., not controlled by the FKTU) labour union
movement and labour protests centred on the labour-intensive sector, especially
among the young female workers who put in long hours under authoritarian
oppression only to get paid less than half the male workers' wage.[21] The development in the rate of unionization by sex confirms that the female workers
spearheaded unionization in the 1970s (Table 4.13). This rather unusual
phenomenon can be explained by the lack of a craft union tradition and the fact
that female workers bore the brunt of the authoritarian oppression under the
scheme of dualistic growth.

Table 4.13   Union membership (in thousands) and unionization rate

	1963	1970	1973	1977	1980	1985	1988[a]
Unionization rate[b]							
Total	20.2	20.0	20.4	24.3	20.1	15.7	19.4
Male	20.0	20.1	20.4	22.7	18.5	15.9	20.4
Female	17.3	19.7	20.5	28.5	23.6	15.2	16.3
Union membership	224	473	548	955	948	1,004	1,510

Notes:
[a] As of 30 June 1988.
[b] Union membership as a percentage of regular employees in non-farm sector.

Sources: Korea Labour Institute (KLI); EPB; MOL.

Chun's ultimate sacrifice for his young female fellow workers was also
indicative of the paternalistic element within the labour movement itself. The
independent labour movement in the 1970s was nurtured by the support and
resources of church and student activists, who were aroused by the great
injustices done to the young workers. The rapid increase in union membership

and unionization rate during the latter half of the 1970s reflected this middle-class paternalism as well as the state policy of mobilizing labour unions for FSM.

The Economic Crisis and Labour Protests in the 1980s

By the late 1970s there were a significant number of independent local unions exerting pressure on the FKTU and challenging the authoritarian labour regime under Park. Along with the rejection of the implicit social compact by a growing portion of the urban middle class whose chief complaint was the rising inflation rates, the independent labour movement contributed to the political crisis which led to Park's assassination in 1979. The subsequent eruption of popular demands for political democratization and economic equity was once again crushed by the military led by General Chun in May 1980.

The new government faced a severe economic crisis. After years of boom the economy was slowing down in 1979, as inflation was accelerating and export performance deteriorating. Then came the second oil shock and the Volker deflation. Inflation rose to 28 per cent and GNP declined by more than 2 per cent in 1980. Soaring oil import bills and interest payments brought about a rapid accumulation of foreign debt, raising the debt/GNP ratio from 28.5 per cent in 1978 to 53.5 per cent in 1982. Although growth resumed in 1982, the performance of the economy during the period 1979–85 was flat by Korean standards (see Table 4.1 in Section II).

A key element in the Chun government's responses to the economic crisis was a strong wage restraint designed to bring down inflation and restore competitiveness. Given the growth of the labour unions in the 1970s, brutal repression was necessary to accomplish this and put the burden of adjustment on the part of the workers. Labour leaders were sent to 'purification' camps, independent unions were crushed, national industrial unions were divested of any meaningful role, and the involvement of church groups and other activists was outlawed in 1980 (Deyo, 1989). As a result, the rate of unionization declined sharply in 1980, from 23.6 per cent in 1979 to 20.1 per cent, and continued to slide to 14.3 per cent in June 1987 when the process of 'democratization' began (Table 4.13). Unionization became so tough that the total union membership never regained the 1979 level during this period. The same holds for the wage share of income (see Table 4.9 in Section IV).

Despite these setbacks under Chun's repressive campaign, the labour movement did not remain dormant. In fact, the workers began to develop class consciousness and the labour movement underwent important qualitative changes, as they struggled against the naked oppression by the state and capital. The strike at the Daewoo Motor Company (DMC) in 1985 illustrates aspects of those changes. First, it signified that the centre stage of labour protests was moving away from the labour-intensive sector with a predominantly female labour force towards the capital- and skill-intensive sector with mostly male workers. DMC, jointly owned by the General Motors and the Daewoo *chaebol*, is one of the leading automobile makers in Korea, and its production workers are all male with relatively high levels of education. Second, the striking workers at DMC demanded a direct election of the union officials, thus raising the issue of union democracy which was soon to become very important. Third, students-turned-workers played an active role in leading the DMC strike, reflecting the rise of the radical left and the decline of middle-class paternalism. Finally, another incident in 1985 in which 2500 workers from ten different plants waged sympathy strikes to protest the arrests of union leaders of Daewoo Apparel Textile Co. demonstrated the militancy and organizational strength of the independent labour movement.

Labour repression in the Chun era, therefore, succeeded in stopping the quantitative growth of the labour unions but not these qualitative developments. These developments and the large increase in strike activity in 1985–86 from the trend level of about 100 per year (except 1980–81 when the state's labour-control system was in disarray after Park's assassination) marked the beginning of the end of authoritarian capital–labour relations. If disputes of a clearly defensive nature – those caused by wage non-payment or shop closure – are excluded, the increase since 1985 is even more pronounced than the increase in 1980 when more than half of the disputes were caused by wage non-payment amidst a severe recession (Table 4.14). From 1985 the authoritarian capital–labour relations were in crisis and the final rupture was soon to come.

Table 4.14   Number of labour disputes, 1975–89

Year	75	76	77	78	79	80	81	82	83	84	85	86	87	88	89
Total no.	133	110	96	102	105	407	186	88	98	113	265	276	3,749	1,833	1,616
Total – defensive disputes	94	65	62	70	64	109	106	58	54	72	192	217	3,693	1,790	n.a.

Source: MOL.

The Breakdown of Authoritarian Capital–Labour Relations

With the government concession to the opposition demand for a direct presidential election on 29 June 1987, the 'era of democratization' began.[22] As if they had been waiting for the right moment, strikes broke out immediately and on an unprecedented scale; more than three thousand disputes erupted during July and August alone, involving more than a million workers all over the country. Although a substantial increase in labour unrest was expected to follow the political changes as in 1980, the explosiveness and the scale of the strike wave was beyond anyone's imagination. The working class made it clear that they were a major force to be reckoned with rather than the subservient to be bossed around or the unfortunate to be pitied.

The massive and simultaneous occurrence of the disputes and the organizational expansion of labour unions plunged the old system of authoritarian capital–labour relations into an open crisis.[23] Tables 4.14 and 4.15 show the dramatic increase of capital–labour confrontations since 1987, which signals the end of the industrial peace imposed by repression and state controls. Since one of the key objectives of the disputes was gaining recognition for new independent unions (Park, 1988), the wave of confrontations led to a tremendous growth of new unions; the number of enterprise unions nearly doubled from 2725 in June 1987 to 5062 in June 1988, and the union membership increased from about one million to about one and a half million during the same period and reached almost two million in 1989. Moreover, various solidarity organizations outside the legal framework (i.e. the FKTU) sprang up to strengthen the new independent unions, culminating in the founding of a new independent national union centre, *Chun-no-hyup* or the Korean Alliance of Genuine Trade Unions (KAGTU), in January 1990.

Table 4.15   International comparison of stoppage incidence

Low:	Japan	Germany	Hong Kong	Thailand	Malaysia	Korea-I
	4.8	1.4	1.1	9.7	5.5	4.5

High:	US	UK	Canada	Philippines	Chile	Mexico	Korea-II
	78.4	186.0	463.4	254.0	76.5	89.4	473.4

Notes: Stoppage incidence = number of work days lost due to labour disputes per year per 1000 non-agricultural employees. Reported figures are the average annual figures during 1985–87 except Korea-I and Chile (1984–86) and Korea-II (1987–88).

Source: You (1990).

Characteristics of the New Independent Unionism

The rise of the independent union movement and the consequent breakdown of the authoritarian capital–labour relations in the post-'democratization' era are marked by important changes in the nature of the labour union movement. First is the shift in the organizational base and lead role of the union movement from labour-intensive to capital-intensive heavy industries, from female to male workers. The strike wave of the summer of 1987 was led by workers in large-scale heavy manufacturing plants in Korea's biggest industrial areas in sharp contrast with the 1970s.[24] It is also notable that the leading *chaebol* firms, which had been largely immune from labour disputes, came to be involved in some of the bitterest strikes. Table 4.16 reports the shift in sexual and industrial composition of the union membership since 1987. The increase in union membership among male workers is proportionately greater than among female workers (see also the change in the unionization rate by sex in Table 4.13). Among the major manufacturing sector unions, the Metal Workers' Union whose membership draws from the iron and steel, machinery, automobile and shipbuilding industry, etc. experienced a tremendous growth. In contrast, the Textile Workers' Union – the leading union in the 1970s – stagnated in this period. The sharp increase in the membership of the Financial Workers' Union and the United Workers' Union, which includes unions at hospitals, news media, universities and research institutions, reflects the rise of trade unionism among the white-collar workers in this period.

Table 4.16 Change in sexual/industrial composition of union membership

	Total	Female	Male	TWU	MWU	CWU	FWU	UWU	Other
1979	1,088	364	724	168	128	165	60	78	489
1986	1,036	311	725	115	136	154	98	60	473
1988.6	1,510	430	1,080	127	327	216[a]	156[b]	146	558
% increase during									
86–88	45.8	38.3	49.0	10.4	140.4	40.3	59.2	143.3	18.0

Notes: TWU = Textile Workers' Union, MWU = Metal WU, CWU = Chemical WU, FWU = Financial WU, UWU = United WU.
[a] Includes the membership of the Rubber WU which split from CWU in 1988.
[b] Includes the membership of the Insurance WU and the Office and Financial WU, both of which split from FWU in 1988.

Source: KLI.

The shift in the organizational base of the union movement reflects in part changes in the industrial structure. As shown in Table 4.17, since the mid-1970s the employment share of the light manufacturing industries has continuously declined. In the 1980s the growth of the machinery and equipment manufacturing sector (SIC code 380) which forms the basis of the Metal Workers' Union has been especially rapid, while the textiles and apparel industry (320) has declined significantly.

Table 4.17   Structure of manufacturing industry by employment

Industry	1963	1973	1977	1981	1985	1987
31–34, 39	60.7	60.6	55.4	51.7	47.0	43.9
(32)	(32.4)	(34.0)	(34.1)	(32.3)	(29.8)	(28.2)
35–38	39.3	39.4	44.6	48.3	53.0	56.1
(38)	(15.3)	(19.7)	(24.4)	(26.6)	(31.2)	(36.7)

Sources: EPB for 1963–81; MOL for 1985–87.

The growth of independent unionism among male workers in capital-intensive heavy industries signifies the workers' rejection of authoritarian paternalism. As leading beneficiaries of higher wages and various paternalistic perks, their revolts meant rejection of authoritarian controls that came as a part and parcel of paternalistic benefits. For them, militaristic management style was an even more fundamental reason for the uprising than wages. As one observer of the epic 109-day Hyundai shipyard strike in 1988 put it, 'Although they wanted higher wages, money wasn't their top grievance. Above all, they hate the way bosses order them around: They want their human dignity reaffirmed.'[25] Workers' rejection of authoritarian paternalism is reflected in their demands voiced during the disputes. The far-ranging demands included not only bread-and-butter issues. Among the 15,000 demands raised in 3311 disputes during the strike wave of 1987, demands for wages and other compensation accounted for 50.2 per cent; demands related to working conditions such as work hours, holidays and safety conditions 24.8 per cent; demands regarding union recognition and autonomy 8.1 per cent; demands regarding management and personnel policies 8.1 per cent (of which 2.9 per cent was demand for 'humane treatment'); and other demands 8.5 per cent.[26]

Since 1987 workers have begun to challenge hitherto unquestioned management prerogatives. More and more unions are calling for equal control over personnel management and profit distribution. For instance, workers at Young Chang Musical Instrument Co. fought successfully for a direct election of team leaders and foremen. In the 1987 strike, DMC workers demanded, among other things, the repeal of the unequal contract with GM. The seriousness of this challenge is reflected in the fact that the National Employers' Association, which was formed in 1989 to counter the independent union movement, took it as its main objective to defend management prerogatives. The independent union movement has also challenged the ban on unions' political activities – another cornerstone of authoritarian capital–labour relations – by openly engaging in anti-government struggles.

While workers' refusal to submit to employers' discretion and state controls has been made clear, it is not clear if paternalism *per se* is being rejected. Some paternalistic elements have been reinforced. No attempt has been made to change the old practice of union officials getting paid by company.[27] Paternalistic remuneration such as family allowances and scholarships for children are among the popular demands. The majority of workers seem to find the Western-style strictly contractual employer–employee relationship unattractive. One survey conducted immediately after the 'great labour struggle' finds that only 12 per cent of the surveyed workers preferred strictly contractual relationships, 38 per cent paternalism, 50 per cent mutual respect and cooperation/codetermination (K.B. Lee, 1987). The survey shows the aversion to contractual relationships is shared by both management and workers.[28] While workers reject authoritarian paternalism and ask for justice and human dignity, most of them do not think a strictly contractual relationship with management provides a solution.

VI   THE CAUSES AND THE CONSEQUENCES OF THE BREAKDOWN

Apart from the magnitude of the unrest, the rise in labour militancy since 1987 seems a repeat of the historical pattern of increasing labour militancy during periods of political crisis as happened during 1960–61, 1969–71 and 1978–81 (Deyo, 1989). It is, however, only the beginning of the story. Profound political changes underlie the recent crisis of the legitimacy of state power, and recent labour militancy reflects a substantial increase in working-class power.

Politics of Democratization

Underlying the 'democratization' since 1987 is the crisis of the implicit social compact between the military-dominated state and the citizenry. The image of the state as the promoter of economic development aloof from particularistic interests was increasingly marred by corruption scandals and a conspicuous rise in the power of *chaebols* in the 1980s under Chun's reign (Bello, 1990). Table 4.18 shows that the share of the top five *chaebols* in manufacturing shipment increased discontinuously in 1981, even as their share of employment decreased. Moreover, the *chaebol* groups acquired substantial shares of the commercial banks in 1984 after they were privatized as a part of financial liberalization policy. The seemingly limitless concentration of economic power in the hands of the *chaebols*, together with the intrusive expansion of privileges for the military, increasingly alienated the urban middle class that was getting less tolerant of the infringement of their rights.

Table 4.18   Chaebols' *shares in manufacturing, 1977–83*

| | In shipment | | | | In employment | | | |
	1977	1980	1981	1983	1977	1980	1981	1983
Business groups								
Top 5	15.7	16.9	21.5	22.3	9.1	9.1	8.9	8.5
Top 10	21.2	23.8	28.4	29.3	12.5	12.8	12.8	11.9
Top 20	29.3	31.4	35.3	36.0	17.4	17.9	17.0	15.3
Top 30	34.1	36.0	39.7	39.9	20.5	22.4	20.8	17.9

Source: K.U. Lee (1986) p. 239.

On the other hand, workers were subjected to extremely harsh repression under Chun's political and economic stabilization programme. As shown earlier, labour unions were crushed and labour's share of income fell from the late 1970s level, while the average work week increased from around 52 hours in the 1970s to around 54 hours in the first half of the 1980s. On top of these was a considerable increase in work intensity: the number of work days lost due to injuries increased from 2.9 million days in 1982 to 15.3 million days in 1985 (You, 1990). Farmers also suffered a sharp decline in their relative economic status. Above all, they were hurt by import liberalization pursued under Chun, which turned the terms of trade against farmers (see Table 4.19). Mounting debts led to numerous suicides of farmers in this period, while many more were killed from chemical poisoning.

Table 4.19   *Agricultural terms of trade, 1976–86*

	1976	1978	1980	1982	1984	1986
PR	35.2	53.5	72.4	99.2	100.7	97.8
PP	31.6	48.2	68.3	98.8	102.5	99.4
TOT	111.4	111.0	106.0	100.4	98.2	98.4

Notes: PR = index of prices received by farmers; PP = index of prices paid by farmers (1985 = 100); TOT = 100*PR/PP.

Source: BOK.

It was therefore only a matter of time – time needed for people to cope with the fears inflicted by the massacre in 1980 – that the Chun regime would face challenges from a wide variety of social groups: workers, farmers, small and medium industrialists, intellectuals and, especially, students who led the anti-government struggle with legendary courage and tenacity. The decades-old implicit social compact disintegrated and Chun's surrender became inevitable when the urban middle class actively supported anti-government demonstrations in June 1987. Thus came the beginning of the 'democratization' and a search for a new social order. It was the working class who made the most swift and powerful move – the massive strike wave of the summer of 1987 – for which political changes were only a necessary condition. The increased strength of the working class provided a sufficient condition.

Increase in the Strength of the Working Class

Despite authoritarian repression, the underlying strength of the working class – in terms of market power, structural capacity and cultural strength – increased tremendously during the export-led industrialization. The rapid industrialization brought about a rapid absorption of surplus labour and consequently a decline in unemployment and underemployment rates (Table 4.20). The resulting increase in the market power of the workers made possible not only high real-wage growth rates but a growing challenge to the authoritarian oppression of employers. The labour market has been especially tight since 1987, which was undoubtedly a factor in boosting militancy among workers. The rate of unemployment was 3.1 per cent in 1987, 2.5 per cent in 1988 and 2.6 per cent in 1989.

Table 4.20   Rates of unemployment and underemployment, 1963–86

	1963	1968	1973	1978	1983	1986
A: Unempl.	8.2	5.1	4.0	3.2	4.1	3.8
B: (Non-farm)	16.4	8.9	6.8	4.7	5.4	4.7
C: Underempl.	8.7	5.4	3.8	1.0	0.5	0.9
D: (Non-farm)	4.6	1.6	1.5	0.4	0.4	0.8
A + C: Sum	16.9	10.5	7.8	4.2	4.6	4.7
B + D: (Non-farm)	21.0	10.5	8.3	5.1	5.8	5.5

Note: Underemployment = employed less than 18 hours per week.

Sources: EPB; MOL.

Not only the market power but the structural capacity of the working class increased due to the structural changes towards heavy capital-intensive industries referred to earlier. Workers in these industries have a stronger commitment to their job as well as greater resources. Thus, they show a much higher degree of solidarity and militancy than the predominantly female labour-intensive sector workers with low skill, minimal advancement opportunities and little anticipation of long-term employment with their current employers. Therefore, workers in male-dominated heavy industries have been more successful in mounting strong opposition to and gaining concessions from their employers than the secondary-sector workers whose protests were poorly organized, mainly defensive in nature, and highly vulnerable to employer and police repression (see Deyo, 1989, pp. 77–81). It is also notable that many of the independent unions in the light manufacturing industries which were active in the 1970s depended heavily on the resources of church-linked liberal labour rights organizations, while the recent independent union movement led by male workers in heavy manufacturing is much less dependent on outside resources.

The increase in the structural capacity of the working class is due also to the development of working-class communities. In large concentrated industrial areas such as Seoul-Inchon, Masan-Changwon, Ulsan and Pusan the workers developed a strong sense of belonging to the working-class communities, which had been present only among the miners. In addition to the geographical concentration of industries, the increase in second-generation workers in recent years helped the development of working-class communities. In earlier days of industrialization most of the young workers had migrated from rural areas, and the continuous influx of these workers hindered development of working-class communities and their capacity to organize. But the second-generation workers with urban backgrounds are less influenced by traditional patriarchal values and better able to mobilize community resources in the urban context.

Finally, the cultural strength or 'class consciousness' of the working class increased over the years. This led workers to reject authoritarian paternalism, thereby shattering the basis of authoritarian capital–labour relations. Apart from the development of working-class communities and the dedicated work of students-turned-workers armed with leftist ideologies to raise consciousness among workers, two other factors have contributed to this development. First, the educational level of the workers rose considerably, as shown in Table 4.21. While schooling in Korea, where schools often enforce military-style discipline, helped create a productive and disciplined workforce, the increasing spread of high-school education also raised the expectations and the assertiveness of the workers.

Table 4.21   Educational composition among entrants in manufacturing (per cent)

	Elementary or lower	Junior high	Senior high	College or higher
1973	45.2	37.9	14.2	2.7
1986	9.2	40.0	45.1	5.7

Note: Each category includes drop-outs from a higher-level institution.

Source: EPB, *Korea Statistical Yearbook*, 1975 and 1987.

Another factor which contributed to increasing the confidence and the independence of the workers is skill accumulation, especially in the technologically dynamic capital-intensive sector. Rather than desperate resistance to technical changes rendering their skills obsolete, the recent revolt of workers seems a proud demand for the social recognition and respect for their contribution to economic growth through their learning efforts. Many workers in Korea go to evening classes in various educational institutions, studying to get skill certificates or to excel in their job. According to a labour administrator, young workers today have a 'sense of pride and high motivation for achievements' (Han-kuk Il-bo, 9 November 1988). A natural counterpart of this new sense of pride is a heightened sense of their rights.[29]

Workers are, in a sense, mounting a challenge to the social disregard for manual work and technical skills rooted in the traditional Korean culture, which is often contrasted to the Japanese culture which puts a high value on skilled trades. This cultural tradition may well be responsible for the much bigger wage differential between high school graduates and college graduates and that between production workers and non-manual workers than in other countries: for instance, the ratio of the average wage of college graduates to that of high school graduates was 2.3 in Korea in 1980 compared with about 1.2 in Japan in 1978 (J.W. Lee, 1983).[30] Once a debilitating influence to the relatively passive workers in the past, this cultural tradition is now adding fuel to labour disputes as production workers are reacting to discrimination between office workers and them.

Korea in the Light of the OECD Experience

Just as the workings of the Korean model of capital–labour relations differed from the Fordist model, the unravelling and subsequent changes of the model exhibit differences from those of the Fordist model. While the limits to Fordism unfolded in various economic difficulties (Boyer, Chapter 2, this volume), the authoritarian capital–labour relations in Korea unravelled due to political difficulties before any economic limits of the model asserted itself. However, the profit squeeze thesis which seeks the origin of the economic difficulties in the OECD countries in the rise in labour militancy due to full employment points to a common element in the unravelling of both models.

It is true that the political difficulties in Korea are rooted in the economic changes which undermined the state power *vis-à-vis* social classes, but the nature of the difficulties that surfaced in Korea is not economic. While changes in the capital–labour relations of the OECD countries are spurred by the continuing stagnation and the onset of deindustrialization, changes in Korea are prompted by healthy growth based on rapid expansion of mass production. In terms of the weight of political factors in causing the changes the Korean case is closer to the Brazilian case, although the economic situation is very different in Brazil (Amadeo and Camargo, Chapter 5, this volume).

Naturally, the direction of the changes differs as well. In the OECD countries changes are taking place in search of flexibility in the labour market and the production system: for instance, weakening of labour unions and social welfare system, and moving away from mass production in favour of flexible specialization. The changes taking place in Korea are in the opposite direction: unions are getting stronger and mass production is very much in progress. Perhaps an even more significant difference is that the future possibilities are much wider open in Korea, depending on the outcome of political battles. In OECD countries, where the changes are to a larger extent governed by economic imperatives, different political regimes have produced similar changes (Boyer, 1988).

The Economic Consequences

The full economic consequences of the breakdown of authoritarian capital–labour relations have yet to materialize. The most obvious change concerns wage formation. Labour unions clearly exert a much stronger influence over wage determination now. One result of this is big increases in real wages: real wages in manufacturing rose 8.2 per cent in 1987, 12.1 per cent in 1988 and 19 per cent in the first nine months of 1989, exhibiting a marked increase from the average annual real-wage growth rate of 5.7 per cent during 1981–86. Whether this development will lead to a reduction in real-wage flexibility is unclear. The acceleration of real-wage growth in 1989, in spite of the business downturn and the increase in the rate of inflation, may be a sign of a change in real-wage behaviour. But one year's observation can hardly provide conclusive evidence. The impact of stronger labour unions on wage polarization is also unclear. Although the wage differential between production workers and office workers has been reduced, the wage dispersion may be increasing. As labour unions' bargaining power rose, though most of the bargaining remained fragmented, the wage settlements began to reflect to a greater extent employers' ability to pay. Table 4.22 shows that wage increases were consistently higher in smaller firms than in large firms during 1983–86, but this pattern was disrupted in 1987 and reversed in 1988. If the wage bargaining gets more centralized, this trend could be reversed in the future.

The large increases in real wages and consequent rise in the labour share of income (see Table 4.9 in Section IV), along with a sharp appreciation of won from 890 won/$ at the end of 1985 to 670 won/$ in mid-1989, brought about a change in the macroeconomic structure from export-led growth to domestic demand-led growth. As shown in Table 4.23, until 1986, the growth rate of export demand far outpaced the growth rate of domestic demand, especially consumption demand. The changes since 1987 are quite clear. Domestic demand has replaced export demand as the engine of growth as consumption growth accelerated and export growth declined, while the growth of investment demand remained high.

Table 4.22   Wage bargaining settlements by size of employer (percentage increase)

	Total	100–299	300–499	500–999	1,000–
1983	6.9	7.4	6.9	6.9	6.5
1984	5.4	6.4	5.4	5.1	4.6
1985	6.9	7.1	7.0	7.0	6.7
1986	6.4	6.7	6.5	6.5	6.1
1987	17.2	18.2	17.1	15.9	17.1
1988[a]	13.5	11.7	12.5	14.0	14.7

Note: [a] Until 31 October.

Source: KLI.

Table 4.23   Decomposition of real GDP growth rates

	GDP	C	I	G	X	M
1970–78	10.1	7.7	15.0	8.0	24.7	17.9
1979–86	7.2	5.1	5.5	4.8	10.3	6.1
1987	11.8	8.4	15.1	6.9	21.6	19.4
1988	11.3	9.6	13.0	11.8	13.1	12.2
1989[a]	6.0	10.0	23.2	8.8	–4.3	13.2

Notes:
Growth rates for 1970–86 are calculated from data in 1980 constant prices; for 1987–89, from data in 1985 constant prices. 1988 and 1989 data are preliminary.
[a] First three quarters; growth rates from the figures for the same period of the previous year.

Source: BOK.

There are also microeconomic adjustments as firms try to cope with rapidly rising labour costs by factory automation, technological upgrading, and moving toward products of higher value-added; or by relocating labour-intensive production activities to lower-wage countries in Southeast Asia and elsewhere. Despite a rapid increase in R&D expenditure – in manufacturing, R&D expenditure as a share of total sales increased from 0.33 per cent in 1979 to 1.67 per cent in 1986 (Ministry of Science and Technology) – the weakness of indigenous technological capability, especially in assimilating information technologies and flexible manufacturing systems, has emerged as the major obstacle to further economic growth.

VII CONCLUSION

This paper has examined the role of authoritarian capital–labour relations in Korea's rapid industrialization. The conventional – both from the right and from the left – view finds the linkage between authoritarian capital–labour relations and export-led growth in the role of labour repression to ensure export competitiveness based on low wages. This view, however, has little to say about the indisputable fact that Korea has been able to maintain competitiveness over the years, with the real wages rising extremely rapidly, if from a low base. The open secret, of course, is the equally rapid rise in productivity propelled by structural and technical changes. If there were any functional linkage between authoritarian capital–labour relations and rapid industrialization, it cannot be long-term repression of wages.

This paper suggests a different view. The authoritarian capital–labour relations established labour controls and discipline on the shop floor, which provided a sound basis on which to build an efficient manufacturing system and improve productivity. They also gave rise to flexible and polarized wage formation. The latter were associated, especially, with the sexual division of labour and permitted export expansion of labour-intensive products based on predominantly female relatively low-wage labour. At the same time there was a growth of higher-productivity capital-intensive industries, based on cheap capital provided in part from the surplus created in labour-intensive export industries. This dualistic growth generated a greater degree of technological dynamism than a pure specialization in labour-intensive industries would achieve.

The crumbling of this model of development did not come as a result of exogenous shocks but as an inevitable manifestation of the inherent contradiction of the model. The economic performance in the 1980s before 'democratization' was quite satisfactory; in fact, Korea's economic performance was the envy of the debt-ridden developing world. The contradiction developed in the political sphere instead. The dominance of the state, which was at the heart of the model, was bound to face challenges from both the capitalists and the workers, whose increasing relative strength *vis-à-vis* the state was, ironically, a direct result of the very success of the model in achieving rapid industrialization.

The rise of capitalist power, especially the power of the giant business conglomerates, became apparent under the liberalization policies of the 1980s. The state looked increasingly unable or unwilling to tame the power of the *chaebol*, and this undermined the implicit social compact in which the state would harness the social forces and mobilize the economic resources to the goals of economic development and the citizenry would tolerate banishing of their political and labour rights (Bello, 1990). In the minds of the younger-generation Koreans with no living memory of the wars and the starvation, the military-dominated state outlived its purpose, if it had any. Such was the political reality which, along with the increased strength of the popular classes, led to the demise of the authoritarian politics or the beginning of 'democratization' in 1987. The ensuing explosion of labour militancy reflects a significant increase in the structural capacity and the cultural strength of the working class.

With the fall of the old sociopolitical order, a battle for a new order began. The working class emerged as a key participant in this battle, putting an end to authoritarian capital–labour relations. It is true that the political scene is clouded by uncertainties. Since the formation of the Grand Conservative Coalition government in January 1990, there are signs of retreat from the path of democratization and reform. Forceful intervention to end strikes has re-emerged, and steps are being taken to slow down the wage increases. In addition, the reforms designed to improve equity – a reform of the taxation on real estate and a financial reform which would ban the current practice of holding financial resources under an assumed name – which were pushed forward during 1988–89, have been effectively stalled. However, going back to the old days of authoritarianism is not a serious possibility. Any new stable order of political economy that emerges out of the current capital–labour confrontations and political uncertainties will have to accommodate the changes in capital–labour relations.

NOTES

1. It is estimated that more than 11 million migrated during 1963–82 (see Table 2 in Bai, 1987).
2. In 1984, the average wage in manufacturing establishments with 500 or more employees was only 130 per cent of the average wage in firms with less than 100 employees. While the inter-industry wage differential in Korea is very high by international standards (Krueger and Summers, 1986), the wage differential by firm size is lower than in the US or Japan (J.W. Lee, 1983).
3. The overwhelming majority of workers in the export zones are female. For example, in 1980 86.4 per cent of the unskilled workers in the Masan export processing zone were female.
4. See also Jones and SaKong (1980), Amsden (1989), and Bello (1990).
5. See Woo (1988). Limited penetration by foreign direct investment was also conducive to the relative autonomy of the state. Indeed, 'it is a distinctive feature of South Korea's dependent development that the state has the upper hand over both local capital and the multi-nationals' (Lim, 1982, p. 139). These features contrast with the Latin American countries, where the influence of landlords, multinationals and financial openness is strong (Evans, 1987).
6. See You (1990) for an account of the evolution of labour policies during the export-led industrialization.

7. The best developed welfare scheme in Korea is the Industrial Accidents Insurance, whose rate of coverage reached 66 per cent of the workforce in 1980. Note that, unlike measures which reduce the cost of job loss, the IAI encourages hard work.
8. The national industrial unions in Korea were never much more than paper organizations. Though they came to play a more active role in the late 1970s it was reversed in the 1980s when their involvement in collective bargaining was legally prohibited.
9. Bai (1982) argues that the Korean economy passed the Lewis-type 'turning point' in the mid-1970s. Even after that, new labour reserves appeared due to the absolute decline in agricultural employment and the increase in the female labour force participation rate (Amsden, 1987).
10. Often militaristic discipline is imposed on workers. For example, Hyundai is run like a boot-camp, with a regulation Hyundai haircut and uniform (Bello, 1990). According to T. Hattori's study, cited in Amsden (1989, p. 168), 29 out of 556 cases of recruits into the ranks of top managers during the period 1962–78 came from the military and the KCIA. Due to the lengthy compulsory service and continued military dictatorship, Korean society is permeated by militaristic culture.
11. Corporate paternalism is a managerial strategy to mitigate capital–labour conflict and increase employee attachment by joining the authority of the employer and the paternal authority symbolically and creating a family-like environment.
12. The first story is adapted from 'Min-ju No-jo: South Korea's New Trade Unions', AMRC, 1987 (originally from Hedberg, 1978). The second story is from 'We Are Not What We Used To Be Anymore: A Collection of Workers' Writings', Seoul, 1986.
13. The essence of Taylorism is that 'all possible brain work should be removed from the shop and centered in the planning and laying out department' (F. Taylor, *The Principles of Scientific Management*, pp. 98–9, cited in Kaplinsky, 1988, p. 454).
14. See Amsden (1989), pp. 171–3. Similar observations have been made with respect to Japanese management. A revealing example is found in I. Magaziner and M. Patinkin, 'Fast Heat: How Korea Won the Microwave War', *Harvard Business Review*, Jan.–Feb. 1989. In 1983 it cost General Electric $218 to make a typical microwave oven, while the unit cost for Samsung, a Korean manufacturer, was $155. Per unit assembly labour cost was $8 for GE and 63 cents for Samsung. Much more significant was the differential in overhead labour cost: $30 for GE vs 73 cents for Samsung. The biggest source of this differential was *line and central management*, which cost $10 for GE and only 2 cents for Samsung.
15. There are disagreements as to how radical a departure from Taylorism the Japanese-style management is. For sympathetic views, see Aoki (1990) and Kaplinsky (1988). Critical views can be found in Dohse et al. (1984). They all seem to agree, however, that a successful application of the Japanese model requires the absence of an independent trade union and/or the development of compliant company unions.
16. See K. Kim (1986), which defines import-substitution (IS) industries as those in which the relative contribution of IS to output growth is higher than 10 per cent and concurrently higher than the relative contribution of export expansion. By this criterion, transportation equipment manufacturing among the capital-intensive industries is excluded from IS industries. However, this kind of study grossly underestimates the contribution of IS to output growth by conceptualizing IS as a one-time activity rather than as a stream of activities. For instance, IS of automobiles would be counted as such when they began to be assembled from kits. Later replacement of imports through quality improvements would be counted as an expansion in domestic demand (Amsden, 1989).
17. Frequently, this flow of surplus takes place within a *chaebol*, when investments in capital-intensive operations are made out of profits from domestic sales as well as exports of labour-intensive products.
18. Whether real-wage flexibility helps macroeconomic stability is controversial. J.M. Keynes's view certainly casts doubts on the conventional wisdom. But if the economy is highly dependent on export, downward adjustments of real wages to recessions are likely to stimulate demand and thus stabilize growth (see You, 1991, Chapter 4).
19. See Shirai (1983) and Lazonick, Chapter 3, this volume, for Japanese industrial relations in general. For employment security, see Hashimoto and Raisin (1985). See Dore (1984) for consensus building and Koike (1987) for a description of the 'worker-manager'.

20. In one survey, only 30 per cent of the representatives of the workers in the workplaces which experienced labour disputes in the summer of 1987 said they were receiving briefings on company matters (MOL, 1988). Internal labour markets for blue-collar workers are not well developed in Korea: the promotion ladder is usually short, and managerial positions are off the limit.
21. Major exceptions are the strikes at Hyundai shipyard in 1974 and 1977.
22. For a review of this process, see West and Baker (1988). The following discussion on recent capital–labour confrontations is based on various Korean publications and my interviews with labour activists and union officials.
23. Also note that the recent strikes are of an offensive nature, whereas in the past they were mostly defensive in nature (disputes over wage non-payment or shop closures). But during 1987–88 less than 2 per cent of the disputes were caused by wage non-payment.
24. When tens of thousands of Hyundai workers waged street demonstrations with forklift trucks in front rows, they were like an army and easily overwhelmed the riot police forces. The nation was stunned. The jailed leader Kwon Yong Mok recounts, 'What can we possibly be afraid of, if we truly unite?' – quite a change from Chun Tai-il's self-immolation.
25. John Gittelsohn, 'Shattering Glass', *Korea Business World*, May 1989, p. 18, cited in Bello (1990), p. 16.
26. Data from MOL (1988). If we assume that one dispute raised only one demand regarding union rights, about 36 per cent of the total disputes raised this issue. The same applies to the demands regarding management and personnel policies.
27. In the US, the Wagner Act prohibited employer support for employee organizations in order to preclude the company unions.
28. For the managers, the corresponding numbers were 6 per cent, 31 per cent, and 63 per cent. It seems that they were more attracted to the euphemism of the last answer, which was vaguely phrased.
29. An influential labour organizer, Chang Myung Kook, told me that 'union leaders at the enterprise level are often the most hard-working and intelligent high school graduates who take great pride in their skills'.
30. This may also account for the anomaly of the higher return to college education than basic education in Korea (see J.W. Lee, 1983). Marglin (1990b) argues that the ideological dominance of *episteme* (theoretical knowledge) over *techne* (knowledge embedded in practice) in Western culture has played a role in the success of the capitalist project to take control of the production process. In Korea, its impact has been more apparent in wage distribution than in the production process.

REFERENCES

Amadeo, E. and T. Banuri (1990) 'Worlds within the Third World: Labor Market Institutions in Asia and Latin America', in T. Banuri (ed.) *Economic Liberalization: No Panacea*, Oxford: Clarendon Press.

Amsden, A.H. (1989) *Asia's Next Giant: South Korea and Late Industrialization*, Oxford: Oxford University Press.

Amsden, A.H. (1987) 'Stabilization and Adjustment Policies and Programs, Republic of Korea', Country Study 14, WIDER.

Aoki, M. (1990) 'A New Paradigm of Work Organization and Co-ordination? Lessons from the Japanese Experiences', in S. Marglin and J.B. Schor (eds), *The Golden Age of Capitalism*, Oxford: Clarendon Press.

Asia Monitor Resource Center (AMRC) (1987) *Min-Ju No-Jo: South Korea's New Trade Unions*, Hong Kong.

Bai, M.K. (1982) 'The Turning Point in the Korean Economy', *The Developing Economies*, XX- 1.

Bai, M.K. (1987) 'Export-led Industrialization, Wages and Labor Conditions in South Korea', in A. Addison and L. Demery (eds), *Wages and Labor Condition in the NICS of Asia*, London: Overseas Development Institute.

Bank of Korea (BOK) *Economic Statistics Yearbook*, Seoul, various issues.

Barone, C.A. (1986) 'Dependency, Marxist Theory, and Salvaging the Idea of Capitalism in South Korea', *Review of Radical Political Economics*, vol. 15, no. 1.

Bello, W. (1990) *Dragons in Distress: Crisis and Conflict in the East Asian NICs*, San Francisco: Food Research Institute.

Bowles, S. et al. (1986) 'Power and Profits: The Social Structure of Accumulation and the Profits of the Postwar US Economy', *Review of Radical Political Economics*, pp. 132–67.

Bowles, S. and R. Boyer (1988) 'Income Distribution, Labor Discipline and Unemployment', *American Economic Review*, Papers and Proceedings, May.

Boyer, R. (ed.) (1988) *The Search for Labour Market Flexibility*, Oxford: Clarendon Press.

Cha, H. (1985) 'Labor Process and Work Control in Electronics Industry', unpublished M.A. thesis, Seoul National University.

Choi, J. (1983) 'Interest Conflict and Political Control in South Korea: A Study of the Labor Unions in Manufacturing Industries, 1961–80', unpublished Ph.D. dissertation, University of Chicago.

Cummings, B. (1984) 'The Origin and Development of the Northeast Asian Political Economy', *International Organization*, Winter.

Deyo, F.C. (1989) *Beneath the Miracle: Labor Subordination in the New Asian Industrialism*, Berkeley: University of California Press.

Deyo, F.C. (1987) 'State and Labor: Modes of Political Exclusion in East Asian Development', in F.C. Deyo (ed.) *The Political Economy of the New Asian Industrialism*, Ithaca: Cornell University Press.

Dohse, K. et al. (1985) 'From "Fordism" to "Toyotism"? The Social Organization of the Labor Process in the Japanese Automobile Industry', *Politics & Society*, vol. 14, no. 2.

Dore, R. (1984) *The Social Sources of the Will to Innovate*, London: Technical Change Centre.

Economic Planning Board (EPB), *Major Economic Indicators*, Seoul, various issues.

Edwards, R. (1979) *Contested Terrain*, London: Heinemann.

Evans, P. (1987) 'Class, State, and Dependence in East Asia', in F.C. Deyo (ed.) *The Political Economy of the New Asian Industrialism*, Ithaca: Cornell University Press.

Fields, G.S. (1984) 'Employment, Income Distribution, and Economic Growth in Seven Small Open Economies', *Economic Journal*, vol. 94.

Fields, G.S. and H. Wan, Jr. (1989) 'Wage-setting Institutions and Economic Growth', *World Development*, vol. 17, no. 9.

Haggard, S. and C. Moon (1983) 'Liberal, Dependent or Mercantile? The South Korean State in the International Economy', in J. Ruggie (ed.) *The Antinomies of Interdependence*, New York: Columbia University Press.

Hashimoto, M. and J. Raisan (1985) 'Employment Tenure and Earnings Profiles in Japan and the United States', *American Economic Review*, September.

Hedberg, M. (1978) *The New Challenge: South Korea*, Seoul: Chongno Book Center.

Hodgson, G. (1988) *Economics and Institutions*, Cambridge: Polity Press.

Ito, T. and K. Kang (1989) 'Bonuses, Overtime, and Employment: Korea vs. Japan', NBER Working Paper no. 3012.

Jones, L.P. and I. SaKong (1980) *Government, Business, and Entrepreneurship in Economic Development: The Korean Case*, Cambridge, Mass.: Harvard University Press.

Kaplinsky, R. (1988) 'Restructuring the Capitalist Labor Process', *Cambridge Journal of Economics*, no. 12.

Kim, H. (1988) *Monopoly Capital and Wage Labor in Korea*, Seoul: Kachi.

Kim, K. (1986) 'Relative price Changes and Industrial Growth Patterns in Korea', in K.U. Lee (ed.) *Industrial Development Policies and Issues*, Seoul: KDI Press.

Kim, L. (1987) 'Technological Transformation in Korea: Progress Achieved and Problems Ahead', mimeo, Korea University.

Koike, K. (1987) 'Human Resource Development and Labor-Management Relations', in K. Yamamura and Y. Yasuba (eds) *The Political Economy of Japan*, vol. 1, Stanford: Stanford University Press.

Koo, S. (1982) 'Iron and Steel Industry', in S. Kim and T. Ha (eds) *Case Studies on Labor-Management Relations*, Seoul: KDI Press.

Korea Employer's Association (1979) *A Survey of the Wage Policy*, Seoul.

Korea Labour Institute (KLI) *Quarterly Labour Review*, Seoul, various issues.

Kreye, O. (1980) 'World Market-oriented Industrialization and Labor', in Fröbel et al. *The New International Division of Labor*, Cambridge: Cambridge University Press.

Krueger, A. (1988) 'The Relationships between Trade, Employment, and Development', in G. Ranis and T. Schultz (eds) *The State of Development Economics*, Oxford: Basil Blackwell.

Krueger, A. and L.H. Summers (1986) 'Reflections on the Inter-Industry Wage Structure', in K. Lang and J. Leonard (eds) *Unemployment and the Structure of Labor Markets*, London: Basil Blackwell.

Lee, J.W. (1983) 'Economic Development and Wage Inequality in South Korea', unpublished Ph.D. dissertation, Harvard University.

Lee, K.B. (1987) 'Cultural Attitudes in the Labor–Management Relations', in Social Science Research Center, *Labor–Management Relations in Korea*, Seoul National University.

Lee, K.U. (1986) 'The Concentration of Economic Power in Korea', in K.U. Lee (ed.) *Industrial Development Policies and Issues*, Seoul: KDI Press.

Leibenstein, H. (1987) *Inside the Firm*, Cambridge, Mass.: Harvard University Press.

Lim, H. (1982) 'Dependent Development in the World System: the Case Study of South Korea. 1963–1979', unpublished Ph.D. dissertation, Harvard University.

Lipietz, A. (1986) *Mirages and Miracles*, London: Verso.

Luedde-Neurath, R. (1986) *Import Controls and Export-Oriented Development: A Reassessment of the South Korean Case*, Boulder: Westview Press.

Marglin, S.A. (1990a) 'Lessons of the Golden Age: An Overview', in Marglin and Schor (eds).

Marglin, S.A. (1990b) 'Losing Touch: The Cultural Conditions of Worker Accommodation and Resistance', in F.A. Marglin and S.A. Marglin (eds), *Dominating Knowledge*, Oxford: Clarendon Press.

Marglin, S.A. and J.B. Schor (eds) (1990) *The Golden Age of Capitalism*, Oxford: Clarendon Press.

Ministry of Labor (MOL) (1988) *Report on the Labor Disputes in the Summer of 1987*, Seoul.

Ministry of Labor (MOL) *Labor Statistics Yearbook*, Seoul, various issues.

North, D. (1990) *Institutions, Institutional Change and Economic Performance*, Cambridge: Cambridge University Press.

Ohno, K. and H. Imaoka (1987) 'The Experience of Dual-Industrial Growth: Korea and Taiwan', *The Developing Economies*, XXV-4.

Park, K.-K. and S.-I., Park (1984) *The Wage Structure in Korea*, Seoul: KDI Press.

Park, S.-I. (1988) 'Labor Issues in Korea's Future', *World Development*, vol. 16, no. 1.

Pyo, H. (1988) 'Estimates of Capital Stock and Capital/Output Coefficients by Industries for the Republic of Korea (1953–1986)', Seoul: KDI Press.

Ranis, G. (1984) 'Determinants and Consequences of Indigenous Technological Activity', in M. Fransman and K. King (eds) *Technological Capability in the Third World*, New York: St. Martin's Press.

Shirai, T. (ed.) (1983) *Contemporary Industrial Relations in Japan*, Madison: University of Wisconsin Press.

US Bureau of Labor Statistics (1990) *International Comparisons of Hourly Compensation Costs for Production Workers in Manufacturing, 1989*. Washington, DC.

West, J.M. and E.J. Baker (1988) 'The 1987 Constitutional Reforms in South Korea', *Harvard Human Rights Yearbook*.

Woo, J. (1988) 'State Power, Finance, and Korean Development', unpublished Ph. D. dissertation, Columbia University.

World Bank (1987) *World Development Report 1987*, Oxford: Oxford University Press.

You, J.-I. (1990) 'South Korea', in S. Herzenberg and J. Perez-Lopez (eds) *Labor Standards and Development in the Global Economy*, US Department of Labor.

You, J.-I. (1991) 'Capital–labor relations and economic development: Theoretical essays and a case study of South Korea, unpublished Ph.D. dissertation, Harvard University.

5. 'New unionism' and the relations among capital, labour and the state in Brazil

Edward J. Amadeo and José Márcio Camargo

I INTRODUCTION

Until 1980, Brazil was one of the most dynamic and fastest growing economies in the world. Between 1955 and 1985, the average rate of growth of industrial output was close to 7 per cent a year. In 1950, agriculture accounted for 60 per cent of total employment, and by 1980, had shrunk to 29 per cent of the labour force. In the same period, the industrial sector as a share of total employment increased from 9.4 per cent to 17.2 per cent. This sharp change in the composition of employment was accompanied by equally drastic changes in the relations between capital and labour in the country. This paper analyses the evolution of these relations in Brazil, examines what has caused these changes over the 1980s, and offers some prospects for the future.

First, the rapid growth of the economy and its structural transformation generated a heterogeneous labour market. Workers in the new industrial sectors are organized into strong unions, while in traditional sectors, services (except banking) and commerce workers are not organized, and a large share of employees work on a non-signed contract basis. The nature of labour relations varies across economic sectors and geographical regions. On average, half of the workers are employed on a non-signed contract basis and 25 per cent are self-employed. In the industrial sector, however, about 80 per cent of the workers have a signed contract job. In Section II of this paper we discuss the heterogeneity of the labour force.

In Brazil, capital–labour relations were, until 1988, regulated by a set of laws approved during the 1930s and unified into a labour code named the Consolidação das Leis do Trabalho (CLT). It was a comprehensive set of rules regulating almost every aspect of wage policy. Social as well as individual rights were included. Approved during the Vargas dictatorship, the code was authoritarian and paternalistic. These rules were characterized by the notions that conflicts between capital and labour in the workplace should be avoided, and that the control of workers' organizations by the state was an important instrument to reduce labour militancy. Paternalistic institutions and authoritarian rules, combined with the idea that conflicts should be directed to the labour courts left almost no room for negotiations between workers and employers. In Section III we discuss the institutional setting of the labour market up to the 1980s and the means by which the state tried to avoid conflict between capital and labour.

The change in the structure of production and employment and the democratization process, which started in 1975, generated drastic changes in the relations among capital, labour and the state in Brazil. Using modern technology and Taylorized methods of production and labour processes, the growth of the 1970s gave rise to a rapid increase in labour productivity. However, this growth was not accompanied by a corresponding increase in real wages nor an increase in social benefits to labour. As a result, the share of labour in output declined over the 1960s and early 1970s leading to workers' discontent. In the late 1970s and early 1980s workers' dissatisfaction exploded into violent strikes. This process, which we explore in Section IV, marks a turning point in capital–labour relations in Brazil.

After the labour turmoil of the late 1970s, the structure of unions' organization moved towards greater centralization at the national level. Although the law forbade the existence of such organizations, two national unions were created, Central Unica dos Trabalhadores (CUT) and the Confederaçao Geral dos Trabalhadores (CGT). Even before the appearance of the central unions, a Workers' Party (PT), linked to the most combative union leaders, was created and became an important channel through which the unions took their demands to the parliament.

Until 1988, when the new constitution was approved, the old labour code was not revised. As unions became more organized, and the law did not favour direct bargaining between capital and labour, it became more and more difficult to avoid confrontation. Unions considered the code too authoritarian, and the strongest and most organized ones simply did not respect it. In many instances, not even the Ministry of Labour followed the code. A truly institutional vacuum was created thus generating a period of strong confrontation between capital and labour.

The new constitution, approved in October 1988, liberalized the relations between capital and labour, legalized the right to strike, and forbade state intervention in union activity. This was an important step towards democratization of capital–labour relations in the country, but many problems still remain. In section V we examine the emergence of the 'new unionism' in Brazil.

In the early 1980s the Brazilian economy was in the process of adjusting to the external debt crisis. This meant a drastic reduction in employment and real wages, and in the bargaining power of unions. However, in 1984–85 when the economy recovered and the military regime ended, unions re-established their power. The improved ability of unions to secure better wages and the decentralized structure of wage bargaining help to explain two important phenomena of the 1980s in Brazil. The distributive conflict between organized labour and capital led to a high degree of industrial conflict and the acceleration of inflation. However, this also entailed a redistribution of income from the less organized segments of society (both employers and workers in the competitive and less organized segments of the economy) to the more organized sectors (unionized labour and oligopolist enterprises). We elaborate on these phenomena in Section VI.

In the last section we draw conclusions from the analysis and discuss the prospects for the relations among capital, labour and the state in Brazil. We conclude that the current crisis in these fundamental relations can be explained by the rapid economic growth and transformation of the production structure, the conflict between different segments of society due to the unequal distribution of income, the re-emergence of the union movement with a radically new structure and the democratization process. Although it is difficult to pinpoint causal relationships between these aspects, the new organization of the union movement, and in particular the tendency towards centralization, is the critical aspect of the current process of transformation of Brazilian society, and in particular, the changing relations among capital, labour and the state.

As for the prospects, although there are some indications that Brazilian society will follow a route towards a less 'exclusive system', two basic obstacles still exist. Employers in Brazil have been quite resistant to changes, and might be able to block the growth of labour participation. Moreover, there is a huge number of workers whose relation with capital does not have a legal status, and it will take some time before they become part of the organized segment of the labour force.

II THE STRUCTURAL HETEROGENEITY OF THE BRAZILIAN LABOUR MARKET

The Brazilian labour market is quite heterogeneous. Strong and organized unions coexist with a large percentage of workers who are without a signed contract and have no union representation. In addition, the labour market is heterogeneous across sectors and regions. Table 5.1 shows that although 72.4 per cent of the workers in the industrial sector had a signed contract in 1986, in agriculture this percentage was only 6.9 per cent and in services 21.9 per cent. On the other hand, self-employment, which represents only 6.6 per cent of the employment in industry, reaches 33.2 per cent in services and agriculture.

Table 5.1   Composition of the labour force by sector in Brazil, 1986

	Signed contract	Non-signed contract	Self-employed	Without remuneration	Employers
Agriculture	6.9	33.2	33.2	25.2	3.5
Industry	72.4	15.9	6.6	1.3	3.8
Construction	39.3	27.9	29.6	0.7	2.5
Commerce	42.5	16.3	30.9	3.5	6.8
Services	21.9	40.7	33.2	1.5	2.7
Transport & communication	60.2	11.9	25.1	0.7	2.1
Public admin.	52.5	47.0	0.3	–	0.2
Total	38.2	27.9	22.9	7.6	3.4

Source: Sabóia (1988).

This heterogeneity is also evident across regions. In São Paulo, the most industrialized region of the country, 82.6 per cent and 25.5 per cent of the workers employed in the industrial and the agriculture sectors, respectively, had a signed contract job in 1986. In the northeast, the least industrialized region, the corresponding figures were 41.7 per cent and 3.3 per cent. As noted in Tables 5.2 and 5.3, the non-signed contract jobs were much more important in the northeast than in São Paulo.

Table 5.2   Composition of the labour force by sector in São Paulo, 1986

	Signed contract	Non-signed contract	Self-employed	Without remuneration	Employers
Agriculture	25.5	36.0	13.9	18.9	5.7
Industry	82.6	11.6	1.5	0.7	3.6
Construction	42.0	22.5	30.8	0.5	4.2
Commerce	47.7	16.7	24.0	2.6	9.0
Services	28.1	36.5	30.7	1.3	3.4
Transport & communication	68.2	8.7	19.2	1.1	2.8
Public Admin.	42.0	57.9	–	–	0.1
Total	54.8	23.5	14.7	2.6	4.4

Source: Sabóia (1988).

Table 5.3   Composition of the labour force by sector in the northeast, 1986

	Signed contract	Non-signed contract	Self-employed	Without remuneration	Employers
Agriculture	3.3	33.0	38.5	23.1	2.1
Industry	41.7	27.9	23.2	3.9	3.3
Construction	32.4	37.6	28.2	0.6	1.2
Commerce	25.1	17.6	48.4	5.4	3.5
Services	12.0	46.3	37.6	2.2	1.9
Transport & communication	42.9	19.4	35.3	1.0	1.4
Public admin.	59.7	39.6	0.5	–	0.2
Total	21.8	32.5	32.2	11.4	2.1

Source: Sabóia (1988).

Table 5.4   Distribution of employed workers by occupations in non-agricultural activities, Brazil, 1979–84

	1979	1981	1982	1983	1984
Signed contract	53.2	50.0	49.1	45.5	47.6
Non-signed	23.2	24.9	25.2	29.5	26.9
Self-employed	17.9	19.5	20.2	19.8	20.3
Non-paid	2.1	1.9	2.3	2.1	1.9
Employers	3.8	3.0	3.2	3.1	3.3

Source: Sabóia (1988).

By contrasting the evolution of the various segments of the labour market over the period 1979–84, an interesting picture emerges. As Table 5.4 indicates, the rate of open unemployment and the percentage of workers employed on a non-signed contract basis increased during the recession (1981–83) and declined in 1984, while the share of self-employment was virtually constant over this period. Thus, during recessions, the rate of unemployment and also the share of non-signed contract workers in the labour market are forced to adjust. This occurs because in Brazil there are no unemployment benefit programmes, so that if a worker is fired he must find a job in the non-signed segment of the market. These jobs usually require fewer qualifications but also pay much less.

However, the effect of changes in the level of activity on the share of self-employment is quite small, implying that the segmentation between waged workers and self-employed workers is a structural phenomenon. Indeed, self-employment as a share of total employment in Brazil in the last three to four decades has been relatively stable.

The heterogeneity of the labour force is quite important in understanding the recent developments in the relations among capital, labour and the state. In this sense, a further and crucial distinction must be made between unionized and non-unionized workers. Unions are important in those sectors where the signed contract jobs dominate (industry, banking and government) and not as important in those sectors where the non-signed contract and self-employment jobs dominate (services, construction and commerce). Also, unions in the most industrialized regions are stronger than in the less industrialized regions. Finally unionized workers, who are in general better qualified, are usually laid off rather than fired during recessions; they tend to accept unemployment rather than a non-signed contract job. The opposite holds true for non-unionized workers.

Most of the unionized workers are in the dynamic industrial sectors which also correspond to the tradable sectors. Non-unionized workers as well as workers without a signed contract and self-employed workers are in the traditional and non-tradable sectors. As we shall note in Section V, most of the strikes between 1979 and 1985 occurred in the industrial sectors, implying that these workers are more active and mobilized.

This interaction between the labour and goods market, together with the introduction of unionization as another dimension in the segmentation of the labour market, has important implications for the analysis of the economic and social changes which took place in the 1980s. During this period, the government persistently promoted exports. If we associate changes in relative prices in favour of the tradable sectors with a reduction of the wage : exchange rate ratio, and we recognize that workers in the signed contract/unionized segment were able to resist reductions in their real wages better than other workers, then it seems clear that the non-unionized workers of the non-tradable sectors bore the costs of government policies.[1]

III   THE PRODUCTION SYSTEM AND THE RULES OF COORDINATION

In the following analysis of the capital–labour relations in Brazil we consider two sets of elements: first, the 'rules of (macroeconomic) coordination' of the economic system which relate to the set of rules which determine the structure of union organizations and the collective bargaining process; and second, the 'system of production' which relates to the technology used and control over the labour process, and therefore affects labour productivity.

The Rules of Coordination

Until 1988, regulation of the relations between capital and labour in the Brazilian economy was in large part determined by a set of laws approved during the 1930s and consolidated into a general labour code known as the Consolidation of the Labour Laws or Consolidção das Leis do Trabalho (CLT) in 1943. At that time, Brazil was an agrarian economy with a small but growing industrial sector. The laws were approved by an authoritarian civilian government (the Getúlio Vargas dictatorship) and was an adaptation of the Italian labour code of the time. The structure of the code had a 'state corporatist' character in that it regulated almost all aspects of capital–labour relations both at the individual and social level.[2]

The code defined a union structure founded on an occupational and a geographical basis. The set of occupational unions in a state defined a federation and a set of federations defined a confederation for each sector (industry, commerce, banking and agriculture) at the national level. This was the highest level of centralization allowed by the code. There was no central union at the national level. There was a similar structure on the employers' side.

Each union, to acquire jurisdictional existence and the right to represent workers on collective bargaining, had to be approved directly by the Ministry of Labour. After approval, the union monopolized the representation of the respective occupation at the city level. A financial contribution by workers was compulsory, independent of union affiliation. The results of the negotiations between unions and employers were extended to all workers, regardless of membership.

The revenue of the contributions collected by the state was shared among the union itself, the federations, the confederations and the Ministry of Labour. A law regulated the use of this fund, and control over its use by the unions was the responsibility of the Ministry of Labour. It could be used for assistencial objectives, but not for some objectives, such as financing a strike or paying unemployment benefits.

The Ministry of Labour could intervene in union behaviour for administrative or political reasons. It could depose the board of directors, nominate a new board, call new elections, and regulate and control the electoral process.

There was a system of labour courts composed of labour lawyers, a worker and an employer representative. At the federal level, the members were named by the president and approved by the federal senate. The labour courts had jurisdiction over the social and individual rights of the workers.

Collective bargaining was conducted between labour unions and employers' representatives at the occupational and city level. If the negotiations were made through an employers' association, the agreement was called a 'convention'. If an individual employer signed an agreement with a union, it was called an 'agreement'. Each occupation had a different date for collective negotiation, legally once a year. The Ministry of Labour approved any agreements reached. If approved, the agreement was law. The law stipulated that any agreement should be in line with the economic policy followed by the government.

If an agreement was not possible, at any time one of the parties could unilaterally call a 'dissídio', and the dispute would be sent to the labour court at the state level. The sentence at this level could be appealed to the superior labour court and a suspensive effect on the state court decision was obtained by the claimant. While this suspensive effect was in force the previous labour contract continued in effect. The superior labour court decision was final.

Another important characteristic of the Brazilian labour code was its paternalistic character regarding the individual rights of workers. A large number of regulations dealing with working conditions and pay was part of the code. These included maximum hours of work time, maximum overtime work, minimum payment for extra-time work, minimum wage clauses, rules of job security, etc. There was, however, no provision for workers' representation at the plant level. The protection of individual rights was a function of the state and not of the unions.

The main objectives of this institutional framework were to create a fragmented collective bargaining process and a decentralized union structure, to avoid confrontation between capital and labour, and to minimize workers' representation and influence at the plant level. The lack of provisions for workers' representation at the firm level and the pre-emption of workers' demands regarding individual rights were important instruments in reducing unions' influence in the workplace. As most of the individual rights were given to the workers by law, the existence of representation at the workplace was considered by most labour lawyers as unnecessary and the action of the unions tended to be directed to the state.

This institutional structure created a union movement controlled by and dependent on the state. The movement was involved with national politics but had no important links with the day-to-day problems of the workers. The plant was considered a 'domain of the employers, whose limits of action were only determined by the Labour Justice' (Rodrigues, 1979, p. 134). If workers were unhappy they should go to the courts. The demands for workers' representation at the plant level were considered by labour lawyers as 'absurd demands' (from a labour lawyer quoted in Castro, 1988, p. 92).

This system was quite effective until 1964, when the military coup reduced its paternalistic character and reinforced the authoritarian aspects of the code. The coup was preceded by an increase in union militancy cultivated by the previous government links with the official union structure. The first years of military rule were characterized by persecution and imprisonment of labour leaders and the closing of more militant unions (see Souza and Lamounier, 1981). At the same time, three laws were approved which changed capital–labour relations in the country in important ways.

The first was a restrictive strike law approved in 1964 (Law 1330). Strikes had to be approved in a formal convention by secret ballot by more than 50 per cent of the workers and employers had to receive previous notification. Political and solidarity strikes were forbidden. A strike could be declared illegal by the labour courts and if the workers did not return to work, the Labour Ministry could intervene in the union and its leaders could be jailed. Strikes were also strictly forbidden in a large number of sectors of the economy considered 'essential'. This law rendered any attempt to strike impossible.

The second law reduced the costs of dismissing workers. And the third introduced a wage adjustment law. These three important changes in the law increased the discretion of employers to contract and dismiss workers, reduced even further union militancy and, given the authoritarian climate, increased the capacity of the government to coordinate the process of wage formation in the economy. These changes essentially rendered collective bargains irrelevant and created the opportunity to impose an incomes policy which in part caused the tremendous concentration of the distribution of income in the 1960s and early 1970s.

Before we turn to the effects of these institutional changes on capital–labour relations, it is important to consider the development of the structure of production and the labour process.

The Structure of Production and the Labour Process

Over the last three decades deep structural changes have occurred in the Brazilian industrial sector. Between 1955 and 1985, industrial output grew at an average rate of 6.7 per cent. However, the following aggregates grew even faster: the durable consumption goods sectors (automobiles, electric appliances, etc.) had an average rate of growth of 12.6 per cent a year, industrial inputs (metallurgy, machinery, cement, etc.) 8.4 per cent a year, and the capital goods sectors (machines and industrial equipment) 9.4 per cent a year. In the same period the average rate of growth of non-durable consumer goods (food processing, textiles, etc.) was less than 4 per cent a year (Table 5.5).[3]

Table 5.5   *Average rates of growth of industrial output by sectors in Brazil, 1955–85 (in per cent)*

| | Consumption goods | | Industrial sector | | |
| | | | Industrial | Capital | |
	Durables	Non-durables	inputs	goods	Industry
1955–62	23.9	6.6	12.1	26.4	9.8
1962–67	4.1	0.0	5.9	–2.6	2.6
1967–73	26.6	4.9	13.4	18.0	12.7
1973–80	9.3	4.4	8.3	7.4	7.5
1980–83	–8.1	–1.3	–4.5	–17.3	–6.2
1983–85	3.3	4.9	8.7	13.8	6.7

Source: IBGE and FGV.

A variety of growth strategies followed by the Brazilian governments explains the structural change that occurred in this period. Between 1955 and 1964, an aggressive import-substitution strategy resulted in the first wave of growth of the modern and capital-intensive industrial sectors. During this period, the automotive and appliances industries as well as the capital goods industries were developed in the country. The financing for these projects was mainly based on foreign direct investment of multinational enterprises.

The second wave of growth in 1967–73 was based on changes in the industrial development strategy and resulted in growth in two particular areas: first, a sharp concentration in the distribution of income led to a 26 per cent average rate of growth in the demand for durable consumption goods and luxury goods, and second, the import-substitution strategy was replaced with an export-oriented strategy which created production incentives to the industrial sector. Foreign direct investment as well as indebtedness were the main sources of financing. During this period the durable consumption goods industries were consolidated in the Brazilian industrial structure.

Finally, beginning in 1975, the Brazilian government implemented an ambitious import-substitution programme of capital goods and industrial inputs. This programme operated through direct state investment and subsidized credit from the government to the private sector. The programme was mainly financed by foreign indebtedness. This process is seen as the 'last phase' of the import-substitution strategy, and is an important factor in attaining commercial surpluses of approximately $18 billion a year since 1984.

There are two aspects which all three of the growth phases have in common. First, foreign technology was used either directly through multinational investments or indirectly through licensing from these firms. Given the amount of resources available for R&D investment and the capital-intensive technology used in these sectors, the technological basis was mainly imported and was quite similar to that used in the industrialized countries. Second, all three phases of growth required a redistribution of income away from the low-income groups to high-income groups and profits.

As we would expect, the change in the industrial structure towards more capital-intensive sectors, and based on imported technologies, implied an important change in the dominant labour process. Taylorized methods of production, division of labour, separation of conception and execution, regulation of the rhythm of work through assembly lines, and gradual substitution of machines for men became important elements of the work process in Brazilian industry. In what follows we provide some quotations from industry workers on the adoption of Taylorized methods of production in Brazil.[4]

An operator of an assembly line of the Fiat automotive industry says:

> the most important element of the automotive industry is the conveyor, called the assembly line. The worker stays on a given position, he is fixed and it is the conveyor that moves the cars. It is the same with the production of engines ... The rhythm is controlled by the company, in accordance with its needs ... There are hundreds of assembly lines in the factory. The worker must adapt himself to this. (Quoted in Le Ven, 1988, p. 539)

The testimony of other workers points out that the rhythm of production is determined by the foreman who receives orders from the production manager: 'The velocity of the assembly line is [determined] according to what production department demands. There is a maximum and a minimum velocity, but it is the foreman who determines the rhythm of work (quoted in Le Ven, 1988, p. 540). Further, 'The rhythm of work is imposed by the machine. It is inhumane. The worker adapts himself to the machine to the point of being able to control it as if it were a part of his brain' (an assembly line worker quoted by Le Ven, 1988, p. 547).

The separation between conception and execution is also an important characteristic of the work process. The production process is

> organized in such a way that [the worker] receives everything finished. It is the FIAT standard, it is the FIAT technology and program, developed and decided in Italy. The company sends people to Italy but I do not know for what reason since everything arrives here ready to be used ... The car is produced here, but the project comes from abroad. (Words of a qualified worker quoted in Le Ven, 1988, p. 551)

Another worker refers to the policy in his company according to which 'the idea is to divide the workers, to create an atmosphere of rivalry between workers with different functions. To maintain the worker uninformed about the technology being used ... It gives no chance for a worker to learn more than one type of job' (a worker quoted in Le Ven, 1988, p. 550). In general, firms invest very little in human capital. The skill level of the labour force is low in Brazil, except in cases of very specialized workers. In two automobile firms surveyed in São Paulo in the late 1970s, 70 per cent of the workers were classified as non-skilled or semi-skilled. Of 15 toolsmiths surveyed, 10 workers were hired, 3 had technical school training and 2 had night school training without the firm's support (Humphrey, 1988, p.14). As noted by a worker at Fiat, 'what (the workers) know here ... (they) learned by (them)selves. Nothing was taught to them' (a worker quoted in Le Ven, 1988, p. 550).

Because the costs for dismissing a worker in Brazil are practically nil, many companies use the turnover of workers, especially those less skilled, to reduce their operating expenses. Firms do not have incentives to invest in employee skills. Indeed, given the high rates of turnover observed, one is led to conclude that it is more economical to fire a trained worker and hire another one with less experience than to try to increase the productivity of workers by improving their skills. Table 5.6 shows the number of new admissions and dismissals in the first half of 1977, in the automotive industry.

Table 5.6   Labour turnover in the automotive industry, January–June 1977

	No. of workers	Admissions	%	Dismissals	%	Net change
Chrysler	3,777	426	11.3	531	14.0	–2.8
FNM	3,377	1,003	23.0	631	14.4	8.5
FIAT	5,326	2,614	49.1	871	16.4	32.7
Ford	231	1,315	5.7	3,603	15.6	–9.9
GM	19,795	454	2.3	3,552	17.9	–15.7
Mercedes Benz	16,460	3,314	20.0	2,558	15.5	4.6
Volkswagen	39,057	2,141	5.5	3,698	9.5	4.0
Auto industry	117,900	12,456	10.6	16,226	13.8	–3.2

Source: SINE, quoted in Humphrey (1988), p. 16.

As the table indicates, the percentage of admissions and dismissals in proportion to total employment during the first half of 1977 was quite high. For the industry as a whole, 10.6 per cent of the workers were admitted and 13.8 per cent were dismissed in six months. As noted by workers of Ford Motor Company and Scania, quoted by Abramo (1986),

Every last Wednesday of the month, Ford fired workers. It was a great calamity ... Everybody talked about that. It was terrible. Folks only woke up to the question of turnover when the union started to talk about it. (p. 106)

Friday was marked by the expectation of the relief of the weekend, and mainly because the worker was certain that he would not be fired. He knew that he would have another weekend paid by the company and was going to rest. He would be tortured again only on the next Wednesday or Thursday ... The turnover was very high. (p. 105)

In the case of the Brazilian economy, unlike most OECD countries, the adoption of Taylorist methods of production was not accompanied by a significant increase in job security. The high rate of turnover is still a characteristic of the modern and more capital-intensive sectors, as well as that of the traditional sectors of the economy.

IV   TAYLORISM WITHOUT THE 'FORDIST COMPROMISE'

Capital–labour relations in some OECD countries after the Second World War were characterized by what came to be called the 'Fordist compromise'. According to this compromise, Taylorist technology and organization of the working process led to fast productivity growth and high employment stability. The growth in productivity was shared by wages and profits so that consumption expenditure became as important as investment demand in keeping high levels of aggregate demand and employment. The improvement of working conditions was another important element of the compromise. 'Collective bargaining', on the other hand, reduced wage differentials and created a sense of solidarity amongst workers. The social compromise also entailed a gradual increase of the social wage, that is, the generalized access to social services (such as health, education, social security, etc. – see Boyer, Chapter 2, this volume).

This compromise was, at least in part, a result of union activism, both at the macro-level and at the workplace, and the existence of (social) democratic governments. In Brazil, the combination of Taylorist technologies, the lack of union activism in the workplace and an authoritarian government led to a perverse system. This system has the worst aspects of Taylorism and no social compromise between capital and labour, resulting in poor working conditions at the firm level, total control of the production process by employers and a very unequal distribution of the benefits from productivity growth. These conditions have caused the explosion of union activism and the breakdown of the production system in Brazil over the last ten years.

As an example of the poor working conditions, we look at the number of on-the-job accidents which increased sharply during the period 1969–75 – the years of the Brazilian 'economic miracle'. The number of registered on-the-job accidents by the Brazilian social security institute (INPS) increased from 1,059,296 in 1969 to 1,797,000 in 1974 – an increase of 70 per cent. This represented an increase from 14.6 per cent to 22.8 per cent in the number of workers who suffered on-the-job accidents in relation to the total number of workers insured by the institute. See Table 5.7.

Table 5.7   *On-the-job accidents in Brazil, 1969–74*

	On-the-job accidents, total	As % of insured workers
1969	1,059,296	14.6
1970	1,220,111	16.7
1971	1,330,523	17.6
1972	1,504,723	19.4
1973	1,800,000	22.8
1974	1,797,000	–

Source: INPS, in Abramo (1986), p. 78.

Discipline, overtime, an exhausting rhythm of work and rigid control of the labour process characterized working conditions even in the most dynamic sectors of industry. In what follows, we provide a few quotations from workers expressing their feelings about their working conditions:[5]

It was common for a worker to work 160 hours a month besides his normal work time. This meant a 14 working hour work day plus travel time. If we compute the time needed to go to work and go back home, it represented a 16 to 17 hour day. It was not too different from the time of slavery. (p. 93)

The over-time work was always an element of oppression in the firm. In my sector there was a black-board where the department head used to write down the names of the workers [who were selected to work on] Saturday and Sunday. And if the person for any reason could not come, a situation of discomfort and pressure was created. (p. 96)

The firms … are driving workers like slaves, offending their dignity and destroying their physical and mental health. In fact, they are genuine factories of mad people, suppliers of patients to the INPS [the social security system] … They seem to have lost the notion of what is a human being. (p. 153)

You should see [the workers] anguish, when on Friday the department head comes and asks [them] to work on Saturday and Sunday. If [the worker] could not come, [the head] would ask why not. No one accepts when [the worker] says that he needs a rest, or needs to stay with his family. Then [he] has to look for thousands of excuses. I think the weekend rest is a human right. If [the worker] becomes exhausted and has to go to the INPS, when [he] comes back, they fire him ... (p. 154)

The system is militaristic, with hierarchy and everything else. It is ruled by a colonel and a lieutenant. It is absolutely repressive. In the factory exit, the worker is humiliated and examined as if he were a dangerous delinquent. If he protests he is threatened and his number is written down by the security officer. All his belongings are examined. (Quoted in Le Ven, 1988, p. 560)

In Brazil, the turnover of workers has been used as an important element for reducing costs. But more important than that, it is extensively used as an instrument to control the labour force. Even today union leaders complain that employers threaten the workers with dismissals during strikes or movements on the shop floor. Only where the labour movement is stronger, workers have a certain degree of job security. In general, however, there is nothing to prevent firms from dismissing workers either for economic or political reasons. The following testimony of a worker quoted by Abramo (1986) is evidence of how the threat of dismissal is used to control workers:

There was a feeling of insecurity and, more than that, injustice, mainly when they demanded over-time work from the workers ... The insecurity regarding the next wave of dismissals helped to maintain the discipline. The turn-over of labour force is one of the most ruthless aspects of the automobile industry management ... (p. 49)

If conditions at the workplace were bad, the situation at the macro-level was not better. The introduction of Taylorist methods of production resulted in a sharp increase in labour productivity in the industrial sector.

Since 1964, the government had centrally determined wages through a wage policy. However over the last ten years, the policy has been losing its effectiveness. In the 1960s and early 1970s the wage adjustment formula was based on the estimated rate of inflation. Although the explicit objective of the wage adjustment policy was to maintain the share of labour in total income, it was in fact used as an anti-inflationary instrument.[6] The official nominal wage adjustment was always below the actual rate of inflation since the future rate of inflation was recurrently underestimated. As noted by Simonsen (1983), an important policy maker during the military regime,

From 1965 through 1979 the wage law imposed a binding constraint on collective bargaining, leaving no degree of freedom to employers to negotiate the wage adjustment or increases in real wages. Indeed, the wage policy became an incomes policy device because both productivity gains and the expected rate of inflation were decreed by the government leaving no room for collective bargaining or strikes. (pp. 118–19)

Fast productivity growth and the reduction of real wages resulted in a declining share of wages in net national income. In 1970, wages represented 40.73 per cent of net income, and in 1975, this share had declined to 36.55 per cent (Census data, FIBGE). The deterioration in the functional distribution of income was accompanied by a worsening of the personal distribution of income in the 1970s and 1980s. In Table 5.8 we look at the ratio of the average real income of different income brackets to the average income of the first three deciles. We note that there was a considerable concentration of income, with the ratios increasing from 1960 to 1970 to 1976, with the exception of the second group (from the fourth to the seventh deciles). The average income of the tenth decile was 17 times the income of the first three deciles; in 1976 this ratio was 26, thus increasing by more than 50 per cent.

Table 5.8   *Personal distribution of income (ratio of average income of selected deciles to average income of first three deciles) in Brazil, 1960–76*

	1960	1970	1976
1st–3rd deciles	1.00	1.00	1.00
4th–7th deciles	2.49	2.69	2.51
8th–10th deciles	9.59	11.54	12.89
10th decile	17.24	22.47	26.00

Source: Bonelli and Sedlacek (1989).

Table 5.9   *Social security and health expenditures as percentage of GDP in Brazil, 1970–75*

Year	%
1970	8.21
1971	7.07
1972	7.31
1973	6.68
1974	6.08
1975	6.72

Source: National Accounts.

The reduction in the share of wages in national income and the worsening of the distribution of income was also followed by a reduction in the percentage of government expenditures on social security and health. In 1970, government expenditures on these services represented 8.21 per cent of total output. In 1974, this percentage had declined to 6.08 per cent (Table 5.9).

Thus, from the workers' perspective, although the economy was growing fast, economic and social conditions were deteriorating. The feeling of social injustice was an important source of dissatisfaction in the labour force. There were many manifestations of this discomfort, but the wave of strikes in 1978 and 1979 was certainly the most vivid. As early as September 1971, the newspaper *Tribuna Metalurgica*, published by the metallurgy workers union in São Bernardo (the centre of the labour movement in Brazil) printed the following: 'we have to make ourselves aware of our responsibilities as workers. We have to make ourselves present in the national scenario ... and demand our share in the fruits of progress ...'. Then in 1972 the newspaper called for the recognition of the role of workers in the process of accumulation: 'The social peace will be possible when the bosses recognize our dignity as workers and do not pay a vile price for our labour power'.

Although the unions were completely repressed, there were democratic and progressive forces fighting in the political arena. In 1974, a national election for the federal senate and for the federal chamber of representatives resulted in an overwhelming victory for the opposition, anti-military, party. It won in all but one state in the country. Dissatisfaction with the military regime was mounting and the government decided to initiate the democratization of the political process. The plans were slowly to retire from politics and return the country to a civilian government, but without losing control of the process.

The democratization process and the feeling of social injustice described above gave rise to a new union movement in the most developed regions of the country. Independent union leaders, not linked to the official union structure, became the focus of high rates of labour militancy. The 'new unionism', characterized by close links to the workers at the firm level and a very activist posture in relation to government policies in collective bargaining, originated in São Paulo in the late 1970s.

In 1978, after more than a decade of 'industrial peace', a strike movement exploded in the industrial belt of São Paulo. In May of 1978, an estimated 100,000 workers downed tools in São Paulo, Santo André, Osasco, Guarulhos, São Caetano and São Bernardo. This represented about 50 per cent of the total number of industrial workers in this region (Abramo, 1986, p. 232). The movement continued for three months. Surprised by the violence of the movement, the employers tried to avoid confrontation by sending workers' demands to the Labour Justice and refusing to negotiate. However, the tactic was insufficient and the strike continued until the employers conceded to most of the union's demands. The victory of this first attempt at confrontation sparked the development of a new union structure. The intensity of the strike movement increased sharply.

This marked an important structural change in capital–labour relations in the Brazilian economy.

V   THE 'NEW UNIONISM' OF THE 1980s

Former unions were characterized by fragmented union structure, no representation at the workplace, a lack of attention to the day-to-day problems of the workers on the shop floor and a dependent relationship to the state. The new union structure moved rapidly towards a more centralized organization, with decentralized collective bargaining, and created workers' councils at the firm level and established complete independence from the state.

After the success of the 1978 strike, the movement followed two opposite but complementary routes. As it spread to other regions of the country, the necessity to organize the activities of the movement generated demand for more *centralization* of the union structure. Union leaders also perceived that if they wanted to improve workers' conditions and increase political power, the Consolidção das Leis do Travalho (CLT) would have to be changed drastically. This required an investment in parliamentary politics to change the existing institutions and approve laws which could facilitate workers' organization.

The other route was to increase the level of organization at the plant level, creating councils and concentrating collective bargaining in the firm. In addition to being closer to the workers' problems, this strategy also forced employers to negotiate with unions, instead of going directly to the Labour Justice. This meant a *decentralization* of the collective bargaining process.

In a survey of workers' leaders in São Paulo in 1981, 72 per cent of those interviewed considered the organization at the plant level an important instrument to increase unions' strength. Sixty-one per cent considered changes in the law to legalize the existence of a strike fund and 76 per cent considered changes in the strike law as other important aspects to attain this objective (CEDEC, 1981, quoted in Castro, 1988, p. 121).

The first move in the direction of a more centralized union organization was the creation of a central union, at the national level, the Central Unica dos Trabalhadores (CUT). This was followed by the creation of another central union, the Confederaçao Geral dos Trabalhadores (CGT), linked to a different political group. The objective was to unify labour demands, assist affiliated unions in the process of collective bargaining, and elect new labour leaders. Some specific demands of the CUT are a multi-annual collective labour contract with national coverage, minimum wage adjustment clauses, better working conditions and simultaneity of collective bargaining for all workers.

Even before the creation of the CUT, a political party was also created, the Party of the Workers (PT), which was intimately linked to the labour movement. Candidates for parliamentary and executive elections all over the country were backed by this party. Since the beginning, it was composed of different groups, a minority representing the extreme left, and most of the party affiliates linked to the CUT and to the left of the Catholic Church. Instead of being dependent on the state (which characterized the labour movement until 1975) the new unionism linked itself to the parliamentary process.

This link between unions and the party transformed most of the demands of the CUT into important political issues in parliament. The rapid growth of the CUT in the labour movement and that of the PT in the political dimension generated an impressive process of union centralization and increasing political importance of labour *qua* social group in Brazilian society. The change to a civilian government in 1985 reinforced this process.

The increasing importance of the labour movement and its close link to the parliamentary process became quite clear during the debates over the new Brazilian Constitution, voted in 1987–88. Although the PT elected only a small minority of representatives, capital–labour relations and workers' rights turned out to be one of the most important issues in the discussions. Many suggestions were presented by the PT and a large part of the workers' demands were approved after a heated public dispute with the employers' representatives, where the traditional arguments were raised about increasing rigidities in the labour market, instability of the economic process and effects of the increase in labour costs on employment and inflation.

The main changes in the institutions affecting capital–labour relations were freedom to organize unions, autonomy from the government, and the almost unrestricted right to strike. These are now inscribed in the constitution as rights of the workers. After the promulgation of the new constitution, the old labour code became practically irrelevant, although parts of it (such as the compulsory contribution and the monopoly of representation) were maintained. It should be noted that the two central unions could not reach agreement on these aspects of capital–labour relations.

Also very important were the creation of workers' councils at the plant level, the greater importance given in bargaining to the day-to-day problems of the workers and decentralization of collective bargaining. The decentralization of collective bargaining can be inferred by the comparison of the number of conventions (the result of a negotiation between a union and an employer organization) in relation to the number of accords (the result of a negotiation between a union and one individual employer). In 1982, the number of conventions signed was 42 per cent higher than the number of accords. In 1985, the number of accords was three times that of conventions (see Castro, 1988, p. 139). In São Paulo, the accords represented 42 per cent of the total in 1979, 66 per cent in 1983 and

77 per cent in 1987 (Pastore and Zylberstajn, 1983, p. 113). Thus, in 1987, 77 per cent of all negotiations in the industrial sector of São Paulo were completed at the firm level.

The unions also implemented workers' organization at the firm level through the shop steward, and workers' councils. Data on the number of these institutions in Brazil are difficult to obtain, but some indications are available. In 1981, in a research conducted by the CEDEC in São Paulo, 31 per cent of the workers interviewed said there was a workers' council in their occupation. From these, 53 per cent were introduced by the union's initiative and 23 per cent by the workers directly. Sixty per cent of the workers interviewed said the workers' councils maintained contact with the occupational union. Finally, 35 per cent of the workers said the objective of the workers' councils was to deal with questions specifically related to the firm. As for shop stewards, 30 per cent said they existed in their occupation and 60 per cent of them were identified directly by the workers in the firm. Given that the research was conducted in 1981, the numbers are quite expressive.

The firms resisted the growth of union activity at the firm level in many ways. In the same research, 43 per cent of the workers interviewed said the firms did not hire workers affiliated with the unions, 43 per cent said the most active workers in their firms were dismissed and 42 per cent said firing workers was a way to avoid workers' activity at the firm level. Items such as constant surveillance in the plant, prohibition to circulate union newspapers and denunciation of activists to the police were cited by more than 40 per cent of the workers as means commonly utilized by firms to reduce workers' militancy (see Castro, 1988, pp. 125–36).

In an analysis of a sample of conventions and accords registered in the Ministry of Labour office in São Paulo, Castro also found a sharp increase in the number of demands to create workers' councils and shop stewards after 1982, as well as to increase protection for the members of these institutions from their employers' discretion. This increase was particularly important in 1984 and 1985, the last year the research covered (Castro, 1988, pp. 134–48).

VI THE CRISIS OF THE 1980s: CONFLICT, INDEXATION AND WAGE DISPERSION

The 1980s in Brazil were characterized by a progressive increase in the degree of conflict between the most important social groups, in particular organized labour and capital, as well as a gradual process of disorganization of the economic system. As a result, the country entered the 1990s immersed in a social and economic crisis. In this section we discuss the origins and developments of this crisis.

After a decade of authoritarian military governments, political dissension emerged in the second half of the 1970s. As in other countries, the transition to democracy in Brazil was marked by an increase in popular mobilization against the economic and political exclusion of the masses. The transition in Brazil was gradual, and it took almost a decade before a civilian government was elected. Hirshman (1986), commenting on the political opening process in Brazil, refers to the social tensions which generally show up during transitions to democracy:

> When a civilian, democratic government first comes into power after a long period of repressive military rule, it is normal for various, newly active groups of the reborn civil society – particularly the long-repressed trade unions – to stake substantial claims for higher incomes ... New inflationary and balance-of-payments pressures are of course likely to result from the granting of such demands ... (p. 39)

The increase in strike activity between 1978 and 1986 indicates how dissatisfied workers were with their standard of living and the degree of distributive conflict. As Table 5.10 indicates, during this period the number of strikes grew continuously (with the exception of 1980 and 1982), and increased significantly in 1979, 1983 and 1986. It is also clear that the most active groups were the industrial workers and the middle-class wage-earners. In the first group, the workers of the most organized segment – those in the metallurgy industry – were responsible for 34 per cent of the strikes. Also, 74 per cent of the strikes between 1978 and 1986 took place in the southwest of the country where the most active and organized unions were based.

Table 5.10   Number of strikes in Brazil, 1978–86

	1978	1979	1980	1981	1982	1983	1984	1985	1986
Industrial	84	77	43	41	73	189	317	246	534
workers	(72)	(31)	(29)	(27)	(50)	(54)	(64)	(39)	(53)
Middle-class	8	55	43	46	31	85	84	211	237
workers	(7)	(22)	(29)	(3)	(21)	(24)	(17)	(34)	(23)
Housing	8	20	19	7	4	10	18	23	45
industry	(7)	(8)	(13)	(5)	(3)	(4)	(4)	(5)	(5)
Others	5	44	18	34	11	16	11	14	1
	(4)	(18)	(12)	(22)	(8)	(5)	(2)	(2)	(0)
Total	118	246	144	150	144	347	492	619	817
	(100)	(100)	(100)	(100)	(100)	(100)	(100)	(100)	(100)

Source: NEPP/Unicamp, reproduced from Tavares de Almeida (1988)

Over the last three years up to time of writing, union militancy has spread out over the country. The movement began in the industrial sectors of São Paulo and gradually other sectors of the labour force organized and demanded wage adjustments and improved working conditions. In 1984, the strikes of metal-lurgical workers in São Paulo accounted for almost 40 per cent of the total number of strikes in Brazil. In the following years this percentage was 15 per cent (1985), 30 per cent (1986), 10 per cent (1987) and 5 per cent (1988).[7] The growth of the union movement around the country is part of the strategy of the most active central union (CUT).

As a response to the mobilization of the labour movement, the government has altered its wage policy many times since the mid-1970s. Two alterations in the policy deserve consideration. First, the adjustment period of money wages was gradually reduced from one year to six months in 1979, and since then has fallen to its current one month period in 1988–89. The progressive indexation of wages through the wage policy can be seen as the government's attempt to reduce the degree of dissatisfaction of workers, and thus the degree of conflict. However, with increasing inflation, the reduction of the adjustment period is never sufficient to protect the purchasing power of wages. As a result, the degree of conflict has been growing during the late 1980s.

The second change is an attempt to mitigate inflation by reducing the degree of indexation of higher wages. Between 1979 and 1985 the rate of adjustment of wages at the lower end of the distribution was higher than the past rate of inflation, whereas the rate of adjustment for higher wages was smaller than inflation. In doing this the government was able to undermine the capacity of the most organized unions to obtain wage increases above the inflation rate or even in line with it. However, these unions, whose workers' wages were higher than the average, were usually able to negotiate adjustments with their employers which were above those determined by the policy.

Thus the central elements in understanding the relation between conflict, inflation and the distribution of income in the 1980s relate to the political dissension and transition into a democracy, the re-emergence of labour activism (and the centralization of the movement), and the progressive indexation of wages. The combination of these elements explain the acceleration of the rate of inflation, and the increase in wage dispersion between the wages of the less and those of the more organized groups. Hence, in the last decade there has been a tendency towards a deepening of the economic dualization of the labour market.

When we associate the above elements with the acceleration of inflation, it should be clear that the progressive indexation of wages and the rise of labour activism are not the only factors affecting prices. In fact, they may be seen as a response to the acceleration of inflation. The attempts to change relative prices in favour of tradables through devaluations of the domestic currency and the resistance of the unions to reduced real wages are central to explain changes in the rate of inflation in the early 1980s. On the other hand, the behaviour of firms plays an important part in fixing prices, and the effect is growing uncertainty over this decision.[8]

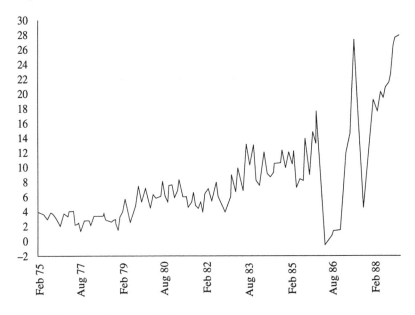

Figure 5.1   Monthly rate of inflation

The acceleration of inflation in the last decade can be seen as the result of an attempt by the different social groups to protect the purchasing power of their incomes. The capacity of the groups within the labour force and that of employers to resist reductions in their incomes differ significantly. In Figure 5.1, where the trajectory of the monthly rate of inflation is depicted, there are five points of inflection corresponding to:

1. The first half of 1979 after an attempt to increase the domestic price of energy.
2. The second half of 1983 after a maxi-devaluation of the domestic currency.
3. The second half of 1985, one year after the economy recovered from a long recession, when the level of union activism increased and firms were anticipating a price freeze.
4. The first half of 1987 after one year of the price freeze.
5. The first half of 1988, after six months of the price freeze.

During these ten years, the functional distribution of income, and the distribution of the wage income in particular, changed dramatically. These changes resulted from a combination of different economic policies and the heterogeneity of the labour force (in terms of the degree of organization of the different segments) and of the capitalists (in terms of the capacity to mark-up costs of firms in different sectors of the economy).

In Figures 5.2 and 5.3, which refer to data for the industrial sector in Brazil, we look at the movement of the productivity of labour; the real wage; the product wage; the wage share in industry; and the ratio of the real wage to labour productivity. In Figures 5.4 and 5.5, we look at the same data for the industrial sector in São Paulo.[9]

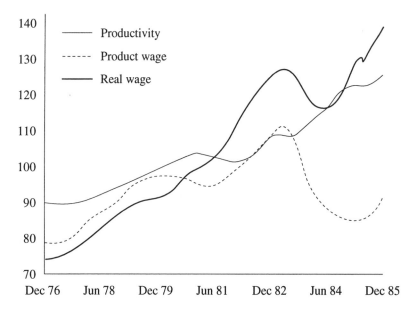

Figure 5.2 Data for the industrial sector in Brazil: productivity, real wage and product wage

The first point worth noting is that productivity (as measured by the relation between output and employment) grew continuously over the period. Between 1976 and mid-1979 the product wage grew faster than labour productivity, implying an increase in the share of labour in industrial output. Over 1980, the product wage and the share of wages fell due to the first maxi-devaluation of the cruzeiro and the acceleration of inflation. The real wage grew from 1976 to 1980, which implies that the wage in the industrial sector was growing faster than the price index of the consumption basket.

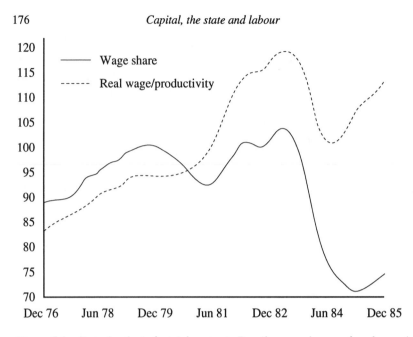

*Figure 5.3   Data for the industrial sector in Brazil: wage share and real wage/
                productivity*

In 1981 and 1982, despite a strong recession, the real wage and product wage
increased. However, after the second maxi-devaluation of the currency early
in 1983, and after two years of growing unemployment, they fell, and only started
to recover in mid-1984.

In São Paulo the share of wages in industry fell almost continuously from
March 1979 to August 1985. In the industrial sector for Brazil as a whole, it
recovered in 1981 and 1982, but then plunged, by more than 30 per cent in 1983.

What is interesting to note in these figures is that while the product wage
exhibits volatile behaviour over the period and the share of wages in industrial
output falls (continuously in São Paulo and abruptly in Brazil in 1983), the real
wage grew almost continuously over the whole period. The reason for this is
that the prices of the non-industrial sectors (agriculture, commerce, services)
were growing more slowly than wages in the industrial sector.

There are clear indications of changes in the distribution of income between
agents in the industrial and agents in the non-industrial sectors. As can be seen
in Table 5.11, the wages paid in the non-industrial sectors fall over the period in
relation to the average wage paid in industry (data for Brazil). This may be taken
as an indication that there is a redistribution of the wage fund from workers in
the agriculture, services and commerce sectors to workers in the industrial sector.

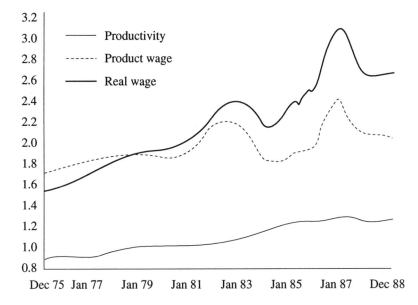

Figure 5.4 Data for the industrial sector in São Paulo: productivity, real wage and product wage

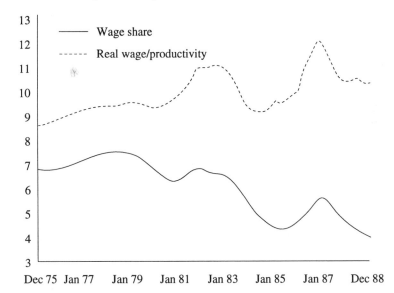

Figure 5.5 Data for the industrial sector in São Paulo: wage share and real wage/productivity

Table 5.11   Relative wages in Brazil (wage of sector over average wage in industry), 1980–86

	1980	1981	1982	1983	1984	1985	1986
General industry	1.00	1.00	1.00	1.00	1.00	1.00	1.00
non-metal minerals	0.78	0.78	0.78	0.78	0.76	0.82	0.77
metallurgy	1.22	1.23	1.24	1.23	1.21	1.22	1.24
mechanics	1.31	1.31	1.31	1.32	1.30	1.31	1.37
electrical material	1.31	1.33	1.34	1.37	1.40	1.38	1.35
transport material	1.46	1.49	1.57	1.62	1.67	1.65	1.59
wood	0.52	0.51	0.51	0.51	0.49	0.48	0.49
furniture	0.61	0.61	0.60	0.58	0.57	0.57	0.59
paper	1.07	1.08	1.10	1.11	1.12	1.14	1.17
chemical	1.92	1.92	1.99	2.03	2.04	2.05	2.00
plastic material	0.97	0.92	0.94	0.90	0.90	0.90	0.88
textile	0.75	0.76	0.76	0.76	0.77	0.78	0.81
clothing	0.52	0.52	0.51	0.50	0.50	0.48	0.51
foodstuff	0.69	0.70	0.69	0.70	0.69	0.67	0.67
publishing	1.07	1.06	1.05	1.03	0.99	1.01	1.05
Public utilities	1.78	1.79	1.80	1.77	1.69	1.72	1.96
Construction	0.79	0.77	0.76	0.74	0.73	0.71	0.77
Commerce	0.71	0.69	0.68	0.66	0.65	0.66	0.66
Services	1.20	1.16	1.19	1.13	1.06	1.06	1.06
transportation	0.99	1.00	0.99	0.98	0.94	0.94	0.93
communication	1.33	1.35	1.34	1.43	1.33	1.41	1.44
housing and food	0.47	0.46	0.45	0.44	0.43	0.41	0.44
personal	0.76	0.73	0.72	0.70	0.65	0.64	0.68
commercial	1.01	0.97	1.03	0.92	0.90	0.86	0.89

Source: RAIS.

We note that the relative wages of workers in the electrical materials, transport materials, paper, chemicals and metallurgy industries were above the average in 1980 and grew relative to the average wage paid in industry over the succeeding years. The wages of workers in the furniture, plastics, clothing, and foodstuff industries were below the average and suffered a relative reduction. The same is true, although the tendency is considerably stronger, for wages in the public utilities, construction, commerce and services sectors. Hence there was an increase in wage dispersion in the economy.

The same conclusion can be drawn if we look at the relationship between the average wage paid in the industrial sector (data for São Paulo) and the institutional minimum wage. The latter can be seen as a proxy for the wage paid to workers in the lower bound of the distribution of wages in the economy. As seen in Figure 5.6, the ratio increased continuously over the period, growing 68 per cent in twelve years.

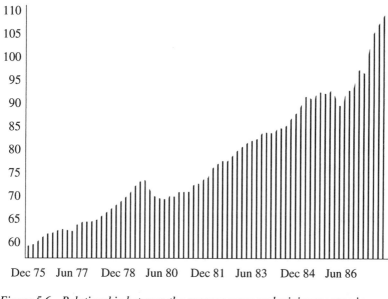

Figure 5.6   Relationship between the average wage and minimum wage in São Paulo

Wage dispersion as measured by the coefficient of variation of wages paid in the industrial sector (data for São Paulo) also confirms the conclusion that the distribution of wages became more unequal during the last years. In Figure 5.7 the coefficient of variation grew continuously between 1978 and 1987.

As Table 5.12 indicates, the relative wages paid to workers outside the industrial sector fell. Also the relationship between the components of the consumer price index[10] and the average industrial price index fell continuously over the period. As an example, in ten years, the ratio of the consumer price of foodstuff to the industrial price index fell 40 per cent.

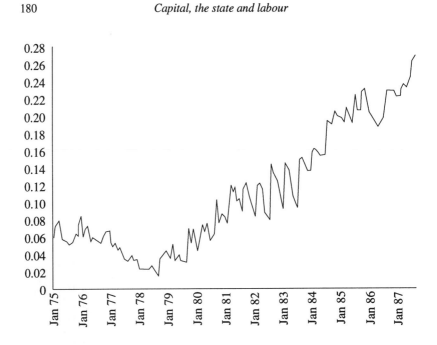

Figure 5.7   Coefficient of variation of wages in São Paulo

Table 5.12   Relative prices in Brazil, CPI components/WPI (base 1977 = 100)

	Foodstuffs	Housing	Transport	Clothing	Health	Personal Services	Education
1977	100.00	100.00	100.00	100.00	100.00	100.00	100.00
1978	101.50	101.15	102.04	106.14	98.56	99.88	104.81
1979	100.70	103.43	98.09	108.83	92.58	98.11	102.74
1980	93.38	100.77	83.90	118.93	81.18	90.03	89.94
1981	83.98	91.24	72.13	124.20	68.99	83.81	78.87
1982	79.25	83.24	66.44	121.28	64.78	85.19	80.60
1983	76.71	82.79	61.01	118.88	59.42	80.63	79.87
1984	69.44	83.86	48.53	108.12	45.67	70.22	67.44
1985	58.99	71.48	38.69	100.45	45.04	59.82	57.35
1986	57.95	75.69	34.58	90.41	53.88	59.02	54.51

Source: FIGBE/INPC.

In 1986 these tendencies changed dramatically. Both wages and prices in the non-industrial sectors grew relative to wages and prices in the industrial sectors, respectively. This was a result of a price freeze imposed for one year during the Cruzado Plan.[11] Since 1986, two other price freeze plans were launched and the economic stabilization results were disastrous. These plans resulted in a further disorganization of the economic relations, and an increase in the degree of distributive conflict. The data available for São Paulo indicate that in industry the product wage and the share of wages have been falling continuously, whereas the real wage fell in 1987 and stabilized in 1988.

We conclude from this analysis that the relationships among capital, labour and the state are immersed in a deep crisis. The acceleration of inflation, the increase in wage dispersion and the recurrent changes in the distribution of income between profits and wages (as illustrated by the ups and downs in the share of wages in the industry) reflect this crisis.

The re-emergence of labour activism in certain sectors of the economy is an important part of understanding the developments over the last ten years. The resistance of capitalists to accept this new reality and their attempt to block the progress of labour is at the root of the conflict. Weak actors both amongst capital and labour have been suffering from losses in their share of income.

VII CONCLUDING REMARKS

This analysis began by demonstrating that the Brazilian labour market is quite heterogeneous. There is a modern segment where workers are unionized, and other sectors in which capital–labour relations may or may not have legal status. We noted that the state through the Ministry of Labour and the Labour Justice played a paternalistic role, and that the labour code induced a very corporatist structure. We argued that even in the modern sectors working conditions are quite bad and workers' rights are almost non-existent: job security is absent, labour turnover is high, workers' representation at the firm level is prohibited, the rhythm of work is exhausting and there is rigid control of the labour process.

At the macro-level, we noted that nothing like a 'Fordist compromise' can be identified in Brazil – not even in the most modern sectors. Real wages do grow occasionally in certain sectors but the share of wages in industry (even in São Paulo) is extremely low, and has fallen over the 1980s. The structural transformations which took place in the last three decades gave rise to an industrial labour force. Workers' dissatisfaction with the distribution of the fruits of progress has led to the formation of a strong union movement which has been demanding changes in the conservative labour relations as prescribed in the labour laws.

The 'new unionism' of the 1980s has changed the face of the relationship among capital, labour and the state. The movement has grown quickly during the 1980s, and has resulted in a new union structure which has strong ties with the workers in the factories and is centralized at the national level. Their demands for better working conditions, and rights such as job security and workers' representation have met strong opposition from employers. The strongest unions have been able to succeed in most of their demands. However there is still a long way to go before the majority of the workers have the same rights.

In those sectors where workers maintain a legal relation with their employers, the central unions (especially CUT) have been able to mobilize workers. In recent years, the distributive conflict between organized labour and capital can be seen as a positive-sum game in which gains have been shared by the two groups. But the conflict between organized and non-organized segments of society is a zero-sum game which the latter group has been losing.

The centralization of the union structure and the creation of a very active Workers' Party may extend the benefits of the stronger unions to all workers with a legal status. Hence, we are led to believe that the widening of the wage dispersion in the 1980s will give place to a more egalitarian distribution of the wage income. On the other hand, there are indications that the growth of the movement at the national level will force employers to share productivity gains with workers, and maybe even lead to a redistribution of income in favour of wages.

The optimism of the last paragraph should not be exaggerated. Employers in Brazil have been quite resistant to change, and so far they have been able to partially block the growth of the labour movement. However, there is a huge number of workers whose relation with capital does not have a legal status. It will take some time before they can become part of the legal system and part of the organized segment of the labour force.

NOTES

1. Indeed, we shall note in Section VI that over the period 1975–88 both the profit margins and the purchasing power of wages in relation to productivity gains grew almost continually in the industrial sectors in the state of São Paulo.
2. In an interesting analysis of labour-market institutions in Latin America, Collier and Collier (1979) note that in the region 'governments have commonly sought to exercise control over labor movements and that within this context of control, the concept of corporatism captures an important aspect of the network of hierarchical relationships through which labor organizations come to be dependent and penetrated by the state'. They use the distinction between state corporatism and societal corporatism due to Schmitter. In the former, which they associate with the Latin American case, the state creates institutional structures in order to control certain groups which then become dependent on the state. Societal corporatism refers to systems in which the legitimacy of the state depends on the support of independent social groups. For another view of the development of the labour institutions in Latin America, see Banuri and Amadeo (1989).

3   This pattern of growth has a counterpart in the distribution of income which has deteriorated since the early 1960s.
4.   The quotations were translated by the authors.
5.   The quotations are taken from a study of the labour movement in Brazil after 1978 (Abramo, 1986). They are the words of workers in large companies such as Volkswagen, Perkings Motor Company, Ford, Scania, etc.
6.   Explicitly, the objective of 'the wage policy is to maintain the share of workers on the benefits from growth', quoted from the 1965 government economic plan (PAEG).
7.   See La Rocque (1989).
8.   See Amadeo and Camargo (1989a) for a formal analysis of the inflationary process and stabilization policies in Brazil.
9.   We define:

   - productivity of labour as the ratio $x = X/N$ where X is the level of output and N the level of employment;
   - real wage as the ratio $r = W/CPI$ where W stands for money wage and CPI for consumer price index;
   - product wage as the ratio $w = W/WPI$ where WPI stands for wholesale price index; and
   - wage share as the ratio w/x.

10. Foodstuffs, clothing, personal services, health and shelter.
11. See Amadeo and Camargo (1989b) for an analysis of the Cruzado Plan in Brazil, and especially the changes in the distribution of income and relative prices.

REFERENCES

Abramo, L. (1986) 'O Resgate da Dignidade', M.A. dissertation, USP, São Paulo.

Amadeo, E. and T. Banuri (1990) 'Policy, Governance, and the Management of Conflict', in T. Banuri (ed.) *Economic Liberalization: No Panacea*, Oxford: Clarendon Press.

Amadeo, E.J. and J.M. Camargo (1989a) 'A structuralist model of inflation and stabilization', mimeo, WIDER/UNU, Helsinki.

Amadeo, E.J. and J.M. Camargo (1989b) 'Market structure, relative prices and income distribution: an analysis of heterodox shock experiments', mimeo, WIDER/UNU, Helsinki.

Amadeo, E.J. and J.M. Camargo (1989c) 'Choque e Concerto', forthcoming in *Dados*.

Amadeo, E.J. and J.M. Camargo (1989d) 'Política salarial e negociaçöes: perspectivas para o futuro', mimeo, OIT/Ministério do Trabalho.

Bacha, E. and L. Taylor (1978) 'Brazilian income distribution in the 60's: facts, model results, and the controversy', *Journal of Development Studies*.

Banuri, T. and E. Amadeo (1990) 'Worlds within the Third World: labour market institutions in Asia and Latin America', in T. Banuri (ed.) *Economic Liberalization: No Panacea*, Oxford: Clarendon Press.

Bonelli, R. and G.L. Sedlacek (1989) 'Distribuição de renda: evolução no último quarto de século', in Sedlacek and Paes de Barros (1989).

Bontempo, H.C. (1987) 'Transferências externas e financiamento do governo', *Pesquisa e Planejamento Econômico*, São Paulo: USP.

Boyer, R. (ed.) (1986) *La Flexibilidad del Trabajo en Europa*, Ministerio del Trabajo y seguridad Social, Madrid.

Camargo, J.M. (1980) 'A nova política salarial, distribuição de renda e inflação', *Pesquisa e Planejamento Econômico*, São Paulo: USP.

Camargo, J.M. (1981) 'A nova política salarial, distribuição de renda e inflação – uma réplica', *Pesquisa e Planejamento Econômico*.

Camargo, J.M. (1989) 'Informalização e renda no mercado de trabalho', in Sedlacek and Paes de Barros (1989).

Cardoso, E. and E. Reis (1986) 'Deficits, Dívidas e Inflação no Brasil', *Pesquisa e Planejamento Econômico*, São Paulo: USP.

Castro, A. B. and F.E. Pires (1985) *A Economia brasileira em marcha forçada*, Rio de Janeiro: Paz e Terra.

Castro, M. (1988) *Participação ou Controle: o dilema da atuação operária nos locais de trabalho*, São Paulo: IPE.

Collier, R. and D. Collier (1979) 'Inducements versus Constraints: disaggregating "corporatism"', *American Political Science Review*, vol. 73, no. 4.

FIGBE *Indice National de Precos ao Consumidor*, various numbers, Rio de Janerio.

Hirshman, A. (1986) 'The Political Economy of Latin American Development: Seven Exercises in Retrospect', paper for the XIII International Congress of the Latin American Studies Association, Boston, October 1986.

Hoffman, R. (1989) 'Evolução da distribuição da renda no Brasil, entre pessoas e entre famílias, 1979–86' in Sedlacek and Paes de Barros (1989).

Humphrey, J. (1988) 'Gênero e Processo de Trabalho', in *Anais do Seminário sobre Padröes Tecnológicos e Políticas de Gestão*, São Paulo: USP.

Jatobá, J. (1989) 'A dimensão regional da pobreza urbana e os mercados de trabalho: o caso brasileiro, 1970–83', in Sedlacek and Paes de Barros (1989).

Langoni, G. (1973) *Distribuição de Renda e desenvolvimento econômico no Brasil*, Rio de Janeiro: Expressão e Cultura.

La Rocque, E. de (1989) 'Sindicalismo Brasileiro', undergraduate monograph.

Le Ven, M. (1988) 'Padröes Tecnológicos e Formas de Uso e Controleda Força de Trabalho', in *Anais do Seminário sobre Padröes Tecnológicos e Políticas de Gestão*, São Paulo: USP.

Ministerio do Trabalho, *Registro Anual de Informacoes Sociais (RAIS)*, various numbers, Brasilia.

Pastore, J., H. Zylberstajn, and C. Pagotto (1983) *Mudança social e pobreza no Brasil 1970–1980*, São Paulo: FIPE/USP.

Reisen, H. and A. Trotsenburg (1988) 'Developing countries' debt: the budgetary and transfer problem', Paris: OECD.

Rodrigues, L.M. (1979) 'Tendencias futuras do sindicalismo brasileiro', *Rivista de Administracao de Empresas*, vol. 4, October–December.

Sabóia, J. (1988) 'Dualismo ou Integração do mercado de trabalho?', Texto para Discussão, UFRJ.

Sedlacek, G. and R. Paes de Barros (1989) *Mercado de trabalho e distribuição de renda: uma coletânea*, Rio de Janeiro: IPEA.

Simonsen, M.H. (1983) 'Indexation: current theory and the Brazilian experience' in R. Dornbush and M.H. Simonsen (eds) *Inflation, Debt and Indexation*, Cambridge, Mass.: MIT Press.

Souza, A. and B. Lamounier (1981) 'Governo e sindicatos no Brasil: a perspectiva dos anos 80', *Dados*.

Tavares de Almeida, M.H. (1988) 'Dificil caminho: sindicatos e politica na contruacao da democracia' in F.W. Rice and G. O'Donnell (eds) *A democracia no Brasil: delamas e perspectivas*, São Paulo: Vertice.

Werneck, R. (1986) 'Poupança estatal, dívida externa e crise financeira do estado', *Pesquisa e Planejamento Econômico*.

Werneck, R. (1987) 'Public sector adjustment to external shocks and domestic pressures in Brazil', Discussion Paper, PUC/RJ.

6. Capital, the state and labour in Malaysia

K.S. Jomo

I INTRODUCTION

Since being appointed in mid-1981, Malaysian Prime Minister Mahathir Mohamad has tried to reshape capital–labour relations in Malaysia in line with his desire to accelerate economic growth and modernization, especially industrialization. His early efforts to promote heavy industries as part of a second round of import substitution (after the first round petered out from the mid-1960s onwards) involved a rapid increase in government-guaranteed foreign borrowing. The resulting debt and fiscal crisis (see Jomo, 1990a) led to various structural adjustments and economic liberalization from the mid-1980s. Since the late 1980s, economic growth – based on export-orientated industrialization under foreign, especially East Asian, auspices – has picked up.

Although Mahathir's economic, and especially his industrialization policies changed dramatically in midstream, his administration's labour policies have been far more consistent. Soon after becoming Prime Minister, he announced various new policies, including a highly controversial 'Look East' policy (see Jomo, 1985). His Look East initiative has been variously interpreted by both supporters and detractors. Initially, this policy was widely believed to refer to changing foreign orientation in a wide variety of matters. Fairly or unfairly, it has been associated with other policy changes of the early 1980s, e.g. state intervention to develop heavy industries (Pura, 1985), state encouragement for the establishment of large Japanese-style sogososha trading agencies (Chee and Lee, 1983), privatization and efforts to improve relations between the ethnically Malay-dominated government and the predominantly Sino-Malaysian business community known as the 'Malaysian Incorporated' policy. Looking East has also been seen as favouring Japanese and South Korean construction – an estimated six billion ringgit of construction projects are believed to have been given to such companies in the early 1980s (e.g. Chang, 1985) – and other firms, particularly at the expense of Britain, the former colonial power, after a series of inter-governmental tiffs in the early 1980s.

However, the Look East policy emphasis from the outset was clearly on labour. After considerable criticism (not least by those disfavoured by the new preferences) and some experience (much of which has been very costly, e.g. with heavy industries and the sogososha experiments), Mahathir emphasized that the main thrust in Looking East should involve the inculcation of Japanese-style work ethics, mainly referring to efforts to increase productivity through harder work and greater loyalty to the company, and presumably management as well (Muto, 1985). Malaysians, especially Malay workers, were exhorted to work harder to raise productivity. Workers were told to abandon antagonistic British-style trade unionism in favour of loyalty to the company as a citizen is expected to be loyal to the nation. To further this other aspect of 'Malaysian Incorporated', the government would officially encourage 'in-house' or company unions instead of the existing national or (in the case of textiles and clothing) regional/statewide unions. Quality control circles (QCCs) as well as several other Japanese labour management institutions were encouraged, while selected workers – mainly those employed in the recently established heavy industries – were sent for brief training and exposure stints in Japan and, to a lesser extent, in South Korea.

There was little or no mention of other key aspects of Japanese industrial relations, notably guaranteed lifelong employment and the seniority wage system (see Jomo, 1985). As Lazonick has pointed out in Chapter 3 of this volume, these features have proved to be crucial complements to company unionism in a system where wage determination is undertaken at the enterprise, rather than at the industry level. For the Malaysian private sector, collective bargaining, in so far as it exists, is largely conducted at the enterprise level, except for the still sizeable plantation. However, the number of employees in most Malaysian companies is so small that most in-house unions are relatively ineffective. Also there are no industry-wide trade union federations which might help overcome the disadvantages of minuscule company unions. Hiring and firing are management prerogatives which workers cannot legally challenge since the relevant laws were introduced. Hence, employment security does not exist outside the public sector in an economy very vulnerable to the vicissitudes of global business cycles. Without a seniority wage system to reward experience and company loyalty, it is not surprising that job-hopping and mobility are common when employment conditions are favourable.

In other words, the Look East policy exhorted Malaysian workers to work harder, produce more and serve their managements loyally without requiring or conceding any significant or substantial material incentives by way of company welfarism. And while the Japanese 'achievement' in this regard has involved complex culturally and historically rooted systems of material incentives (e.g. including guaranteed lifelong employment and the seniority wage system), the Malaysian version has emphasized virtually costless work ethics (Chandra,

1983a), quality control circles (QCCs) (Ryder, 1985) and in-house unions (Chandra, 1983b). Not surprisingly, then, most Malaysian workers have not been converted to the Look East policy although there has not been any significant trade union or other resistance or opposition to it. Nevertheless, the Look East policy has significantly shaped and defined the Malaysian government's labour policy in the 1980s as it well might for the 1990s.

Mahathir's own attitude to labour is long-standing. In the 1960s, he clashed with the leaders of the Transport Workers' Union (TWU) – who now identify with the parliamentary opposition and lead the Malaysian Trade Unions' Congress (MTUC) – and tried to get the predominantly Malay workers of the Sri Jaya bus company to form their own in-house union. One of his most trusted business allies, Eric Chia, successfully crushed a union-organizing effort by the Transport Equipment Industry Workers' Union in the mid-1970s by setting up a management-sponsored in-house union. Shortly before becoming premier, Mahathir personally intervened in the Malaysian Airlines System (MAS) workers' industrial actions in 1978–79, that were harshly put down by the government, which resorted to using the Internal Security Act (ISA) to arrest, interrogate and detain the MAS employees' leaders without trial.

To further reduce the possibility of the recurrence of such industrial actions, the government amended the labour laws in 1980 and encouraged a split between government and private-sector unions. Influenced by the low unemployment levels and rising wages of the period and the neighbouring Singapore government's so-called Second Industrial Revolution – which attempted to attract 'high-tech' industry at the expense of older, more labour-intensive manufacturing (Rodan, 1989) – the government offered better overtime pay rates and retrenchment benefits as a sop, only to withdraw them in 1988 as part and parcel of creating a more attractive investment (including industrial relations) environment.

After more than two decades of the electronics industry's existence, workers there remain largely unorganized. If allowed to form a single national union, it could potentially have about 100,000 members, i.e. certainly the largest in the manufacturing sector, and possibly throughout the country because of declining membership in the National Union of Plantation Workers (NUPW) to about 70,000. The Labour Ministry has consistently refused to allow the Electrical Industry Workers' Union (EIWU) to unionize them, claiming that the electrical and electronics industries are distinct. In the 1980s, employees in a Japanese electronics factory in Penang quietly formed an in-house union, but American firms, which dominate the industry, have been particularly adamant in opposing unionization.

In 1988, the AFL–CIO (American Federation of Labour–Congress of Industrial Organization) petitioned the US Congress to withdraw Malaysia's GSP (General System of Preferences) privileges for violation of worker rights, particularly because of the Malaysian government's refusal to allow the 100,000 workers in the electronics industry to unionize. In late 1988, the Malaysian Labour Minister hastily agreed to unionization, only to qualify this shortly afterwards by only allowing in-house unions (Grace, 1990). Hence the protracted efforts to establish a national union for the electronics workers continue to be frustrated. Even the solitary effort to form an in-house union for employees of RCA (now Harris Solid State) has been repeatedly frustrated by management intransigence. However, although the AFL–CIO was unsuccessful, it is quite likely that pressure will continue to be exerted on the Malaysian government to recognize workers' rights. And it is likely that such pressure will have some favourable effect in strengthening labour's position.

From 1989, the Malaysian government has sought to further weaken the MTUC, still the main labour centre in the country, especially for private-sector employees. After the 1980 split between MTUC and CUEPACS (Congress of Unions of Employees in Public and Allied Civil Services) over the 1980 labour law amendments, the government recognized both as labour centres of equivalent status for representation at the annual international Labour Organization (ILO) meetings, i.e. effectively diminishing the MTUC's previous status as the sole labour centre for the country. Then, in 1989, it encouraged the National Union of Bank Employees (NUBE) secretary, Shanmugam, to form a third labour centre, the Malaysian Labour Organization (MLO). The MLO now claims fifteen union affiliates with a 100,000 members, compared to CUEPACS and the MTUC, each of which claims 2.5 to 3.5 times as many members and many more union affiliates. After the October 1990 general election, the MLO was officially sanctioned by the government, and by February 1991, Shanmugam was the sole labour representative in the Mahathir-appointed Malaysian Business Council, comprising government ministers, senior civil servants and prominent businessmen. In 1991, the law was amended to allow the unions for employees of government statutory bodies to affiliate with CUEPACS after serious conflicts between their leaders and leaders of CUEPACS, which previously only included government employees. Again, this move was intended to further erode MTUC affiliation and membership.

Hence, unlike the 'quasi-corporatism' of the early 1970s, official labour policy since the 1980s has deliberately undermined the already moderate and largely ineffectual trade union movement. Not surprisingly, then, MTUC leaders have increasingly identified themselves with the parliamentary opposition, although labour laws require that trade unionists cannot hold positions in political parties and vice versa.

However, it may well be the case that labour laws and the politics of official labour policy follow rather than determine capital–labour relations in Malaysia. For example, there is considerable evidence that labour flexibility in the manufacturing sector increased significantly between 1985 and 1988 (Standing, 1989).

(Recent unpublished research by Khong How Ling and Siti Rohani Yahya points to similar trends in the service sector as well as other sectors of the economy.) Presumably this is partly due to the weakening of labour's bargaining position as unemployment grew from 1983 when the government adopted deflationary policies, and especially during the severe 1985–86 recession (Jomo, 1990). However, there is also evidence of changing management policies and practices *vis-à-vis* labour, e.g. involving greater contracting out of supplies, and even of labour. Labour contracting is very common in plantation agriculture, land development and construction (Rema Devi, 1987), while the increasing use of cheaper illegal and legal immigrant workers from neighbouring Indonesia, the Philippines and Thailand has grown in recent years.

With greater economic specialization and sophistication, some increase in services and supplies contracting has been inevitable. The increased role of East Asian, especially Japanese investments, particularly in manufacturing, since the mid-1980s has been accompanied by the growing adoption of Japanese management techniques as well as product and process innovations. Hence, for instance, the increasing popularity of 'just-in-time' (JIT) production methods – requiring considerably reduced inventories with the availability of flexible and prompt supply sources – has strengthened domestic economic linkages while requiring greater supplier, especially labour, flexibility.

The preceding review of the last decade and the following overview of the historical development of capital–labour relations in Malaysia suggest that due to the relative openness of the Malaysian economy in terms of both international trade and foreign investments, Malaysia confirms somewhat broadly peripheral Fordist propositions about changing capital–labour relations (Lipietz, 1987). However, a fuller understanding of the Malaysian experience must be rooted in an appreciation of its history, especially as it has shaped the present.

II   CAPITAL–LABOUR RELATIONS IN HISTORICAL PERSPECTIVE

Employment of wage labour in Malaya on a large scale began as a consequence of growing capital investments in agriculture and mining, especially in the last century. These investments spread from commercial agriculture and international trade into tin mining in the late nineteenth century and rubber in the early twentieth century. The development of tin mines and rubber plantations required an abundant pool of labour. As most indigenous Malays preferred to remain as yeoman peasants rather than become subordinated as wage-earners with poor wages and living conditions, the colonial government and employers turned to the poverty-stricken rural masses in China and India for labour. With the large pool of immigrant labour available from India and China, the colonial Malayan government encouraged and even forced the Malay peasantry to produce more rice, rather than compete with capitalist interests involved in rubber and tin production. Until the early twentieth century, indentured labour was extensively used. With the decline of indenture, other usually informal modes of labour control – often related to immigration and credit – served to strengthen employers' control over labour. Only after the Great Crash of 1929 did labour immigration begin to stabilize.

Ethnic identification with occupation and employment status today has its roots in the racial division of labour which developed under British colonialism (Lim, 1984). In the interest of political stability to consolidate colonial rule, the British decided to allow and even encourage indigenous Malays to remain as yeoman peasants, preferably growing cheap rice to feed the growing immigrant labour population. The British-preferred source of labour was another colony, India, recruiting mainly Dravidians, especially Hindu Tamils, from the south. The colonial rulers also allowed, and sometimes even encouraged Chinese business interests to bring in their own labour supply from South China.

Trade expansion – especially after the British establishment of the Straits Settlements from the end of the eighteenth century – encouraged voluntary as well as involuntary (labour) immigration to service trade, the colonial state and commercial production. However, it was not until the massive expansion of tin mining – mainly using the labour-intensive open-cast method – in the second half of the last century and the rubber boom in the early part of this century that labour immigration, from China and India respectively, rose. And for a brief period, as Indian workers began to resist the oppressive conditions they were subjected to, the British sought to further diversify labour supply in order to better control it, by bringing in Javanese labour from the Dutch East Indies.

The ethnic breakdown of labour in the colonial period, especially before the Japanese Occupation, clearly reflected these labour immigration policies. For example, in 1911, 96 per cent of the 196,520 tin mine labourers were Chinese. With the subsequent decline of the more labour-intensive Chinese tin mining, in the face of the state-backed British dredging interests, employment in the industry declined, with the ethnic composition beginning to change correspondingly. By the Depression years of the early 1930s, total employment in tin mining had fallen by almost three-quarters to about 52,000 on average, with the Chinese proportion down to 85 per cent. As employment picked up in the late 1930s to about 75,000, the Chinese share continued to decline to 81 per cent. A decade later, after the disruption caused by the Japanese Occupation, the Chinese proportion had dropped to 69 per cent of the 45,000 employed, and by the first half of the 1960s, this share had fallen further to 61 per cent, with the total employment and ethnic ratios more stable until the tin collapse of the mid-1980s. As the Chinese share of employment in tin mining declined, Indian workers accounted for most of the increase before the war, i.e. from 2 per cent in 1911 to 13 per cent during 1936–40 and 12 per cent during 1961–65, with the Malay share rising after the war from 1 per cent in 1911 and 5 per cent during 1936–40 to 26 per cent in 1961–65 (Jomo, 1990b).

The number of workers employed in plantations has been only slightly less volatile while their ethnic breakdown remained more stable, at least until the 1950s. The number of estate labourers in the Federated Malay States first shot up from 57,070 in 1908 to 188,050 in 1912 and 237,134 in 1919, before falling to 156,341 in 1921, and then rising again to 258,780 in 1929, before falling again to 125,600 in 1932. The Indian share declined from 76.2 per cent in 1908 to 66.0 per cent in 1911, owing to rapid increases in recruitment of Chinese, Javanese and other labour, with the latter two declining thereafter, and the Chinese proportion continuing to rise only until the late 1920s, i.e. until the Great Depression (Parmer, 1960). For the next three decades until the Japanese Occupation, the Indian share of total estate employment fluctuated between two-thirds and 80 per cent, beginning to decline steadily after the war to about half by the 1980s (Jomo, 1986a).

However, it was not until 1940 that the British colonial government began to legally recognize trade unions as it belatedly attempted to seek popular support in the face of the Axis threat and the imminent Japanese invasion. Pre-war labour regulations had been primarily concerned with regulating labour supply, and with ensuring the welfare of employees in this connection. Labour administration was conducted along racial lines, with the colonial government in India displaying far greater concern for Indian labour in Malaya than the government of China for Chinese workers in the British colony. Although the recruitment and employment of Indian labour were far more centralized and regulated than for the Chinese, neither were substantially better off than the other. Both Indian and Chinese immigrant labour were often locked into dependent relations with their recruiters or employers. While Chinese labourers generally earned higher wages, this was partly offset by the accommodation and other facilities provided for most Indian labourers. All labourers suffered insecurity of employment, and were liable to be dismissed at the whim of their employers. Most had little protection against employers who defaulted on wage payments or failed to comply with labour regulations. However, subject to different employment conditions and more independent of the colonial government, Chinese immigrant labourers were generally better organized than their Indian counterparts – a factor which partly explains the uneven development of the labour movement among the different ethnic groups.

Rapid economic recovery after the Japanese Occupation in Britain's most valuable colony was complemented by militant labour organization under the leadership of the Communist Party of Malaya (CPM) until 1948, when all radical nationalist organizations were driven underground by the British colonial administration. The rebuilding of the colonial economy was followed by some socioeconomic reforms from the early 1950s as part of the British counter-insurgency strategy. After independence in 1957, the post-colonial government emphasized industrialization, agricultural diversification and infrastructural development without directly threatening the colonial economic structure. State intervention and the public sector grew from the early 1970s until the mid-1980s, largely for the purpose of inter-ethnic redistribution in favour of the majority indigenous Malay community. Economic 'liberalization' since then has been followed by a manufacturing-based boom since the late 1980s.

The Malaysian economy's considerable economic fluctuations have been exacerbated by its very open nature. (More than half of its GDP has been exported and a similar proportion has been imported for many years.) Nevertheless, on average, it has achieved a fairly high growth rate by international standards. While the agricultural sector has been relatively stagnant in the 1980s, the industrial and service sectors have grown tremendously in the post-war period, especially in the 1970s and since the late 1980s. Needless to say, such tremendous economic change has involved the labour force, with a growing proportion becoming waged employees, i.e. directly employed by capital.

Official data, including labour statistics, do not easily lend themselves to class analysis. There are several specific reasons for this in the Malaysian case. Besides the obvious fact that both colonial and post-colonial officials have simply not been interested in class analysis, there are several other factors which complicate the task. Pre-war data were very unevenly collected, reflecting the uneven development of colonial authority in Malaya. Even by the time the whole of Peninsular Malaysia was under direct and indirect British control at the outbreak of the First World War, colonial jurisdiction was not uniform between the three Straits Settlements (SS) ports of Penang, Malacca and Singapore (colonized by the British between 1786 and 1819), the four Federated Malay States (FMS) of Perak, Selangor, Negeri Sembilan and Pahang (indirectly ruled by the British from between 1874 and 1888) and the remaining five Unfederated Malay States (UMS) of Kedah, Perlis, Kelantan, Trengganu and Johore (which officially received British 'advice' from between 1909 and 1914). The varied quality of colonial statistics, especially before the Japanese Occupation, also reflected the uneven development of colonialism in Malaya.

The following discussion will primarily employ post-war data, which do not involve some of these earlier problems. Unfortunately, the census data are not evenly spaced, though in retrospect, the uneven timing offers certain advantages. The census data for 1947 offer a glimpse of the post-war situation, after a couple of years of recovery and before the disruption associated with the counter-insurgency known as the Emergency. The 1957 Census provides a picture in the year of Independence, while the 1970 Census offers a demographic profile of the country just before the New Economic Policy came into effect after the *laissez-faire* policies of the 1960s. The 1980 Census captures the situation after another decade of rapid growth, inflation and greatly increased wage employment before the impact of the generally recessionary 1980s. Unfortunately, there seem to be various differences in definition, categorization and modes of data collection, which greatly impair the overall picture. For example, the 1957 and 1970 Censuses did not distinguish between employers and own-account workers, while the number of unpaid family workers is inexplicably much larger in 1970 compared to the other census years, probably because of a more comprehensive definition employed. Nevertheless, the data by employment status do provide us with a crude, but useful picture of major categories in the census years.

According to official census data, the percentage of employees rose from 48 per cent in 1947 to 57 per cent in 1957, declining to 49 per cent in 1970, and then rising again to 61 per cent in 1980. The unexpected dip in 1970 is partly due to the sudden increase in the percentage of unpaid family workers to 17 per cent (476,624) in 1970, from 9 per cent (178,762) in 1947 and 8 per cent (176,864) in 1957; by 1980, this figure had dropped to 7 per cent (275,201). More significantly, the number of Malay unpaid family workers more than doubled from 141,436 in 1957 to 328,643 in 1970, while their Chinese counterparts quadrupled from 31,500 in 1957 to 129,689 in 1970 – presumably due to a more comprehensive definition used, which probably still does not include those engaged in 'housework' types of domestic labour. With increased wage employment through the 1970s, it is possible that though this broader definition was retained in 1980, unpaid family labour besides housework has declined in significance, both absolutely and relatively, as wage-labour relations displace petty commodity relations, including both peasant and artisan production as well as petty commerce.

As Tables 6.1, 6.2 and 6.3 show, the number of employees grew from 912,472 in 1947 to 1,200,881 in 1957, 1,374,164 in 1970 and 2,327,837 in 1980. These figures suggest that the number of employees rose by almost 290,000 during 1947–57, by over 170,000 during 1957–70, and by almost a million during the 1970s. One would expect these trends as wage employment picked up after the economic disruption caused by the war, followed by a period of relatively slow expansion of wage employment in the Alliance period of *laissez-faire* development and capital-intensive import-substituting industrialization after Independence in 1957. In the 1970s, employment in export-led manufacturing and the services (including public services) grew tremendously.

As we can see in Table 6.1, the number of own-account workers rose from 780,672 in 1947 to 1,039,538 in 1980, though the percentage of own-account workers dropped from 41 per cent in 1947 to 27 per cent in 1980, as shown in Tables 6.2 and 6.3. Such a relative decline in self-employment would reflect the other trends associated with capitalist transformation identified earlier. The number of employers also increased from only 24,220 (1.3 per cent) in 1947

Table 6.1   Employment status by ethnic group and gender, 1947, 1957,
*   1970 and 1980*

Employment Status	Malays			Chinese		
	Males	Females	Total	Males	Females	Total
1947						
Employer	3,334	752	4,086	15,858	860	16,718
Own-account worker	396,737	85,397	482,134	227,109	38,013	265,122
Unpaid family worker	54,684	86,613	141,297	18,618	14,531	33,149
Employee	186,714	44,701	231,415	314,410	83,446	397,856
In employment	641,469	217,463	858,932	575,995	136,850	712,845
1957						
Employer ⎫ Own-account worker ⎬	395,488	94,307	489,795	181,475	32,130	213,605
Unpaid family worker	55,492	85,944	141,436	19,278	12,222	31,500
Employee	301,366	68,965	370,331	369,526	141,264	510,710
In employment	752,346	249,216	1,001,562	570,279	185,616	755,815
1970						
Employer ⎫ Own-account worker ⎬	476,490	154,918	631,408	215,138	49,565	264,703
Unpaid family worker	136,608	192,035	328,643	71,865	57,824	129,689
Employee	418,425	117,869	536,294	408,815	186,537	595,352
In employment	1,031,523	464,822	1,496,345	695,818	293,926	989,744
1980						
Employer	36,993	16,423	53,416	62,734	14,725	77,459
Own-account worker	459,879	210,222	670,101	247,119	80,131	327,250
Unpaid family worker	82,602	104,307	186,909	35,362	36,690	72,052
Employee	792,688	331,322	1,124,010	560,106	289,796	849,902
In employment	1,372,162	662,274	2,034,436	905,321	421,342	1,326,663

Note: The 1957 and 1970 Censuses do not distinguish between 'employer' or 'own-account worker'. Instead both 'employer' and 'own-account worker' are categorized together as 'self-employed'.

Sources: Department of Statistics, *Population Census of Malaya* (1947), *Population Census of Federation of Malaya* (1957), *Population Census of Malaysia* (1970, 1980).

Indians			Others			Total		
Males	Females	Total	Males	Females	Total	Males	Females	Total
3,006	33	3,039	355	22	377	22,553	1,667	24,220
25,471	1,162	26,633	5,900	833	6,783	655,217	125,455	780,672
985	294	1,279	998	2,039	3,037	75,285	103,477	178,762
188,813	79,702	268,515	12,835	1,851	14,686	702,772	209,700	912,472
218,275	81,191	299,466	20,088	4,795	24,883	1,455,827	440,299	1,896,126
29,095	986	30,081	6,976	1,024	8,000	613,034	128,447	741,481
1,427	234	1,661	1,007	1,260	2,267	77,204	99,660	176,864
194,854	79,873	274,127	41,340	3,693	45,033	907,086	293,795	1,200,881
225,376	81,093	308,869	49,323	5,977	55,300	1,597,334	521,902	2,119,226
37,678	5,243	42,921	5,352	1,955	7,307	734,658	211,681	946,339
7,616	5,478	13,094	1,976	3,222	5,198	218,065	258,559	476,624
161,441	68,081	229,522	10,544	2,452	12,996	999,225	374,939	1,374,164
206,735	78,802	285,537	17,872	7,629	25,501	1,951,948	845,179	2,797,127
12,954	5,588	18,542	918	191	1,109	113,599	36,927	150,526
27,938	5,638	33,576	5,248	3,363	8,611	740,184	299,354	1,039,538
6,917	6,643	13,560	1,198	1,482	2,680	126,079	149,122	275,201
221,483	118,018	339,501	10,523	3,901	14,424	1,584,800	743,037	2,327,837
269,292	135,887	405,179	17,887	8,937	26,824	2,564,662	1,228,440	3,793,102

to 150,526 (4.0 per cent) in 1980, though these figures presumably include small
employers employing only a few workers.

*Table 6.2   Peninsular Malaysia: employment status by ethnicity, 1947 and 1980
             (percentages)*

Employment status	Malays	Chinese	Indians	Others	All races
1947					
Employer	0.5	2.3	1.0	1.5	1.3
(% of total in category)	(16.9)	(69.0)	(12.5)	(1.6)	(100.0)
Own-account worker	56.1	37.2	8.9	27.3	41.2
(% of total in category)	(61.8)	(34.0)	(3.3)	(0.9)	(100.0)
Unpaid family worker	16.5	4.7	0.4	12.2	9.4
(% of total in category)	(79.0)	(18.6)	(0.7)	(1.7)	(100.0)
Employee	26.9	55.8	89.7	59.0	48.1
(% of total in category)	(25.4)	(43.6)	(29.4)	(1.6)	(100.0)
In employment	100.0	100.0	100.0	100.0	100.0
(% of total in category)	(45.3)	(37.6)	(15.8)	(1.3)	(100.0)
1980					
Employer	2.6	5.8	4.6	4.1	4.0
(% of total in category)	(35.5)	(51.5)	(12.3)	(0.7)	(100.0)
Own-account worker	32.9	24.7	8.3	32.1	27.4
(% of total in category)	(64.5)	(31.5)	(3.2)	(0.8)	(100.0)
Unpaid family worker	9.2	5.4	3.3	10.0	7.2
(% of total in category)	(67.9)	(26.2)	(4.9)	(1.0)	(100.0)
Employee	55.3	64.1	83.8	53.8	61.4
(% of total in category)	(48.3)	(36.5)	(14.6)	(0.6)	(100.0)
In employment	100.0	100.0	100.0	100.0	100.0
(% of total in category)	(53.6)	(35.0)	(10.7)	(0.7)	(100.0)

Sources: Department of Statistics, *Population Census of Malaya* (1947), *Population Census of
Federation of Malaya* (1957), *Population Census of Malaysia* (1970, 1980).

The uneven involvement of different ethnic groups in wage employment can
be clearly seen in Tables 6.1 and 6.2. In 1947, less than 3 per cent of working
Malays were employees, compared to 56 per cent of Chinese and 90 per cent
of Indians. Only 9 per cent of Indians were self-employed, compared to 37 per
cent of Chinese and 56 per cent of Malays. Presumably, most of these Malays
and a high proportion of these Chinese were peasant farmers or fishermen, while
the rest were artisans or small traders. By 1980, however, this distribution had

changed dramatically, with 84 per cent of Indians, 64 per cent of Chinese and 55 per cent of Malays working as employees. Thus, between 1947 and 1980, the proportion of Malays among all employees rose from 25 per cent to 48 per cent, while the Chinese and Indian shares declined from 44 per cent to 37 per cent and from 29 per cent to 15 per cent respectively. Official labour force data show that while the overall class structure of the Indian and Chinese working populations has changed moderately, reflecting differential opportunities and access within the modernizing capitalist sector of the economy, the Malay working population underwent the greatest transformation, with its rapid incorporation into wage employment, especially during the 1970s.

Table 6.3   Peninsular Malaysia: percentage distribution of employment status by gender, 1947 and 1980

Employment Status	1947			1980		
	Males	Females	Total	Males	Females	Total
Employer	1.5	0.4	1.3	4.4	3.0	4.0
(% of total in category)	(93.1)	(6.9)	(100.0)	(75.5)	(24.5)	(100.0)
Own-account worker	45.0	28.5	41.2	28.9	24.4	27.4
(% of total in category)	(83.9)	(16.1)	(100.0)	(71.2)	(28.8)	(100.0)
Unpaid family worker	5.2	23.5	9.4	4.9	12.1	7.2
(% of total in category)	(42.1)	(57.9)	(100.0)	(45.8)	(54.2)	(100.0)
Employee	48.3	47.6	48.1	61.8	60.5	61.4
(% of total in category)	(77.0)	(23.0)	(100.0)	(68.1)	(31.9)	(100.0)
In employment	100.0	100.0	100.0	100.0	100.0	100.0
(% of total in category)	(76.8)	(23.2)	(100.0)	(67.6)	(32.4)	(100.0)

Sources: Department of Statistics, *Population Census of Malaya* (1947), *Population Census of Federation of Malaya* (1957), *Population Census of Malaysia* (1970, 1980).

Tables 6.4, 6.5 and 6.6 only provide a rough idea of ethnic distribution by sector, type of economic activity and work category since they do not distinguish by employment status. Nevertheless, the tables suggest that Malay labour involvement has increased faster than the employment increase in both secondary and tertiary sectors since 1970. It is quite possible that employment expansion in these sectors itself may have been more important than the government's ethnic redistributive efforts (e.g. by imposing ethnic employment quotas) in bringing about this change. According to Table 6.5, the number of Malays rose in all economic activities between 1957 and 1976, especially in plantation agriculture, manufacturing, construction, commerce and services. Table 6.6 suggests

Table 6.4 Peninsular Malaysia: employment by sector and ethnicity, 1970 and 1985 ('000)

Sector	1970					1985				
	Malays	Chinese	Indians	Others	Total	Malays	Chinese	Indians	Others	Total
Primary	902.3	265.4	154.0	12.9	1,334.6	1,450.1	350.8	194.5	18.3	201.3
%	(57.6)	(19.9)	(11.5)	(1.0)	(100.0)	(72.0)	(17.4)	(9.7)	(0.9)	(100.0)
Secondary	215.6	394.3	57.1	4.7	671.7	500.4	600.5	96.2	9.6	1,206.7
%	(32.1)	(58.7)	(8.5)	(0.7)	(100.0)	(41.5)	(49.8)	(17.9)	(0.8)	(100.0)
Tertiary	359.7	383.9	90.3	10.1	844.0	1,151.2	875.3	205.5	16.1	2,248.1
%	(42.6)	(45.5)	(10.7)	(1.2)	(100.0)	(51.2)	(38.9)	(9.2)	(0.7)	(100.0)
Total employed	1,477.6	1,043.6	301.4	27.7	2,850.3	3,101.7	1,826.6	496.2	44.0	5,468.5
%	(51.8)	(36.6)	(10.6)	(1.0)	(100.0)	(56.7)	(33.4)	(9.1)	(0.8)	(100.0)
Labour force	1,608.3	1,122.4	338.7	28.6	3,098.0	3,397.3	1,931.9	541.6	46.3	5,917.1
%	(51.9)	(36.2)	(10.9)	(0.9)	(100.0)	(57.4)	(32.6)	(9.2)	(0.8)	(100.0)
Unemployment	130.7	78.8	37.3	0.9	247.7	196.3	65.5	29.0	1.2	292.0
%	(8.1)	(7.0)	(11.0)	(3.1)	(8.0)	(67.2)	(22.4)	(10.0)	(0.4)	(100.0)

that the proportion of Malays in all work categories rose between 1957 and 1983, especially in clerical work, sales and production, and least of all in agriculture.

Tables 6.1 and 6.3 both reflect the tremendous post-war incorporation of women into wage employment, rising from 209,700 or 23 per cent in 1947 to 743,037 or 32 per cent in 1980. While only 48 per cent of working women, i.e. other than those only doing unwaged domestic work, were waged employees in 1947, this proportion had risen to 61 per cent by 1980. (In 1980, women still comprised the majority of unpaid family workers, and had risen as a proportion of the self-employed compared to 1947.) Increasing female labour force participation was a feature of all ethnic groups, and the same can be said for wage employment. The ethnic trends described earlier also influenced differential female participation.

Rapid structural change in the Malaysian economy in the 1970s is reflected in Table 6.4, which clearly shows the rapid expansion of employment in the secondary and tertiary sectors, especially in the 1970s, as well as the virtual stagnation of employment in the primary sector. With recessionary trends more pronounced in the 1980s, structural change in employment slowed down somewhat, especially in the middle of the decade. Interestingly, over the 1970s, the Malay percentage rose in all three sectors, while the Chinese percentage declined in these sectors, although the latter's proportion of the labour force declined only slightly. These apparently paradoxical developments make sense once we note that the primary sector was virtually stagnant while the other two sectors grew rapidly.

The general trends suggested by Table 6.4 for the period from 1970 are also reflected in greater detail in Table 6.5. These trends reflect the broader sectoral trends shown in Table 6.4, and clearly suggest that structural changes in employment accelerated in the 1970s. By 1976, agriculture accounted for only 30.2 per cent of the working population, compared to 58.5 per cent in 1957, while manufacturing's share had risen to 16 per cent, compared to only 6.4 per cent in 1957, and commerce and services together had risen to 32.6 per cent, from only 24.2 per cent in 1957.

Table 6.6 also provides a rough idea of the effects of structural change and some stratification trends in the Peninsular Malaysian labour force since 1957. The proportion of professional and technical workers has risen with technological change and modernization of the economy (from 2.8 per cent in 1957 to 9.1 per cent in 1993), while the proportion of administrative and managerial workers – which remained remarkably constant between 1957 and 1970 at around 1.2 per cent – rose to 2.7 per cent in 1993. Similarly, the proportion of clerical workers has risen (from 2.9 per cent in 1957 to 9.8 per cent in 1993), while the proportion in services has risen more than the percentage in sales. Predictably, the proportion in agriculture has fallen tremendously (from 56.2 per cent in 1957 to 25.4 per cent in 1993), though the proportion in production, transport, etc. has risen less

Table 6.5   Peninsular Malaysia: labour force by ethnic group and activity, 1957, 1970 and 1984

	1957[1]								1970[2]		
	Malays		Chinese		Indians		Total		Malays		Chinese
Activity	'000	%	'000	%	'000	%	'000	%	'000	%	'000
Agri., forest., livestock & fish.	459.8	45.8	100.9	13.3	4.5	1.5	572.8	26.9	495.2	34.5	100.0
Agri., products[a]	289.5	28.8	209.5	27.6	170.0	55.3	672.0	31.6	427.1	29.8	192.9
Mining & quarrying	10.3	1.0	40.0	5.3	6.8	2.2	58.5	2.8	13.3	0.9	37.1
Manufacturing	26.6	2.6	97.5	12.8	10.1	3.3	135.7	6.4	73.1	5.1	164.5
Construction	21.8	2.2	32.6	4.3	12.3	4.0	67.8	3.2	13.0	0.9	43.1
Utilities[b]	3.8	0.4	3.0	0.4	4.2	1.4	11.6	0.5	9.5	0.7	3.6
Commerce	32.0	3.2	127.1	16.7	32.8	10.7	195.2	9.2	64.3	4.5	179.8
Transport and communications	26.9	2.7	29.2	3.8	16.1	5.2	74.8	3.5	41.5	2.9	39.1
Services	127.6	12.7	110.0	14.5	48.1	15.7	319.8	15.0	223.9	15.6	173.5
Miscellaneous activities	5.9	0.6	9.4	1.2	2.4	0.8	18.1	0.9	74.1	5.2	55.6
Total	1,004.3	100.0	759.2	100.0	307.2	100.0	2,126.3	100.0	1,435.0	100.0	990.0

Notes:

[a] Requiring substantial processing (e.g. rubber, coconut, oil palm, etc.).

[b] Including electricity, gas, water and sanitation.

Sources: 1. Department of Statistics (1960), *1957 Population Census of the Federation of Malaya*, Report No. 14, Kuala Lumpur.
2. Department of Statistics (1970), *Population Census of Malaysia*.
3. Department of Statistics (1988), *Report on the Labour Force, 1984*, Kuala Lumpur, January.

					1984[3]							
	Indians		Total		Malays		Chinese		Indians		Total	
%	'000	%	'000	%	'000	%	'000	%	'000	%	'000	%
10.2	6.0	2.1	611.3	22.3	834.0	34.0	215.9	13.5	153.0	30.7	1211.6	26.5
19.5	125.7	43.9	747.8	27.3	–	–	–	–	–	–	–	–
3.8	4.6	1.6	55.3	2.0	17.1	0.7	16.4	1.0	4.2	0.8	38.5	0.8
16.6	13.3	4.6	251.9	9.2	352.5	14.4	341.4	21.4	95.4	19.2	792.9	17.3
4.4	3.6	1.3	59.9	2.2	138.8	5.7	189.7	11.9	25.8	5.2	359.1	7.8
0.4	6.4	2.2	19.8	0.7	19.4	0.8	1.9	0.1	4.6	0.9	26.1	0.6
18.2	29.1	10.2	274.6	10.0	292.6	11.9	461.8	28.9	67.0	13.5	824.8	18.0
3.9	16.7	5.3	98.0	3.6	107.0	4.4	70.7	4.4	31.1	6.2	210.0	4.6
17.5	66.3	23.2	472.6	17.3	71.4	2.9	82.8	5.2	23.2	4.7	179.6	3.9
5.6	14.3	5.1	145.2	5.3	–	–	–	–	–	–	–	–
100.0	286.1	100.0	2,736.4	100.0	2,449.3	100.0	1,598.4	100.0	497.5	100.0	4,575.2	100.0

Capital, the state and labour

*Table 6.6   Peninsular Malaysia: labour force by ethnic group and
work category, 1957, 1970 and 1993 ('000)*

| Category[a] | 1957[b] | | | | Malays |
	Malays	Chinese	Indians	Total (%)	
Professional/technical	2.7	3.3	2.3	2.8	4.3
workers[d]	(41.0)	(38.0)	(11.0)		(47.1)
Administrative &	0.4	2.0	1.0	1.2	0.5
managerial workers[e]	(17.6)	(62.4)	(12.2)		(24.1)
Clerical and	1.7	3.7	4.0	2.9	3.4
related workers[f]	(27.1)	(46.2)	(19.9)		(35.4)
Sales and related	2.9	15.9	10.0	8.6	4.7
workers[g]	(15.9)	(66.1)	(16.8)		(26.7)
Service workers[h]	7.3	8.0	7.6	8.6	6.8
	(39.7)	(33.3)	(12.8)		(44.3)
Agricultural workers[i]	74.2	38.3	50.2	56.2	62.3
	(62.1)	(24.3)	(12.8)		(72.0)
Production, transport	10.6	28.3	24.6	18.9	18.0
& other workers[j]	(26.5)	(53.5)	(18.9)		(34.2)
Total workers	1,004.3	759.0	307.2	2,126.2	1,477.6
	(48.2)	(36.3)	(14.7)		(51.8)

Notes:
a   Classification of the occupations had been based on the Ministry of Labour and Manpower,
Dictionary of Occupational Classification, 1980.
b   Value in brackets shows percentage by ethnic group.
c   Includes workers who cannot be classified.
d   Includes professions such as architects, accountants, auditors, engineers, teachers, nurses, doctors,
dentists, veterinary surgeons, surveyors and lawyers. For the Malays, a substantial proportion
of those employed in this occupational group are made up of teachers and nurses. These two
groups are estimated to account for about 76,000 or 53 per cent of their total in 1980.
e   Includes legislative officials, government administrators and managers.
f   Includes clerical supervisors, government executive officials, typists, book-keepers, cashiers,
telephone operators and telegraph operators.
g   Includes managers (wholesale and retail trade), sales supervisors and buyers, technical salesmen,
commercial travellers and manufacturers' agents.
h   Includes managers of catering and accommodation services, working proprietors, housekeeping and related service supervisors, cooks and related workers.
i   Includes plantation managers and supervisors, planters and farmers, agricultural and animal
husbandry workers, forestry workers, fishermen, hunters and related workers.
j   Includes production supervisors and general foremen, miners, quarrymen, well drillers, motor-
vehicle drivers and related workers.

Sources: 1.   Jomo and Shari (1986) pp.329–55.
2.   Malaysia (1994), *Mid-Term Review of the Sixth Malaysia Plan, 1991–1995*,
Government Printers, Kuala Lumpur.

| 1970[c] | | | 1993 | | | |
Chinese	Indians	Total (%)	Malays	Chinese	Indians	Total (%)
5.2	4.9	4.8	9.7	8.1	8.2	9.1
(39.5)	(10.8)		(63.2)	(27.6)	(7.7)	
1.9	0.8	1.1	1.5	5.1	1.6	2.7
(62.9)	(7.8)		(32.5)	(60.0)	(5.0)	
6.3	8.1	5.0	9.2	11.4	9.1	9.8
(45.9)	(17.2)		(55.7)	(36.2)	(7.9)	
15.3	9.5	9.1	7.4	21.9	9.3	12.1
(61.7)	(11.1)		(36.6)	(56.4)	(6.6)	
8.6	10.9	7.9	13.2	10.6	12.6	12.4
(17.3)	(14.6)		(63.5)	(26.5)	(8.7)	
21.2	41.0	44.8	33.5	11.0	19.9	25.4
(55.9)	(9.7)		(78.5)	(13.5)	(6.7)	
41.6	24.7	27.3	25.5	31.9	39.3	28.5
(55.9)	(9.6)		(53.1)	(34.9)	(11.8)	
1,043.6	301.4	2,850.3	4,409.7	2,309.2	632.0	7,410.6
(36.6)	(10.6)		(59.5)	(31.2)	(8.5)	

dramatically (from 18.9 per cent in 1957 to 27.3 per cent in 1970 and 28.5 per cent in 1993!).

III   POST-WAR LABOUR LAW AND POLICY

Growing labour and nationalist militancy in the immediate post-war period culminated in the colonial government's declaration of a state of emergency in June 1948. By the end of 1948, most of the more militant unions had been deregistered, and other repressive measures had caused trade union membership to decline to about a third of what it had been at the beginning of that year. While subsequent independent labour organizations were curbed by various means, 'responsible' alternative unions were groomed under colonial tutelage. New legislation by the colonial authorities was designed to further labour control and weaken the unions. For instance, the Trade Disputes Ordinance of 1949 severely curbed the workers' right to strike; the subsequent Employment Ordinance of 1955 provided for the summary dismissal of workers on spurious grounds, such as alleged misconduct. Nevertheless, union membership and labour militancy picked up once again as independence became increasingly imminent, though never reaching its earlier 1948 peak. In 1956 and 1957 alone, the colonial government deregistered 45 unions.

In 1959, the post-colonial Malayan government passed the Trade Union Ordinance, which embodied legislation passed during the Emergency since 1948. Another 'state of emergency' during the 'confrontation' with Indonesia (1963–66) paved the way for the reimposition of many of the more severe restrictions of the previous Emergency (1948–60). In response to growing labour militancy in the early and mid-1960s, new industrial relations legislation was introduced in 1965, including compulsory arbitration, thus effectively limiting the right to strike in a wide range of 'essential services', with the definition of 'essential services' including industries such as pineapple canning. Government employees were effectively barred from industrial action after several disputes involving railway, postal and fire fighting service workers in the mid-1960s.

The subsequent Industrial Relations Act of 1967 subsumed previous legislation affecting industrial disputes. The bloody communal riots of May 1969 led to a third 'state of emergency', during which the normal operation of law was once again officially suspended. In October 1969, the government introduced amendments to the Industrial Relations Act precluding certain issues – such as management prerogatives over dismissals, transfers, etc. – from negotiation. Procedures for collective bargaining and for settlement of industrial disputes by conciliation and arbitration were stipulated. In 1971, when parliament was reconvened for the first time after the post-election riots of 1969, these and other regulations were incorporated into comprehensive new legislation prohibiting union officials from holding office in political parties, and preventing unions from maintaining 'political funds'. It also further limited the right to strike (e.g. by designating various issues, such as union recognition, as 'non-strikeable' issues), strengthened the power of management (e.g. by no longer requiring employers to state reasons for dismissal), fragmented labour unity, and provided more means to bolster collaborating unions and curb the emergence of new, independent unions (e.g. by enhancing the power of the relevant government-appointed authorities in matters such as union registration). Many of these changes in the late 1960s and early 1970s reflected changes in labour policy in line with the switch to export-oriented industrialization.

There has never been minimum wage legislation in Malaysia. The Malaysian (formerly Federal) Industrial Development Authority assures prospective investors in pioneer industries of safeguards against 'unreasonable demands' from unions during their first five years of existence, or for 'any such extended period'. While there is no legislation actually prohibiting unions in pioneer industries (as is sometimes mistakenly alleged), it is indeed suggestive that about 100,000 electronics workers – who would be able to form the largest industry-based union in the manufacturing sector – have not been allowed to register a union for more than two decades since the first electronics factory was set up in Malaysia in the late 1960s.

Meanwhile, it has become increasingly evident that the establishment of the Social Security Organization (SOCSO) in 1969 – to compensate victims of industrial accidents regardless of responsibility – has actually shifted responsibility for compensation away from employers even if the latter have been negligent. Furthermore, since the compensation rates have been kept minimal, SOCSO payments have become an additional cheap source of financing for the government. Total SOCSO membership rose from 1.7 million workers in 1980 to 2.4 million in 1983. With the wage ceiling increased from RM (Malaysian ringgit) 500 to RM1000 per month from 1984, SOCSO membership increased to 4.2 million by 1989. The large and growing SOCSO membership has helped SOCSO's assets to grow rapidly from virtually nothing in 1971 to over RM700 million by the end of 1985. However, compensation paid out to workers has been comparatively small, amounting to only about one-eighth of their contributions. During 1971–80, SOCSO collected RM243 million in contributions, but only paid out about RM17 million as benefits and RM6.5 million for medical expenses, i.e. roughly 9 per cent of total contributions. By 1984, SOCSO had collected RM621.8 million, but had only paid out RM81.2 million, i.e. about 12 per cent, even after improving the compensation scheme in that year. The balance of RM540.6 million has since been invested in government securities. By the end of 1984, SOCSO investments in government securities totalled RM711.5 million, while its fixed deposits amounted to RM2.5 million;

during 1972–84, SOCSO earned RM207.8 million from its investments. By 1989, SOCSO was collecting about RM200 million, with annual expenditure rising even faster to RM93.4 million (Paguman, 1991, p.32).

During the 1960s and 1970s, there were several government efforts to portray itself as a neutral arbiter standing above and mediating between capital or management and labour, though by and large the state generally favoured capital over labour, e.g. as reflected in various amendments to the labour laws or the government's role in industrial relations. In the 1980s, however, the anti-labour character of the state has become even more blatant, as can be seen in the following brief review of the more important recent labour policies.

After the tightening up of the labour laws in 1980, the industrial relations machinery and labour policies have also changed, largely at the expense of labour. The 1980 amendments to the labour laws not only reflected the government reaction to the protracted Malaysian Airlines System (MAS) industrial dispute of 1978–79, but also envisaged the government's view of an even more sub-ordinate role for labour in Malaysia's development strategy in the 1980s. Malaysian trade unions, already docile by international standards, were to be further circumscribed. Unlike the admittedly half-hearted efforts in the early and mid-1970s to promote 'tripartism' and other reforms to coopt moderate trade union leaders with the semblance of a new social contract for labour, the new initiative sought to further limit labour's political and legal rights while providing some economic benefits – in the buoyant circumstances prevailing then – to sweeten the bitter medicine. The 1980 amendments thus represented a somewhat systematic effort to anticipate and curb possible threats to the envisaged industrial order desired by the government in its efforts to try to become a 'newly indus-trializing country' (NIC).

The blatant government promotion of in-house unions in the 1980s also represents a departure from previous labour policy. In-house unions have existed for some time in Malaysia, though mainly in the statutory bodies. As noted earlier, in the mid-1970s, the government intervened on behalf of management to facilitate the establishment of an in-house union for employees of United Motor Works (UMW), although many of the workers involved had already joined another union, not unlike what happened a few years later with the MAS employees. However, despite ostensible government support for in-house unions, very few new in-house unions have been registered where no unions existed before. Instead, it appears that in-house unions are being encouraged to replace 'troublesome' unions already in existence. Seen in this light, then, government encouragement of in-house unions for the private sector appears to be intended to further weaken the already weak trade union movement in the country. The penalties for those who step out of line have been sufficiently severe to discourage labour militancy.

With relatively high economic growth – especially the development of labour-intensive, export-oriented industries and the public sector – in the 1970s, the official unemployment rate reached a post-Independence low in the early 1980s. With considerable emigration of Malaysian labour to Singapore and elsewhere, especially the Middle East, increasing in the mid- and late 1970s, real wages actually rose and pockets of labour shortages emerged, usually in activities offering low wages, poor work conditions and the option of out-migration. To offset the pressure on wages, and ostensibly to overcome these labour shortages, the government adopted several measures. The increased use of illegal contract labour and immigrant workers – primarily from Indonesia, Southern Thailand (especially to the northern states of Peninsular Malaysia) and the Southern Philippines (to Sabah) – has depressed real wage trends. The magnitude of such recent illegal immigration is difficult to measure, but estimates varied from 0.5 million to 1.5 million by the mid-1980s – compared to a national population of 18 million and a labour force of about 7 million. Although sometimes justified in terms of the need for the Malay-dominated government to strengthen itself further by increasing the number and the proportion of ethnic Malays, the tacit approval of such massive illegal labour immigration has adversely affected wages. Poorly paid immigrant workers have become increasingly widespread in plantation agriculture, land development schemes and construction.

Recession, as well as the freeze on recruitment and subsequent attempts to reduce the public sector, resulted in increasing unemployment in the mid-1980s as well as other pressures on wages. Membership of trade unions actually declined in the early 1980s, while the official unemployment rate rose from 4.6 per cent in 1983 to 8.1 per cent in 1987. There was a virtual freeze in wage increases, including those awarded by the industrial court. In his 1987 Budget speech, delivered in October 1986, the finance minister called for a voluntary wage freeze for the following three years. The government made no commitment, however, to instituting a freeze on prices; nor did it try to explain why the wage freeze was needed for three years. Instead, a mandatory wage freeze was threatened if the call for a voluntary freeze was not heeded. In the context of rising prices and productivity, the wage freeze enabled capital to increase its share of the product at the expense of labour. However, the economic boom and declining unemployment since 1987 have pushed up wages since that time.

In the seven collective agreements made in 1985, the industrial court awarded increases averaging less than 3 per cent, declining to 2 per cent in early 1986. Wages in the plantation sector fell by 16 to 26 per cent during 1985, largely due to poor rubber and palm oil prices, though they have not risen as much as commodity prices since 1987. Meanwhile, 787,000 public-sector employees were given wage increases of about 1 to 12 per cent in July 1985, against a rise in the official Consumer Price Index (CPI) of over 25 per cent since the last wage review in 1980. Allowances for government employees were increased in mid-1990 before the October general election, while wage increases averaging 5 per cent were announced in early 1991 as fixed incomes continued to be increasingly eroded as inflation began to pick up from the late 1980s after a brief lull during the recession in the middle of the decade.

IV TRADE UNION MEMBERSHIP AND INDUSTRIAL DISPUTES

The history of trade unionism in Peninsular Malaysia does not, however, neatly reflect the growth of wage labour. A variety of factors have influenced unionization among Malaysian wage workers besides the uneven growth of wage labour itself. As in many other parts of the world, there has been a greater likelihood for employees of large enterprises to be unionized compared to their counterparts in smaller firms. Also, once unions are officially permitted, public-sector employees are often able to unionize more easily than workers in the private sector, though this does not necessarily mean that they enjoy all the rights enjoyed by other unionized workers.

The economic, social and political history of Peninsular Malaysia has also been an important influence on unionization. Immigrant workers often brought with them traditions of labour organization, whether they were from China, British India or Indonesia, then the Dutch East Indies. In contrast, indigenous Malays were often discouraged by colonial policy from leaving the peasantry to join the ranks of wage labour. Hence, traditions of labour organization have been unevenly influential in different ethnic and sub-ethnic worker cultures. With wage labour before the Great Depression mainly involving males, gender differences in working-class tradition and culture have also been very important. Such historical differences have, in turn, been reinforced or eroded by subsequent developments, especially in employment patterns and government policies.

Though trade unions were not officially recognized by the British colonial government before 1940, nevertheless, labour organizations of various types, including trade unions, had already come into existence from the end of the last century to serve workers' interests. At war with Germany in Europe and with the looming threat of a Pacific war with Japan, the British Empire reluctantly accepted the Communist Party of Malaya's (CPM) call – after the invasion of China by the Japanese in the mid-1930s – for a united front to face the fascist Axis threat. Abandoning the call for an independent socialist republic, the CPM offered to work with the British against the imminent Japanese threat. These overtures were initially rebuffed until Germany's belligerent intentions became unmistakable in the late 1930s.

With the Japanese invasion of Malaya from December 1941, it became clear that the British gestures had been too little and too late. The Japanese Occupation (1942–45) is usually overlooked in most discussions of Malaysian social and economic history. The surrender of the Japanese after the war to the communist-led Malayan People's Anti-Japanese Army (MPAJA) and the returning British military forces set the stage for a new phase of nationalist agitation and unrest. The immediate post-war years – 1946 and 1947 – witnessed the peak of these unsuccessful efforts to gain independence as the colonial government faced difficulties trying to restore its authority and administrative apparatus.

Labour statistics in Malaya date back to the early part of the century, but union statistics only begin from 1947. These statistics tell a rather interesting story about the rise and fall of trade union membership. Union membership dropped from 195,113 to 69,134 in 1948 alone and to 41,305 in 1949 with the repression accompanying the declaration of a state of emergency in June 1948. Union membership remained very low for several years until the early 1950s, when the colonial government decided to actively promote an anti-communist labour movement. The establishment of the Malayan Trade Unions Council (MTUC) and the Labour Party of Malaya were important components of this new initiative, which soon saw the resurgence of trade union membership. As Table 6.7 shows, union membership rose to 127,946 in 1952, but then dropped in 1953 to 109,557, with the collapse of the post-Korean War boom.

However, the resurgent unions could not be too easily controlled from above by the more compliant British-sponsored leaders. Instead, a new wave of labour agitation developed around economic issues – especially after the early 1950s Korean War boom - and the struggle for Independence. Union membership rose again to 232,174 in 1956, on the eve of Independence. Ironically, membership fell again after Independence to 172,704 in 1959, before increasing again in the first half of the 1960s to 328,331 in 1965. Rising union membership had to be tolerated because of public recognition of labour's key contribution to the Independence struggle. However, with the resurgence of labour agitation, the second state of emergency declared during the mid-1960s confrontation with Indonesia provided the pretext for renewed labour repression. Furthermore, with the third state of emergency declared after the post-election race riots of May 1969, the draconian changes to the labour laws later that year essentially emasculated the trade union movement; hence union membership declined in the latter part of the 1960s to 275,238 in 1970. With the rapid increase of Malays in wage employment, especially in the public sector, and the desire of the new Razak regime to project a new consensus or social contract, union membership was allowed to rise again after 1970 to 424,626 in 1975, before rising more slowly to 503,686 in 1980 and to 533,921 in 1988.

*Table 6.7   Peninsular Malaysia: trade union[a] membership by ethnicity,
1949–86*

	Malays	Chinese	Indians	Others	Total
1949	5,370 (13%)	9,913 (24%)	23,957 (58%)	2,065 (5%)	41,305 (100%)
1950	6,549 (12%)	14,191 (26%)	31,656 (58%)	2,183 (4%)	54,579 (100%)
1951	12,184 (11%)	15,789 (15%)	77,117 (71%)	3,164 (3%)	108,254 (100%)
1952	16,924 (13%)	19,543 (15%)	88,264 (69%)	3,215 (3%)	127,946 (100%)
1953	n.a.	n.a.	n.a.	n.a.	n.a.
1954	20,189 (18%)	17,489 (15%)	73,482 (65%)	2,310 (2%)	113,470 (100%)
1955	29,425 (20%)	22,795 (16%)	90,734 (62%)	2,795 (2%)	145,749 (100%)
1956	49,505 (21%)	37,137 (16%)	143,048 (62%)	2,484 (1%)	232,174 (100%)
1957	45,851 (20%)	46,497 (21%)	128,675 (58%)	1,021 (1%)	222,044 (100%)
1958	47,373 (22%)	35,427 (17%)	127,072 (60%)	1,756 (1%)	211,628 (100%)
1959	38,595 (22%)	29,130 (17%)	103,673 (60%)	1,306 (1%)	172,704 (100%)
1960	36,106 (21%)	27,646 (16%)	103,840 (62%)	1,588 (1%)	169,180 (100%)
1961	43,355 (24%)	30,709 (17%)	105,400 (58%)	1,721 (1%)	181,185 (100%)
1962	38,718 (18%)	55,269 (26%)	117,925 (55%)	2,375 (1%)	214,287 (100%)
1963	68,105 (28%)	46,592 (19%)	124,591 (52%)	2,217 (1%)	241,505 (100%)
1964	56,936 (21%)	84,170 (31%)	131,959 (48%)	2,747 (1%)	275,812 (100%)
1975	200,507 (47%)	94,979 (23%)	124,547 (29%)	4,593 (1%)	424,626 (100%)
1976	206,805 (47%)	100,012 (23%)	125,559 (29%)	4,651 (1%)	437,027 (100%)
1977	228,972 (49%)	103,635 (22%)	130,834 (28%)	5,156 (1%)	468,597 (100%)
1978	184,039 (39%)	130,881 (27%)	159,992 (33%)	6,220 (1%)	481,132 (100%)
1979	208,710 (43%)	117,686 (24%)	158,019 (32%)	5,229 (1%)	489,644 (100%)
1980	254,563 (50%)	108,843 (22%)	135,716 (27%)	4,564 (1%)	503,686 (100%)
1981	267,717 (51%)	112,067 (22%)	134,896 (26%)	4,151 (1%)	518,831 (100%)
1982	273,517 (51%)	114,803 (22%)	135,965 (26%)	4,761 (1%)	529,046 (100%)
1983	281,016 (53%)	98,964 (19%)	145,536 (27%)	3,705 (1%)	529,221 (100%)
1984	285,172 (55%)	92,075 (18%)	130,776 (26%)	3,221 (1%)	511,244 (100%)
1985	295,083 (57%)	92,174 (17%)	130,650 (25%)	3,441 (1%)	521,348 (100%)
1986	301,297 (57%)	89,423 (17%)	130,853 (25%)	3,518 (1%)	525,091 (100%)

Note: [a] Excluding employers' trade unions.

Sources: Ministry of Labour, *Annual Report*, various years; *Annual Report of the Trade Unions
Registry*, various years.

The ethnic composition of union membership has also changed very dramatically over the years. In the 1940s, unions mainly involved Chinese and
Indians, with the latter especially highly represented compared to their share
of the Malayan population. This high representation can largely be explained
by the colonial employment pattern, where Indians were mainly recruited into
the government sector and the British-owned private sector, especially the
plantations, whereas unionization was less widespread among the predominantly

Chinese employees of the generally smaller Chinese firms. Both colonial and post-colonial governments also did not particularly want to encourage union-ization among the Chinese-educated, who were considered to be far more susceptible to communist influence. Also, since Independence, there has been relatively less upward and outward social mobility among Indian workers compared to the Chinese. However, contrary to the popular impression that trade unions are dominated by Indians, the distribution of trade union principal officers by ethnic origin has by and large reflected the changing ethnic com-position of unionized labour.

Table 6.8   Peninsular Malaysia: trade union membership by gender, 1952–88

	Males	Females	Total
1952	101,022 (79%)	26,924 (21%)	127,946 (100%)
1953	n.a.	n.a.	n.a.
1954	91,740 (81%)	21,730 (19%)	113,470 (100%)
1955	137,649 (94%)	8,100 (6%)	145,749 (100%)
1956	178,611 (77%)	53,563 (23%)	232,174 (100%)
1957	169,642 (76%)	52,402 (24%)	222,044 (100%)
1958	153,853 (73%)	57,775 (27%)	211,628 (100%)
1959	128,399 (74%)	44,305 (26%)	172,704 (100%)
1960	124,755 (74%)	44,425 (26%)	169,180 (100%)
1961	136,111 (75%)	45,074 (25%)	181,185 (100%)
1962	163,060 (76%)	51,227 (24%)	214,287 (100%)
1963	186,038 (77%)	55,467 (23%)	241,505 (100%)
1964	212,495 (77%)	63,317 (23%)	275,812 (100%)
1978	357,416 (74%)	124,242 (26%)	481,658 (100%)
1979	358,804 (73%)	131,521 (27%)	490,325 (100%)
1980	367,280 (73%)	136,406 (27%)	503,686 (100%)
1981	382,088 (74%)	136,743 (26%)	518,831 (100%)
1982	388,753 (73%)	140,293 (27%)	529,046 (100%)
1983	384,043 (73%)	145,178 (27%)	529,221 (100%)
1984	373,346 (73%)	137,898 (27%)	511,244 (100%)
1985	381,457 (73%)	139,891 (27%)	521,348 (100%)
1986	382,355 (73%)	142,736 (27%)	525,091 (100%)
1987	375,850 (71%)	152,447 (29%)	528,297 (100%)
1988	374,465 (70%)	159,456 (30%)	533,921 (100%)

Sources: Ministry of Labour, *Annual Report*, various years; *Annual Report of the Trade Unions Registry*, various years.

There have also been very interesting changes in the gender breakdown of union membership, with a slow but clear increase in female participation, albeit unevenly, and not quite reflecting increased female participation in the labour force, as Table 6.8 shows. This may be largely due to the fact that one of the largest manufacturing industries in terms of female employment since the 1970s has been electronics, where no union was allowed until 1988, when the government reluctantly announced that in-house unions could now be set up. Also, while about 200,000 people, mainly women, are believed to be involved in the textiles and garments industry, the majority are not regularly or directly employed, and hence not eligible for union membership. Hence, female trade union membership has lagged considerably behind female participation in the labour force, even as wage employees. Still more regrettable, however, has been the even lower representation of women as principal officers in trade unions, which was only about 7 per cent in 1988.

The degree of unionization in the public sector has generally been greater than for the private sector, although industrial actions have generally been higher in the private sector, with some exceptions, of course. Nevertheless, since the public sector is still much smaller than the private sector, even after its rapid expansion under the NEP, there were more unionized private-sector employees until 1984, when the number of government as well as statutory body and local authority unionized employees first exceeded private-sector union members.

This development reflects the relatively lower rate of unionization and slower increase in union membership in the private sector compared to the public sector. Although trade unions in Malaysia have been increasingly emasculated by changes in the labour laws and labour policy in the post-war period, public-sector unions generally have even fewer rights than private-sector unions, with government-sector unions even denied the basic right of collective bargaining in the 1980s.

Both the government sector as well as statutory bodies and local authorities have witnessed a proliferation of unions, resulting in a situation of many more unions in the public sector than in the private sector. The government's efforts to promote in-house unions since the 1970s has resulted in the proliferation of trade unions generally, with relatively small corresponding increases in union membership. For instance, the number of unions in the private sector rose from 98 in 1977 to 149 in 1979, with total membership rising from 252,167 to 281,223 over the same two-year period. Similarly, the number of private-sector unions rose from 153 in 1984 to 161 in 1985 and 170 in 1986, while membership crept up from 286,882 to 291,313 and 291,464 respectively. Between 1977 and 1979, government-sector unions also increased from 114 in 1977 to 140 in 1979, with a small increase in membership from 151,226 to 175,093 respectively. Similarly, unions in statutory bodies and local authorities increased from 53 in 1977 to 73 in 1979, with membership increasing from 57,730 to 69,659. In other words, the number of unions increased much faster than the number of union members in the late 1970s. This phenomenon emerged in the private sector in the mid-1980s with the government's policy to promote in-house unions. Hence increasing union membership and the number of unions has not correspondingly strengthened trade unions generally.

Table 6.9   Peninsular Malaysia: trade union membership by union size, 1962–88

	<100	100 to 200	201 to 500	501 to 1,000	1,001 to 2,000	2,001 to 5,000	5,001 to 10,000	>10,000	Total
1962	5,192	8,369	18,030	20,182	31,729	26,120	23,803	124,061	257,486
1963	4,429	7,944	18,010	20,032	32,098	45,866	16,530	131,161	267,070
1964	4,136	8,876	14,798	21,492	35,759	58,489	13,459	166,199	323,208
1965	4,347	8,438	16,144	25,670	37,092	63,310	5,141	168,189	328,331
1966	3,893	8,227	17,551	26,472	36,900	59,111	11,869	151,687	315,710
1967	3,702	6,157	14,260	26,017	41,757	53,458	38,086	123,508	306,945
1968	3,344	5,984	14,217	21,741	46,937	65,983	26,295	114,988	299,489
1969	3,390	5,132	16,056	20,048	37,922	53,689	49,469	104,162	289,868
1970	3,436	4,166	15,854	19,025	36,234	60,771	31,205	103,942	274,633
1971	3,170	4,715	16,993	24,847	41,341	50,515	47,105	94,309	282,995
1972	3,267	4,743	14,098	17,082	54,756	53,544	54,544	94,309	296,223
1973	3,631	3,883	15,477	21,213	50,054	72,816	56,571	94,270	317,915
1974	3,467	5,443	14,728	21,468	51,538	85,756	54,321	136,339	373,060
1975	3,021	4,281	17,605	24,665	45,042	93,769	54,681	181,827	424,891
1976	3,078	4,700	15,824	28,357	46,838	98,302	82,959	150,238	430,296
1977	2,993	4,430	19,081	26,705	54,445	83,978	101,272	168,219	461,123
1978	2,439	4,509	18,908	27,275	58,095	93,913	103,846	172,149	481,134
1979	2,529	5,563	18,851	24,683	59,515	77,087	129,100	172,316	489,644
1980	2,663	5,281	19,713	27,260	60,870	88,960	125,024	173,228	502,999
1981	2,355	5,868	17,385	28,141	57,153	91,927	130,213	184,574	517,616
1982	2,660	5,988	16,150	28,856	53,917	92,260	136,693	191,891	528,415
1983	2,139	5,449	12,426	27,558	51,299	90,676	128,481	211,193	529,221
1984	1,955	5,304	18,490	34,203	51,790	100,876	126,448	208,200	547,266
1985	1,891	5,718	21,906	36,354	50,865	107,068	122,226	214,311	560,339
1986	3,153	7,727	27,748	46,509	65,131	117,149	112,889	225,518	605,824
1987	3,926	7,504	25,960	43,393	74,850	104,251	120,981	225,048	605,913
1988	4,284	7,593	29,951	40,333	72,145	118,095	122,392	222,124	616,917

Sources: Ministry of Labour, *Annual Report*, various years.

Tables 6.9 and 6.10 also suggest a tendency between 1970 and 1980 for a higher proportion of union members to be found in the relatively larger unions with between 5000 to 10,000 members. However, as Table 6.11 shows, the number of small unions with less than 200 members seemed to be declining in the mid-1970s, after which they have been growing in number, probably due to official efforts to promote in-house unions.

Table 6.10　Peninsular Malaysia: total trade union membership by union size, 1962–88 (percentages)

				Number of union members				
	<100	100 to 200	201 to 500	501 to 1,000	1,001 to 2,000	2,001 to 5,000	5,001 to 10,000	>10,000	Total
1962	2.0	3.3	7.0	7.8	12.3	10.2	9.2	48.2	100.0
1963	1.6	2.9	6.5	7.3	11.6	16.6	6.0	47.5	100.0
1964	1.3	2.7	4.6	6.6	11.1	18.1	4.2	51.4	100.0
1965	1.3	2.6	4.9	7.8	11.3	19.3	1.6	51.2	100.0
1966	1.2	2.6	5.6	8.4	11.7	18.7	3.8	48.0	100.0
1967	1.2	2.0	4.7	8.5	13.6	17.4	12.4	40.2	100.0
1968	1.1	2.0	4.7	7.3	15.7	22.0	8.8	38.4	100.0
1969	1.2	1.8	5.5	6.9	13.1	18.5	17.1	35.9	100.0
1970	1.3	1.5	5.8	6.9	13.2	22.1	11.4	37.8	100.0
1971	1.1	1.7	6.0	8.8	14.6	17.9	16.6	33.3	100.0
1972	1.1	1.6	4.8	5.8	18.5	18.1	18.3	31.8	100.0
1973	1.1	1.2	4.9	6.7	15.7	22.9	17.8	29.7	100.0
1974	0.9	1.5	3.9	5.8	13.8	23.0	14.6	36.5	100.0
1975	0.7	1.0	4.1	5.8	10.6	22.1	12.9	42.8	100.0
1976	0.7	1.1	3.7	6.6	10.9	22.8	19.3	34.9	100.0
1977	0.6	1.0	4.1	5.8	11.8	18.2	22.0	36.5	100.0
1978	0.5	0.9	3.9	5.7	12.1	19.5	21.6	35.8	100.0
1979	0.5	1.1	3.8	5.0	12.2	15.7	26.5	35.2	100.0
1980	0.5	1.1	3.9	5.4	12.1	17.7	24.9	34.4	100.0
1981	0.5	1.1	3.4	5.4	11.0	17.8	25.2	35.6	100.0
1982	0.5	1.1	3.1	5.5	10.2	17.4	25.9	36.3	100.0
1983	0.4	1.0	2.4	5.2	9.7	17.1	24.3	39.9	100.0
1984	0.4	1.0	3.4	6.2	9.5	18.4	23.1	38.0	100.0
1985	0.3	1.0	3.9	6.5	9.1	19.1	21.8	38.3	100.0
1986	0.5	1.3	4.6	7.7	10.8	19.3	18.6	37.2	100.0
1987	0.6	1.2	4.3	7.2	12.3	17.2	20.0	37.1	100.0
1988	0.7	1.2	4.9	6.5	11.7	19.1	19.8	36.0	100.0

Source:　Calculated from Table 6.9.

Table 6.11   Peninsular Malaysia: trade unions by union size, 1962–88

	<100	100 to 200	201 to 500	501 to 1,000	1,001 to 2,000	2,001 to 5,000	5,001 to 10,000	>10,000	Total
				Number of union members					
1962	112	56	60	31	23	9	3	1	295
1963	99	55	59	29	22	15	2	2	283
1964	96	62	48	33	27	19	2	3	290
1965	106	59	49	36	26	18	1	3	302
1966	81	55	52	38	25	17	2	4	274
1967	81	44	44	36	27	15	6	3	256
1968	72	41	42	31	31	18	4	3	242
1969	75	35	49	28	26	16	8	2	239
1970	78	31	48	27	26	19	5	2	236
1971	71	33	50	32	29	17	7	1	240
1972	69	34	44	24	40	18	8	1	238
1973	69	27	48	30	35	23	8	2	242
1974	66	36	46	30	36	26	7	2	249
1975	60	29	55	34	32	30	8	4	252
1976	59	34	49	40	33	31	12	4	262
1977	56	31	55	37	39	26	15	5	264
1978	51	31	56	38	41	28	15	5	265
1979	47	37	57	35	41	26	18	5	266
1980	51	37	58	36	42	27	18	5	274
1981	49	40	58	40	40	26	18	6	277
1982	46	39	50	42	39	30	20	6	272
1983	39	37	51	46	42	31	20	7	273
1984	37	37	57	48	37	33	18	8	275
1985	35	39	64	50	36	33	17	8	282
1986	69	54	82	65	47	37	16	9	379
1987	81	52	76	63	54	34	18	9	387
1988	79	49	90	57	51	39	18	9	392

Source: Ministry of Labour, *Annual Report*, various years.

Industrial Disputes

Perhaps more significant than levels of unionization have been the trends in industrial actions taken by workers. It might be argued that fewer industrial actions could reflect greater worker satisfaction with job conditions or greater disinclination to take industrial action because of the difficulties and sacrifices involved. Certainly, the changing industrial relations environment in Malaysia – particularly the role of legislation and its implications for mounting industrial action – have gradually and systematically limited workers and union rights while

Table 6.12   Peninsular Malaysia: number of strikes, workers involved, working days lost, total union membership, percentage involved, 1947–88

	No. of strikes	No. of workers involved	No. of working days lost	Total union membership	Percentage of membership involved
1947	291	69,217	696,036	195,113	4
1948	181	34,037	370,464	69,134	5
1949	29	2,292	5,390	41,305	6
1950	48	4,925	37,067	54,579	9
1951	58	7,454	41,365	107,171	7
1952	98	12,801	44,489	127,946	1
1953	47	7,524	38,957	109,557	7
1954	78	10,011	50,831	113,470	9
1955	72	15,386	79,931	145,749	1
1956	213	48,677	562,125	232,174	2
1957	113	14,067	218,562	222,173	6
1958	69	9,467	59,211	210,688	4
1959	39	6,946	38,523	175,647	4
1960	37	4,596	41,947	184,627	2
1961	58	9,045	59,730	211,801	4
1962	95	232,912	449,856	257,486	9
1963	72	17,232	305,168	276,070	6
1964	85	226,427	508,439	323,208	7
1965	46	14,684	152,666	328,331	4
1966	60	16,673	109,915	316,609	5
1967	45	9,452	157,984	307,663	3
1968	103	31,062	280,417	300,183	1
1969	49	8,750	76,779	290,549	3
1970	17	1,216	1,867	275,238	1
1971	45	5,311	20,265	283,594	2
1972	66	9,701	33,455	296,782	3
1973	66	14,003	40,866	318,459	4
1974	85	21,830	103,884	373,572	6
1975	64	12,124	45,749	425,408	3
1976	70	20,040	108,562	430,790	4
1977	40	7,783	73,729	461,637	2
1978	36	6,792	35,032	481,658	1
1979	28	5,629	24,868	490,325	1
1980	28	3,402	19,554	503,686	1
1981	24	4,832	11,850	518,831	1
1982	26	3,330	9,621	529,046	1
1983	24	2,458	7,880	529,982	1
1984	17	2,437	9,269	547,936	1
1985	22	8,710	34,773	560,952	2
1986	23	3,957	14,333	561,099	1
1987	13	2,192	n.a.	560,725	0
1988	9	2,912	n.a.	568,408	1

Source: Ministry of Labour, *Annual Report*, various years.

strengthening management and government prerogatives. The result has been an overall decline in industrial disputes, particularly strikes, over the last four decades, especially since the mid-1970s, although this process has hardly been a gradual or smooth one, of course.

Table 6.12 lists the number of strikes, workers involved and working days lost by year. It suggests that while strike actions in the late 1940s and mid-1950s may have been economically inspired, they were supported by and contributed to the Independence struggle. Both were effectively suppressed by the state of emergency declared in 1948 and lasting until 1960. The subsequent upsurges of industrial action in the mid- and late 1960s met with two more states of emergency during the Indonesian Confrontation and after the May 1969 race riots. The table also shows that the percentage of trade union members involved in strikes declined from the mid-1950s, and especially after Independence in 1957, before rising in 1962 and 1964, and then declined again from the mid-1960s, especially in the 1970s, and even more so from the late 1970s. The evidence points to increasing strike activity being met by greater repression legitimized by the declared states of emergency.

Table 6.13 breaks down the strikes by sector and industry, clearly showing that most strikes have involved workers in 'agricultural products requiring substantial processing', though manufacturing-sector strikes have become increasingly significant since Independence, especially since the 1970s. The declaration of a state of emergency in June 1948 dramatically reduced the number of strikes, workers involved and working days lost in the agricultural sector from 231 strikes, 46,282 workers and 402,655 days in 1947 to 19 strikes, 2026 workers and 4753 days in 1949. The resurgence of labour activity in the plantations in the early and mid-1960s has not been seen again since then, resulting in a decline in tappers' real wages between 1960 and 1981 despite a 128 per cent increase in productivity (Jomo, 1986b). The organization of an alternative plantation workers' union in the form of the United Malayan Estate Workers' Union (UMEWU) in the mid-1960s partly accounts for the resurgence of strike activity after the crushing of militant unions in the late 1940s and subsequent colonial government support for the establishment of the National Union of Plantation Workers (NUPW).

The issues leading to strikes are broken down in Table 6.14. Pay disputes appear to have declined in significance over the years until the 1980s, whereas strikes due to worker dismissals rose in significance from the mid-1950s and through the 1960s. Other employment conditions have also been important, while 'other' strike issues not related to collective bargaining have become more significant since the 1970s. The outcomes of strike actions are summarized in Table 6.15, which suggests that since the 1970s worker demands have generally been less likely to be successful as 'indeterminate' or 'unknown' outcomes became more commonplace. While there is no clear pattern of total or partial rejection

Capital, the state and labour

Table 6.13   Peninsular Malaysia: percentage of strikes by industry, 1947–88

	Agriculture	Agricultural products requiring substantial processing	Mining & quarrying	Manufac- turing	Building & construction
1947	–	78.0	3.7	11.5	–
1948	–	88.9	4.2	0.5	0.5
1949	–	65.5	–	3.4	–
1950	–	77.1	2.1	–	–
1951	–	79.3	1.7	–	–
1952	–	90.8	–	6.1	–
1953	4.2	87.5	–	6.3	–
1954	–	82.1	3.8	–	–
1955	–	68.1	6.9	–	–
1956	0.5	77.0	4.7	6.6	0.9
1957	–	62.8	3.5	19.5	0.9
1958	–	55.1	8.7	26.1	–
1959	–	74.4	–	23.1	–
1960	–	81.1	–	5.4	8.1
1961	–	87.9	3.4	3.4	3.4
1962	–	82.1	–	7.4	–
1963	–	83.3	1.4	4.2	1.4
1964	–	76.5	–	9.4	–
1965	–	71.1	2.2	2.2	2.2
1966	–	65.0	3.0	25.0	1.5
1967	–	58.0	4.0	20.0	9.0
1968	–	87.0	–	8.0	1.0
1969	–	80.0	2.0	8.0	–
1970	–	70.0	–	30.0	–
1971	–	68.7	–	28.7	–
1972	–	46.8	3.4	33.3	–
1973	–	47.0	1.5	37.9	–
1974	–	44.7	–	36.5	2.4
1975	–	54.7	3.1	25.0	3.1
1976	–	25.7	–	48.5	5.7
1977	27.5	–	0	45.0	7.5
1978	–	58.3	2.8	30.6	5.6
1979	46.4	–	0	32.1	0
1980	–	25.0	–	71.4	3.6
1981	–	50.0	–	37.5	8.3
1982	–	57.8	–	23.1	11.5
1983	–	75.0	4.2	8.3	8.3
1984	–	76.5	5.9	17.6	–
1985	–	60.9	–	17.4	8.7
1986	–	61.0	8.7	21.7	4.3
1987	84.6	–	0	7.7	7.7
1988	55.6	–	33.3	0	0

Source: Ministry of Labour, *Annual Report*, various years.

Electricity water, etc.	Commerce	Transport & communications	Services	Activities omitted	Total
0.3	0.7	2.4	3.4	–	100.0
–	–	1.1	0.5	4.2	100.0
–	–	–	3.4	27.6	100.0
–	–	–	–	20.8	100.0
–	–	–	–	19.0	100.0
–	–	3.1	–	–	100.0
–	–	–	2.1	–	100.0
–	–	–	–	14.1	100.0
–	–	–	–	25.0	100.0
–	–	8.5	–	1.0	100.0
–	1.8	8.8	–	2.7	100.0
–	1.4	7.2	1.4	–	100.0
–	–	2.6	–	–	100.0
–	–	5.4	–	–	100.0
–	1.7	–	–	–	100.0
–	5.3	5.3	–	–	100.0
2.8	2.8	2.8	1.4	–	100.0
–	1.2	5.9	7.1	–	100.0
–	6.7	6.7	8.9	–	100.0
–	3.0	–	1.5	–	100.0
–	4.0	–	2.0	–	100.0
–	1.0	–	3.0	–	100.0
–	6.0	–	4.0	–	100.0
–	–	–	–	–	100.0
–	2.6	–	–	–	100.0
–	4.5	7.5	4.5	–	100.0
–	6.1	3.0	4.5	–	100.0
–	3.5	5.9	7.0	–	100.0
–	3.1	6.3	4.7	–	100.0
–	8.6	8.6	2.9	–	100.0
0	5.0	12.5	2.5	0	100.0
–	–	2.7	–	–	100.0
0	17.9	3.6	0	0	100.0
–	–	–	–	–	100.0
–	–	–	4.2	–	100.0
–	–	3.8	3.8	–	100.0
–	–	4.2	–	–	100.0
–	–	–	–	–	100.0
–	–	8.7	4.3	–	100.0
–	–	4.3	–	–	100.0
0	0	0	0	0	100.0
0	11.1	0	0	0	100.0

Table 6.14 *Peninsular Malaysia: percentage of strikes by dispute issues, 1953–88*

		Strike related to collective bargaining		Dispute issues
	Refusal to conclude a collective agreement	Wages	Hours of labour	Other conditions of employment
1953	–	40	2	19
1954	–	36	4	26
1955	–	36	1	14
1956	–	40	4	10
1957	–	45	2	11
1958	–	28	3	19
1959	–	13	3	26
1960	–	30	3	32
1961	–	20	2	50
1962	–	19	3	34
1963	–	20	4	17
1964	–	27	1	23
1965	–	26	2	17
1966	–	18	–	25
1967	–	2	–	18
1968	–	17	2	32
1969	–	22	2	31
1970	–	18	–	23
1971	–	11	9	35
1972	8	12	2	32
1973	6	21	3	25
1974	5	31	2	28
1975	–	15	2	33
1976	10	41	–	16
1977	–	20	–	30
1978	8	30	6	11
1979	n.a.	n.a.	n.a.	n.a.
1980	4	75	7	7
1981	4	21	4	8
1982	8	34	8	8
1983	–	13	–	33
1984	–	24	–	29
1985	14	86	–	–
1986	22	78	–	–
1987	n.a.	n.a.	n.a.	n.a.
1988	n.a.	n.a.	n.a.	n.a.

Source: Ministry of Labour, *Annual Report*, various years.

Strike not related to collective bargaining

Trade union recognition	Engagement or dismissal of workers	Sympathetic dispute	Political dispute	Others
–	15	2	–	22
–	18	8	–	8
2	32	1	–	14
2	33	4	–	7
–	31	4	–	7
1	38	1	–	10
3	41	3	–	11
3	19	3	–	10
–	19	2	–	7
1	35	2	–	6
3	40	8	–	8
2	45	2	–	–
5	50	–	–	–
5	40	10	–	2
13	60	2	–	5
3	39	2	–	5
–	31	2	–	12
–	47	6	–	6
–	16	2	–	27
–	30	6	–	10
–	17	2	–	26
–	14	1	1	18
–	17	2	–	31
–	23	–	–	10
15	35	–	–	–
–	14	–	–	31
n.a.	n.a.	n.a.	n.a.	n.a.
–	–	–	–	7
–	4	–	–	59
–	15	–	–	27
–	4	–	–	50
–	6	12	–	29
–	–	–	–	–
–	–	–	–	–
n.a.	n.a.	n.a.	n.a.	n.a.
n.a.	n.a.	n.a.	n.a.	n.a.

Table 6.15   *Peninsular Malaysia: percentage of strikes by outcome*
when strike ended, 1953–88

Year	Workers' demands entirely accepted	Workers' demands partially accepted	Workers' demands rejected	Employers' demands entirely accepted
1953	17	25	31	2
1954	22	40	23	4
1955	19	39	14	8
1956	20	39	26	–
1957	18	43	21	–
1958	23	35	19	–
1959	23	31	31	–
1960	19	35	16	–
1961	33	28	22	7
1962	32	27	11	8
1963	32	47	6	1
1964	25	53	11	–
1965	20	23	20	4
1966	18	52	5	2
1967	11	47	40	–
1968	25	26	6	4
1969	14	33	16	2
1970	12	12	41	6
1971	22	13	16	2
1972	4	33	17	2
1973	9	27	21	2
1974	5	36	19	4
1975	20	28	17	5
1976	18	36	16	–
1977	15	35	12	0
1978	17	30	42	3
1979	22	32	25	–
1980	7	25	68	–
1981	4	29	21	9
1982	12	8	23	4
1983	9	33	33	–
1984	17	24	24	–
1985	30	30	40	–
1986	13	13	70	4
1987	–	–	–	–
1988	–	–	–	–

Source: Ministry of Labour, *Annual Report*, various years.

Employers' demands partially accepted	Employers' demands rejected	Indeterminate or unknown results	Strikes still ongoing in that year
6	–	19	–
4	1	6	–
13	–	6	1
8	–	5	2
–	–	18	–
–	–	23	–
–	–	15	–
–	–	30	–
2	–	3	5
6	–	3	3
–	–	8	6
6	–	4	1
7	–	26	–
–	–	21	2
–	–	2	–
1	34	4	–
4	–	31	–
–	–	29	–
2	–	45	–
–	–	44	–
3	–	38	–
1	–	35	–
2	–	28	–
–	–	30	–
0	0	38	0
–	–	8	–
–	–	21	–
–	–	–	–
4	–	33	–
–	–	53	–
–	–	25	–
–	6	29	–
–	–	–	–
–	–	–	–
–	–	–	–
–	–	–	–

of workers' demands, strike outcomes seemed to become more unfavourable for the workers involved in the 1980s.

All these trends, however, should be seen against the overall trend of declining industrial action, especially strike activity, in the late 1950s and then from the mid-1960s, especially in the 1970s, and even more so in the 1980s. There is little reason to believe that this trend has been primarily due to improved labour conditions or greater worker satisfaction. While working conditions have undoubtedly improved generally with rapid economic growth, rising productivity, improved workers' bargaining position due to lower unemployment and tighter labour-market conditions, there is also evidence that labour's share of the growing output has declined, at least in the agricultural and manufacturing sectors (see Jomo and Ishak, 1986). In other words, more powerful and effective trade unions could have ensured that workers would have enjoyed more of the fruits of rapid economic growth, especially since Independence. A stronger labour movement would probably also have stemmed the communal tide in Malaysian politics, especially since the late 1960s, and helped ensure a more democratic polity, greater public accountability and more respect for civil liberties and human rights generally.

V   CAUSES OF CHANGE IN CAPITAL–LABOUR RELATIONS

Available official data do not allow systematic and rigorous analysis of changes in capital–labour relations, let alone their causes. Nevertheless, fragmentary evidence from various sources provides valuable insights into the possible factors involved. Such evidence will be utilized to evaluate various propositions which have been suggested to explain the supposedly recent breakdown of capital–labour relations associated with the Golden Age. Perhaps most importantly, the Golden Age in the central theatres of capital accumulation has had very diverse implications, not unrelated to the character of uneven development at the global, national and regional levels, as well as other specific conjunctural developments, with particular spatial or locational implications.

Internal Developments

As the preceding survey suggests, the rapid growth of wage labour in the last two decades – especially in manufacturing and services – has not resulted in a corresponding strengthening of worker organizations, including the trade union movement. On the contrary, the already weak trade union movement has been further weakened by increasingly repressive labour policy and legislation, ethnic mistrust and other debilitating factors. Hence labour struggles in themselves have not been generally important in improving the welfare of workers since the 1960s, although there have been some important exceptions. Industrial action or the threat of such action has secured small, but significant gains for workers, e.g. for plantation employees in early 1990.

Instead, however, declining unemployment from the early 1970s, with the growth of public-sector employment, export-oriented industrialization and other services, as well as labour emigration to Singapore and the Middle East (especially in the late 1970s), greatly strengthened labour's bargaining position and brought about some significant wage increases. However, the slowdown in manufacturing growth and the government's austerity drive from the early 1980s, and the severe recession of 1985 and 1986 – due to the collapse of primary commodity prices and exacerbated by deflationary fiscal policies – caused the unemployment rate to rise from 4.6 per cent in 1983 to 8.1 per cent in 1987. This upsurge of unemployment and the negative demonstration effect of stagnant wages in the public sector adversely affected labour's bargaining position and wage levels more generally.

Owing to the weak trade union movement, ethnic divisions among the working class as well as other deterrents to labour mobilization, and the effective elimination of much of the parliamentary left from the mid-1960s, there has been a decline of class conflict since the late 1960s. Nevertheless, the reduction of unemployment in the early and mid-1970s enabled labour to gain from near full employment and the tighter labour market.

This situation was mainly due to factors including:

1. The rapid growth of the public sector from the early 1970s ostensibly to advance inter-ethnic redistributive policies.
2. The growth of manufacturing employment with the success of export-oriented industrialization under foreign auspices.
3. The generally more rapid growth of the economy with increased public spending, especially with the expansion of oil revenues from the mid-1970s due to the oil price increase and additional production with the discovery of new deposits.

Hence, in the late 1970s and early 1980s, real wages grew as money wage increases outstripped the high inflation at the time. However, this trend was unsustainable for a variety of reasons, especially the massive deficit financing from foreign sources, particularly in the early 1980s. Hence, after the Volcker-triggered increase in interest rates in the early 1980s, like many other debtor economies, the Malaysian government was forced to reduce public spending, setting off deflationary pressures. At the same time, the real property market boom – which had been sustained by generous and low-interest facilities, especially for public-sector employees – was another casualty of the government spending cuts.

The structural adjustment policies introduced by the government from the mid-1980s have included a commitment to providing more attractive incentives for investors, especially in manufacturing and modern services. With the Plaza II agreements of September 1986 leading to the depreciation of the US dollar against the Japanese yen, the Deutschmark and other major currencies, the Malaysian authorities decided to stop supporting the Malaysian dollar, the ringgit, allowing it to depreciate even against the US dollar. While this massive depreciation almost doubled the size of the Malaysian foreign debt, it also served to reduce production costs, especially labour costs in Malaysia by international comparison. With the rise of the Japanese yen and other East Asian currency values (against the ringgit), and the increase of production costs more generally in the East Asian newly industrialized economies, there has been significant relocation of manufacturing activities in Malaysia. This has been further encouraged by a new round of attractive investment incentives, relatively good infrastructure facilities as well as other incentives to relocate in Malaysia, such as the lifting of existing curbs on foreign ownership of real property in Malaysia (though subsequent opposition has forced the authorities to tighten up once again). The result has been a tremendous growth of manufacturing investment and activity, especially under foreign auspices, mainly from Japan, Taiwan and Singapore.

This has been encouraged by changing production arrangements requiring closer location of ancillary industries, thus strengthening linkages within the manufacturing sector, which have long remained weak, owing to the foreign-dominated character of manufacturing activity in the country. The new circumstances have encouraged medium and small manufacturing firms supplying larger firms in Japan to relocate abroad as the larger firms had already begun to do so much earlier. Hence, ironically, the foreign domination – which had previously been responsible for the poorly integrated nature of the Malaysian manufacturing sector – has recently contributed to the strengthening of linkages, although not with all the usual features normally accompanying such developments.

Meanwhile, labour policy reforms have further weakened labour rights and existing trade unions. The recent spate of investments in the Malaysian manufacturing sector in the late 1980s has been the outcome of global, or at least East Asian industrial restructuring. This has been accompanied by greater labour flexibility without any concomitant improvement in income security for labour. There has been, for instance, a much greater casualization of employment, which has undoubtedly weakened the bargaining position of workers *vis-à-vis* management. Hence it is unlikely that improved labour organization in itself would be able to significantly contribute to enhancing workers' welfare in the near future. Rather, such an improvement may lie in favourable labour-market conditions and enhanced labour productivity, e.g. due to skill development. New manufacturing linkages have developed in line with the requirements of the new production and process technologies. For instance, just-in-time (JIT) production arrangements require input supply sources which are close by, incurring minimal delivery delays, and thus encouraging ancillary industries to relocate nearby. It is still unclear whether Taylorism has exhausted itself in these situations as mass production for export (i.e. consumption abroad) is still growing, although not as rapidly as smaller batch production involving greater flexible special-ization (Grace, 1990).

Economic Crisis

Given the very open nature of the Malaysian economy, where about three-fifths of the GDP is exported (and an almost equivalent proportion of expenditure is spent on imported goods and services), external demand is as important, if not more important than domestic demand. During the 1985–86 recession, inter-national demand for many Malaysian primary exports collapsed, resulting in considerably lower commodity prices. In early 1985, palm oil prices declined precipitously from an all-time high in 1984. In October 1985, the International Tin Agreement buffer stock operations ceased, causing the price of the metal to collapse. Malaysia had long been the world's greatest exporter of both these commodities. In early 1986, the petroleum price collapsed internationally, again adversely affecting Malaysia's export earnings. Meanwhile, Malaysia's manufactured exports were under pressure; the electronics industry, in particular, was severely buffeted as the industry's business cycle reached its nadir.

As indicated earlier, domestic demand too had been adversely affected from the early 1980s. The mid-1980s' decline and slowdown in growth of aggregate demand was also due to significant reductions in public spending. This was largely a matter of policy choice, rather than compelling economic circumstances owing to the highly open nature of the Malaysian economy. After the general elections of 1982, the government announced an austerity drive, cutting public, especially development expenditure immediately, and for several years to come throughout the mid-1980s. More generally, this marked the end of an era of public-sector expansion from the early 1970s. It also marked the beginning of a series of structural adjustments, guided by international agencies such as the World Bank, International Monetary Fund and the Asian Development Bank. Rising interest rates, tighter credit facilities and cuts in public spending induced generally deflationary consequences for the rest of the economy.

The greatest impact of the decline in aggregate demand was on 'non-tradables', e.g. real property and construction. This was manifested particularly in the collapse of the real property market, with serious implications for the domestic construction industry. The industry had already suffered from the award of numerous lucrative construction contracts to Japanese and South Korean firms which had lost jobs in the Middle East in the early 1980s as the price of petroleum began to decline. The overall decline in aggregate demand was, in turn, exacerbated by the growth of unemployment. It is very likely that the economic crisis of 1985–86, which was the culmination of a wide-ranging malaise from the early 1980s, accelerated changes in capital–labour relations which had already begun, although the empirical evidence does not allow more definite evaluation of this hypothesis.

In view of Malaysia's very open economy, greater weight should be placed on the significance of external constraints. There is little doubt that historically, Malaysian economic growth has been very much influenced by international growth trends, especially in the OECD economies. However, Malaysian growth rates have historically been higher than OECD growth rates, both in boom and bust phases, with occasional exceptional periods. The Malaysian economy has been particularly vulnerable to primary commodity price trends, especially for its main exports, which now include petroleum, timber, rubber and palm oil. Employment in logging is very poorly regulated and logging workers have never had a union to protect their interests, unlike their colleagues further downstream in the wood industry. Petroleum and the related natural (petroleum) gas industries are very capital-intensive and the workers they employ are quite cut off from the rest of the labour force.

However, the rubber and oil palm plantation industries employ a quarter of a million people in Peninsular Malaysia alone who are very much affected by these international vicissitudes. Wage incomes in the plantation industry are among the most stagnant in real terms despite tremendous productivity increases. Since the late 1970s, plantation wages have been successfully depressed by the use of disenfranchised immigrant workers willing to work for lower wages. There is also evidence of generally lower wages in the export-oriented industries, e.g. electronics, textiles and garments, compared to the capital-intensive import-substituting industries. However, greater productivity gains in the former have helped to reduce the income gap among manufacturing-sector workers, although the gap between manufacturing-sector wages and plantation incomes has continued to grow.

The decline in domestic and external demand clearly affected the industries concerned, and inevitably, capital–labour relations as well. However, there is little evidence to suggest that the impact on capital–labour relations in these industries has been qualitatively different from the impact of similar earlier crises. This is not to suggest that history is simply repeating itself with every crisis. Clearly, there have been changes, and important ones at that. However, it does not appear that the main qualitative changes in capital–labour relations which have occurred in the last decade have been primarily due to adverse shifts in aggregate demand, whether domestically or abroad.

Changing International Division of Labour

The changing international division of labour, with the relocation of manufacturing activities in the south since the 1960s, has been the subject of much attention and discussion. However, the growth in Malaysia of export-oriented industries in this connection only really took off in the early 1970s, although a new policy and legal framework for its promotion had emerged in the late 1960s. This included the activation, from 1967, of the Federal Industrial Development Authority set up in 1965. A new Industrial Incentives Act – superseding the Pioneer Industries Ordinance of the late 1950s which was oriented towards promoting import-substituting industries – was passed in 1968. During the state of emergency after the May 1969 race riots, new labour legislation was introduced to complement the new framework for export-oriented manufacturing growth.

As noted earlier, there was a tremendous growth of labour employed in the manufacturing sector in the 1970s, notably including a high proportion of women. The growth of the public sector in the same period contributed significantly to the expansion of employment in services. Hence the growth in manufacturing and services as well as other secondary and tertiary activities more than compensated for the relative decline in employment in agriculture (and mining). Consequently, aided by labour emigration, unemployment declined significantly in the late 1970s. The majority of the labour force were now wage-earners, rather than self-employed, whether in peasant agriculture or in the urban informal sector.

The growth of formal education contributed to labour productivity as well. However, although labour market conditions due to these factors strengthened labour's position and workers' welfare, especially in the late 1970s and early 1980s, this trend was not accompanied by a strengthening of the labour movement. On the contrary, as noted earlier, repression from the mid-1960s had broken the back of militant leftist labour activism, leaving the field open to 'moderate', 'responsible' and collaborative union leaders. The Malaysian regime in the early 1970s softened this trend by making some minor concessions to labour and rhetorically encouraging corporatism in the form of 'tripartism', involving the state, management and labour.

However, since the late 1970s, and especially during the early 1980s, the labour movement has been further weakened by government policies and legislation. Less than a tenth of the labour force has been unionized, although a large majority now comprises wage labour. Among waged employees, only one sixth are in trade unions. More than half the unionized workers are in the public sector, and are hence denied basic collective bargaining rights by law.

Of employees in the private sector, the single largest union, the National Union of Plantation Workers (NUPW) was set up under British colonial auspices in the early 1950s and has remained under the same leadership to this day. Only in 1990 did it finally make a little progress in trying to establish a monthly wage for plantation workers after taking some industrial action. However, official data suggest that despite tremendous increases in plantation labour productivity, real wages may have actually declined due to the inability of the union to secure substantive gains for the workers. The union is also notorious for its undemocratic and unaccountable leadership and administration as well as for imposing the highest union rates on its still large membership, which was halved over the 1980s.

Most of the manufacturing-sector unions have remained small, although some have been reasonably effective, compared to public-sector unions and the NUPW. However, economic restructuring from the mid-1980s has taken a considerable toll on at least some of these unions. For example, the relatively small Transport Equipment Industry Employees' Union had its membership reduced by half with the government's launching of Proton, an ostensibly Malaysian-made car actually controlled by Mitsubishi. Other existing car assembly plants have been forced to close down or reduce their workforce as Mitsubishi has increased its market share from under 10 per cent to almost two-thirds in less than half a decade with government protection. Proton workers have not been allowed to join the existing national workers' union, though they have been told they can eventually form an in-house or company union.

In fact, the government has been encouraging the formation of in-house unions since the early 1980s in an attempt to weaken the trade union movement. In the mid-1940s, the British colonial government banned General Labour Unions (GLUs) by requiring that unions be organized along trade or industry lines. However, in the 1970s, a potentially large union in the manufacturing sector was avoided by only allowing textile and garment workers to join state-wide or regional unions. From the late 1970s, Prime Minister Mahathir Mohamad has been directly involved in encouraging in-house or company unions, instead of national unions. While company unions may not necessarily be ineffective, and may even encourage a greater degree of accountability on the part of the leadership, the in-house unions envisaged by the government are expected to be easily controlled by management.

There has been significant growth in the employment of illegal workers, especially from Indonesia, since the late 1970s, particularly in plantations, land clearance and development as well as construction. Such recruitment has undoubtedly weakened the NUPW and undermined the position of the other two sectors which have remained largely un-unionized.

Recent findings (Standing, 1993) suggest that there has been significant casualization of labour in the manufacturing sector between 1985 and 1988, which is probably related to higher unemployment, structural adjustments in the economy and management initiatives in response to new labour-market conditions. The trend of recent manufacturing investments in the late 1980s is also ominous.

Many of the new investors from Japan tend to be medium-sized or smaller firms seeking relocation to more effectively complement the larger firms they supply, which have already relocated in Malaysia. In general also, Taiwanese, Hong Kong and Singaporean firms tend to be smaller in size. Such firms are more likely to prioritize labour flexibility at the expense of worker security, and ultimately, the potential for effective mobilization and organization of the workers employed.

Exogenous Political Factors

Two external political developments are particularly worth noting when considering changes in capital–labour relations in Malaysia during the 1980s. First, as is now well known, the ascendance of the Third World, or the South, in the 1970s was effectively reversed in the 1980s. One hardly hears any more the rallying cry of the 1970s to establish a New International Economic Order (NIEO). While the NIEO's substantive demands still remain relevant – for example, higher and more stable commodity prices, more generous debt-financing facilities, greater and more meaningful technology transfer – the economic agenda of the 1980s was increasingly determined by private business interests, often transmitted through governments as well as international economic agencies. The clearest manifestation of this was the handling of the international debt crisis in the early 1980s, which in turn forced reluctant debtor governments to execute structural adjustment programmes imposed by such international agencies. Another clear example is the Uruguay round of GATT (General Agreement on Tariffs and Trade) negotiations which has just been ratified, in which the North, led by the US, is seeking to extend the scope of coverage from international trade in commodities to include trade in services as well as foreign investment flows and intellectual property rights, all of which are likely to constrain the likelihood of more autonomous, domestic-led industrialization in the South.

Faced with such a difficult external environment and reluctant to encourage the development of a domestic industrial community likely to be dominated by ethnic Chinese, the Malaysian government has voluntarily gone along with much of the economic agenda imposed by the North. Other influences on capital–labour relations are more indirect. The changing character of the world economy in the 1980s, including the resurgence of protectionism as well as the emergence of new trading blocs, is likely to affect international trade patterns and international investment flows as well. Furthermore, recent developments in China are likely to affect investment flows in East and Southeast Asia, especially among the ethnic Chinese minorities, including those operating through Singapore and Hong Kong. Recent developments in Eastern Europe are likely to divert funds which might otherwise have flowed to the South. All these are especially important for an economy such as Malaysia, which is very open, even by Third

World standards. Market access is extremely important since Malaysia exports well over half of what it produces, including an increasingly large share of manufactures. Also, investment in modern activities, especially manufacturing and services, has been largely dominated by foreign capital. After all, the Malaysian economic slowdown of the first half of the 1980s was partly caused by the decline of foreign investment during that period.

From Mass Production to Flexible Specialization

At the global level, there has undoubtedly been a fairly significant trend towards greater product differentiation, involving a shift from Taylorist mass production to smaller batch production, often involving some degree of flexible specialization in product and process technologies. This global trend has also been reflected in Malaysia, especially since much of Malaysian manufacturing is for export, and most of this is under transnational auspices. Owing to the highly open character of the Malaysian economy, society and culture, global trends in product differentiation have also been reflected in Malaysian consumption patterns. This has, of course, been encouraged by the rapid growth of income, especially in the 1970s and into the 1980s, which has in turn influenced the structure of demand in favour of differentiated, rather than standardized products.

This trend towards flexible specialization in production has probably been influenced by manufacturing technological developments internationally as well. Since most of the export-oriented industries in Malaysia are owned by or dependent on transnational corporations for their production technologies, technological developments abroad have greatly influenced product and process technologies used in Malaysia as well. Most notably, the shift to flexible specialization has been accentuated by more rapid information flows between consumer markets and product design and development centres, which have in turn become more closely integrated with actual production. This trend may have encouraged some relocation in the North to ensure closer integration with R&D centres as well as consumer markets, especially with robotization and greater automation, reducing direct human labour input. However, where considerable human labour is still required in the production processes, it has resulted, for example, in the greater linkages in the South, noted earlier for the Malaysian manufacturing sector since the mid-1980s.

VI   CONCLUDING REMARKS

Clearly, the significant changes in capital–labour relations in the Malaysian economy in the post war period are only partly related to developments associated with the earlier Golden Age and its subsequent demise. There are also significant differences reflecting uneven development within the Malaysian economy, for example, between sectors (primary/secondary/ tertiary), between activities (agriculture/mining/ manufacturing/construction/commerce/services), between industries, between regions, within industries (e.g. between high-tech electronics and consumer electronics) and so on. The highly varied nature of the Malaysian economy has, in turn, spawned a great variety of capital–labour relations which do not lend themselves to simple or convenient summary descriptions.

The extremely open nature of the Malaysian economy has also meant that the economy as a whole, including capital–labour relations, is very much subject to external influences. In some instances, such external influences have even been internalized as official policy, for example, the 'Look East' policy from the early 1980s has sought to emulate ostensibly Japanese work ethics and labour practices.

There have also been conflicting pressures on the Malaysian authorities to bring industrial relations in line with international trends. On the one hand, the neoclassical economists of the World Bank, IMF and Asian Development Bank have sought to reduce and eliminate supposed labour-market 'distortions', for example, by urging the reduction of public-sector wages and other emoluments in line with private-sector remuneration trends. Such pressures have also been responsible for the substantial depreciation of the Malaysian ringgit after September 1985, which has greatly reduced production, especially labour costs, from an international comparative perspective. On the other hand, however, diverse international labour organizations, such as the ILO and the international trade union secretariats, have sought to put pressure on governments to bring their labour policies and practices into line with international standards to ensure minimum levels of labour security and welfare. The record thus far clearly suggests that the Malaysian authorities themselves are more inclined to the former, rather than the latter.

Domestically, however, despite the tremendous expansion of wage labour over the last couple of decades, especially in manufacturing and services, it appears that labour organization and mobilization has become less significant since the 1960s. Hence trade unions have not been seen as particularly effective in significantly improving the welfare of the workers they represent. The government and managements have also worked quite effectively to discourage the more widespread and effective unionization of Malaysian workers. It thus appears that collective bargaining has not been particularly influential as a means of significantly advancing the position of labour *vis-à-vis* capital over the last two decades. It has also been argued (Standing, 1993) that labour legislation and policy have not been especially effective in influencing actual labour practices in Malaysian economy. Rather, the evidence seems to suggest that labour-market conditions have been the major determinant of the welfare of workers, a great majority of whom are not unionized, and many of whom do not enjoy job security in labour contracts which are being increasingly casualized.

Although prophecy is best left to those claiming divine or clairvoyant powers, it may not be too hazardous to suggest some likely developments in the near future. The Malaysian economy has picked up since late 1986, as commodity prices recovered and with the tremendous growth in new manufacturing invest-ments, especially from East Asia. By 1990, commodity prices had begun to decline again, although this impact was more than compensated for by increased timber output from 1987 and the continued strong resurgence in export-oriented manufacturing growth.

Some of the problems of the early 1980s are beginning to re-emerge as the government gets carried away by the longest sustained boom since Indepen-dence. Already, several unnecessary prestige projects – e.g. the proposed Highland Highway and the KL Telecommunications Tower, touted to be the tallest in the world – have been announced. Other very expensive projects of dubious value and feasibility have also been proclaimed, such as the West Coast Land Reclamation Scheme. Despite the expensive and unhappy experience with the heavy industry projects of the early 1980s, the government has recently approved further similar investments.

Yet simultaneously, the government seems quite interested to continue to privatize the more profitable and lucrative enterprises and activities it controls. In most instances, this has not involved arm's-length transactions, but rather political nepotism involving beneficiaries closely related to the ruling clique. Also, there has been fairly significant deregulation and other efforts since the mid-1980s to favour private-sector expansion more generously.

These two trends seem to suggest that the sustainability of the current expansion is in doubt. Although it is unclear how severe the next downturn is likely to be, there is general agreement that Malaysian growth is likely to continue to be quite cyclical. Past experience in medium-term economic fore-casting has generally been poor because of the highly open character of the Malaysian economy, both in terms of international trade and the dominance of foreign investments. In light of the changing role of state intervention in the economy since the early 1980s, it is probable that compensatory or counter-cyclical measures are less likely to succeed in the foreseeable future.

Public-sector expansion from the early 1970s has been accompanied by quasi-corporatism at the national level. The remaining pretensions to such cor-poratism *vis-à-vis* labour have been virtually destroyed over the 1980s under the Mahathir regime. A revival of tripartism at this stage may therefore not nec-essarily enhance labour's interests, as it might have done in the early 1970s. Under the general auspices of the 'Look East' policy from the early 1980s, one might think that the government was encouraging an alternative corporatism at the firm or enterprise level. However, the general environment has not significantly changed in order to favour such corporatism. There have been no outstanding measures beyond rhetoric to ensure greater management concern for and protection of employee interests, for example, in terms of guaranteed employment, or even wage increments based on seniority or productivity increases. The encouragement of in-house unions without any other accompanying measures to enhance workers' welfare will mean that employees will remain unorganized or less effectively organized in such unions, which are likely to be controlled by management.

Nevertheless, this bleak scenario does not necessarily condemn labour to immiserization despite the growing hegemony of capital. It is quite possible, in fact likely, that low unemployment levels will force management to better remunerate workers, especially those who are more highly skilled. In general, as skill requirements rise with the increasing sophistication and complexity of production processes, and in light of the existing skill bottlenecks in the country due to the nature of the school system, it is quite likely that the lot of skilled workers in particular will improve in the foreseeable future, especially those in the more dynamic and technologically progressive industries.

The fate of the rest, however, is more at risk. The lot of unskilled workers is likely to continue to be undermined by illegal immigrant labourers, who are generally prepared to work hard for lower wage rates than those that their Malaysian counterparts expect. Also, in so far as skilled workers are more likely to be ethnic Chinese, whereas less skilled workers are more likely to be Malays and Indians, the likely growing gap in worker remuneration may exacerbate existing inter-ethnic tensions among workers, which might in turn be manipulated by ambitious ethno-populist politicians, with potentially tragic consequences.

The foregoing discussion suggests that capital–labour relations in Malaysia remain quite diverse, although the nature of this diversity has changed significantly with the transformation of the national economy. At the sectoral level, there has been a significant growth of employment in services and manufacturing, with agricultural employment relatively stagnant and mining employment declining with the collapse of the tin industry. In plantation agriculture, the shift from rubber to palm oil has meant different labour requirements. But perhaps more important, the stagnation of plantation agricultural wages (Jomo, 1985) has involved increasing casualization of labour and employment of immigrant contract workers.

In manufacturing, import-substituting industries have generally employed relatively few workers, using imported technology on comparatively favourable terms made possible by heavy protectionism. In contrast, export-oriented industries generally employ many workers with relatively poorer remuneration, usually organized in Taylorist assembly lines. The growing labour flexibility noted in the manufacturing sector in the late 1980s coincides with new investments by smaller East Asian industrialists and the adoption of new production processes requiring greater supply flexibility. Also, with technological upgrading in the older export-oriented industries, it might be said that a trend away from traditional Taylorism has begun, although the significance of this development should not be exaggerated.

It is also clear that despite the rapid growth in wage employment since Independence, and especially in the last two decades, there has not been a corresponding strengthening of labour's bargaining position in industrial relations or even politically. Instead, a variety of developments related to government policy has ensured the contrary. Hence an important precondition for Fordism – namely a strong labour-based social democratic movement able to institute a 'Fordist' social contract with capital – is simply non-existent in Malaysia. Instead, it appears that favourable labour-market conditions during periods of rapid growth and low unemployment have been far more significant than either the strength of the labour movement or 'sympathetic' (or even corporatist) state intervention in improving workers' welfare.

The problem is exacerbated by the very open nature of the Malaysian economy – both in terms of international trade and foreign investments – which has meant that capital, especially in export-oriented manufacturing, remains foreign-dominated and uncommitted to deepening the national market. While foreign-dominated import-substituting manufacturers obviously gain from a larger national market and have generally been more willing to tolerate unions and concede better wages because they employ fewer workers with their imported technology and gain most of their profits from the protectionism they enjoy, there is no evidence that they are seriously committed to a Fordist national market-oriented growth strategy. In any case, export competitiveness has been the dominant theme for growth and manufacturing strategy since the advent of export-oriented industrialization, and especially since the mid-1980s. This has frequently been invoked to justify recent labour policies.

In light of recent developments and trends, labour's interests may be served by extending social security beyond the existing provisions for occupational disease and employment injury to cover unemployment benefits, sickness, maternity benefits, family allowances, invalidity pensions, old age pensions and survivors' pensions – as originally envisaged in the late 1960s (Paguman 1991). This should involve reasonable means testing and replacement of existing, highly politicized government patronage. Wage indexing to consumer prices and productivity increases would also protect and enhance workers' welfare without undermining capital's profits. However, the effective advocacy and advancement of labour's interests requires an institutionalized framework reflecting a social contract between capital and labour, which does not appear anywhere on Malaysia's political horizon for the time being.

REFERENCES

Chandra, Muzaffar (1983a) 'Hard Work: The Cure-All?', in Jomo (1985).

Chandra, Muzaffar (1983b) 'Overkill? In-house Unions for Malaysia', in Jomo (1985).

Chang, Yii Tan (1985) 'Tilting East: The Construction Problem', in Jomo (1985).

Chee, Peng Lim and Lee Poh Ping (1983) 'Japanese Joint Ventures in Malaysia', in Jomo (1983).

Grace, E. (1990) *Shortcircuiting Labour: Unionising Electronic Workers in Malaysia*, Kuala Lumpur: Insan.

Jomo, K.S. (ed.) (1985) *The Sun Also Sets: Lessons in Looking East*, Kuala Lumpur: Insan.

Jomo, K.S. (ed.) (1986a) 'Estates of Poverty: Malaysian Labour on Rubber Plantations', *Ilmu Masyarakat*, vol. 10.

Jomo, K.S. (1986b) *A Question of Class: Capital, the State and Uneven Development in Malaysia*, Singapore: Oxford University Press.

Jomo, K.S. (1990a) *Growth and Structural Change in the Malaysian Economy*, London: Macmillan.

Jomo, K.S. (1990b) *Undermining Tin: The Decline of Malaysian Pre-eminence*, Transnational Corporations Research Project, University of Sydney, Australia.

Jomo, K.S. and Ishak Shari (1986) *Development Policies and Income Inequality in Peninsular Malaysia*, Institute of Advanced Studies, University of Malaya, Kuala Lumpur.

Jomo, K.S. and Patricia Todd (1994), *Trade Unions and the State in Peninsular Malaysia*, Kuala Lumpur: Oxford University Press.

Kuppusamy, S. (1995), 'Employee Welfare' in Jomo (ed.) *Privatizing Malaysia: Rents, Rhetoric, Realities*, Boulder and London: Westview Press.

Lim, Teck Ghee (1984) 'British Colonial Administration and the Ethnic Division of Labour in Malaya', *Kajian Malaysia: Journal of Malaysian Studies*, vol.2, no.2.

Lipietz, Alan (1987) *Mirages and Miracles: The Crisis of Global Fordism*, London: Verso.

Mohd, Shahari Ahmad Jabar (1985) 'Government Support for Private Enterprise', in Jomo (1985).

Muto, Ichiyo (1985) 'Japanese Labour in the "Company World"', in Jomo (1985).

Paguman, Singh (1991) 'Social Security in Malaysia', in Colin Nicholas and Arne Wangel (eds) *Safety at Work in Malaysia: An Anthology of Current Research*, Institute of Advanced Studies, Universiti Malaya, Kuala Lumpur.

Parmer, J. Norman (1960) *Colonial Labour Policy and Administration: A History of Labour in the Rubber Plantation Industry in Malaya*, Locust Valley: Association for Asian Studies.

Pura, R. (1985) 'Doubts Over Heavy Industrialization Strategy', in Jomo (1985).

Rema Devi, P. (1987) 'Contract Labour in Peninsular Malaysia', M. Phil. Thesis, Institute of Advanced Studies, University of Malaya.

Rodan, Garry (1989) *The Political Economy of Singapore's Industrialisation: National State and International Capital*, London: Macmillan.

Ryder, W. James (1985) 'QCCs: Management's New Velvet Glove', in Jomo (1985).

Standing, Guy (1993) 'Labour Flexibility in the Malaysian Manufacturing Sector' in Jomo (ed.) *Industrialising Malaysia: Performance, Problems, Prospects*, London: Routledge.

Wad, Peter and K.S. Jomo (1994), 'In-House Unions: "Looking East" for Industrial Relations' in Jomo (ed.) *Japan and Malaysian Development: In the Shadow of the Rising Sun*, London: Routledge.

7. Capital, labour and the Indian state

J. Mohan Rao

I INTRODUCTION

Modern industry in India constitutes only an island within a predominantly traditional and backward economy. Yet, the 10–15 million workers it employs make it appreciably large by international standards. Although the pace of diversification and economic growth has quickened since Independence, per capita GDP in 1983–84, at purchasing power parities, was only one-third the mean for developing countries and one-thirteenth that for developed countries. It would be quixotic to regard this period as anything like a Golden Age. While India has managed to sustain nearly uninterrupted electoral democracy, there are great inequalities of power and wealth. State-guided capitalism in such a setting has allowed the manipulation of state institutions for the privileged and the powerful, and has divided the working classes. Nonetheless, industrial labour has posed serious challenges that neither capital nor the state has been able to surmount. This not only is a paradox that political economy must explain but should also inform any explanation of the pattern of economic growth in post-Independence India.

Towards these ends, the present chapter makes a case for a distinctive Indian model of capital–labour relations. The bulk of the labour force, working outside the formal sector, is subject to high rates of unemployment and underemployment, long and hard hours of work (when work is available) and to the virtual absence of social security. A large, impoverished reserve army of labour indicates a potentially quiescent and easily disciplined working class. This is certainly the case in the segment of industry where firms are small and workers unorganized. The high premium on job security is effectively utilized to buy the worker's loyalty and the employer's task of extracting labour is lightened.

However, among firms in the formal or organized sector, both public and private, labour unions and state laws all but erased the employer's ability to sack the worker. Given employment security, state regulation of both bargaining and the union movement have effectively delinked wages and job tenure from productivity. Symmetrically, an economy largely closed to foreign trade has allowed large firms considerable monopoly power in product markets while a framework of investment regulation has restrained the mobility of capital. This structure has significantly circumscribed the role of the market in economic coordination and defined the parameters of bargaining between capital and labour.

A conspicuous oddity of the Indian model is the simultaneous attempts by the state to enhance and limit the power of capital while similarly institutionalizing job security and manipulating unions and bargaining. This is explained by the conflicting demands of stability and growth in a mixed economy undergoing planned development. The conflict is greatly amplified by the pulls and pushes of powerful classes on state policy, the vulnerability of large segments of the population to inflation and the restraints of electoral democracy.[1] To these must be added the state's direct interest, by virtue of its leading role in growth and of owning over half the organized sector's capital stock, in containing wage differentials and other elements of the wage contract.

Production relations in the formal sector – featuring strict hierarchy, minimal worker participation and the attempt to separate knowledge from execution – faithfully conform to the Taylorist model. But the Taylorist project has been mostly thwarted due to the insecure basis of managerial authority, the continuing influence of paternalism and both formal and everyday resistance by workers. Unresolved workplace conflicts spill over into wage bargaining which assumes salience. Sheltered markets and industrial regulation have focused wage bargaining on issues of parity. Another implication of this structure is the markedly reduced flexibility of these firms in responding to changing markets and technologies. The attenuated link between job security, wages and productivity together with its implications for capital–labour conflict forms the first main theme of this chapter.

The other principal theme relates to the mutual determination and interaction between capital–labour relations in industry and the larger political economy of India. It is evident that the larger economy has conditioned industrial relations especially via state policy. However, their form is not reducible to the imperatives of state policy. Indeed, the latter cannot be understood apart from the structural influences of capital and labour. Over time as well, this mutual determination has played an influential role by compelling changes in both the overall economic regime and capital–labour relations. Again, given the structure of the economy, it is to be expected that the course of economic growth exercises a strong influence on capital–labour relations. Thus, by the mid- to late 1970s, important changes in economic strategy and policy were initiated which have weakened organized labour and enhanced capital's manoeuvrability. But the very initiation of these changes cannot be dissociated from growing contradictions in the relations of production.

In what follows, Section II is devoted to developing the first theme noted above through a focused account of capital–labour relations between 1947 and 1980. Work processes in large and small firms, in public firms and private, are discussed in the larger context of segmented labour markets. An analysis of the main features of the labour movement follows together with a consideration of the constitutive role of the state's legal and regulatory framework. This part of the study ends with a brief review of the course of wage and workplace conflicts over time to set the stage for an analysis of changes in capital–labour relations during the 1980s.

The joint evolution of industrial relations and accumulation eventually reached an economic and political impasse by the mid-1970s. Section III examines political and economic policy shifts that signified important changes in the parameters governing capital's relations with labour. It also outlines the nature of pressures upon capital that had built up over time and contradictions internal to the labour movement. Although political changes have played a very important role, we argue that these are related to evolutionary changes in the accumulation process.

The course of capital–labour relations in the aftermath of these changes is examined in Section IV. While the 1980s present a picture of disarray in industrial relations, dominant elements of continuity and change are hypothesized. We suggest that there is a developing pattern of new employment relations within the formal sector and a shift of activity to the small-firm sector. The chapter concludes with a brief assessment of what these changes portend for the future course of industrialization and industrial relations.

The study incorporates some observations from field visits during the winter of 1988. The larger portion of my time was spent with various textile units in Ahmedabad, 'the Manchester of India'. The composite (spinning and weaving) units that I visited include Arogya Mills, a long-established mill that has managed to remain in good health over six decades; Jupiter Mills, a comparable but 'sick' unit, managed by the government for over a decade; and Naveen Mills, a unit that has been in existence only fifteen years. I also visited two small powerloom units owned by PL Weaving and two textile-processing houses of PH Processing. I spent the rest of my time at the machine-tools and watch factories of HMT Limited, a public-sector company, in Bangalore.[2]

II   AN INDIAN MODEL OF CAPITAL–LABOUR RELATIONS?

This section develops several interpretive hypotheses concerning industrial relations in India. The first part describes work processes in large and small firms, in public and private enterprises, against a backdrop of large wage differentials and mobility barriers across segments of the labour market. The second part considers the labour movement in relation to capital and the state. Rejecting the view that the state dominates industrial relations, it provides an alternative, class-based interpretation. The third part analyses the joint evolution of capital–labour relations and the growth process. It concludes with the hypothesis of capital–labour stalemate which sets the stage for Sections III and IV.

Economic Structure and Production Relations

Segmented markets and labour supplies

Recorded statistics fail to capture the massive extent of unemployment and under-employment in the Indian economy. A rough estimate puts the sum of recorded and unrecorded unemployment at about 25 per cent of the labour force (Robinson, 1983). Both underemployment and women's participation are masked by the large share (55 per cent) of self-employment (Brahmananda, 1983). The incidence of seasonal unemployment and part-time employment is similarly widespread. This situation simply reflects the continuing inability of capitalist growth to absorb surplus labour even as it undermines the viability of traditional sources of employment. Employers, urban and rural, face 'unlimited' supplies of labour.

However, segmented labour markets, customarily classified into formal and informal (or organized and unorganized), structure the matching of labour demands with labour supplies. For our purposes, it is modern technology, relatively large-scale wage employment and attempts to separate conception from execution that define the formal sector. Labour mobility between segments is restricted despite rather large wage differentials and high rates of unemploy-ment. Wage and salaried employees in the organized sector earn substantially more than workers elsewhere. In 1974–75, taking wages in factories employing more than 50 workers to be 100, the wage index for smaller factories was 45, for urban unorganized sector workers 36 and rural workers 19. Wage differ-entials are due mainly to firm-size effects rather than to skill, education or occupation.[3]

Social and economic factors, some specific to the traditional economy, serve as gatekeepers to the formal sector citadel. This was shown in a study of the Bombay labour market in the late 1970s. About 50 per cent of the labour force was occupied in the organized sector. Only 11.2 per cent of these workers started in the unorganized sector. For every additional formal job created, there were three additional migrants into the city. Few of these could expect to move into the formal sector at any time and the rate of return migration was also large.[4] Moreover, workers in the organized sector came predominantly from the landed classes, far more so than did casual workers (Deshpande, 1983, p. 90). This seg-mentation is perpetuated across generations as access to education is greater for the children of formal-sector workers. Segmentation also reproduces the modern/traditional polarities: there is little transfer of traditionally skilled workers into the modern sector; instead newly skilled workers are created as needs arise in the formal sector (Papola, 1981).

In the rest of this chapter, we focus on the manufacturing sector. In 1983–84, industry – including manufacturing, construction, mining and utilities – accounted for 25 per cent of GDP with manufacturing contributing 16 per cent. Nearly a third of manufacturing value-added was due to small enterprises, using little capital and low levels of technology, in the 'unregistered' sector (Sundrum, 1987, pp. 27–51).[5] Manufacturing units may be classified under household industries including rural cottage and handicrafts; large factories (employing 50 or more workers) and the small-firm sector, which encompasses the smaller factories and small workshops outside the household sector.

Manufacturing employed some 27 million workers in 1981, constituting about 11 per cent of the total labour force. Household manufacturing absorbed about 8.6 million workers in 1981, down from 9.7 million in 1961. The employment share of non-household enterprises within manufacturing has increased from 45 per cent to 67 per cent over the same period. Table 7.1 shows the distribution of employment within the non-household sector. In 1981, small firms accounted for 66 per cent of non-household employment, the share declining over the 1960s and then rising significantly over the 1970s. The rise of the small-firm sector's share was mostly at the expense of private large firms. The employment share of public firms within the large-firm sector rose from 12 per cent in 1961 to 25 per cent in 1981.

Table 7.1   Non-household manufacturing employment (millions)

	1961	1971	1981
Large firms	3.05	4.77	6.05
%	(39)	(44)	(34)
Public sector	0.37	0.81	1.50
%	(5)	(7)	(8)
Private sector	2.68	3.96	4.55
%	(34)	(37)	(25)
Small firms	4.82	5.97	11.97
%	(61)	(56)	(66)
Total non-household	7.87	10.74	18.02

Source: Census and Economic Surveys.

Given wide differences in labour productivities, value-added shares of the three sub-sectors differ considerably from their employment shares. In 1974–75, large firms contributed as much as 58 per cent of manufacturing value-added while household production contributed only 23 per cent (Sundaram and Tendulkar, 1988).[6] Table 7.2 shows the distribution of resources and output within the factory sector. The divergence in the public sector's shares of value-added and productive capital is particularly notable. Public firms are, on average, much larger than private firms and also much more capital-intensive, being concentrated in modern intermediates and capital-goods industries.

Table 7.2   Ownership structure of factories, 1978–79

	Employment	Productive capital	Value-added index	Labour/capital
Public sector	26.7	62.1	29.5	100
Joint sector	5.1	5.8	5.9	204
Private sector	68.2	32.1	64.6	494
(of which firms with capital < Rs lm)	32.1	7.5	14.5	995

Source: Annual Survey of Industries.

Work processes in large firms

Higher wages and stable employment in large enterprises may be rationalizations, in one version or another, of the efficiency-wage hypothesis. Larger enterprises, with heavy investments in newer technologies, attempt to internalize training and learning benefits (Taira, 1977). Smaller enterprises, by contrast, can afford to be more open to the labour market. Mazumdar's (1973) study showed that mills in Bombay's early textile industry employed permanent workers with relatively high wages while also maintaining a significant proportion of workers on a casual, daily-wage basis. But legislative developments in the post-independence period sharpened and generalized this division. On the whole, employment in the large-firm sector has assumed the character of a fixed factor barring variations in daily-wage or temporary employment. Thus, the high wages of formal-sector firms cannot serve as a worker-discipline device because sacking a permanent[7] worker has to be justified according to elaborate legal procedures. Unions too are organized mostly around the goal of employment security and dismissals for 'disciplinary reasons' are a major cause of work stoppages. Larger firms are also subject to a whole range of labour laws that make even lay-off, let alone retrenchment or closure, impossible or expensive.[8]

Firms' inability to sack workers is only the most visible type of institutional restraint. Work practices too adapt to a pre-existing or developing situation. A good example is adaptation to an acknowledged situation of labour redundancy. Though many textile mills are operating with a surplus of permanent workers, recruitment from the ranks of the *badlis* (temporary substitutes) has not declined perceptibly, nor has absenteeism among the permanent workers increased markedly to account for the phenomenon. Instead, management yields to the pressure of the *badlis* and learns to accept increased underutilization of its employees. Managements have been obliged to accommodate the workers'/union's desire for work sharing, not unlike similar practices that rule in the informal sector.[9]

Capital–labour relations impinge in more direct ways on labour utilization and productivity growth in the formal sector. Early industrialization in India relied on technology imports, replicating technical and organizational features typical of industrialized countries. The knowledge acquisition process was not informed by significant adaptation to local conditions. Thus there was a strong proclivity to vertically integrated firms and against Japanese-type subcontracting (Nagaraj, 1984, p. 1441). Firms relied on full-time, permanent workers and in-house supervisors. But in other respects, the acquisition and learning process was quite dissimilar. The abrupt transition from agricultural to factory production without any intervening merchant-craftsman stage meant that the deskilling process of early Taylorism was obviated. Yet the labour force had to be trained and adapted to industrial conditions and adaptation ultimately hinged on the workers themselves and their supervisors, i.e. on shop-floor relations. And here the influences of broader social and political changes left their mark.

While hierarchy, minimal worker participation and separation of knowledge from execution have prevailed, managerial control of the work process has rested on insecure foundations. In an earlier period, before Independence, the labour force was recruited largely from the socially depressed classes/castes but not, in significant numbers, from among the highly skilled, traditional artisanate.[10] Employer paternalism was the norm, and given the economic and political circumstances of the time, succeeded. But times have changed. Newer generations of workers are more exposed to industrial culture and to political changes than older workers. Besides, as in the Bombay study, more of them come from the better-off strata of the population, perhaps because of the growth of population and the scarcity of (now) well paid industrial jobs. Many are also better schooled than earlier generations. Experienced managers at both Naveen Mills and Arogya Mills told me that whereas yesterday's workers were easily controlled by ties of kinship and personal obligation, newer workers are a 'risk'. While they may turn out, on average, to be more productive, they are more likely to create 'trouble'. This difference must be explained by the changing cultural and political context of work relations.

Contemporary workers have been more willing and able to contest managers' prerogatives in the workplace. Workers are able to create a measure of autonomy for themselves in the workplace with little risk of losing their jobs. And most large firms, public and private alike, have enjoyed sheltered markets. At the same time, shortages of power, materials and inputs as well as demand deficiencies have plagued industry. Managerial incentives for running a tight ship, from the viewpoint of skill and knowledge acquisition, have therefore been weak. While workplace conflict has varied over time, and often spilled over into other areas of bargaining, decisive confrontations were thus avoided.

At HMT's machine-tool factory, the practice of scientific management has been greatly impeded by worker resistance and managerial indisposition to open conflict. In the mid-1950s, while initial standards were met within a couple of years of start-up, standards could not be revised over time as learning and improved work practices took effect. Industrial engineers noted that adequate standards were easier to set when new products were introduced or machines and methods radically changed.[11] The existing individual incentive system has contributed much to workplace friction and little to productivity. To begin with, workers are entitled to a bonus for achieving a minimum of only 35 per cent of available standard hours. Even at 70 per cent achievement, which more than half the employees manage, the bonus amounts to only 5–8 per cent of their gross income. Besides, the union has won allowances for involuntary idle time. Managers felt much of this idle time, in fact, was not involuntary but due to 'worker indiscipline'. Workers and union leaders, on the other hand, blame managerial ineptitude in materials and production planning for the poor loading of men and machines. Shop-floor managers argued, in turn, that headquarters restricts their authority in order to avoid ugly confrontations with the union.

In an older industry such as Ahmedabad textiles, the story is not much different than at HMT. Weavers' basic pay is set as a piece rate. But since basic rates have not been revised in over 20 years, they have been dwarfed by the rising cost-of-living adjustments (broadly unrelated to basic pay) over the years. Thus, the basic-wage difference between the best and worst piece-rate weavers at Arogya Mills is less than 10 per cent. Meanwhile, managers and workers differ widely over the revision of work norms when machinery is proposed to be modernized, and these are tied to longstanding disputes over wage revisions. These instances do not necessarily define the norm for all industries. The setting of work standards is reported to be tighter in some private firms, particularly in the newer industries. Work incentives, often set on effort/workload calculations rather than on output, also produce substantial differences in pay. But as we shall argue later, the record of total productivity growth in industry is consistent with our view that managerial authority has been inadequate to permit the reproduction of Taylorism, i.e., the continuous attempt to replace the worker's discretion, knowledge and responsibility with machine-paced and rule-directed systems.

Experiments in so-called 'worker participation' in industrial management have failed everywhere in India. Such schemes have frequently been promoted by top management and/or government agencies and have not allowed real power to workers. They do not amount to much more than consultations with workers about peripheral matters (Ramaswamy and Ramaswamy, 1981, p. v). Among the complaints that Jupiter Mills' workers levelled against the recognized union (which is alienated from most of the rank and file), the chief one related to collusion between union leaders and management with the 'worker participation' scheme being an important vehicle.

State-owned firms constitute only 5 per cent of all factories; yet they command a quarter of all employment and over one half of the capital stock. Much of this investment is in capital- and skill-intensive industries (Sundrum, 1987, p. 98). While this sector's share of total investment has risen from 33 per cent in the early 1950s to 47 per cent in the late 1970s, it has contributed only marginally to savings. A widely held view is that this is due to employment and pricing policies that reduce public sector surpluses and, directly or indirectly, benefit no more than the upper two deciles (the so-called middle class) of the income distribution, whether as workers or as consumers.

There are two related considerations from the standpoint of capital–labour relations and productivity in this sector. First, public firms are easy prey to political pressures for generating well paid jobs. This has allowed productivity to be governed by employment targets rather than vice versa. Second, industrial relations are influenced by political interference in the day-to-day management of these enterprises. Apart from the basic problem of Taylorization, which is not unique to these firms, the greater problem in the public sector is probably that of managing managers. Even as layers in the hierarchy have increased, at both factory and office, there are severe morale problems among officers. At Arogya Mills and Naveen Mills, sacking managers is considered exceptional but the carrot of promotion is important, though probably less so than in Western corporations. At HMT, the sack is unthinkable and promotions are used very sparingly as a reward for effectiveness: for the most part, promotions are a routine affair governed by years spent on a particular job.

Top managers are appointed, by the executives of government, with a multifarious mandate that allows for routine political meddling and limits the managers' autonomy. In particular, managers' dealings with unions are constrained by prevailing political winds and by the wishes of politicians, national or local. Similarly, major investment decisions are manipulated for political advantage. In HMT's case, the technical manager cited the location of expansion units away from the mother unit as having hampered the learning and technology acquisition process. Government had also coerced management into accepting an unprofitable and unrelated acquisition. These influences are well understood by employees and, one suspects, must have an enduring adverse impact on work attitudes.[12] The direct links between union leaders (or their political backers) and top managers also lead to a sense of disaffection among both middle managers and workers, easily detectable in the HMT case.[13]

Within the public sector, there has been an abiding tension between a policy of relative wage uniformity and a policy of differentiated wages according to effort and productivity. It cannot be asserted, however, that the latter policy necessarily contributes to greater productivity growth since much unrest and lack of morale of public sector workers has in fact been attributed to the discontent over wage differentials within the sector (Rudolph and Rudolph, 1987, p.265). Workers and their unions have sought parity in wages and employment conditions within the sector. When these demands are fulfilled, as they frequently are, it leaves the impression that public sector workers 'get whatever they demand'. But, on the other hand, firm-level bargaining is usually constrained by management appeals to parity. The crux of the matter is that bargaining in public firms is much more subject to government influence; understandably so since the state's interest is more immediate. The Bureau of Public Enterprises issues wage norms (particularly maxima) which are generally binding. Neither managers nor plant-level leaders can stray too far from sector-wide norms unless they are willing collectively to confront the government. This also explains the much lower frequency of work stoppages in the public sector. Long before conflicts develop, government steps in to settle the matter by applying norms; in the private sector, as a rule, government has to be 'invited in'. Public-sector workers seem to demand what they get.

All the same, average wages and benefits tend to be higher in public than in private firms. Part of the difference may be attributable to higher skill and education levels of public-sector workers or to the much larger size of public than of private firms. Comparable private firms are believed to pay as much, if not more. Nevertheless, one study concluded that 'For industries with strong representation of both public and private firms ... public-sector wages are substantially higher in almost every case' (Vermeulen and Sethi, 1982, p. 156). We can only suggest a hypothesis: the issue of parity goes beyond industrial enterprises and encompasses workers in public administration; government workers as a class wield considerable political influence on government wage setting.

Small versus large firms

Work processes in the small-firm sector present a sharply contrasting picture relative to the situation in large firms. Consider the case of PL Weaving, a small powerloom unit. Production operations at PL are run entirely by a head jobber with a dozen workers. The owner, who manages marketing, visits daily only to place his output demands. The jobber recruits workers, trains them, supervises them, pays them and is free to extract work from them as he chooses. Himself an ex-worker of PL, the jobber earns a fixed salary over three times the wages of his workers but he is often on the job for two shifts. There is real economy in supervision because the weavers' wages are entirely determined by piece rates. The firm is free to lay workers off or close down as the situation demands. But stable employment is very attractive to workers who would otherwise be severely underemployed; in return, the firm is assured of their loyalty. Thus efficiency wage arguments appear to be more relevant in the small-firm sector.

Working conditions are generally much inferior in small than in large enterprises (Holmstrom, 1985). Whereas workers in Ahmedabad Mills get three official breaks totalling 70 minutes in an eight-hour day, PL's weavers are allowed only two breaks of 20 minutes each. Besides, it is reported that many powerloom workers work twelve-hour days. While conditions in weaving sheds with ordinary looms are oppressive in mills, they are noticeably worse in powerlooms: less space and ventilation, more work hazards, poor amenities, etc. It is quite impossible to explain the prevailing wage differential (more than 2:1 in favour of the mills) as a compensating differential. Nor can it be explained in terms of efficiency wages since powerloom workers produce more cloth than their mill counterparts. But powerloom workers have no unions to demand better conditions or enforcement of their legal rights; mill workers do.

The extent to which such 'disembedded' capitalist relations prevail within the labour-hiring small-firm sector is difficult to assess. The difficulty arises from the great diversity within this sector and our limited knowledge. In many small workshops, both urban and rural, with no more than five or ten workers, there is no very clearcut division of labour as tasks overlap in team work. This is true, for instance, of the smaller units found in the Tiruppur knitting industry. There is little room here for Taylorization. In the larger factories in the same industry, by contrast, job fragmentation and specialization are much more extensive but this appears to be a fairly recent phenomenon (Krishnaswami, 1989, p. 1355). By breaking down whole tasks, employers are able to achieve considerable economies through deskilling, better control over the work process and the use of cheaper children's and women's labour.[14] Presumably, these practices produce an impersonal work culture. Yet, recruitment and rewards follow traditional patterns based on loyalty and caste affinities even among the larger factories.[15] A remark made by a Coimbatore mill-hand is typical of the situation in many factories, large and small, particularly in older industries: 'Since most of us have got jobs through recommendation, [the employers] complain to our superiors if we protest' (Ramaswamy, 1977, p. 44).

Are loyalty to the employer and deference to authority liable to be more pronounced in labour-hiring small firms? We suggest, tentatively, that this is less a matter of the size of firms than of changes over time. Thus, paternalism was more in evidence at Arogya Mills than at PL Weaving. This is accountable more by the difference in age (and possibly, turnover rates) of their workforces than by their difference in size.

Is the Labour Movement Dominated by the State?

The labour movement in India is based on the relatively easily organized formal-sector workers; there have been only scattered efforts at organizing workers outside this sector. The union movement remains heavily fragmented because of internal factors and external influences. The typical union in India is plant-based though there are important exceptions. Many leaders are, or aspire to be, professional politicians. There is an elaborate legal machinery to permit disputes to go to government conciliation and, beyond that, to mandatory adjudication – and they often do. It is easily accepted that the state has played a distinctive role in this evolution. What is debatable is that the state has been the dominating force.

A notable feature of the union movement is its fragmentation both at the local or plant level and at the apex level of union federations. Typically, multiple unions coexist at the plant level; closed shop arrangements develop rather exceptionally where a strong union prevails. Industry-wide unions are also to be found in some, particularly older, industries – the major textile centre unions, steel, plantations, railways and postal services among others. Given the historical circumstance of a direct transition from agricultural to industrial work, craft unions have not developed and there has been greater scope for rivalrous general unions (Monappa, 1988, p. 50). Union federations are sharply divided along party lines. Although the number of registered unions and union membership has grown impressively, the average membership of unions declined from the early 1950s by a fifth to only 634 members in 1976.[16]

The present shape of the union movement must be viewed against the backdrop of its historical evolution and the considerable involvement of the state. The movement began hesitantly in the early part of this century when the average worker was a rural, usually illiterate, immigrant faced with a radical change in his work situation. Pay and working conditions were dismal. Employers colluded even as they used their political influence to prevent the legalization of unions. Paternalistic employers were sometimes sympathetic to worker demands but unwilling to deal with unions. The Trade Unions Act, assuring the legality of unions, was not passed until 1926, 75 years after the birth of modern industry. When unions became a reality in many industries, employers sought to use them as a vehicle for their paternalism as in the case of Ahmedabad's Textile Labour Association which was heavily influenced by Gandhian ideology. Where this did not succeed, as in Bombay's textile unions, the influence of the Communist Party rose. As the labour movement became enmeshed with the anticolonial movement, the leadership – mostly of middle-class, non-worker origins

– of the two movements tended to coalesce. But the political divisions within the latter movement carried over into the labour movement.

The state's role is intimately tied to the legal framework that evolved from the pre-Independence period. This framework allowed for procedures that were unfavourable to an independent union movement while allowing government a key role in conflict resolution. Under the Trade Unions Act of 1926, which remains effective, it takes only seven members to form a union. The Industrial Disputes Act (1947) does not require union recognition or compulsory collective bargaining, a remarkable omission considering the weight and reach of labour legislation.[17] On the contrary it institutionalized government interventionism by creating an elaborate machinery for officially mediated conciliation and arbitration. It allowed several registered unions (irrespective of strength!) to operate simultaneously by giving them equal access to this machinery. Strikes are deemed illegal if they are called before (cumbersome and lengthy) procedures for conciliation are exhausted. These procedures diverted unions and managements away from bargaining to manipulating procedures, politicians and the labour courts (Ramaswamy and Ramaswamy, 1981, p. 94).

There undoubtedly were partisan reasons for such procedures. Before Independence, the dominant Congress Party created a trade union wing Indian National Trade Union Congress (INTUC) in an attempt to displace the leading position of the communists in many key unions. This campaign was substantially helped by the ruling government's executive powers coupled with the laws relating to union recognition. Thus the 1950s and 1960s saw a certain weakening of the movement due to the increasing role of the ruling government. In a few states (and restricted to some industries), the local law allows for recognition, not by secret ballot but by official 'verification' of records. But here too, the ruling party has been able to manipulate records in order to foster the INTUC. The creation of Rashtriya Mill Mazdoor Sangh (RMMS) [National Mill Workers Union], an INTUC member, in 1945 and its recognition, under the Bombay Industrial Relations Act, as sole bargaining agent, served to curb the strong position of the communist union in Bombay's textile industry. When the recognized union becomes institutionally entrenched even when it has lost worker support, it suppresses the emergence of internal leaders.[18] At Naveen Mills, virtually every major work stoppage or slowdown over the past fifteen years or so was occasioned by workers' attempts to displace the recognized union – and they have all failed due to the employer's insistence on 'abiding by the law'. In such situations, the rise of internal leadership and external challenges to the institutionalized union remain episodic.

The identification by unions with narrow party and factional interests has served to fragment the movement. Internal divisions within general unions were probably important as well. The predominance of mostly non-working-class union leaders is also due to the social and economic gulf between managers and ordinary workers that has allowed such outsiders a key role that workers have not been averse to accepting. The more important reason lies in the function of the union/party leader as an intermediary between workers and the state apparatus (Ramaswamy, 1988).

Notwithstanding these considerable obstacles erected by the state in the path of the labour movement, it would be a mistake to conclude that the state has thus acquired a dominating role over it. The reasons are twofold. First, other provisions of the law have, we would maintain, gone considerably farther in providing organized labour a secure footing in the industrial system and we may learn more from examining why this is so. Second, the procedural hurdles have not always been sufficient to hobble the movement.

Existing law is largely responsible for making formal-sector labour a fixed production factor and, thereby, curtailing capital's most important weapon against labour. Even dismissals of individual workmen, who have worked more than 240 days, are subject to elaborate procedures of adjudication by industrial courts or tribunals. Over time, the courts have tended to shift the burden of proof on to employers. A vital provision of the Industrial Disputes Act is that firms with more than 100 workers require official permission for layoffs or retrenchment. Governments have preferred to let units turn sick or even take them over rather than permit employers to have their way. The commitment to security of formal-sector jobs has been one of the remarkable features of state law and government policy. We attempt an explanatory hypothesis for this commitment later in this section.

To the Indian worker, job security is above everything else. Apart from wages, the most notable difference between unionized workers and others relates to job security. While temporary workers in large firms or workers in the small-firm sector suffer acute uncertainty and high actual rates of unemployment, unionized workers generally have tenure. Many unions are also able to impose hiring clauses favouring the kin of members. Dismissals of workers figure prominently in strikes and other forms of 'union trouble'. What the worker values highly, employers find most onerous. To quote the chief executive of Naveen Mills: 'The ills of Indian industry will vanish if the law is changed to permit managers to fire, with no questions asked, at most 1% of union workers'. Without job security laws, the difficult problem of organizing even formal-sector workers would be appreciably more difficult whether or not industrial ills would be resolved thereby.

Government influence has also been substantial in raising organized-sector wages. In covered firms, the legal minima relating to leave, bonus,[19] medical and pension fund contributions add up to over 40 per cent of the wage (D.C. Mathur, 1989). Hence, about one half of the 2.5:1 wage differential between organized- and unorganized-sector firms can be explained by such direct interventions alone, quite apart from the indirect effects of job security laws that also probably work in the same direction. Government has also appointed *ad hoc* commissions of inquiry and wage boards for many industries, especially during the 1950s and 1960s, whose non-binding recommendations have generally been accepted by both sides. Such measures, however, have not necessarily raised wages further as some allege. Government has been more concerned with parity across major organized-sector industries in the interest of stability.

And it may have influenced production by limiting the scope of productivity bargaining (and bargaining generally). Where multiple unions exist, inter-union rivalry is a major reason for stalled productivity and bargaining stalemates. Much the same holds where the single recognized union has potential rivals. Thus, the recognized union in the Ahmedabad textile industry has been unable (not unwilling) to allow a shift in the composition of pay from dearness allowance to basic rates. For piece-rate-based weavers, such a shift would probably raise earnings differentials by tying a greater part of pay to productivity. This has been prevented only because workers would organize effectively against it with the support of potential rivals of the recognized union. Union rivalries, compounded by the influence of local politicians, produced bitter conflict involving both workers and their managers about a decade ago at HMT. This was cited as the root cause of the present state of 'indiscipline' among workers and morale problems among middle managers. The presence of multiple unions, as the weaving master at Arogya Mills told me, 'increases the pressure on management'. But such pressure does not always mean that workers get what they want. In fact, managers are known widely to foster company unions and thus divide workers. It does mean, however, that government has been unable to fine-tune industrial relations to produce favourable effects on shop-floor productivity.

Even in procedural terms, government's restrictive role on labour in conflict resolution must not be exaggerated. Strikes do occur and continue long after they are declared illegal. A study of 80 employers and 86 unions in 1972–73 found that about 70 per cent of disputes were resolved through collective bargaining without government intervention. Larger unions are better able to rely on their own ability while smaller firms tend often to resort to government machinery (Vermuelen and Sethi, 1982).

What, then, has been the role of unions in winning workers' demands? At a minimum, they have been necessary to ensure the enforcement of laws favouring labour. Where unions are weak or absent, employers have evaded the law. Employers terminate workers temporarily before they have completed 240 days; alter the names of employees over successive periods; and maintain the fiction of having employee strength below the limits at which certain laws take effect. PL Weaving, for example, is split into two units barely a kilometre apart so as to avoid provisions of the Factories Act and other laws. The lengths to which employers go to evade the law is clear indication that legal provisions, not profit or efficiency considerations alone, determine the capital–labour contract. But the reported success, in many cases, of their attempts would be difficult if workers were unionized. Where unions are strong, they provide a protective umbrella to most workers within the enterprise. The fact that wages, virtually across all skill and occupational categories, are strongly correlated with firm size (and therefore unionization) belies the claim that unions in India protect the privileged. And, by the same token, management's ability to adjust wage structures according to its own needs is circumscribed. The 'privileged' place of union workers has required a century-long struggle in the workplace and in the political arena. Organized labour's autonomous role is by no means confined to the determination of wages alone. Perhaps more important has been its contestation of managerial prerogatives in structuring work relations: the content of jobs, the pace of work, the deployment and disciplining of labour, the conditions for modernization, etc.

Outside the formal sector, there are serious obstacles to unionization. As long as mass unemployment remains, the prospect for unionization appears remote indeed. Workers at PL Weaving believe that even where unions exist, they make little difference to wages or job security. The most they can do is to take up individual grievances or to press for legal rights; but organizers would have to risk their jobs (and more) in the face of employer hostility. On occasion, unorganized workers especially in urban industrial areas form a large protest group to agitate for minimum wages but these have generally failed.[20]

Summing up, it is evident that the state has played an important role in setting key parameters for the capital–labour relationship and these have also had substantive effects. These interventions have institutionalized certain structural conditions for collective bargaining between capitalists and workers. But they have not been sufficient to ensure that such bargaining will take place or that legal provisions will hold. This has depended on the actual struggles waged by workers and their unions against employers, and on the limits on enforceability of the law. Moreover, we have observed that the state has also institutionalized an activist role for itself in the more routine affairs of conflict resolution rather than allow full and free bargaining. Such interventionism has not gone uncontested by labour, although the state has been sometimes able to deflect the contestation by playing one union or federation against another.[21] The self-contradictory nature of these interventions is most evident between the commitment to job security and the refusal to allow democratic union-recognition provisions.

Why has the state played such a distinctive role? Why was a commitment to job security realized and union-recognition laws never amended? This is not the place to enter into a political analysis of the state itself which these questions require. Yet, they are important, perhaps crucial, questions and we shall suggest a tentative hypothesis. The state's stance has elements of ruling party partisanship, paternalism (cultural resonance, some might say), and even of the imported fabianism characteristic of Nehru and his ilk. Without wishing to deny the influence of these factors, we argue for a hypothesis that takes class interests seriously.

At Independence, national capital was aware of its inability to go it alone either economically or politically while the rural élite was discredited as a comprador/reactionary class.[22] Whereas the bulk of surplus produced accrued to these classes, there was no assurance of their accomplishing a capitalist transformation autonomously. Neither was socialism – whether as a radical transformation of the countryside or nationalization of capital – on the political agenda. What emerged was an attempt at state-guided capitalist development in industry first and then, haltingly, in the countryside as well.

State guidance of this process was a delicate affair considering the conflicting claims of the dominant classes, and the potential for destabilization through popular mobilization. Electoral democracy did not help but could scarcely have been avoided. Hence, planned development and the maintenance of wage, price and economic stability became the state's primary interests. But how was the state to ensure economic stability in a mixed economy? Instruments of policy deemed necessary for planned development may not also assure 'stability', defined here as the maintenance of relative incomes at least among classes which could be expected to resist erosion of their income position. We now consider two such areas of conflict.

Strict regulation of foreign trade and investment was thought necessary for planned industrialization. But this would confer significant monopoly power on domestic industry in the home market and have unequalizing effects between capital and labour, whose strengths were unmatched and/or among different segments of the working class. The state was also expected to create and command leading sectors of industry. For one thing, this would expand profit opportunities for private capital. For another, it would raise difficult issues of parity in wages and job security among organized workers in private industry, public enterprises and the civil service.

Short of an incomes policy, at least within organized industry, which would in any case have other undesirable consequences, the state needed additional instruments to control the stability of the growth process. Regulating private capital was one part of the answer. Socialist rhetoric helped the regulatory process while also harnessing populist forces to the state's agenda. The other, analysed at some length above, lay in the regulation of industrial relations however imperfect the available instruments. This presupposes that organized-sector workers could and would pose challenges to stability. But history, both before and after the launching of planned development, did not prove otherwise.

The hypothesis seems plausible not only in explaining the general problem posed but also the specific issue of an apparent contradiction between regulated collective bargaining and the commitment to job security. The latter addressed the problem of structural inequality between capital and labour, defined by oligopolistic market power and unlimited labour supplies, while also securing parity within the organized sectors, private and public. Regulated bargaining was intended to give the state a handle on the day-to-day issues of wage conflicts and also create a more pliable union movement.

The industrial relations system that emerged reflected these designs of the state. But they are scarcely the designs of a 'self-determining' entity working in a class vacuum, where both labour and capital are just marginal players (Rudolph and Rudolph, 1987, p. 400). The Rudolphs take labour's inability to mount a working-class challenge against prevailing ideology as proof that such a class-free state dominates labour. On the contrary, the rise to power of communist governments in the states of Kerala and West Bengal shows that this sort of challenge has not been absent. Leaving aside radical ideological challenges, the failure of the labour movement to realize 'even' the modest ideals of, say, Swedish social democracy cannot be dissociated from an analysis of capital, labour and the state. How else explain the fact that organized labour in India has escaped the institutionalization of capital's anti-labour stance typical of late-industrializing nations?

Conflict and Stalemate

The limits on the state's capacity to control industrial relations become evident when we examine the course of employment, wages, profits and productivity which is what we propose to do in this section. This will serve also to set the stage for an analysis of changes in capital–labour relations during the 1980s. Much of the following discussion focuses on the organized sector of industry for which evidence is easier to come by. This sector's importance derives from the fact that it absorbs the lion's share of investment and is expected to be an engine of growth for the rest of the economy.

Apart from the low rates of growth of industry and economy, the most remarkable aspect of the 1950–80 period was the deceleration in industrial growth from 6.85 per cent during 1950–65 to only 2.5 per cent over 1966–80. Excess capacity rose during the latter period and public investment slowed down significantly. Between the two halves of the 1950–80 period, the deceleration was greater (from 7.0 per cent to 4.5 per cent) for registered manufacturing than for unregistered manufacturing (from 5.1 per cent to 4.7 per cent). The investment share of the registered sector in manufacturing has fallen from 90 per cent in the 1950s to 74 per cent in the 1970s.

Whereas economy-wide employment between 1961 and 1981 grew at the rate of 0.83 per cent, industrial employment in the non-household sector grew at 4 per cent, household employment declining at the compound rate of 2.25 per cent.[23]

Paradoxically, non-household employment grew faster in the 1970s, at 4.99 per cent, compared to 3.02 per cent in the 1960s. A breakdown of the data suggests that this acceleration of employment growth in the non-household sector is accounted for almost entirely by the small-firm sector (see Table 7.3). No doubt the growth of the small-firm sector was aided by congenial public policies and subsidies. But the faster growth of wages in the unionized, large-firm sector, which is analysed below, was also probably responsible.

Table 7.3   Manufacturing employment growth, 1961–81 (non-household sector)

	Non-household sector	Large firms	Small firms
1961–71	3.0	3.1	3.0
1971–81	5.0	3.4	5.8
1961–81	4.0	3.2	4.4

Source: Census and ASI.

Further evidence for this argument is the dispersal of factory employment growth away from the older established industrial states.[24] Factory sector employment has grown significantly slower than the national average in the most industrialized states of Maharashtra, Tamil Nadu and West Bengal, and in Kerala, a state reputed for the strength of its organized labour movement. The only traditionally industrial state which had rapid employment growth is Gujarat, where the union movement is not known for its militancy. In contrast, the regional distribution of non-factory, non-household employment has remained roughly stable (Mohan, 1989, p. 2495) suggesting that there has been a shift, in the traditional industrial states, from the formal to the small-firm sectors. Much of the dispersal of industrial activity has been of the labour-intensive sort implying the growing significance of labour costs.[25]

Table 7.4 (first two columns) gives trends in real wage and real salary indices for the large-firm sector during 1960–82. Real salaries fell over the period of industrial deceleration, recovered briefly, fell again after the first oil shock and stagnated thereafter at 80 per cent of their 1960 level. Real wages, on the other hand, fell only for the years following the oil shocks (1974 and 1980); they stagnated during the emergency (1976–77) years. For the period as a whole, the growth of wages in the large-firm sector has been higher than the growth of per capita income.

Table 7.4   Real wages, salaries and workforce composition, 1960–82 (large enterprise sector)

| | Index* of | | Salary to | Wage workers/ |
	Real salary	Wage ratio	salary earner	salary earners
1960	100	100	3.3	7.0
1961–65	105	102	3.2	7.5
1966–70	109	89	2.6	4.9
1971	117	107	3.0	4.3
1972	–	–	–	–
1973	117	106	3.0	4.0
1974	101	82	2.6	3.9
1975	115	81	2.3	3.7
1976	121	82	2.2	3.7
1977	120	89	2.4	3.7
1978	137	82	1.9	3.7
1979	161	82	1.6	3.6
1980	138	79	1.9	3.4
1981	137	80	1.9	3.5
1982	143	85	1.9	3.6

Note: *Mean wage and salary rates deflated by industrial workers' CPI.

Source: *Annual Survey of Industries* (census factories).

These numbers on mean wage and salary rates must be treated with caution as they are unadjusted for the changing skill or industrial composition of the workforce. There is no compelling reason, however, to suppose that such compositional shifts should cause real wages to rise faster than salaries within the formal sector.[26] But the salariat (including most supervisory personnel) is neither protected by labour legislation that applies to wage-earning workers nor nearly as well organized to press its demands as workers are. We suggest tentatively that this may underlie the growth differential between wages and salaries. We return to the question of falling salaries below.

Although real wages have grown, they have not grown as fast as labour productivity. Labour productivity, over the 1950–70 period, grew at 4.0 per cent per annum in the unregistered sector and only 3.2 per cent in the registered sector (Choudhury, 1983). Productivity in the manufacturing sector as a whole grew at the rate of 4.4 per cent. For the 1960–80 period, manufacturing productivity growth slowed to 2.5 per cent which compares favourably only in relation to the 1.5 per cent growth rate for real wages over the 21-year period (ASI census firms). Reliable data for the small-firm sector are hard to come by but there is evidence suggesting lower real wage growth than in large firms. Clearly, manufacturing productivity grew faster than real wages but the lag in wages was significantly smaller for the large- than for the small-firm sector. That is, organized labour has been able to capture a larger share of growth in productivity than unorganized labour and the salaried class.

Import-substituting industrialization was a factor in allowing or raising monopoly profits in the large-firm sector. This no doubt gave large firms discretion in setting wages. The presumption must be that this allowed unions to win wage concessions as productivity grew. It was noted previously that there is a pronounced effect of the size/type of firm on the level of wages: wages rise successively as we move up the ladder of firm size or from private to public firms. Within the corporate sector, there has been some increase in asset concentration during the period as a whole (Chandra, 1981). It may be inferred, therefore, that there would also be a tendency towards greater wage dispersion in the formal sector. This is confirmed by a recent study of wage differentials which found that over a broad range of industries in the factory sector, the mean value of the coefficient of variation in wages doubled from 26 per cent to 52 per cent (Chatterjee and Sen, 1988, p. 221).[27]

A closer look at the period of industrial deceleration reveals the effects of trends in the wider economy on wage bargaining. This period coincided with an increase in the average rate of inflation caused by supply shocks in agriculture and budgetary deficits. Given the large weight of food and other agricultural commodities in workers' consumption, workers' money wage demands grew. On the other hand, there have been persistent increases in industry's product wage (see Table 7.5). The squeeze on industrial price/cost margins is related to several factors other than increases in nominal wages: administrative price restraints; a rising relative price of capital goods; and, with rising excess capacity, the reduced ability of firms to pass on rising costs. Much of the growth in labour productivity, besides, was the result of a rapid rise in the capital–labour ratio.

The upshot was a squeeze on profits. For the private sector, the share of profits and interest fell from 40.1 per cent in the 1960s to 36.8 per cent in the 1970s; for the public sector, this share rose from 18.8 per cent in the 1960s to 21.2 per cent in the 1970s (Sundrum, 1987, p. 168). Based on ASI data for census firms (those with more than 50 workers), our calculations show that the aggregate return on capital (total surplus relative to the value of productive capital) fell sharply from 16.5 per cent to 10.6 per cent over the 1960s. Recovery has been slow and modest over the 1970s. These numbers understate the relative drop and recovery in the private sector because the trend in the public sector has been positive.

The squeeze on profits dampened employers' profit expectations and made them less willing to countenance wage increases. Consequently, there was a marked and steady rise in the incidence of work stoppages, the number of work days lost per 1000 workers rising fivefold from 1966 to its peak in 1974. The rise in industrial conflict was also witnessed in other parts of the organized sector (such as insurance, banking, railways, government administration, etc.). Such conflicts affected blue-collar unions and organizations of white-collar workers. Apart from the stagflation, this is also related to a spate of nationalizations that brought certain wage disparities onto the agenda for negotiation. 'Violence and indiscipline' grew in importance among disputed issues and there was a progressive decline in the proportion of cases won by labour.

Table 7.5   The product wage in manufacturing, 1961–87

Year	Product wage index	Year	Product wage index
1961	100	1978	153
1962–65	109	1979	140
1966–70	121	1980	131
1971	124	1981	138
1972	–	1982	139
1973	126	1983	154
1974	115	1984	170
1975	128	1985	178
1976	127	1986	176
1977	132	1987	188

Note: *The product wage is the nominal wage deflated by the WPI for manufacturing. For 1961–81, nominal wage refers to the mean wage of ASI (census factories) workers; for the 1982–87 period, it refers to the mean emoluments of public-sector employees.

Source: Annual Survey of Industries (census factories) and *Economic Survey*, 1987–88.

The growing ineffectiveness of strikes was due not only to the unwillingness of employers to make wage concessions but also to their growing ability to resist workers' demands. Given the weak capacity of unions to provide significant strike benefits, excess capacity in industry swung the pendulum increasingly in favour of management as its holding power grew. A related factor was the continued splintering of the union movement. But the rising trend in open conflict was ruptured in 1975 when, following a massive strike of railworkers, the government declared a national emergency. We resume the story in Section III below.

Although we have been examining the effect of the industrial slowdown on wage conflicts, the failures in accumulation themselves are not independent of capital–labour relations. We wish to emphasize two types of effect in this connection. First, capital–labour relations probably had a direct effect on productivity growth. Second, slower growth, accompanied by greater conflict, worsened the prospects for investment and modernization with serious effects that the economy has had to confront after the late 1970s.[28]

Rising industrial labour productivity, it has been observed, was accompanied by a marked increase in the capital–labour ratio. In fact, total factor productivity in Indian industry is estimated to have declined at an annual rate of between 0.2 per cent and 1.3 per cent during the 1960–80 period. This cannot, for the most part, be explained by shifts in industrial composition (Ahluwalia, 1985, pp. 127–46). Neither can it, we hasten to add, be taken as an unalloyed measure of declining technical efficiency, technical 'unlearning' and the like.[29] The larger issue of sorting this finding into its component causes – including demand constraints, agricultural and infrastructural bottlenecks, state regulation of private investment, etc. – need not detain us here.[30] Suffice it to note that it is highly probable that some part of the result owes to problems of generating increases in productivity on the shop floor.[31]

The failure to achieve mastery over technology has been adduced as a major cause (Ghosh, 1989a). Undoubtedly, pure managerial failures have played a part. Ghosh cites uncritical acceptance of 'technological' solutions to productivity problems as having been an important type of managerial failure. But the uncertain basis of managerial authority, oscillating between paternalism and repressive union-busting tactics, has not been conducive to reproducing Taylorism once technologies were acquired. Managerial initiatives in the workplace were limited to producing feeble copies of Taylorist techniques, as we have noted (see also Ramaswamy, 1988). Bureaucratic control too yielded to various forms of paternalism and social pressure. Managerial concern was to limit the demands of organized labour rather than drive hard cash-for-productivity bargains. The inability of employers to adjust employment to output not only induced them to raise the capital–labour ratio but also allowed them to restrict wage growth as unions traded wage rises for less work.

With slowed growth, some part of both capacity and the workforce became redundant. Inducements to improved efficiency were thus absent or weak. Permanent workers accustomed to overtime could not be compelled to scale down their expectations. Unavoidable shortages of inputs including power and transport (products of the commanding heights in the faltering public sector) also caused idleness and counterproductive adaptation. These conditions also slowed the pace of replacement and modernizing investments while managers learnt to live with a poorly utilized labour force. For example, workers at Naveen Mills responded to lowered incentive wages (due to lowered utilization rates) by slowing down production until management settled for an *ad hoc* compensation formula. But the responsibility for lack of modernization can also be blamed on unions: the general secretary of the Majoor Mahajan admitted as much when he said that his union had failed to compel management to modernize when the need and the opportunity existed. These changes were bound to make managers revise their estimates of labour's reliability and productivity.[32]

Table 7.4 (last two columns) reveals a dramatic shift in the composition of employment away from wage-earning 'workers' to salary-earning 'non-workers'. The number of workers per salary-earner was cut in half between 1960 and 1982. This cannot be satisfactorily explained in terms of 'technical' considerations. Thus, the average size[33] of factories actually fell over time from about 140 workers in 1950 to fewer than 60 workers in 1976. The employment share of factories with more than 500 workers also fell from 83 per cent in 1956 to only 65 per cent in 1977 (Nagaraj, 1985). The presumption, arising from the learning curve in an industrializing country, would also be a fall in the need for technical and non-technical supervision. As opposed to this, the number of very large, mostly public-sector enterprises also rose during this period. Although such firms have a higher proportion of salaried workers, this cannot account for the shift noted as the employment share of the public sector remained small.[34]

What, then, explains this trend? One possibility flows straight out of Table 7.4: as salaries fell relative to wages, employers substituted supervisory employees for workers. Such substitutability is implausible since it would not be easily permitted by the wide gap in status between blue- and white-collar workers in India. On the other hand, the narrowing wage–salary ratios within company hierarchies could be a factor reducing the effectiveness of supervision. Coupled with the increasing need for such supervision which is implied by our earlier arguments, this would explain the observed trend. This is consistent with the stories I heard repeated a number of times at HMT. Finally, we cannot rule out the influence of social pressures, especially on larger firms, to satisfy the job demands of the educated middle classes.

By the mid-1970s, the continuing problems of slow growth and rising conflict signalled a political–economic stalemate. It would be too much to claim that the Emergency was the result solely of industrial ills. That these played a critical part cannot be doubted, however. Even by the limited criterion of managing industrial peace, not all the procedural interventionism of the state succeeded. The growth slowdown revealed deeper contradictions within the system including capital–labour relations. The Emergency turned out at best to be a prelude to restructuring. Changes that appeared eventually, as we argue in the following section, cannot be described as a radical restructuring either. They have been halting, stealthy and indirect.

III EASING OUT OF THE IMPASSE

The unprecedented assumption of emergency powers by the state in 1975 reflected a sense of crisis in both polity and economy. The trigger for this suspension of democracy was the increase in social conflict accompanying the price rise due to the first oil shock; its deeper source lay in the internal contradictions of the growth process. The stalemate in capital–labour relations was but a partial manifestation of this crisis. In some measure too, the Emergency gave an opportunity for the ruling classes to reassess economic strategy and this continued beyond the emergency years (1975–77) through the displacement of the ruling Congress in 1977 and its subsequent recovery of power in 1980. A significant revision of some key parameters governing the accumulation process emerged and is considered here. Changes in capital–labour relations have been mostly a consequence of or reactions to these revisions and these are taken up later.

Changes in the Growth Regime

Before we consider the changes themselves, it is necessary to note the interests that have shaped them. The fundamental concern of private capital was to create conditions favourable to the resumption of its own growth. This required addressing the problems of the previous accumulation regime: demand, infrastructure, low productivity and the regulatory environment. The 'middle class' – which, together with the upper class, forms the top decile or two of the income distribution – had been frustrated by the failure of growth to deliver the consumer goods it desired. It is these two interests[35] that policy reforms were intended to satisfy and in a complementary way. Reforms were expected to promote industrial investment and modernization, increase exports to pay for the needed imports, and increase domestic competition and efficiency.

   The diagnoses of economic policy failures largely reflected these interests; had the deciding interests been different, the diagnoses too would have differed. Where the previous regime had been led by public investment, the new one was to be led by the consumption demand of the middle class. Where previously the state had regulated the private sector and foreign trade, the new call was for freeing up the policy environment for private investment, modernization and imports. The public sector's efforts would be focused on improving the supply of infrastructure. Other failures of growth were not addressed as enthusiastically or directly: slow growth of mass demand, incomes and employment; continuing problems of transforming agriculture and stagnation of per capita food intake; and massive regional and class inequalities of income. Class pressures from below and above impinged unequally on the state, which responded accordingly.[36]

   At the core of the resulting policy initiatives have been measures to raise the domestic mobility of capital. In years past, the state had controlled big corporate capital in particular by placing licensing restrictions on capacity expansion and diversification. Under the new dispensation, capacity limits on the large-firm sector have been dismantled and wider opportunities have been opened up for private, including foreign, investment. Both independently and as a necessary concomitant of this, there has been a move away from the heavy quantitative restrictions on imports in a broad range of industries and a rapid expansion in imports. Until the mid-1970s, there was across-the-board import substitution in Indian industry. The imports–domestic production ratio fell in most industries and, by the end of the period, India was a substantially closed economy with an imports–GDP ratio of only 5 per cent. But from the mid-1970s onward, in part due to rising exports and remittances, and in part due to policy relaxation, imports grew rapidly. The import of capital goods has soared to meet the new demands and to ensure modernization.

The shift in policies, while undoubtedly designed to meet the consumption demands of the rich, has also diminished the public sector's leading role. Given the easier access to imported alternatives, the domestic intermediate and capital goods sectors (much of it in the public sector) have languished. While the private sector was given a relatively free hand to choose between imports and domestic (mostly public sector) substitutes, the public sector was obliged to get its own inputs from domestic, high-cost sources. This bias has been intensified due to the growing reliance on external finance which often requires global tenders (Kelkar and Kumar, 1990, p. 216).

A growing variety of consumer goods is being produced not for the bottom 70 per cent of the population, but for the upper classes. This has gone partly to meet the pent-up demand for such goods; but the new regime is also geared to create the demands which it satisfies, presumably with unequalizing consequences. The bias of policy is apparent in the sectors that have prospered – automobiles, two-wheelers, television, consumer electronics, petrochemicals, synthetic fibres – and those that have stagnated – mass-produced textiles, capital goods, basic drugs (Kelkar and Kumar, 1990). The growth of consumerism is a relatively recent phenomenon, even for the Indian middle class. The perception that the modern sector has shifted from being a suppliers' market to a consumers' market is explained by all of the above changes.

At least from the viewpoint of the dominant class interests, the effect of these new policies on industrial growth has been salutary. For registered manufacturing, annual value-added growth has risen smartly to 10.4 per cent during 1980/81–1986/87, compared to 7.6 per cent in 1959/60–1965/66 and 5.5 per cent in 1966/67–1979/80 (Nagaraj, 1989). Industrial growth in India during 1980–87 was only lower than in China, Pakistan and South Korea among a broadly comparable set of countries, being higher than in such newly industrializing countries as Brazil, Singapore and Indonesia. Use-based disaggregation ranked import-intensive, up-market consumer durables far ahead of consumer non-durables and intermediate goods (Kelkar and Kumar,1990). Changes in the composition of growth have been along all relevant dimensions: from the eastern states to the western, from labour-intensive to capital-intensive sectors, from the public to the private sectors and from investment-led to upper-class, consumption-led industries.

However, the new policies cannot accomplish what they are designed to without also posing a threat to their intended beneficiaries. The old regime had sheltered many among these classes – larger firms, an assortment of rentiers, managers, the middle class – by restricting competition and expanding suitable job opportunities. The new one would remove or reduce the shelters. These classes would benefit as consumers but have to compete as producers. The halting and incomplete nature of reforms is partly attributable to this.

The other factor is the continuing demands of political–economic stability. While government has been willing to reduce barriers to entry into industries, it has not been able to fully unshackle capital: thus, the legal restrictions on closures, retrenchments and lay-offs (the barriers to exit) have remained intact. They have impeded the smooth flow of investments across industries even as, with changing conditions of demand and cost, the pressures for mobility have mounted. This has been a cause of growing industrial sickness and government takeovers. Government takeover of sick textile mills, for example, has contributed further to the growth of sickness in that industry. These barriers have not been insurmountable in all cases, as we later show. But even where they have been overcome, the costs to capital have not been small.[37]

Changes in labour legislation have been frequently proposed and equally often rejected. Even proposals to raise the proportion of workers represented for registering or recognizing unions or to speed up compulsory arbitration have not found acceptance. Few observers believe that such reforms, let alone reforms relating to job security laws, will see the light of day in the foreseeable future. Changes favouring capital – the destruction of measures protecting jobs – will only alienate the labour movement even more and governments are unwilling to pay the political price.[38] On the other hand, reforms that will strengthen the union movement will weaken capital's hand in effecting modernization and facing growing competition. At least in this area, the limits of new state policy appear to be well defined.

Labour Politics in Flux

This is not to say that the capital–labour impasse has not been breached. By liberalizing the growth regime, the state hoped that capital would be sufficiently free to proceed as desired; this expectation has been largely met (see below). Moreover, a change in the state's stance towards labour has been detectable, growing out of the labour unrest of the early 1970s and the subsequent emergency/corporatist attempts to weaken labour. Capital has thus been enabled to ease out of the impasse.

Among the episodes that may have signalled a change in the state's stance are the emergency regime of 1975–77 and the Bombay textile strike of 1982–83. During the emergency, government banned strikes, froze wages and impounded dearness allowance payments. On the face of it, the tripartism of earlier decades gave way to bilateral negotiations between labour and capital: 'While this was promoted in the name of worker participation in management, the formal structures concealed the powerful state corporatism which sought, by repression and intimidation and by the explicit policy of more production for less cost' (Rudolph and Rudolph, 1987, p. 275). Not only did the trains run on time, but managements demanded and got more work from workers without having to raise wages.[39]

The 1982–83 strike in the industry that had launched the labour movement was precipitated by the threat of retrenchment following modernization which management wanted.[40] The suspected complicity of the recognized union led a maverick outsider, Datta Samant, to lead the biggest strike in Indian history: the strike lasted well over a year and involved 250,000 workers. When it was over, nearly 100,000 had lost their jobs and those that remained won only a meagre pay raise. The government's calculated policy of non-intervention – especially its refusal to dislodge the union – cannot be explained simply by an appeal to similar past actions alone. The strike affected the largest sector of industrial employment in the main industrial centre of the country. Government was doubtless aware of the ramifications of the strike and its resolution, not only in Bombay but also in Indian industry as a whole (Bakshi, 1986).

More generally, this change is detectable in the government's willingness to use its executive powers selectively to curb labour.[41] At the very least, government has neglected labour as a political force.[42] These signals were bound to be picked up and give rise to a new employer strategy towards labour. Conversely, the changes were part of a wider sense of disarray within the labour movement. Though this change is not transparent, workers have begun doubting the utility of party affiliation and political connections (Ramaswamy, 1988). During the 1970s and 1980s, the main source of challenge to the established unions has come from anarchist, individualist and even chauvinistic elements. This reflects growing frustration with traditional patterns of union representation and action.

As employment has shifted from the old to the new industries, and as the skill and educational levels of the workforce have risen, workers' demands have shifted to shop-floor issues and their need for a different type of leader has also grown. Though the function of the old-style leaders as a useful conduit to the political regime has continued, such leaders have not been able to satisfy the needs of workers in the face of growing workplace pressures – this is more the case with the growing significance of bilateral bargaining. Workers perceive collusion between union leaders and management as the latter comes under increasing pressure to curb labour costs. While workers are particularly concerned about workloads and job security, management is keener to cut jobs. The unbridled economism of even militant leaders has allowed hefty pay rises on the one hand and declining ratios of permanent workers with rising workloads on the other. Rather than fight the growth of contract and casual labour or subcontracting, these leaders prefer to engage in a bidding game for wage increases. Sensing the insufficiency of union responses to capital's recent initiatives, new worker-leaders have arisen in some industries/areas who can express worker discontent more effectively. While union fragmentation goes on, managers seem to be fearful of growing 'anarchy' as represented by the increasing power of the rank and file. But this challenge has so far led mainly to the frequent replacement of union leaders.[43] Sympathetic observers lament this growth of anarchistic currents within the movement.

Our basic thesis is that labour has been weakened in the process. We have identified state-initiated changes in the growth regime (giving capital a freer hand) and a certain bias in state interventionism in capital–labour conflicts as being responsible. But the reader is reminded that the fundamental source of change lies with the legacy of the earlier growth experience. As market uncertainty and pressures grow, the premium on flexible production arrangements and (in the given labour policy context) reliance on contracting out of permanent labour must also grow. How far the relation between capital and labour will be transformed by such attrition and what organized labour's response might eventually be remain to be seen.

IV   EMERGENT PRODUCTION RELATIONS

During the 1980s, the gap between the formal sector's rates of growth of value-added and employment has widened dramatically. Value-added growth in the factory sector has increased significantly. Yet, if there is any employment growth at all in the large-firm sector since 1979, it is because of some modest growth in public enterprises. In private enterprises, there was actually an 8 per cent drop in the number of workers over 1984–87. On the other hand, available indications for the small-firm sector are that employment and value-added have both grown at a compound annual rate of about 6 per cent which does not represent a break from trends in the 1970s.[44] Together, these observations signify a loss in the rate of growth of manufacturing employment. We argue that these developments reflect not only changes in capital–labour relations within the large-firm sector but also a shift in activity from large to small firms.

Changes within the Large-Firm Sector

Large firms have been under pressure to devise new ways of economizing on permanent labour. While cost increases have not let up, the greater mobility of capital has increased product market competition. Whereas the compound annual rate of growth in the manufacturing product wage was 1.5 per cent between 1960 and 1980, that rate tripled during the 1980s. This erosion of monopoly power in many industries has also necessitated technical modernization, held up during the period of slow growth. It also explains why employers perceive sharply increased labour costs. In enterprises that have reduced employment, wages have grown but work standards have risen as well. Many have also resorted to substitution of cheap, unprotected labour for permanent workers, often through the process of subcontracting work to smaller firms. Where this has not been possible or successful, compounded perhaps by weak market positions, there has been a rising trend in industrial 'sickness'.

The weakening of organized labour noted earlier has allowed managements to push ahead more aggressively than they earlier could. The Bata lockout and the Dunlop strike in West Bengal are but the most prominent recent disputes that culminated in substantial increases in managerial prerogatives. Unions are now widely perceived to be 'finally conceding managements the right to manage'. The law, of course, stands in the way: Arogya's manager observed that his company could not 'afford' to get government's permission to retrench. There are several tactics by which management seeks to get rid of redundancy. Voluntary retirement schemes[45] are sought, particularly in sick industries or where unions are weak. The millworkers' union in Ahmedabad, Majoor Mahajan, has been willing to settle for such schemes. Compensation rates have been low enough to allow several mills to retrench in this fashion and then either modernize or put work out to powerlooms. The Mahajan is allowed to pick who will 'voluntarily' retire: 'The union selects senior workers since they will stand most to benefit from the scheme; management gets to retain the younger, more able workers.'

But such measures have not succeeded everywhere, even where unions are divided. In Bombay's textile industry, modernization came after the longest strike in Indian history. Managements are also compelled to compromise on occasion. In 1984, problems erupted when Naveen Mills replaced ordinary with automatic looms: some 60 workers refused to be 'voluntarily' retrenched and sought the help of a 'real' union from the outside, the recognized union being suspect. Management undertook a conciliatory measure to remedy the situation and get something in return as well. A committee of shop representatives was created and a company-wide productivity bargain made, setting escalating production targets and a rise in basic wages at the end of five years, tied to cumulative performance. But the spinning manager noted that such target-based wage setting had caused worker resentment without improving performance.[46]

Where employers can, they blithely ignore the spirit, if not the letter, of the law: they shut down on a plea of lack of power (by not paying power bills) or of raw materials (by not borrowing enough). Lockouts have become more frequent and more prolonged during the 1980s (Anon, 1989, p. 69). According to Sherlock (1989), the high rate of lockouts in India is an index of the 'ongoing weakness of the country's labour movement' (p. 2312). A more plausible interpretation is that lockouts are the final resort of weak firms faced with redundant workers. One revealing tactic has been to shift blue-collar workers to lower managerial positions without change of job content or of emoluments:

> The expansion has been especially pronounced in such categories as junior engineer, junior manager, supervisor and foreman. The shift is sometimes achieved by a mere sleight of hand: the management may simply confer an imposing new designation on the top crust of the blue collar force ... What would change – adversely, from the employees' viewpoint – is the organizing capacity of the segment, which subserves management objectives. (Ramaswamy, 1988, pp. 3–4)[47]

Perhaps in reaction, there has been incipient unionization among the lower managerial ranks.

Modernization has also been accompanied by increased pace of work. The Majoor Mahajan has long insisted on contractual setting of manning and work standards together with wage or piece rates. But as sophisticated new looms are introduced, the Mahajan has been obliged to negotiate contracts with individual mills as production parameters are more varied. When water-jet and Sulzer looms were introduced at Arogya Mills, there was an experimental period during which both management and union studied worker performance. But lacking information on potential profitability, the union had to strike a bargain in ignorance. The factory manager noted with satisfaction that the bargain was a very good one for the Mill. Politically oriented unions have been more successful in preserving job security than in fighting for new workplace demands (Edgren, 1989).

In public-sector units where the surplus labour problem is more extensive, adaptation has been difficult both because shop-floor unionism tends to be stronger and because, until recently, government has been indecisive. The low rate of capacity utilization at HMT was due to several reasons apart from an alleged over-expansion in the mid-1960s. The principal ones originate from the impulse to open up domestic industrial capacities to competition and from import liberalization. Auto-makers, among the main customers, who have been allowed to expand capacity with foreign collaboration, have preferred to import their requirements under the guise of non-competitive imports. Many customers have also been shifting from conventional to computer-numerically controlled (CNC) tools. At the same time, it appears that management, in anticipation of shop-floor problems, tries not to seek out demand where it exists. The main advantage to automation and computer-integrated management, which are to be implemented over the next five years, will be the ensuing 'reduction in operator discretion'.

With an estimated 50 per cent of surplus labour, the company's strategy is pinned on two hopes: one, which will be fulfilled, is attrition by retirement of a third of the workforce; the other, which is of doubtful viability, is the off-loading of some 50 per cent of parts production to small-scale ancillaries. The latter policy will enable the company to cope better with demand fluctuations, of increasing amplitude lately, in the user industries, and to reduce substantially cycle time due to idleness.

Meanwhile, redeployment has been tried and found problematic: workers either resist retraining altogether, thus scuttling redeployment or, when a few are chosen, the others become disaffected. Another tactic in face of demand fluctuations was to produce to order rather than face rising inventory costs when producing in anticipation of demand. But this increased delivery lags and gave all in the company the impression that there was 'a struggle to produce' as orders were met at the eleventh hour – causing further morale problems.

Recently, government has announced a general policy of voluntary retirement in the public sector and basically frozen employment. But as an HMT worker noted wryly, this will not work because the good workers will leave (to get jobs elsewhere) while the bad remain. Reluctant workers might be induced to leave by segregating them with no work. But this can prompt workers' ire, as has previously happened at HMT or at Naveen Mills. In the public sector, it would seem that the adjustment will be gradual through attrition alone.

As important as actions to reduce the existing permanent labour force have been managerial initiatives to reduce the growth of permanent workers and to raise their productivity. Large private firms have been on a 'war-path' against unions: seeking and reclaiming concessions; winning many battles over rationalization and modernization; creating multiple tiers of employees, including some hired through labour contractors, distinguished by job security and wage levels; vertically disintegrating operations and contracting out to non-union shops. The increasing use of contract labour is pronounced in activities such as housekeeping, loading, materials handling, machine maintenance, transport and security. But its use even for regular production jobs is not uncommon even in large enterprises (Ajit Mathur, 1989). It is not only high wages but also failed Taylorization and, perhaps, a lack of confidence in the manageability of larger workforces that prompts managers to unbundle technologies in this way.

But as their ability to wrest concessions from organized labour grows, this process may reach its limits. As bilateral bargaining has gained in importance, managements seem to be moving from *ad hoc* attempts to limit labour's demands to a systematic strategy for getting more out of workers – Taylorism seems to be on the rise. Where modernization has been accomplished, and their authority is secure, managements are keen to exploit the advantages of scientific management to the hilt. At Naveen Mills, the shift supervisor is linked by computer to every shuttle-less loom in his department; he gets instantaneous read-outs of both worker and loom efficiencies. The contrast with the older weaving sheds could not be sharper. Threats to reduce the permanent labour force – though costly to firms – have become an effective weapon by which capital tries to have its way. As these new strategies for dealing with labour spread, their effectiveness grows cumulatively.

Labour has been mostly reacting to capital's moves, increasingly inclined to compromise and reach agreement without resorting to government machinery. Creatively radical responses have been exceptional.[48] Under government-regulated settlements, the practice had been to follow industry- or region-wide norms, and notions of general equity. With bargaining, there has been a trend towards increased disparity in wages across regions and industries. It is this trend which has also allowed firms to devise wage concessions to extract more worker compliance. The increasing frequency with which workers switch their allegiance between rival unions (in the new industries) must be explained as a response to the union–management deals which secure higher production gains relative to wage increases.

Far from reflecting exhaustion of the 'technical' potential of Taylorism, these changes portend a new birth of Taylorism in Indian industry and the eclipse of paternalism. Working within existing constraints, firms have also been compelled to create new forms of flexibility in response to rising costs and stalled productivity. While the differentiation of capital has probably narrowed, the differentiation of labour has certainly widened. The prospect for a new type of unionism, sufficient in response to these challenges, remains unclear at present.

The Small-Firm Sector

The growth of subcontracting and of small firms generally is scarcely a phenomenon of the 1980s alone. Employment in the small-firm sector (hereafter called SFS) grew much faster during the 1970s than earlier (see Table 7.3). Nevertheless, the practice of subcontracting has become more widely diffused since the mid-1970s. Taking the 20-year period from 1970, available indications are that SFS employment more than tripled while employment in large firms rose by only 40 per cent, virtually all of the latter growth occurring in the 1970s. The dramatic rise in factory sector value-added during the 1980s, much of it in the large-firm sector, was supported to some extent by new links forged between the two sectors. We have already indicated the determining factors earlier: as the effective costs of labour, including its underutilization, have grown in large firms, the SFS's advantages (cheap labour, non-existent or easily evaded labour laws, flexible production and sweated labour) have grown relative to its disadvantages (lack of scale economies and capacity to improve technology). The other major factor, which we cannot go into here, has to do with protective policies (reservation of industries, subsidies and tax concessions) for the SFS, avowedly to raise employment, check monopoly power and improve regional equity. Here, we wish to consider some aspects of the links between the two sectors.

In general, of course, the two sectors may be complementary, competitive or independent, according to the product markets they operate in. This is clearly evident in the textile sector: as the predominant yarn producers, the mills are complementary to the decentralized handloom and powerloom units (here, scale economies militate against small-firm competition); in processing and especially weaving, decentralized units have grown, to a considerable extent, at the expense of the mill sector (all of the aforementioned advantages have given them the competitive edge); finally, in certain lines, especially of exports, the two sectors enjoy more or less independent markets. But where large and small firms face major and growing differences in their access to labour power and effort, an apparent case of complementarity, such as a parent–ancillary relationship, may be induced by these changing conditions. This is better categorized as a case of induced complementarity or, simply, as a competitive relationship.[49] We suggest, by way of a hypothesis only, that the growing links between large and small firms in India, noted by many observers during the past decade or more, fit this sort of induced or endogenous complementarity.

Textile weaving is a good example of what we have in mind, though product market changes (including product differentiation, the growth of synthetic fibres), among others, have also been implicated in this case. Operational costs are not notably different between mills and powerlooms (scale economies, at full operation, and yarn costs in favour of mills are matched by labour cost differences in favour of powerlooms). The primary advantage of powerlooms lies, recalling our discussion in Section II, in their flexibility: the cost of temporary idle capacity is very low as no wages are paid (Anubhai, 1989). While mills such as Jupiter have turned sick, some like Arogya have done well by catering to the demands of the upper end of the market.[50]

PH Processing has two units, one of which is organized much like the composite mills and with similar technology; the other, more recent, venture appears to be a world apart. Of course, it had more recent machinery; but it was actually less mechanized, e.g. in addition to hand drying and washing, it had a large hand-printing section. The contrast with Arogya Textiles was striking: while Arogya's manager took obvious pleasure from the reduction in the workforce brought about by automation, PH's owner said that any investment to reduce labour-intensity would just not be warranted by operational savings. The more outstanding difference was that PH relies on contract labour for virtually all its operations.[51] Not surprisingly, exports (via garment manufacturers and other middlemen) are the main source of the demand for PH-processed cloth.[52]

In the Tiruppur knitwear industry, early entrants relied on integrated units, with permanent workers and supervisors. Newer entrants from the 1960s onwards switched over to smaller units to avoid organized labour, while some of the older units broke down into smaller ones for the same reason. The more supervision-intensive tasks are assigned to subcontractors within the units or put out to smaller shops. Even in a long established industrial centre like Jamshedpur, subcontracting by large firms and the growth of small firms are to a considerable extent a phenomenon of the post-1960s period (Gupta, 1980, cited in Nagaraj, 1984).

It is not implied, of course, that the vibrancy of diverse segments of the SFS is to be wholly accounted for by our hypothesis. Recent successes of small firms in consumer products industries, including consumer durables, that have in many cases achieved market leadership at the expense of long-established firms in a short period of time, are not easily explained by any single factor. Innovative marketing strategies of the new entrants and the complacency of the established players have been identified as important factors (Rao, 1989). But it is also apparent that these firms have been free to choose small-scale, flexible, non-union forms of production with an eye to keeping labour costs down.

It is difficult to identify the extent to which the initiative for growth in the SFS originates from the large firms. In textiles, for example, some believe that powerlooms have largely been the creation of the long established mercantile class and of the rising rural kulaks. They would argue that the increasing or continuing protection (including protection from the law) of the SFS reflects the political influence of these 'middle capitalists'. Others suspect that half or more of the investment has come from mill sector capitalists themselves.[53] In any case, textiles policy has not helped the intended beneficiary, i.e. the self-employed handloom weavers. In studies of Bombay and Ahmedabad, Papola (1981) found that small units that were vertically linked (producing intermediates, parts and services) to the formal sector have grown faster than those that compete with large firms producing consumer goods.

The question of initiative is important because it may be tied to the question of control. Of course, shifting from the high-wage to the low-wage sectors is not a mode of adjustment open to all large firms. The shift is more attractive in labour-intensive sectors; similarly, vertical disintegration will segregate labour-intensive processes from the capital-intensive ones. But this move is driven not solely by differences in labour costs but by the ability of the larger firm to drive hard bargains with the smaller units and the threat that some of the latter may pose if they compete with the large firms in the market for whole commodities rather than produce sub-products for which the parent firm is the only market.

This is brought out in a study of Calcutta's electric fan industry. The earlier, whole-fan assembling SFS (producing lower quality goods sold to low-income consumers) has given way to ancillaries. The large firms rely on their ancillaries to meet sporadic excess demands from domestic and export markets. These transactions allow workers in ancillaries little more than casual-market wages and sweatshop conditions (Banerjee, 1988, p. 198). Thus, while the large firm gives up control over process it retains control over the product. In the end, it retains control over profits. This sort of control even allows the parent firm to appropriate state subsidies intended for its ancillaries, as critics of government's small industries policy have argued. Thus, practices in the dealings between large and small firms, where these dealings are not at arm's length, give the former considerable advantage.[54]

A study of garment production for exports in Delhi noted that much of this growth was organized on the basis of home-based, particularly female labour. The work, mostly low-skilled, piece-rated and monotonous work, is put out through a chain of intermediaries and fetches meagre returns to labour. Seasonal and other variations in demand and the cheap labour of the women allow international firms and their local intermediaries to lower costs. Such a development has also been observed in the case of coir, food processing and electronics (Rao and Husain, 1987). Though the extension of large firms' tentacles over their satellites is mainly motivated by the easier exploitability of unorganized labour and small capital, these examples also show that this motive is often mixed with technical comparative advantage considerations such as demand uncertainty or uneven production cycles.

There is also a general question concerning the interpretation of official statistics that these points raise. Subcontracting and specialization in an extended large or small complex raise the rate of expansion of value-added in the large-firm sector while reducing the growth rate of employment. Likewise, many activities previously carried out in-house in large firms may now be classified outside the manufacturing sector altogether and raise the share of services (Ghosh, 1989b, p. 2528).

However, the view that large firms cannibalize their smaller rivals (or always succeed in protecting themselves) is not universally true. At least in the textile industry, it would be more appropriate to say that the smaller units are parasites on the big mills. Parasitism manifests itself in a variety of forms. The most important, perhaps, is the widespread evasion of excise taxes by the powerlooms and process houses while the mills, ordinarily, do not have the opportunity to do so.[55] Smaller process units frequently entice mill designers to moonlight for them; the owner of PH Processing said proudly that the chief designer of a well known mill brought him his latest and best 'even before it was available at the mill itself'. The head jobber at one of PL Weaving's two units was, at the same time, a fitter in a nearby composite mill. Although he worked 16-hour days, he said he managed to rest at least four hours each day at the mill.

The Bombay textile strike gave a massive fillip to the growth of powerlooms. This shift was not just temporary. Some major mills lost their high-quality, high-price markets because the powerlooms, on whom they relied when the strike was on, reportedly pirated their designs and even their brand names to sell on the grey market. Likewise, Naveen Mills' weaving manager explained the company's reduced dependence on powerlooms (by investing in the mill) as a measure to protect itself against a similar fate.[56]

V CONCLUDING REMARKS

Kuznets showed that industrializing countries normally experience a rise in the proportion of high-wage, modern-sector jobs. Industrialization also normally leads to an expansion in the size of manufacturing units which, many believe, is the foundation for faster accumulation, learning, upgrading of skills and technical change. These developments are also accompanied by the growth of an organized labour movement and of collective bargaining over work and wages. We have seen in this chapter that these expectations have been belied in the recent phase of Indian industrial growth. The average size of industrial firms has fallen, there has been a tendency towards vertical disintegration and organized labour has been considerably weakened. Paradoxically, this phase has also witnessed a notable acceleration in the rate of manufacturing growth but very slow growth even of total industrial employment. While some of these changes certainly signify a shift towards more flexible forms of specialization, this is not due to pressures from the changing global marketplace.

We have offered some (tentative) hypotheses to explain the Indian experience. These spring from peculiar features of India's political economy. In the early phase of industrialization, growth was led by public investment within a largely closed economy. Together with a democratic polity and a complex class structure, this entailed state regulation of private industry. State-regulated industrial relations, in which organized labour won a relatively secure place, also emerged in order to assure economic stability. However, this regime did not succeed in maintaining growth beyond the first ten or fifteen years after it was put in place. Although the reasons lie outside the scope of this chapter, we have tried to show that capital–labour relations need to be seriously considered a part of the explanation for this: specifically, in regard to production rigidities and the slow growth of productivity. At any rate, the growth regime reached an impasse which also threatened stability.

Economic restructuring did not directly address the industrial relations regime; nor did it seek to remedy in any new way the problems of the wider economy beyond industry. Rather, reforms were aimed at freeing up the regulatory environment for private capital and allowing élite consumption to lead growth. Nevertheless, we have suggested that the state added its weight to forces that were tending to weaken the labour movement: at first through a kind of repressive corporatism, and subsequently by using its interventionist powers selectively. These changes added new competitive pressures on capital over and above inherited cost pressures, due in part to a rising product wage.

Capital's response has included new strategies towards dealing with organized labour. Far from reflecting exhaustion of the 'technical' potential of Taylorism, these changes portend a new birth of Taylorism in Indian industry and the eclipse of paternalism. Working within existing constraints, firms have also been compelled to create new forms of flexibility. This includes a growing reliance on small firms, subcontracting, two-tiered workforces and the like. But the relative growth of small firms is not just a product of large firms' designs; there is a genuine element of competition between large and small firms. Opportunities for small firms have grown because of the productivity failures of the large-firm sector.

In large firms, where managements find reducing the workforce difficult, wages perforce stagnate. Where they are successful, this threatens further the growth of high-wage, high-productivity employment. Instead, they lead to islands of even higher wage and productivity levels. Hence, there is a wage–employment trade-off imposed by existing capital–labour relations in this sector. Shifts between the large- and small-firm sectors are a more complex matter. It is far from clear to what extent within-sector adjustments will obviate the need for between-sector adjustments. This would depend on how far the adjustments are reflected in changes in work practices, wages and productivities. Between-sector adjustments may involve substantial redistributions of income within the working class. A shift to the small firms can, in general, be expected to increase employment and reduce (average) wage rates. This would again involve a wage–employment trade-off. But these are not the only effects. There may also be dynamic consequences – on the rates of investment and technical change, on government revenues and hence infrastructure, etc. – and these may be set against the apparent wage–employment trade-off.[57]

The prospect for a reformed labour movement, sufficient to these challenges, remains unclear at present. The basic picture that has been emerging is not very encouraging. Total employment growth has been weak during this period of change. While the differentiation of capital has probably narrowed, the differentiation of labour has certainly widened. Regional shifts in industrial employment have also been in the direction of weakening labour. Meanwhile, under the impact of economic liberalization, the economy shows disturbing signs of trouble: rapidly growing debt, both internal and external, and indications of worsening distribution (Kurien, 1989). Hence, both the short-run stability and the potential long-run consequences of the new regime of growth for capital–labour relations remain uncertain.

NOTES

1. The common underlying element is the complexity of the class structure. Thus, the rural kulak class has ties to the state apparatus that are no less significant than those of bourgeois classes. Similarly, most of the smallholding peasantry are vulnerable to food price increases and inflation as are urban working classes.
2. In accordance with the request of their owners, the names of all except the two public-sector units are fictitious.
3. Workers in large Bombay firms (with employment exceeding 1000) earned about 2.5 times as much as casual labourers after adjusting for these other factors (Mazumdar, 1988, p. 226). These differentials are much above the 30–50 per cent premium that unskilled factory workers are expected to command.
4. However, patterns of mobility between segments vary over time and place. It appears that mobility from the rural and urban informal segments has declined over time among the long established, metropolitan industrial centres (Papola, 1977, p. 143). Similarly, recruitment from the rural hinterland is of greater significance among the smaller or newly established towns (Robinson, 1983, p. 96).
5. Industrial units employing ten or more workers with power and twenty or more workers without power are registered under the Factories Act.
6. Foreign firms account for only about 10 per cent of value-added in the factory sector.
7. Defined by law as a workman who has worked more than 240 days during a year. 'Workman' excludes managerial and administrative personnel and supervisors whose earnings exceed a specified minimum.
8. Papola's (1977) finding that firm size accounts for most of the relatively large wage differentials within occupations, points to the significance of legal restraints, internal labour markets and unions as determinants. We do not know enough to weight these different arguments for observed employment patterns in the formal sector.
9. That the formal sector is not exempt from paternalist practices prevalent in the informal sector deserves emphasis though the social conditions generating or supporting these practices remain unexplored; such work sharing without income sharing does raise costs in the formal sector.
10. Few handloom weavers, for example, have entered the powerloom sector (Mazumdar, 1984). Perhaps craftsmen have stayed away because of the gap that separates traditional work culture from modern industry (Marglin, 1988). But skilled artisans, who stand to lose much from deskilling, were never a large fraction of the population.
11. Similarly, at HMT's watch factory, management's attempt to raise productivity by introducing job cards was rejected by the union on the ground that the proposed standards were unacceptable.
12. The rise of public-sector managerial unionism (see Mamkootam, 1989, for a brief account) may also be a response to these influences.
13. This last point though is by no means special to the public sector (Ajit Mathur, 1989).
14. Supervisors' claims concerning the greater mindfulness of female workers towards work and non-involvement in the traditionally male-dominated unions are confirmed both in bigger factories (as I found at HMT's watch unit) and in smaller ones as in Tiruppur's knitwear firms.
15. See also Sheth's (1968) pioneering study of a Baroda factory.
16. This should not be construed *per se* as a weakening of the average union since the average size of factories has fallen even more.
17. Legislative attempts to provide for compulsory collective bargaining and for determining exclusive bargaining rights failed in the early 1950s.
18. Bakshi's (1986) exhaustive account of the failed Bombay textile strike of 1982 shows clearly that this was the main strike issue. The recognized union (RMMS) had employer support and was also allied with the ruling party. Thus the law was used to block challenges to RMMS.
19. The Payment of Bonus Act stipulates a minimum bonus of 8.33 per cent of wages and a maximum of 20 per cent, the actual rate being governed, in principle, by profits. But the rate, in practice, depends on strike threats and occasionally on arbitration.

20. But local circumstances also matter. In the industrial centres of Bombay, for example, worker consciousness can be expected to be strong. The Bombay labour market study found that while wages were stagnant for migrant/casual workers, wages rose for workers in the small-firm sector, though not as rapidly as for factory workers. Thus, where unions are a real threat, wages have risen even outside the unionized sector.

21. The very struggles between the ruling party-nominated representatives of labour and their opponents reflect labour's attempt to resist state intervention. This point is brought out very well in two recent studies of the Bombay textile industry (Bakshi, 1986 and Bhattacharjee, 1989).

22. See Byres (1988) for an overview of the class-in-itself and class-for-itself characteristics of Indian capital, industrial labour and the rural classes.

23. The losses in household sector employment have been borne significantly more by women than men. The female share of household employment fell from 39 per cent to 10 per cent although their share in the non-household sector rose from 4 per cent to 6 per cent.

24. Mohan (1989) provides a detailed analysis.

25. Dholakia (1989) has argued, on the strength of a significant negative association between capital productivity and the capital–labour ratio across states, that investment allocations by the central government have been politically biased in favour of the northern states and against the south and the east.

26. This cannot, at least as the ASI data are reported, be explained by the alleged growth of in-kind benefits, particularly in the case of managerial employees. The ASI category 'total emoluments' on the basis of which salaries here are computed includes the imputed value of benefits in kind.

27. The study also observed that while 28 per cent of factory workers belonged to the top fifth of the urban population in terms of per capita consumption levels in 1977–78, 23 per cent were below the urban poverty line and 49 per cent 'hovered around the mean level of consumption for the urban population'.

28. Verdoorn's Law – a positive relationship between the pace of growth and the rate of growth of productivity – probably worked with a vengeance in India.

29. We leave aside the methodological problems in Solow-type measures of the growth residual.

30. Sundrum (1987) provides a lucid survey of the key issues. For an explanation integrating aggregate demand and agricultural-supply constraints, see Rao (1987).

31. The literature is replete with explanations for failed accumulation in the 1965–80 period; yet the role of capital–labour relations has been mostly ignored.

32. Their reluctance to recognize their own failures is strong but not complete as I found in my discussions with Ahmedabad managers.

33. Smaller firms and factories tend to have a lower proportion of indirect workers or employees.

34. Rao (1983, p. 132) also found from other evidence that the fall in the ratio of workers to supervisory staff was observable in every sector of the industrial economy.

35. The long period of uneven agricultural growth across states manifests itself as an accentuation of rural–urban inequalities in the country as a whole. Hence the seemingly increased responsiveness of the state to an *urban* élite.

36. Whatever doubts there might have been concerning the independence of state objectives at the time of Independence had been laid to rest by the late 1970s.

37. Nationalization of bankrupt units in the engineering and textile industries, due to inefficiency or technical obsolescence, also reveals the curiously dualistic policy towards labour: a high price is paid to protect organized sector jobs while even elementary legislative protections are not effectively extended to the unorganized.

38. This was made clear after the Supreme Court judgments in the late 1970s striking out clauses in the Industrial Disputes Act requiring prior government approval for plant closures, lay-offs and retrenchments. The resultant 'loopholes' in the law were plugged in 1982 and 1984 by legislative amendments. The decline in closures from 226 in 1983 to 140 in 1986 shows the effect (Ajit Mathur, 1989, p. 25).

39. This explains the sharp rise in wages following the emergency (see Table 7.5).

40. Retrenchments could be concealed in the guise of 'voluntary retirement' agreements signed by the pliant BIRA-recognized union.

41. The incidence of violence in industrial disputes rose sharply during 1979–82 as inflation rates rose again but government machinery failed to resolve numerous disputes (Monappa, 1988, p. 14).

42. A major factor has been the growing political organization and influence of kulak interests in the countryside. Growth in capital's influence cannot be ruled out either.

43. We have relied heavily on Ramaswamy (1987) who gives an insightful account of such tendencies in the labour movement in response to employer initiatives.

44. This estimate is based on data presented in Ajit Mathur (1989).

45. The compensation varies with enterprise and industry but is not much in excess of one month's pay for each year of service.

46. Voluntary retirement is also resisted by individual workers who find compensation inadequate or nurse the hope of getting a member of the family employed.

47. This tendency appears to be a fairly recent phenomenon with little significance for explaining the rise in the worker–non-worker ratio discussed in Section II.

48. Kamani Tubes in Bombay is the only instance where workers, following a concerted union campaign, took over a sick enterprise. Kamani had run into serious trouble during the 1980s when its owners and managers decided to abandon it. By 1988, however, with the help of banks and the state government, the union was able to create an employee cooperative and the business is at the time of writing in full commercial operation (Bhowmik, 1989).

49. In other words, it would be a mistake to classify as competitive only those cases where small and large firms produce identical products.

50. See Chandrasekhar (1984) for a careful analysis of the changing structure of the industry and its determinants.

51. When I asked to see the labour contractors, the factory supervisor denied their presence. This was, the owner later told me, the common practice to avoid 'factory inspectors and other official probers'.

52. The decentralized sector, to be sure, is not free from excess capacity or problems of sickness either (Tulpule, 1989). However, it is immune to the more enduring problems of inflexibility and barriers to exit, not to mention the grosser forms of mismanagement, that mills are subject to. Its long-run advantage and profitability are much less open to doubt than is the case with most mill weaving.

53. I was told that many mills prefer to idle their weaving capacity and workforce and put out their yarn to the(ir) powerlooms. If true, it is unclear whether this is a long-run strategy to improve mill profits (by winning union concessions for retrenchment) or a way of siphoning profits out of the government- and shareholder-financed mills for the benefit of a controlling interest.

54. Such practices include substantial delays in payments as a matter of routine and underpricing of purchases with no relation to sales prices.

55. This allows the small firms to reap government benefits while the big firms foot the bills.

56. None of this is meant to imply that existing structures alone, conditioning the articulation between the two sectors, explain performance in both. In the textiles case, while powerloom competition limits the growth of the mill sector's output for the home market, this does not explain the export performance of mills where they have a comparative (quality and marketing) advantage. If the mill sector supplies more in product lines with non-binding foreign import quotas, its fortunes can improve. This remains in check because of failures to modernize (in turn due to capital–labour problems).

57. Technical innovation may be inhibited in smaller firms more easily because enforceable patents are virtually non-existent. Besides, learning and development cannot be formalized as these are subject to scale economies. Adverse fiscal consequences may also flow from the shift (due to lower tax rates or higher evasion). This may badly affect infrastructure creation and, hence, growth.

REFERENCES

Ahluwalia, Isher (1985) *Industrial Growth in India: Stagnation since the Mid-Sixties*, Delhi: Oxford University Press.

Anon (1989) 'Lessons of Two Major Industrial Disputes in West Bengal', *Economic and Political Weekly*, vol. 24, pp. 68–71.

Anubhai, Praful (1989) 'Sickness in Indian Textile Industry', *Economic and Political Weekly*, vol. 24, pp. 1550–52.

Bakshi, Rajni (1986) *The Long Haul*, Bombay: BUILD Documentation Centre.

Banerjee, Nirmala (1988) 'Small and Large Units: Symbiosis or Matsyanyaya?' in K.B. Suri (ed.) *Small Scale Industries and Industrial Development: The Indian Experience*, New Delhi: Sage Publications.

Bhattacharjee, Debashish (1989) 'Evolution of Unionism and Labour Market Structure: Case of Bombay Textile Mills, 1947–1985', *Economic and Political Weekly*, vol. 24, pp. M67–M76.

Bhowmik, Sharit (1989) 'Workers Take Over Kamani Tubes', *Economic and Political Weekly*, vol. 24, pp. 124–6.

Brahmananda, P.R. (1983) 'The Dimensions of the Problems of Unemployment in India', in A. Robinson, P.R. Brahmananda and L.K. Deshpande (eds) *Employment Policy in a Developing Country: A Case Study of India*, vol. 1, London: Macmillan.

Byres, T.J. (1988) 'A Chicago View of the Indian State: An Oriental Grin without an Oriental Cat and Political Economy without Classes', *Journal of Commonwealth and Comparative Politics*, vol. 26, pp. 246–69.

Chandra, N.K. (1981) 'Monopoly Capital, Private Corporate Sector and the Indian Economy: A Study in Relative Growth, 1931–1976', in A.K. Bagchi and N. Banerjee (eds) *Change and Choice in Indian Industry*, Calcutta: K.P. Bagchi.

Chandrasekhar, C.P. (1984) 'Growth and Technical Change in the Indian Cotton-Mill Industry', *Economic and Political Weekly*, vol. 19, pp. PE22–PE39.

Chatterjee, Partha and Asok Sen (1988) 'Planning and the Political Process in India: Duality and Differentiation', in A.K. Bagchi (ed.) *Economy, Society and Polity: Essays in the Political Economy of Indian Planning*, Delhi: Oxford University Press.

Choudhury, Uma (1983) 'The Behaviour of Capital–Labour Ratios in the Indian Economy, 1950–71', in Robinson, Brahmananda and Deshpande (1983).

Deshpande, L.K. (1983) 'Urban Labour Markets: Problems and Policies', in Robinson, Brahmananda and Deshpande (1983).

Dholakia, Ravindra H. (1989) 'Regional Aspects of Industrialization', *Economic and Political Weekly*, vol. 24, pp. 2563–8.

Edgren, Gus (1989) 'Structural Adjustment, the Enterprise and the Workers', in Edgren (ed.) *Employment and Industrial Relations: Adjustment Issues in Asian Industries*, New Delhi: ILO/ARTEP, forthcoming.

Ghosh, Arun (1989a) 'Productivity and Efficiency: Myth and the Reality', *Economic and Political Weekly*, vol. 24, pp. 279–81.

Ghosh, Arun (1989b) 'Mystery of a Declining Capital–Output Ratio', *Economic and Political Weekly*, vol. 24, pp. 2527–30.

Gupta, L.C. (1980) 'Dynamics of Regional Growth Process: Basic Propositions and a Case Study', Bombay: Industrial Development Bank of India.

Holmstrom, Mark (1985) *Industry and Inequality: The social anthropology of Indian Labour*, Cambridge: Cambridge University Press.

Kelkar, V.L. and Rajiv Kumar (1990) 'Industrial Growth in the Eighties: Emerging Policy Issues', *Economic and Political Weekly*, vol. 25, pp. 209–22.

Krishnaswami, C. (1989) 'Dynamics of Capitalist Labour Process', *Economic and Political Weekly*, vol. 24, pp. 1353–9.

Kurien, C.T. (1989) 'Indian Economy in the 1980s and on to the 1990s', *Economic and Political Weekly*, vol. 24, pp. 787–98.

Mamkootam, Kuriakose (1989) 'Emergence of Managerial Unionism in India', *Economic and Political Weekly*, vol. 24, pp. M175–M177.

Marglin, Stephen (1988) 'Losing Touch: The Cultural Conditions of Worker Accommodation and Resistance', Cambridge, Mass.: Department of Economics, Harvard University.

Mathur, Ajit N. (1989) 'Green Signals, Red Flags and White Elephants: A Review of Contractual, Legal and Customary Regulations Affecting Employment in Indian Manufacturing Industry', in G. Edgren (ed.) *Employment and Industrial Relations: Adjustment Issues in Asian Enterprises*, New Delhi: ILO/ARTEP, forthcoming.

Mathur, D.C. (1989) *Contract Labour in India*, Delhi: Mittal.

Mazumdar, Dipak (1973) 'Labour Supply in Early Industrialization: The Case of the Bombay Textile Industry', *Economic History Review*, vol. 26, pp. 477–96.

Mazumdar, Dipak (1984) *The Issue of Small versus Large in the Indian Textile Industry*, Washington, DC: The World Bank.

Mazumdar, Dipak (1988) 'Labour and Product Markets', in K.B. Suri (ed.) (1988) *Small Scale Industries and Industrial Development: The Indian Experience*, New Delhi: Sage Publications.

Mohan, Rakesh (1989) 'Industry and Urban Employment, 1961–1981', *Economic and Political Weekly*, vol. 24, pp. 2481–505.

Monappa, Arun (1988) *Industrial Relations*, New Delhi: Tata McGraw-Hill.

Nagaraj, R. (1984) 'Sub-contracting in Indian Manufacturing Industries: Analysis, Evidence and Issues', *Economic and Political Weekly*, vol. 19, pp. 1435–53.

Nagaraj, R. (1985) 'Trends in factory size in Indian industry, 1950 to 1980: Some tentative inferences', *Economic and Political Weekly*, vol. 20, pp. M26–M32.

Nagaraj, R. (1989) 'Growth in Manufacturing Output since 1980: Some Preliminary Findings', *Economic and Political Weekly*, vol. 24, pp. 1481–4.

Papola, T.S. (1977) 'Mobility and wage structure in an urban labour market: A study in Ahmedabad (India)', in S. Kannappan (ed.) *Studies of urban labour market behaviour in developing countries*, Geneva: International Institute for Labour Studies.

Papola, T.S. (1981) 'Industrialization, Technological Choices and Urban Labour Markets', in Amiya Bagchi and N. Banerjee (eds) *Change and Choice in Indian Industry*, Calcutta: K.P. Bagchi.

Ramaswamy, E.A. (1977) *The Worker and his Union*, Bombay: Allied Publishers.

Ramaswamy, E.A. (1988) *Worker Consciousness and Trade Union Response*, Delhi: Oxford University Press.

Ramaswamy, E.A. and Uma Ramaswamy (1981) *Industry and Labour*, Delhi: Oxford University Press.

Rao, J. Mohan (1987) 'Distribution and Growth with an Infrastructure Constraint', Amherst, Mass.: Department of Economics, University of Massachusetts.

Rao, Rukmini and Sahba Husain (1987) 'Invisible Hands: Women in Home-Based Production in the Garment Export Industry in Delhi', in A. Menefee Singh and A. Kelles-Viitanen, *Invisible Hands: Women in Home-Based Production*, New Delhi: Sage Publications.

Rao, S.L. (1989) 'Innovative Marketing Strategies: Small Enterprises Fight Large Established Companies', *Economic and Political Weekly*, vol. 24, pp. M127–M130.

Rao, V.K.R.V. (1983) *India's National Income, 1950–1980* New Delhi: Sage Publications.

Robinson, Austin (1983) 'Introduction', in Robinson, Brahmananda and Deshpande (1983).

Rudolph, Lloyd and Susanne Rudolph (1987) 'Involuted Pluralism and State Domination of the Industrial Relations Regime', in *In Pursuit of Lakshmi: The Political Economy of the Indian State*, Chicago: University of Chicago Press.

Sherlock Stephen (1989) 'Railway Workers and their Unions: Origins of 1974 Indian Railways Strike', *Economic and Political Weekly*, vol. 24, pp. 2311–22.

Sheth, N.R. (1968) *The Social Framework of an Indian Factory*, Manchester: Manchester University Press.

Sundaram, K. and S.D. Tendulkar (1988) 'An Approximation to the Size Structure of Indian Manufacturing Industry', in K.B. Suri (ed.) (1988) *Small Scale Industries and Industrial Development: The Indian Experience*, New Delhi: Sage Publications.

Sundrum, R.M. (1987) *Growth and Income Distribution in India*, New Delhi: Sage Publications.

Taira, Koji (1977) 'Internal labour markets, ability utilisation and economic growth', in S. Kannappan (ed.) *Studies of urban labour market behaviour in developing countries*, Geneva: International Institute for Labour Studies.

Tulpule, Bagaram (1989) 'Sickness in Indian Textile Industry: Causes and Remedies', *Economic and Political Weekly*, vol. 24, pp. 377–80.

Vermeulen, Bruce and Ravi Sethi (1982) 'Labour–management conflict resolution in state-owned enterprises: a comparison of public- and private-sector practice in India', in Leroy Jones (ed.) *Public Enterprises in Less-Developed Countries*, Cambridge: Cambridge University Press.

8.   After a dark Golden Age – Eastern Europe

Janos Köllö

I   INTRODUCTION

The first question to answer when one investigates capital–labour relations in Eastern Europe (hereafter EE)[1] might sound artless but is of great importance: what is 'capital' in a Soviet-type society? During 70 years of its history, Soviet rule was unable to change the behaviour of the worker. Workers' attitudes are shaped by the economic interests of their households and by the values and traditions of their social environment. A 'new socialist man' has not emerged in the Soviet Union and its fellow countries.

However, the case is not that simple. Authority over capital goods, the right to hire and fire workers or to set wages, are shared by state officials and enterprise managers, and some very important 'capitalist' functions are only performed by central authorities. Hence the trade-off between consumption and accumulation is perceived only by the centre. For enterprise managers, higher wages do not mean a sacrifice of investment and vice versa. The shift of certain roles from the enterprise level to central decision-making bodies may encourage two types of disputable interpretation.

In the common concept of the *command economy* firms appear as dependent parts of the state's control machinery and capital–labour relations are interpreted as conflicts between workers and 'leaders' irrespective of the concrete position the latter hold. By studying the Soviet systems and recognizing the deep conflicts between the managerial and central levels social scientists abandoned this fundamentalist approach long ago. More attention should be paid to the *corporatist* view, which maintains that if managers do not endeavour to minimize or constrain the level of workers' wages and fringe benefits, a basic community of interest can exist between the two parties. This view of the bargaining process is literally one-sided. It emphasizes the phase of negotiations between the central authorities and managers who 'while negotiating wages behave as "union activists" not as employers' (Kornai, 1980, p. 418), that is, they fight for the highest possible benefits for their workers. What this interpretation neglects is the period between two negotiations when the manager resembles anything but a union activist.[2] Massive evidence supports the survival of perpetual revisions of norms, bitter shop-floor bargaining and open disputes in the factory, even after the abolition of central planning and fulfilment-related managerial premia, i.e. after managers ceased directly to depend on central authorities.[3]

Enterprise directors are deeply interested in using the artfully accumulated wage fund as a scarce resource, even in strictly planned economies, where the rewards of top managers depend on plan fulfilment (Berliner, 1957, pp. 24–56). There is an optimal way to distribute wages and set norms given a definite purpose, such as the fulfilment, overfulfilment or deliberate underfulfilment of particular plan targets, and a set of scarce resources after the negotiations. In achieving the production level and the output mix that produces a maximum reward for top managers (or helps them to improve their bargaining position for the next round of negotiations) they have to constrain wages relative to output. The upward stream of unconstrained wage claims thus goes hand in hand with a downward stream of restriction within the enterprise. Each manager claims higher benefits for his unit but, once the wage fund has been set, each demands definite effort on the part of workers while offering a definite wage rate. As the wage/effort parity can be further improved at any particular wage rate, this is sufficient condition for conflicts and bargaining on the shop floor, and motivates the enterprise or shop manager to establish a powerful system of oppression and control.

Unlike unions or workers' councils, the good boss who 'fights for his team' is interested in reducing the autonomy of his subordinates and in suppressing collective action as well as many forms of individual protest. The repression of 'voice' through the early liquidation of union autonomy in these countries is well known as are repeated attempts to render 'exit'. The awkward practices to reinforce loyalty (socialist competition, brigade movement, etc.) are also famous for their widespread use and doubtful results. The ultimate goal to produce a worker who is 'powerless, but still happy' – a goal not so alien to some Western management techniques[4] – manifested itself in a long series of oppressive measures, supported and often urged by enterprise managers.

The community of interest between workers and managers is in fact restricted to special actions which simultaneously produce more benefits for workers and more resources (loose plans) for managers, simultaneously. When this condition is not met – as, for example, in the case of firing an individual, retiming the work week, resetting the work norms, regrouping manpower for urgent tasks – the conflicting interests of workers and managers become apparent.

Inasmuch as we restrict the problem of capital–labour relations to nominal wage setting at the micro-level, the state socialist regimes might seem corporatist indeed. By acting in their own interest, managers as well as branch ministries or official industrial unions tend to fight for better pay for 'their' workers. But the remuneration of a group of workers in relation to others (or in relation to the plan targets of an enterprise) is obviously only part of the story. At the macro-level, where the relevant question is labour's share in real terms, or if the problem of efforts and disutilities required in exchange for a fair day's wage is considered, then the corporatist scheme will no longer fit. For example, who will act on behalf of workers so as to change resource allocation in favour of the food industry when shops are empty but the arsenals are full? Who is interested in vetoing an unfair dismissal? Which branch of the power hierarchy will feel inclined to protest the tightening of work norms in a neighbouring factory?

According to orthodox political theory, this omnipotent 'mediator' is the Party. We shall resist the temptation to discuss this 'theory' and then draw the triumphant conclusion that it is false. Some lower-level party organizations may sometimes behave as unions, but the apparatus itself is no more than one branch of the party–state's bureaucratic establishment; its distinctive feature is not a mediating role between labour and managers but rather a special *means* of control over both sides. Although a great number of party-controlled 'workers' orga- nizations' exist in all EE countries (unions, women's councils, youth movements) we do not regard them as representative of workers' interests. Neither do workers themselves. Instead we shall interpret the set-up of capital–labour relations as a triad of labour, managers and the party–state and maintain that, unless the already mentioned simultaneous conditions are met, workers are left without any kind of organized representation.

Yet the East European worker is not completely powerless. Despite the fall of collective autonomy, which was regained only for short periods during the last 40 years, the logic of the economic system provided the workers (or at least some of them) with considerable individual bargaining power. We shall refer to this set of small freedoms, forms of resistance and evasion as 'everyday power'. In contrast to organized forms of collective action, everyday power is hidden, informal, and possessed by small groups or individuals. It is based on momentary chances, not on established legal rights. Its rules and constraints are not public, so one has to learn them by trial and error. Whereas organized collective action puts a great emphasis on 'voice', everyday power stems from the chances of silent, often hidden, 'exit'.

What we call everyday power is by no means a special East European or 'socialist' concept. The unorganized forms of resistance, expressed in the form of 'dissimulation, desertion, false compliance, pilfering, feigned ignorance, slander, arson, sabotage, a reduction in effort or pretence of work', were observed in West European industrial plants as well as in Malaysian villages.[5] Attempts were also made to grasp the foundations of 'everyday power' in broad historical and cultural perspective (Kemény, 1967; Marglin, 1988). That workers have no other kind of power is not specific to EE. Not only are large masses of the Third World in a similar position, but so are some marginal groups in the West as well. What is undoubtedly specific to EE is the vital contribution that the economic system makes to the emergence of everyday power. In a seemingly paradoxical way, the creation of a totalitarian political power, which deprives workers of collective rights, also means the creation of an economic system in which 'everyday power' is an inherent part. In Section II we shall briefly discuss three domains of the economy where this limited power is 'built in': the labour market, the second economy and the production process. Then we review the limits of 'everyday power' which evoke the attempts of EE workers to go beyond the dualism of legal deprivation and limited freedoms.

II   ON THE DUALISM OF LEGAL DEPRIVATION AND 'EVERYDAY POWER'

The Sources of 'Everyday Power'

The labour market

As part of a resource-constrained economy (Kornai, 1980) EE labour markets had been characterized by rapidly growing employment before they hit the constraint of available labour. With the absorption of reserves, shortages on the male labour market appeared as early as the late 1920s in the USSR, and in the 1960s in more developed Soviet-bloc countries.[6] In both cases demand exceeded supply in a great number of occupations. As a result total labour demand tended to outweigh the total supply, for men first, but several years later for women as well. Although unemployment still existed when full employment was reached, and unemployment benefits were suppressed, it ceased to be a mass phenomenon within a few years. With the exception of regions with large rural labour surpluses and/or very high birth rates (e.g. Central Asia) urban labour markets became increasingly supply-constrained as the massive outflow of workers from the agricultural sector decelerated. Labour shortages became a steady and widespread concomitant of economic development throughout the Soviet bloc.

Data are scarce but those available suggest very low levels of unemployment. In the USSR the estimated unemployment rates fall between 1.1 and 3 per cent, and recently published emigrée survey results indicate a 1.1 per cent rate of long-term unemployment (Wiles, 1982; Granick, 1987; Gregory and Collier, 1988). In Hungary the registered rate was 0.35 per cent in late 1988, the tenth year of economic stagnation and declining labour demand; this rate remained steady even several months after the introduction of a Western-like unemployment benefit system.[7] Although comparable data are not available for other EE countries there is no reason to expect that the Soviet and Hungarian cases are exceptional.

While these unemployment rates are not unprecedented in the Western world, the vacancy rates probably are. The vacancy inflow/unemployment inflow ratio (v/u) in the depressed labour market of Hungary, for January–March 1989, was 3.6 and regional rates were registered as high as 17.0 and 15.4 in the Komarom and Pest regions, where hundreds of citizens reside. In contrast, the highest national rate registered in Sweden between 1964 and 1986 was 2.8 despite a predictably higher vacancy notification rate and a booming economy in 1965.[8] In Finland, another capitalist country famous for its near full employment, the v/u ratio failed to exceed 1.0 throughout the 1970s (Makela, 1986, p. 14). The comparison with contemporary Hungary seems *a fortiori* because this country was regarded to have 'grave' employment problems in the late 1980s. In 1986–87 the v/u ratios in Hungary were at the national level between 5 and 10 and in late 1987, the highest regional rates were 66.8 (Budapest) and 70.2 (Csongrad region). In comparison to other EE countries scarcely available data suggest these figures were not high at all. The national v/u ratio for Poland in 1979, for instance, was 20.1. The Polish labour exchange system covered only a part of workers, hence a direct comparison with Western statistics would be unjustified. What is known about tight labour markets in Western capitalist countries, however, might lead one to regard 20.1 as an extremely high ratio, which not even the tightest regional or occupational sub-market is likely to produce in a market economy. The UK serves as a good example: in the mid-1970s when the UK was considered to be short of manpower, the highest regional v/u rate was 5.5 in the Southeast and the highest occupational rate was 5.33 for machine-tool operators.[9]

The abundance of available jobs is part of economic welfare *per se* and it provides the workers with an effective means of protest. Even in cases of strict legal restrictions on mobility, quitting is an available option for the worker mainly because after being hired the new manager will not really be interested in enforcing legal sanctions, dictated at the central level. The manager who has lost an employee has every reason to favour tough enforcement, but the manager who gains one has every reason to ignore the 'crime' of voluntary labour mobility. This explains the striking failure of many harsh attacks on voluntary labour turnover. During an overall political campaign of legal and moral sanctions against job hoppers in the USSR from 1929–33 the industrial resignation rate fell from 155.2 per cent only to 122.4 per cent (Schwarz, 1954, pp. 87, 98). In Hungary from 1950–54 even though voluntary resignations were treated as a criminal act (arrested culprits were convicted of embezzlement), the resignation rate exceeded 50 per cent in industry and 100 per cent in construction (Gyekiczky, 1988, p. 50.).

Contemporary resignation rates are obviously much lower: as casual work was slowly replaced by steady employment, and great enterprises with internal labour markets became dominant, the annual rate fell below 20 per cent in Soviet industry and below 25 per cent in construction; in Poland it slightly exceeded 20 per cent at the national level (Adam, 1982, pp. 40, 151); in Hungary in the early 1980s the comparable figure was 20–24 per cent, of which approximately 15–17 per cent was accounted for by voluntary mobility between firms.[10] Labour turnover is predictably less intense in Bulgaria, Roumania, Czechoslovakia and for the most part in East Germany. Scarcely available figures suggest that in Czechoslovakia the voluntary resignation rate was about 8 per cent in 1984, but some firms experienced 13–17 per cent rates.[11] A 'success' has been achieved only in East Germany where the rate of voluntary labour turnover was said to be around 4 per cent in the early 1980s and ambitious plans were under way to reduce it to 2 per cent.[12]

Even in Hungary, Poland and the USSR, these rates do not seem especially high by international comparison. However, it should be noted that because of a great number of unfilled vacancies the EE workers quit without the grave risk of becoming unemployed; this is unlike the situation in market economies, where a considerable number of the jobless are recruited from among voluntarily resigning workers. The main constraining factors in EE are institutional and are aimed at increasing the cost and reducing the expected gain of mobility for the individual. As firms are often reluctant to enforce the sanctions and because voluntary labour mobility may be advantageous for the state (the restructuring of labour without intervention, the easing of dissatisfaction via individual rather than collective action), voluntary labour mobility failed to disappear, or even to drop significantly when the Communists came to power. Mobility remained relatively high in almost every country throughout the history of state socialism. For the majority of the workers of EE the exit option is available, and where restrictions are lenient (Hungary, Poland, the USSR recently) job seekers are in a comparatively good position.[13]

An equally important concomitant of labour shortages is that hiring practices are far less selective than in market economies. Workers thus enjoy great autonomy in determining their individual workplace efforts, without risking their jobs. The weakness of screening has probably much to do with the large dispersion of wages within workers' groups; that is one of the few system-specific features of 'socialist' income distribution.[14]

The second economy
The rigidity of Soviet-type economies (as well as the neglect of consumer goods production and services) gave rise to extensive second economies 'run by the market and constrained by the bureaucracy' in contrast to the first economy that is 'run by the bureaucracy and influenced by the market'.[15] The data about the extent and composition of EE second economies are sporadic and do not provide for direct cross-country comparison. With regard to the

heterogeneity of the activities in question one should distinguish among at least three aspects: legality; the productive vs the redistributive nature of the business; and the time spent engaged in the private activity. The second economies of the Soviet bloc countries are quite different in these three aspects.[16] In the USSR, according to emigrée survey results, private persons account for 18 per cent of the urban consumers' expenditures. The legal full-time second economy was almost non-existent until recently and legal part-time activities were also heavily restricted. Although completely illegal factories and full-time black-market traders are common, part-time farming, moonlighting and 'part-time' black market trade seem to be the predominant sectors of the second economy. The case is becoming similar in Roumania, where the unparalleled deterioration of living standards led to an outburst of illegal trade, barters and desperate attempts to earn additional income mainly in non-monetary forms. The Polish situation is more complex: a much larger and quickly expanding legal private sector exists as well as an inflationary gap which provides a special source of secondary income; also available are semi-legal hard-currency transactions. However, large-scale trading with the products of the first economy has begun because of the poor supply of consumer goods and the widespread use of payment in kind. In Yugoslavia, with a large legal private sector and widespread unregistered part-time work, the second economy also expanded as the country entered a period of three-digit inflation and increasing shortages. Unlike those countries, with either traditionally high or increasing proportion of illegal redistributive activities, Hungary experienced an expansion of the legal and predominantly productive forms of private activities: according to recent estimates, 51.2 per cent of the labour input to the second economy falls on legal private plots and gardens, 35.1 per cent is performed in legal forms in industry, trade and services and only 13.8 per cent of the secondary work is done in an illegal way.[17] More than two-thirds of the participants are part-time workers.

Experts generally agree that while Hungary is at one extreme with slightly less than 700 hours a year performed in the second economy by an average economically active adult and 1022 hours by an average participant of the part-time second economy, East Germany is at the other extreme with 300–500 hours a year worked by small gardeners in the second economy and predictably much less by the rest of the population. In East Germany 30–40 per cent of workers take part in the second economy while 65–70 per cent take part in Hungary (Brezinski, 1987, p. 98; Révész, 1986; Tímár, 1988, p. 244). The comparison of Hungarian and Czechoslovak time budgets suggests that in the latter country active workers spend only half as much time on secondary work as do Hungarians on weekdays, although they spend only five minutes less on holidays (Farkas et al., 1988, p. 1117). For Bulgaria data are not available (except for private farming) but according to newspaper reports and personal experience participation in the second economy seems to fall closer to that of East Germany than to Hungary.

The unevenly distributed access to secondary incomes provides the worker with the opportunity to limit his efforts in the workplace without bearing a loss of total income. The fact that a great and variable part in the family's income comes from secondary sources tends to reduce the responsiveness of the worker and to prevent the manager from 'demanding definite effort at a definite wage rate'. Empirical results from Hungary indicate that a trade-off exists between workplace effort and secondary work within homogeneous workers' groups. (Köllö, 1984, p. 62; Sziráczki, 1984, p. 92). Obviously, this is only one of the many consequences of the second economy but it is one which greatly contributes to transforming power relations from the intended hierarchical and authoritative order to a system of bargaining.

The work process under regular input shortages

The excess demand for materials, components, energy and capital goods exerts a crucial influence on the production process. The competition for capital goods under forced growth favoured 'the labour-intensive variants of capital-intensive technologies' (Ellmann, 1979, p. 14). As a result, productive capacity was implemented without additional technology such as control appliances, feeding systems or programming methods. For the state 'this dualism [had] the advantage of combining modern technology with some savings in scarce investment resources' (Ellmann, 1979, p. 14) and for firms such quantity-oriented projects promised a better position in the race for investment funds. The cost was not only poor-quality output but also the need to transform standardized technologies to firm-specific systems that require perpetual maintenance to keep them working. Although non-standardized operating 'knacks' are essential in any production process, they are of vital importance when a system has missing parts.

Furthermore, frequent shortages of current inputs require immediate and frequent adaptation: the retiming of process plans, the substitution of one material for another, the retooling of machines, the reallocation of workers when there are absences, etc. At the managerial level, this problem has received much attention ('benign plan violation' is a central concept of Soviet studies) and one can often find descriptions of attempts to solve the problem by informal market transactions.[18] Research has been less concerned with intra-firm adaptation despite the fact that workers and foremen themselves must carry out, on the shop floor, the adjustment measures in question. The official system built for standardized mass production is generally too slow for eliminating these unforeseen and incalculable disturbances, and this results in the shift of certain organizational functions from management to workers. Such organizational tasks are, e.g. the substitution of inputs and the necessary modification of the work process; the distribution of tasks among group members otherwise having a clearcut official job description; the collection of tool sets or the preparation of the work-piece by friends on a reciprocal basis.[19] The frontiers between shop-level management and implementation, as well as between production, maintenance and auxiliary jobs, are vague in practice although they are usually clear and Taylorian officially. Because the efficient functioning of the plant requires the permanent active loyalty of core workers, the managers (mainly those responsible for production) are deeply interested in avoiding open conflicts with them:

> The brief description of a plastic rolling mill (Budapest-Nagyteteny, Hungary) can highlight the far-reaching consequences of this reallocation of roles. The mills, producing foil, insulation and linoleum had been equipped with continuous process technology. According to the original design the mills should have been working with automatic feeding of pre-mixed material and with mechanized removal of the final product; in this case one mill would have been run by a skilled calender-operator and one or two unskilled machine workers. By comparing this technology with an older mill in the same factory one could observe a serious reduction of workers' autonomy and the displacement of several skilled jobs by machines. But it can only be design. During the implementation of the technology, the firm 'saved' the cost of the feeding system, most of the control appliance, and replaced automatic removal by hand-crane. The implemented technology required an operator, 5–8 semi-skilled machine workers and 2–3 workers to take off the roll, according to official job descriptions. In fact the real working of the technology divided the group into 3–6 core workers and 4–5 marginal workers in each brigade. The lack of automatic feeding and because of the frequent problems with the availability and quality of raw materials, the mills were run in a way, that the factory jargon called rhetorically but appropriately the 'shovel technology'. Whether or not the material mix was correct or not was judged by 'core' machine workers. They and the operator were responsible for ordering additional materials as necessary. The substitution of missing materials with available ones and the consequent modification of the temperature and speed of the machine also presupposed the active participation of some machine workers. Insistence on the original job design would have meant the immediate collapse of the production and this danger was clearly reflected by the management's attitude towards core workers. They could maintain their advantage in the wage hierarchy in a period of grave shortages and 30–40 per cent turnover rate of unskilled workers; they monopolized the access to regular overtime work on holidays; despite payment by results in the plant their wages practically functioned as stable time rates, etc. It might also be important to note that in contrast to the expected and designed deskilling effect of the new technology, its real working needed a high level of practical knowledge, sensitivity and mental effort on the part of workers.[20]

In the course of their belated industrialization, state socialist countries mainly imported or copied Taylorian technologies and organizational rules. Regarding job content and managerial authority, however, the East-Taylorian factory shows distinctive features.[21] The special kind of 'job enrichment' discussed in this section has eroded formal rules, made the use of scientific management almost completely irrelevant and given bargaining power to large groups of workers.

The Limits of 'Everyday Power' and the Lessons of Open Crises

Disorder 'with a human face', not the strict Taylorian rule in the factory; anomie and slyness, not the Orwellian drill; informal bargaining and individual evasion of unfavourable local conditions, not the complete submission of workers – state socialist systems could not fully realize the goals of their institutions. But the forms of exit and voice we briefly discussed in the previous sections are rather restricted, with informal (sometimes illegal) character and local scope. Excess labour demand cannot protect the worker from repressive managerial and author-itative actions, nor can the second economy and the workers' influence over the production process. The limits these sources of power set for the manager are soft and, unlike legal constraints, easily transgressable in individual cases.

Rights versus chances

Full employment and general job stability only decrease the statistical chance of becoming unemployed or being dismissed. EE firms seldom fire their workers and almost never dismiss large groups; even in the case of (highly infrequent) plant closures the typical solution is to regroup the workers within the enterprise. Individual dismissals, however, are not exceptional and the legal protection of those concerned is insufficient. Written laws on disputes seem fair both in the USSR (Lampert, 1986, pp. 273–4) and in other Soviet-bloc countries. However the lack of union control over disputes opens up many ways in which local author-ities influence labour courts.[22] A thorough examination of the USSR labour law on disputes concluded that, in case of individual dismissals, the defence of the worker by courts is rather restricted (Lampert, 1986). In Poland, unfair dismissal of workers provoked many conflicts throughout the 1970s. It was the firing of a crane-woman (Mrs Anna Walentinowicz) that served as the *casus belli* in the shipyard strike in August 1980. Such cases played an important role in the forming of the KOR (the most important organization of the opposition before Solidarity). In Hungary a detailed analysis of trials in labour courts (Gyekiczky, 1988) suggested that in the initial (pre-court) phase 'neither the union nor other collective bodies participated in the dispute'; 75 per cent of the workers had no legal representative during the first trial (still at the firm level) whereas in 85 per cent of the cases the firm did have one or more. In court, in 80 per cent of the cases the dispute was not interpreted in a legal form and 78 per cent of the workers had no legal representative, whereas 100 per cent of the firms did. The literal defencelessness of the worker who is fired might also be illustrated by my own research (with K. Fazekas as co-author) of collectively dismissed workers. Of the 805 redundant workers, more than 700 were fired without clear explanation, only 2.8 per cent contacted the trade union, 3.2 per cent the Party, 1.6 per cent the Communist Youth Organization, and only 4.4 per cent appealed to the labour court (Fazekas and Köllö, 1989, pp. 474–84). Characteristically, the highest proportion (11.2 per cent) contacted his or her own boss (the person who hired him) or a higher-level official, in search of defence.

Despite the high probability of not being dismissed from an EE factory, workers cannot base a collective strategy of protest on job stability. In case of open conflict the worker will probably find himself alone, with poor hopes of defending himself against a strong, *polymorphous* power.[23] Except for times of open revolt and the recent revival of union activity in some countries, the real chance the labour market can offer is silent resignation or reduction in effort – and only the aggregation of individual actions can influence the behaviour of the employer. The bargaining position of the worker, which is based on secondary income or 'everyday power' on the shop floor, is also vulnerable to changing tolerance or to technological development. Although the persistent deficiencies of the economic system will probably maintain the sources of everyday power, at the individual or group level the gains of resistance are rather uncertain and transient.

Inequality

The strength of everyday power may vary with local conditions, providing rather different scope for evasion or resistance. Large disparities may occur, e.g. across regional or occupational labour markets. In the underdeveloped, labour-surplus republics of the USSR, voluntary mobility is successfully controlled by authorities. This is well shown by the very high proportion using the labour office (71.1 per cent in Kirghizia compared to 21.4 per cent in Latvia in 1977 – Schroeder, 1982). Despite general shortages of labour in industrialized areas small EE countries also have labour-surplus regions with open unemployment or restrictions on leaving villages (suppressed unemployment). Yugoslavia is a good example of the former and Roumania of the latter. But even in those countries where regional differences do not seem so large there might be considerable variation in local occupational labour-market tightness. In Hungary in 1987, qualification- and region-specific vacancy/job seeker ratios ranged from 0.1 (non-manual, Szabolcs–Szatmar region) up to 168.6 (skilled manual, Bacs–Kiskun region).[24]

Like excess labour demand and the second economy, active loyalty is a source of bargaining power for many but not for all. Some workers simply do not participate in the adjustment process and, furthermore, participation is a necessary but not sufficient condition for a good bargaining position. Small, cohesive, hierarchically structured groups which can enforce the 'right' behaviour upon their members can be optimistic about exploiting the role they play in running the factory. Loose groups, lacking the technical and cultural means of collective action, often fail to benefit from an equally promising position.[25] Only for coherent, cooperating groups can their 'everyday power' revive the otherwise missing practice of (shop-floor) negotiations.

The advantages of different sources of power seem positively rather than negatively correlated. The comparison of the already mentioned dismissed workers in Gyor (Hungary) with a sample of élite workers of the same company showed, e.g., that the latter earned more income in the second economy and had a more favourable employment record; discriminant analysis of the two groups suggested that on the periphery of the internal labour market one can observe not only low wages, lack of informal bargaining power, ill-health, reduced job opportunities, intergenerational immobility and poverty but also less chance to earn additional income and more difficulties in getting a stable job.

The price to pay

Table 8.1   Work time, paid holidays and overtime rates, 1985

	USSR	Bulgaria	Czech.	GDR	Poland	Hungary	Roumania
Official weekly work time	41	42.5	42.5	43.8	42/45	40/42	46
Days out of work	104	104	101	104	91	104	52
Paid holidays[1]	8	0	4	7	6	max 6	4
Overtime rate[2]	5.9	–	5.1	–	6.7	7.4	–
– of which work on holidays	–	–	–	–	4.3	2.1	–

Notes:
[1] Saturdays preceding paid holidays are workdays in Bulgaria. In Hungary, the number of workdays must not fall below 260.
[2] Poland: 1983; USSR: 1981.

Sources: Tímár, 1988, p. 200; Mischenko, 1982, p. 109; Frey, 1988, p. 189.

Both active loyalty in the workplace and participation in the second economy require additional effort and the sacrifice of spare time. As shown in Table 8.1, the official weekly work time in EE is long, and the number of paid holidays lags behind European standards (apart from Finland and Switzerland with four days each). In the workplace, a lengthy work day is often extended by extra hours. Despite 1.5–2 times higher wage rates for overtime, its unexpected occurrence during production peaks threatens to disrupt the worker's daily schedule. Considering the high rate of female work activity (42–52 per cent in EE as compared to 23–35 per cent in Western Europe; 78–92 per cent among 40–44-year-old women in contrast to 33–56 per cent)[26] and the inferior shopping conditions, this may cause insoluble problems, mainly for mothers. Enforced overtime work often results in debates. Voluntary or compelled abstention from the extra hours can result in conflicts with the employer.

Reliability ... that means the degree they can count on you. In my department we often have to stay after the workday is over, there can be a lot of things to do, which otherwise do not belong to our workplace duties. Those who do it all the time like me, upon whom they can reckon, they are not threatened by dismissals, in my opinion. (Technician, Gyor, Hungary)

I have always worked with products intended for exports. And it was often the case that I came home at two o'clock and they were here from the factory at four, saying how urgent this or that was. That usually occurred at least once a week. (Locksmith, Gyor, Hungary)

Workers often enforce the extra hours themselves, because this is an efficient way of achieving higher wages. The 'misuse' of their control over the production process is very frequently aimed at this purpose. But, as it is often expressed in interviews, this strategy has serious shortcomings:

1. When overtime work becomes an accepted custom, conflicts arise between volunteers and 'non-volunteers'.
2. The gains from extra hours diminish or disappear, as more and more workers take part.
3. The disutilities attached to overtime work are considerable enough to make extra hours a dubious achievement, even for volunteers.

As shown by several strikes in several countries, the interpretation of the overtime rate as a success indicator of workers' resistance would be a misunderstanding of a more complex problem.[27]

Overtime work outside the factory is widespread and expands as the second economy grows. In the USSR 3.7 million peasants worked 'overtime' on their plots and 10 million urban people worked in 'collective gardens'; proportions of those working overtime in gardens in urban communities were reported as high as 28 and 54 per cent (Moskoff, 1984). In Yugoslavia 24 per cent of the families had at least one moonlighting member in the early 1980s (Bičanič, 1985, pp. 13–20). In Hungary 3.3 million people worked part-time in the second economy in 1985, which equals two-thirds of the labour force or 41.5 per cent of the total adult population (including pensioners and students). According to time budget surveys the total labour input to the part-time second economy grew from 930 million hours in 1963 to 3.3 trillion hours a year in 1986 (Révész, 1986; Tímár 1988, p. 244). The survival of reciprocal exchange of labour mainly in house building and agriculture also provides a customary framework for the extension of worktime.[28]

As shown by Table 8.2, EE workers devote significantly shorter time to leisure and rest than do Austrian or Finnish workers. Well paid overtime work within or outside the company is a manifest sign of workers' informal power, but this is also one of the main reasons why these people feel 'grey and exhausted'.[29]

Table 8.2   *The composition of an average day of the year of adult men in selected countries (minutes)*

	Austria (1981)	Finland (1979)	Czech. (1980)	Hungary (1977)	Poland (1976)
First job incl. travel	313	293	345	353	
Second job	37	42	61	68	
Work altogether	350	335	406	421	434
Housework	73	107	104	106	95
Leisure	313	335	305	247	275
Rest	704	663	625	666	636
(Rest + leisure)/(work + housework)	2.4	2.3	1.8	1.7	1.7

Note: Housework includes all activities attached to the maintenance of the household. Rest includes the time spent for personal hygiene.

Source: Boda and Falussy (1984).

The local scope of 'everyday power'

In addition to the non-legal character, the unequal distribution and time-consuming nature of 'everyday power', another important dimension is that macro-decisions fall outside its authority. The macro-level wage fund is determined at the central level and the wage plan is one of the few taken seriously (See Kornai, 1980, Ch. 16). Informal disputes over wages, work time and work norms at the enterprise level can only influence the distribution of a predetermined quantity of benefits and the effort needed for a fair exchange. Leaving the workplace for the second economy is an available option for many workers, but the regulations influencing the gains from this (restrictions on mobility, fodder prices, taxes on private entrepreneurship) are determined by the authorities and appear for the workers as exogenous factors. Under state socialist conditions there is no hope for the spontaneous inflow of capital to areas with unsatisfied consumer demand. Even official unions are excluded from the decisions about the distribution of capital investment among sectors and industries. Institutions through which the differing preferences of consumers and planners (Olivera, 1960, pp. 229–32) could be confronted and compromises made (unions, parliament, independent media, demonstrations) are tradition-ally missing or manipulated by the authorities. The traditional methods to determine the 'tolerance limits' of the population (reports of lower-level party organizations, regular visits to enterprises by local and, ceremonially, by upper-level party officials) are incomplete and biased toward substituting democratic institutions; the existence of separate shops, hospitals, and other special favours for the decision makers do not help them either in finding out where these limits are. What we call the everyday power of the worker is completely insufficient for exerting influence over macro-decisions; and these are the decisions which have perhaps more to do with satisfaction and dissatisfaction in EE than do industrial relations in the strict sense.

Attempts to regain collective autonomy

Everyday power stems from the effort of millions of individuals, the exploitation of spontaneous chances that occur by the failures of control, and the involuntary concessions the authorities have to make. The emergence of small freedoms undoubtedly contributed to a cynical 'social contract' based on suspended rules, disregarded law and evaded prohibitions. However, both workers and rulers relate to this contract in a purely pragmatic way. For the latter this is a transitional deviation from socialism, and for the former this is a poor substitute for democracy.

The motto of discussing open crises (very briefly) could be a sentence from Lech Walesa's speech on the eve of martial law: 'So far we have had to deal with smaller problems: wages, unemployment and the like. Now we are involved in terribly hard political questions' (*Liberation*, 12 December 1981). The great question during open crises was and is the *political right* to deal with 'small' problems rather than the problems themselves. The revolutionary nature of the East European crises, as well as the fundamentalism of the desperate people, make the claims concerning capital–labour relations difficult to identify. Furthermore, the postwar crises of EE were quite different in depth. In Hungary 1956 and Poland 1980–81 the traditional system of capital–labour relations totally collapsed; central planning, the systems of punishment and reward, and the *nomenclature* stopped working, as did the machinery of the party-state in Hungary, and to a smaller degree in Poland. In Czechoslovakia, in 1968, the self-management concepts came from such institutions as the State Commission for Management and Organization, the Ministry of Heavy Industry, economic society and the government itself, whereas the Hungarian situation can well be characterized by the words of Sandor Racz (the president of the Great-Budapest Workers' Council in 1956): 'We took it obvious that as a result of the revolution the directors should stop ordering; we took the factories in our own hands'.[30]

It is difficult to sum up such complex historical events in a few pages. If we nevertheless attempt to summarize the claims attached to capital–labour relations in one sentence, we might conclude that the central elements were the effort to establish independent workers' organizations with enforceable collective power, and to reallocate decision-making among the state, the firm and the organization. The rather general term of 'organization' practically meant either workers' councils or unions. In Poland 1956, the official union structure remained unchanged during the rise of workers' councils; in Hungary the councils explicitly rejected the discredited union form, although they themselves built their regional and central federations. In Czechoslovakia, in 1968, the formation of the officially supported enterprise councils, where elected worker-members had a formal majority,[31] was accompanied by the decentralization of the official union system (32 industrial federations were formed out of the original 12) and by the founding of a single independent union with 23,000 members (Federation of Engine Crews). In the case of Poland in the spring of 1981, radical workers' councils started to spread in addition to (and to a certain extent in spite of) Solidarity.[32]

In the four cases the workers' councils' claims (or declarations) included the right to strike, to express workers' opinion through the media, to elect or to remove the director, to allocate the firm's resources and to criticize the firm's dependence on central authorities. In Hungary and Poland (1980–81) proposals contained an exclusive right of the workers to elect the manager and the right to general strikes.

It is much more difficult to judge the relation to self-management of these open crises. In Poland (1956–58) and Czechoslovakia (1968) the licences of the councils did not go beyond the level of co-management. In Hungary, a paralysed country, real 'self-management' and the organization of public services and supplies were an economic and political necessity. During the short existence of workers' councils they acted as the main economic force in place of the totally collapsed political and economic establishment. In Poland, many analysts regarded the economic power of Solidarity as paralysing rather than constructive despite the publication of Solidarity's programme of reforms in April 1981, the takeover of firm-level management during 'active strikes', and the attempts to establish a network of self-managing workers' councils (Staniszkis, 1982b). Pragmatically (constructively) and after long debates, Solidarity adopted a structure that could help pragmatic negotiations outside the factory, because it fitted into an official set-up of economic decision making,[33] but under the conditions of a disintegrating economy and sharp political conflicts it proved insufficient for active participation in central or industrial management.

The revolts of EE ended in military invasions, coups d'état and the violent liquidation of workers' organizations.[34] Yet these crises clearly reflected that the workers of EE prefer collective autonomy to the dualism of legal deprivation and restricted 'everyday power'.

III   CRISIS, MODERNIZATION, REFORMS

A superficial first glance at contemporary EE in the early 1980s might suggest basic similarities to the problems of developed countries. EE is facing the problem of modernization; it is in crisis and it is changing. However, the causal structure behind the current situation is unique. Here we make an attempt to outline the problem in its own context, with special reference to challenges and responses in industrial relations. The review of problems cannot be complete, of course, and we shall restrict ourselves to focusing on those issues that can result in systemic change. Many small changes within the frame of the old model (varying forms of central wage regulation or of electing official union activists, etc.) will not be addressed.[35]

The Crisis of the 1980s and the Challenge of Modernization

In the 1980s economic growth in all EE countries slowed. Both accumulation and consumption grew more slowly, or in some countries lagged behind the level of the 1970s. Two decades of steady real wage increases and cyclically fluctuating but expanding accumulation ended with a recession of unprecedented length and depth. Until 1981 the CMEA (Comecon) had accumulated $80 billion in net debt, of which $62 billion belonged to small member countries. The debt decreased significantly in 1981–84 but this transitional improvement was followed by a debt level exceeding $100 billion in the late 1980s. The previous temporary success in reducing the debt could only be achieved by restrictions on imports as attempts to expand exports had failed. In 1980–85, exports to the West fell by 12.4 per cent; imports dropped by 22.1 per cent including, and by 38.8 per cent excluding, the USSR.[36] These changes are measured in current US dollars, a unit of measurement that does not hide the uninterrupted long-run deterioration of the terms of trade, reflecting that these countries were unable to restructure their economies in the decade following the first oil crisis. Only in two out of the eight great domains of world trade (export and import of food, raw materials, fuel and manufactures) could EE increase its market share, notably, in fuel exports and food imports. Between 1973 and 1985 EE's manufactured goods share fell from 9 per cent to 6 per cent in exports and from 10 per cent to 7 per cent in imports.[37] The almost unchanged industrial structure and the persistence of chronic problems in the agricultural sector of some important bloc-member countries (USSR, Poland, Roumania) made these losses and the unfavourable structural change unavoidable. Crisis industries like steel, shipbuilding or textiles survived without cuts or organizational restructuring and met increasing competition from Third World countries. Energy consumption demonstrates the slow adaptation to changing trends. Following the 1973 oil crisis, it took nine years for Western Europe (WE) to decrease total energy consumption by 15 per cent, while it took EE twelve years. The respective figures of oil consumption were four vs ten years. In 1973–85 oil consumption fell by 40 per cent in WE but only slightly more than 20 per cent in EE despite the sharply increasing marginal cost of Soviet oil extraction and the drying up of the Roumanian fields.[38] Energy supply functions irregularly in Roumania,

Bulgaria and, to a smaller extent, in Czechoslovakia. Power stations were put under military control in Poland (1982) and Roumania (1985).

Because of bottlenecks and forced exports, shortages of food and the simplest manufactured goods became or remained acute in Roumania, Poland and the Soviet Union; the deterioration of home supplies led East Germany and Czechoslovakia to prohibit foreign tourists from taking goods out of the country. Hungary avoided a similar deterioration of consumer goods supplies, but incurred an enormous foreign debt, accelerating inflation and sharply decreasing real wages (see later).

The first debt crisis in the early 1980s delayed rather than hastened economic and political reforms. The temporary success of 1981–84 had been achieved with the use of strict central orders and restrictions (and by the traditional means of fuel and raw materials exports) not only in centrally planned economies but also in Poland and Hungary where the authorities intensively used informal means to encourage exports and to eliminate the disturbances due to import restrictions. The net hard-currency debt decreased by 35–70 per cent in 1981–84 in those countries where central planning had survived, unlike in Hungary (–6.4 per cent) or Poland (+ 2.2 per cent).[39] Direct intervention and central management without systemic change proved successful in the short run and supported the forces of central planning in all countries.

After 1984 decreasing debts gave rise to ambitious plans all over the Eastern bloc. The five-year plan of Roumania forecast 7–8 per cent annual growth. Czechoslovakia planned 3 per cent growth. The 13th Party Congress in Hungary announced the end of stagnation, and Gorbachev also announced his programme of 'speed-up' which was then echoed by Bulgarian, East German and Czechoslovak leaders as well. These short-lived programmes of dynamic growth brought about a Great Leap Back to the debt crisis and further deterioration of economic conditions. The current tensions are no longer restricted to economic problems; the crisis is affecting the political establishment and the state of human rights and it also means a revolt against a way of life that, among other things, caused life expectancy to decrease in all EE countries.[40]

From the point of view of this book, however, the main question is whether or not the nature of this crisis is similar to the one experienced in the First or the Third World. It would go beyond the scope of this paper to give an exhaustive answer to this question; here we restrict ourselves to one important dimension of the problem, technological renewal, and a brief East–West comparison. Technological change and the resulting restructuring of capital–labour relations are the prime subjects of several regional chapters in this book. From the perspective of capital–labour relations in the West, the shift from Taylorian mass production to 'flexible specialization' in the 1980s was of crucial importance. It contributed to the transformations of the labour market and of unions; it displaced great masses of factory workers and produced (fewer) jobs for another kind of manpower. In contrast to this two-faced development, which can rightly be interpreted as destructive crisis as well as promising modernization, the EE situation can better be characterized as a crisis of stagnation or of 'non-modernization'.

This is not to say, of course, that EE countries do not apply new technologies or new organizational methods. In some industries (e.g. microelectronics) computer-aided design (CAD) is an indispensable technical device. Automation and robots have also been introduced although slowly and to a different extent in the various countries. East Germany had 48,722 industrial robots in 1985, but Czechoslovakia and Bulgaria had only about 2000 and Hungary had no more than 80 (Bogdán and Páll, 1987, pp. 11–12). However, these minor developments have not as of yet upset the rule of (quasi-) Taylorian mass production, and their influence on capital–labour relations still is of marginal importance. The existing reforms respond to problems other than those related to new technologies and new organizational patterns. Before discussing the reforms themselves we shall briefly consider some of the predictable causes of diverging technical and organizational development in the East and West.

The new trends of development in OECD countries suggest that a successful adaptation to changing costs, demands and international competition brought about the eclipse of Taylorian mass production and the rise of more flexible productive systems. Greater flexibility is acquired either by the use of information techniques within the organization – CAD, computer-aided manufacture (CAM), flexible manufacturing systems (FMS), just-in-time (JIT), materials resource planning (MRP) and the like – or sometimes simply by a more efficient connecting network of traditional units (such as the system of financing, subcontracting and marketing for the small firms of the 'Third Italy'). In both cases productivity gains stem from the growing efficiency of the system as a whole, not from a simple aggregation of local productivity increases. A growing part of investment is, therefore, directed towards connecting a system of parts rather than productive machinery or buildings. State socialist countries face serious difficulties in following this pattern of productivity growth.

Among the abandoned assumptions of Taylorian and Fordian mass production were perfect information, stability, additivity, strict planning, centralization, a functional division of labour and the desire to reach a local optimum. It is not too difficult to identify the spirit of central planning in this world of assumptions. The system of central planning may have serious difficulties in managing decentralized systems composed of autonomous parts, dealing with a rapidly changing set-up, or controlling a flexible network of information and finance. There is an inherent contradiction between the strictly hierarchical system of control and the logic of new industrial systems.

Apart from this deep incongruity, the adaptation of Western technologies has always raised serious problems because of shortages, poor quality of inputs and the resulting problems of cooperation and subcontracting. As is shown by the attempts to adapt Western automobile technologies in the USSR, the efficient use of modern technologies usually required separate systems of control for the new plants.[41] The recent experience of introducing Western techniques of management and work organization in mass-production Hungarian firms also suggested that these models presuppose a 'buyers' market' on both the input and the output side. Applying these techniques in an inflexible system with a rather limited freedom of choice will 'cause the managers to feel that their burdens are increasing [and] the price they pay for increasing productivity – by sur-mounting of difficulties caused by shortages – is too high'.[42]

The inflexible system of 'rationing' inputs via central planning and/or the incidence of shortages make the implementation of the *latest* Western technology even more difficult. Flexible manufacturing systems presuppose the timely availability of inputs more than any previous one. Some new models (such as JIT) are completely irrelevant in cases of input shortages. Furthermore, there are new kinds of 'inputs' required to run the most modern technology, such as a developed network of telecommunication, advanced marketing, flexible organizational forms, finance, subcontracting and employment. None of these more general inputs are easily available in state socialist countries.

Further problems arise on the output side. A closer look at new productive systems suggests that the very centre of the technology design process is either the product (the imagined buyer) or, in some new systems, the real buyer with his special needs (see CAD/CAM versus CIB). Flexible manufacturing systems with small batches and convertible capacities are more likely to accommodate special demands within a short time. In state socialist countries reacting to changing demand is neither a necessity nor a possibility for the firm; accom-modating the product to changing demand, and refining techniques to manipulate the preferences of buyers, are of incomparably less importance. Research into the introduction of CAD/CAM in Hungarian firms showed that computer-fanatic engineers, not the production staff or managers, mainly promote new technologies. A review of EE literature on new technologies concluded that 'profit requirements have a very small part or no part at all, [the process] is dominated by the search of solving momentary problems due to labour shortages. (...) Mechanization and automation keep focusing on basic productive processes and serve for the goal of mass production' (Bogdán and Páll, 1987, pp. 24, 7).

The fourth problem is of an organizational nature. In most EE countries decision making is concentrated in the hands of 'trusts' that serve to mediate between the member-enterprises and the central economic management (VVB in East Germany, VHJ in Czechoslovakia, 'kombinats' or 'associations' in Bulgaria, Poland or the USSR). The almost exclusive role of this strongly concentrated and hierarchical establishment in the domain of technological development leaves no room for small producers and mediators, who are so important in the West;

the small firms specialized in the introduction of new technologies or those engaged in advertising or marketing innovations are missing.[43] Similar concentration can be found in R&D. Research is directed from the central level, after 'screening' the proposals and transforming them into large, centrally financed projects. Hence, for example, East Germany launched 21 centrally coordinated projects on new technologies; in Poland 70 per cent of the R&D funds of enterprises are allocated by the government.[44] The bureaucratic nature of these large projects and their isolation, both from non-mission research and from the market, introduces another obstacle in joining the mainstream of technological development.

Beside the questions of 'what of?', 'what for?' and 'by whom?', technological development in EE can raise the query of 'in what place?' Apart from the slow pace of technological development in EE, its impact on the labour market is less apparent because a great part of investment is spent on eliminating vacant jobs. As mentioned earlier, mitigating labour shortages is a leading motive behind the introduction of new technologies; the aim of maintaining productive capacity, by shifting to less labour-intensive equipment, explains why new technologies are still applied in mass production and are so closely associated with labour shortages. Although *job* displacement in the USSR, for instance, is not much lower than in West Germany, this would be an excessive overestimation for the number of displaced *workers*, especially if we consider that the highest ratios are experienced in dying occupations with a massive voluntary outflow of labour (Pietsh and Vogel, 1982, p. 150). In the USSR, where 14 per cent of the productive capacity of the engineering industry and one-third of the truck stock stopped working because of labour shortages (Aitov, 1985) an annual displacement of 1.7 per cent of jobs can occur without any forced change of employment.

The spectacular concomitants of economic restructuring, so familiar to contemporary Western readers, are thus not present in EE. As discussed earlier, the unemployment rate is very low. Despite resolute plans to close hundreds of unprofitable factories in several countries, until recently shut-downs remained exceptional events.[45] In the early 1980s part-time employment amounted to 0.32 per cent in the USSR and 0.6 per cent in Hungary and similar levels exist in other EE countries, except East Germany where its proportion has been traditionally 'high' (9 per cent in 1961 – see Tímár, 1988, p. 172; Moskoff, 1984, p. 27). Flexible work time is not allowed in East Germany and Roumania; its share is 1 per cent in Bulgaria, less than 5 per cent in the USSR and 6 per cent in Hungary (Frey, 1988, p. 76).

The crisis of EE seems to be one of non-adaptation rather than a crisis accompanying actual economic restructuring. What we called the traditional model of capital–labour relations in the first part of the paper is challenged mainly by economic stagnation, structural rigidity and the resulting political crisis – this can well be regarded as a specific feature of the EE situation.

Reforms

Table 8.3   Selected indicators of East European countries

	USSR	Bulgaria	Czech.	GDR	Poland	Hungary	Roumania
Net hard currency debt (1981 = 100)							
1984	62	31	60	51	102	94	67
1987	136	153	113	79	203	143	48
Net debt/exports to the West							
1985	36	62	63	76	556	175	76
1987	109	333	111	131	700	448	129
Inflation							
1981–5	0.9	0.8	1.9	0.1	31.4	6.8	4.8
1986–7	1.6	1.8	0.3	0.0	21.8	6.9	–0.1
1988	3.0[1]	–	–	–	60.0	11.1	–
Real wages (1975 = 100)							
1981	–	108	103	–	106	102	–
1985	–	113	102	–	84	97	–
1987	–	118	105	–	83	98	–

Note: [1] Jan–Jun.

Sources: *WIWW Mitgliederinformation* vol. 9, 1988; vols 1 and 3, 1989; CMEA Selected Economic Indicators, Die Erste Osterreichische Sparkasse Bank, 1986, G/3; Bauer (1987), p. 1143; Statisztikai Evkonyv, Budapest, 1987, pp. 363–4; Fink et al. (1989), *WIWW Report*, 1987; *Financial Market Trends*, Feb. 1988, p. 24.

The treatment of EE as a homogeneous unit may have been justified concerning traditional capital–labour relations or the modernization problem but it would be certainly misleading with respect to how these countries have responded to the crisis. The challenge of modernization also appears in different ways and varies with economic policies. Table 8.3 highlights these differences. The data reinforce the common perception that the small CMEA countries form at least three distinct groups. The data for Bulgaria, Czechoslovakia and East Germany suggest that despite the slow economic growth after 1984, these countries managed to avoid an open debt crisis and maintained price stability. Real wages in 1985 also seem to exceed the 1975 level (but not the 1981 level in Czechoslovakia). It is important to note, however, that by trying to respond to the deceleration of growth in an orthodox way, i.e. by maintaining price stability, by insisting upon 'socialist achievements', by abolishing the private sector and other forms of capitalist infiltration (e.g. public national accounts) they also managed to eliminate the crisis from statistical yearbooks. Under the conditions of repressed inflation problems tend to appear almost exclusively in unobserved variables such as shortages, length of queues, forced substitution, inferior quality, production bottlenecks, price distortion, a tangle of subventions and special taxes. Doubts about the reliability of success indicators published by these countries are warranted. However, given the lack of any considerable change in the capital–labour relations in this group of countries, we shall drop them from this analysis. Instead, we shall concentrate on Roumania, the USSR, Poland and Hungary, each on the way to transforming traditional industrial relations.

Roumania

The case of Roumania cannot be understood without first considering the extreme political terror. The seemingly freakish reactions of the political power to economic developments are in fact not completely erratic. Roumania has always had serious difficulties in integrating with the Soviet bloc. With an economic structure very similar to that of the USSR (rich natural resources, once including oil, backward agriculture and underdeveloped manufacturing) Roumania could not easily follow the general path of trading with the Soviets, i.e. the delivery of machines and/or food in exchange for fuel, energy and raw materials. This far-reaching problem led the country to adapt the original Soviet path of self-reliant industrialization and this provided an economic basis for the rise of Ceausescu's policy of 'the special Roumanian development'. It was this effort to create its own development path that proved abortive in the early 1980s, when the accumulation of the hard-currency debt ended the policy of opening to the West. Recent developments can be understood as a conscious move toward self-reliance. After the rescheduling of the debt service in 1981, 1982 and 1986 Roumania has been paying back its debt much faster than demanded by the creditors or by the IMF and so the repression is much more draconian than necessary.

At the conceptual level industrial relations shifted towards self-reliance, self-finance and collective responsibility. The institutional framework has been enriched by the introduction of workers' shares and an extended use of payment by (the firm's) results, both providing a legal basis for connecting wages with economic performance. Wages are withheld for two or three months if the firm fails to fulfil the plan. Grave input shortages or lack of wagons or fuel to forward the finished product can cause this to occur at any time. Wage reductions are also 'justified' when, for example, the firm's foreign selling prices lag behind the planned level or when the firm must pay fines for violating a contract. (In the case of delayed delivery, for example, 50 per cent of the penalty is paid from the sharing fund.) Mobility between firms became more difficult because the firm may claim compensation. The free choice of the first employer has been replaced by the allocation of school-leavers and/or competition, where school merits are the only accepted criteria of ordering (bribery can help, of course).[46] Similar regulations were issued many times in the history of state socialism, but unlike in the general case, in contemporary Roumania these rules are actually enforced, and complement a series of other oppressive measures. Wage reductions are accompanied by a national campaign to strengthen the work norms (Dascalescu, 1984, pp. 26–27). Because of frequent input shortages and stoppages of electricity, unnoticed rescheduling of the work day or the work week became usual and many firms received instructions to replace the afternoon shift with a night shift so as to avoid consuming electricity at peak hours.[47] The radical cutting of transportation services led to a worsening in travel-to-work conditions, forcing many workers to travel by bike during winter or to walk several miles a day.

Forced self-reliance is not restricted to one's workplace; it is also enforced at the community level. The Self-Management Act of 1985 introduced the six-day work week for villagers during harvest or engaged in public works.[48] While many village markets have been abolished and villagers have been deprived of the right to shop in urban food stores, livestock and delivery quotas have been introduced, irrespective of the occupation of the family members. Industrial workers living in villages must keep animals or – as fodder is scarcely available – must buy their quotas at black-market prices and sell them at the administered delivery price.[49] In a region visited by the author in 1987 even mushrooms and fruit collected in the mountains were subject to compulsory sale at symbolic prices. The urban population is suffering from food shortages and lack of heat without a real chance to reproduce its working capacity. Meat, sugar, flour and petrol are rationed but workers must pay for the coupons and there is no guarantee of a regular supply. Basic products like salt and bread are difficult to buy, so elderly people are often paid for queuing in empty shops with the hope that a purchase will be made. Dwellings with central heating are officially heated to 16°C, but generally there is no perceptible heating at all. The use of electric devices is either prohibited during winter or between 6 and 8.30 a.m. and 5 and 10 p.m.[50] In case of excess consumption the electricity supply to an apartment can be shut off.

Without adding further details to this interminable list, but mentioning the unrestrained political terror, cultural deprivation or the especially grave burden on ethnic minorities, we can conclude that the traditional system of capital–labour relations, once based on legal deprivation but small freedoms, has collapsed in Roumania. The informal rules of bargaining within the firm lost their importance with the deterioration of supplies. The right to leave an unsatisfactory employer has been curtailed. Earnings or no earnings, secondary incomes are no longer a question of choice, everyone has to adjust to a society which 'now consists of "competing bands" each hunting down scarce resources, trading for others, establishing alliances and re-aligning themselves according to momentary advantages' (Sampson, 1986, pp. 19–20).

The Soviet Union

Following two customary campaigns of 'order and discipline' during Andropov's rule and then in the first year of Gorbachev's leadership, the USSR entered an era of *glasnost* and *perestroika* promising profound reforms of the Soviet economy. The first two years of restructuring brought about great changes in many areas but few in the economic system or in the domain of capital–labour relations. The direct purpose of economic reforms was, and still is, to switch from a strictly hierarchical order of economic control and compulsory plans to a system combining central planning with contractual connections, merging central distribution into wholesale trade, mixing one-man responsibility with forms of workers' participation and allowing a limited role to the legal private sector.

So far the Soviet economic system has stubbornly resisted change in some very important areas. The dissolution of central planning, without the immediate rise of market coordination, may cause difficulties both for the authorities and for firms; and this threat induces the central management to introduce reforms step by step and/or to establish transitory solutions. During such cautious reforms, products and firms 'temporarily' remain under direct control. The problem the USSR is facing now (and has faced several times in the past) is that, in a dual system, strong rules tend to dominate weak rules and so the remnants of central planning prove stronger than the initiatives of the reform. Consider the recent move towards firm-to-firm contracts instead of central plan figures. The authorities introduced the 'transitory' institution of state orders (*goszakaz*): if a good is in short supply and/or of prime importance, the state can submit an order for it. The *goszakaz* cannot be rejected but the firm may apply for compensation if the order causes losses. As a result, *goszakaz* have almost completely ousted firm-to-firm contracts. Eighty-seven to 96 per cent of the total output of industries working under the full *hozraschet* system was produced for state orders, and there is pressure on the state to increase its role. The low (25–59 per cent) shares planned for 1989 will probably meet resistance on the part of firms, too.[51] Similarly the planned reduction of central resource allocation by dropping 4554 items out of the recent 5100 will probably cause problems in cooperation that will require the intervention of one or another 'coordinator', as was explicitly claimed in the annual plan for 1989.[52] Parts of the recent economic system, such as the central control over price setting, will survive in the near future and the connection between productivity increases and wages at the enterprise level will be checked by the Ministry of Finance in every quarter of a year, even more frequently than before.[53]

It is the uncertain outcome of the reform of economic control that makes the interpretation of changes in capital–labour relations rather dubious. If central resource allocation, the strict central control over prices and wages or the decisive role of plan targets and state orders remain in effect, the newly established participatory institutions will probably become as formal as were 'socialist work competition' or 'the movement of creative initiatives' before.

Workers' collectives have existed since 1983.[54] Their general assembly has the right to decide how the wage fund is distributed, the form of wage payment and make suggestions for managerial posts. They can veto the use of the assets or the staff of the enterprise for a purpose other than described in the firm's charter (for example, harvesting and cleaning). During the time between general meetings, an elected council that includes firm-level party and union activists, local council members and the representatives of authorities or banks exercises the rights of the assembly. The workers' collective seems a modest step towards co-management – only the most radical interpretations of their future would claim the subordination of the manager to the collective (see Popov, 1988, p. 3). Considering that the most important decisions still fall outside the authority of the firm, the recent moderate role of the collective is not surprising.

Gorbachev's reform places strong emphasis on collective responsibility and payment by collective results so as to combat the notorious passivity of workers and to achieve local productivity gains. The proportion of workers organized into brigades ranges from 40 per cent (services) up to 90 per cent (construction) but only 20–50 per cent of these brigades are in fact paid collectively. The transition from formal collective brigades to the most advanced system of *brigadnii podrjad*, where there is a contractual connection between the employer and the workers' group, has so far been restricted to construction (67 per cent), agriculture (70 per cent) and transport; its share is only 7 per cent in the whole industry and below 1 per cent in all but two branches of industry.[55] Soviet research on the practice of the brigade system showed that despite their formal rights and duties only 14.5 per cent of all brigades took part, as an institutional partner, in the organization of work, and exactly the same proportion had a role in distributing wages. Most workers in brigades thought they had no impact on hiring and regrouping of workers (68.7 per cent), in designing the brigade's tasks (79.4 per cent), in distributing wages and premia (71 per cent) and in nominating or removing the head of the brigade (83.6 and 93.1 per cent respectively). More than half of those concerned did not even know that they had been involved in an experiment. The survey results suggested that the main constraint on developing a system of collective responsibility with clearcut rules was the persistence of shortages, rushed work and instability, the well known characteristics of the system to be reformed (Skurkho and Meshchorkin, 1987, pp. 1390–92).

Unlike the transformation of the state sector, liberalization in the cooperative and private economies brought about radical changes in qualitative terms. In the course of the year following the liberalization in mid-1987 the number of new small cooperatives increased from 3700 to 32,600. The number of workers approached half a million, of which two-thirds are part-time, and output exceeded one billion roubles in July 1988 (Sillaste and Rääkk, 1988, p. 11). Despite this dynamic growth, cooperatives and legal private artisans still produce only a very small part (0.3 per cent) of the total non-agricultural output and no more than 8 per cent of the estimated illegal industrial output (Sillaste and Rääkk, 1988; Kostin, 1988, p. 4).

The emerging legal private sector will face strong resistance not from just the authorities. The sharp differences among republics and industries suggest that the main hindrance is the reluctance of ministries but, according to survey results, many people also share this cautious view. Thirty-one per cent of survey respondents in Tallin and 54 per cent in Leningrad opposed the spread of new cooperatives. (In a symptomatic way, 77 per cent of those who had never contacted a cooperative were against them, but 85 per cent of those who had were for them – Sillaste and Rääkk, 1988, pp. 18–21). Legal uncertainty also contributes to this reluctance. Taxation changed four times between August 1986 and March 1988; incomes exceeding the 'tolerance limit' of 700–800 roubles per month are confiscated; the police refused to defend the cooperatives against widespread mafia blackmail, etc.[56] Finally the private sector has to face the general problem of input shortages that only enormous efforts or bribery can mitigate. The profound analysis of Sillaste and Rääkk (1988) came to the rather disillusioning conclusion that the legal private sector should be included into the systems of *goszakaz*, central resource allocation and state subventions so as to maintain its dynamism.

What the Soviet reforms have responded to is hardly the challenge of post-Fordian modernization; changes are not directed towards a new system of collective autonomy either. Reforms are in fact restricted to a minor flexibilization of central planning and include attempts to interest workers in work and/or in the higher productivity of their shop. Important as they are, these reforms do not extend traditional capital–labour relations. Moreover, the Soviet reformers do not even raise the questions other EE reforms have been concerned with for decades.[57] It should be added that the social unrest emerging in every corner of the USSR in 1989 may slow down the evolutionary process we tried to detect in this section.

Hungary and Poland

Although Hungary and Poland have recently diverged in their political history, they will be analysed together because of the way they are drifting in the same direction. The economic situation of the two countries is similar. Both are experiencing high inflation, declining real wages (lagging behind the 1975 level in the late 1980s) and grave hard-currency indebtedness (see Table 8.3). Unlike Poland, Hungary escaped the rescheduling of its debt service and maintained its relatively satisfactory supply with consumer goods, but it has been threatened with the danger of Polish-like decline ever since 1982.

The radical political change in Poland and Hungary promises a break with the traditional roles of the Party, the state, firms and workers. The way to 'market socialism' and collective autonomies, however, requires crucial changes, some of them hurting the hard core of the political system. The legal circumscription (and restriction) of the party–state's sphere of authority is certainly the most important and the least complete among these changes. The prime importance of this particular change is attested by the experience that, in the presence of an omnipotent power, market institutions serve as new means of control rather than sources of autonomy for the actors in the economy. This is clearly shown by the especially radical Hungarian economic reforms. Since the mid-1980s Hungary has introduced a series of new market institutions such as the stock exchange, the bond and share markets, commercial banks, share-holding companies and public limited companies, VAT and personal income taxes, bankruptcy laws and unemployment benefits. Hungarian reforms have also subordinated (most) managers to enterprise councils instead of ministries, abolished the compulsory splitting of enterprise incomes into distinct funds, decentralized several monopolies, and liberalized price setting, etc. Optimism attached to these changes has so far been in vain: the attitude of managers towards wages fails to change; bankrupt firms generally survive and unprofitable ones often avoid bankruptcy via obscure manipulation of prices, taxes or debt payments; commercial banks remain reluctant to withdraw capital from many unprofitable (but 'important') activities; decisions are made by ministries or interministerial *ad hoc* committees, and so on. The experience of both countries suggests that without the replacement of state authorities by real capital owners who are intrinsically interested in making profit, market reforms tend to remain 'simulation experiments' without a radical break with central management. (Whether a careful owner can only be a private one, is a matter of sharp debates in both countries, but the problem is beyond the scope of this paper.)

It should be added that besides insistence on power and the survival of the traditional organizations of central control, economic causes also contribute to the continuing dominance of the state. Highly monopolized economies, lacking import competition (as those of Hungary and Poland) are likely to produce distorted prices. Also, economic decisions are always accompanied by barren discussion with the unavoidable participation of many state authorities. Lacking domestic and foreign competitors, production cuts and plant closures are difficult to carry out. Authorities must often suspend the strict official rules of the game, so as to avoid production bottlenecks or commodity shortages. The erosion of managerial autonomy and market rules is further increased by the extended use of fiscal measures. As monetary policy tends to fall short, aggregate demand is also controlled by special (sometimes retroactive) taxes or centrally initiated price increases. The failure of monetary policy leads the authorities to centralize a great part of enterprise profits (e.g. more than 70 per cent in Hungary), and thus further increases the role of the state budget. Moreover, in Poland, the hardly avoidable survival of central resource allocation that influences 80 per cent of the output in one way or another made a decisive contribution to the state's overwhelming role.

The search for an actor in the new play (an independent owner) is thus going on while another – uninvited – actor has already appeared on the scene. In Poland, Solidarity was relegalized in 1989 and many workers' councils were permitted to reconvene during the last few years. Strikes in 1988–89 were also treated with tolerance except the first one in Nowa Huta. In Hungary, a dozen independent trade unions were founded in 1988, mainly by the intelligentsia. A growing dissatisfaction forced the official union to give up the servile attitude it has always had. Similar to Czechoslovakia in 1968, some industrial unions were decentralized and the TUC itself made a few friendly gestures towards the membership (declarations concerned with inflation, real wage decline, minimum wages and cutting of social expenditures). But unlike in Poland the opposition in Hungary is mainly organized along rival party lines rather than in a union. In contrast to expectations and preparations (as, e.g., a new act on strikes) industrial conflicts remained at a modest level; dissatisfaction is mainly directed at the central management and debates are focusing on governmental decisions and general conditions such as prices, taxes or social expenditures (not to mention the overwhelming political, historical or moral issues).

The forthcoming organizational form of the labour movement as well as the future set-up of collective bargaining seem rather uncertain now, in both countries. The knock-out victory of Solidarity in the senate elections and the results of public opinion polls in Hungary suggest that most people feel sympathetic towards a plural political system with autonomous collective actors and open debates. At the same time, the economic system, and the ways in which one can gain 'everyday' advantages, remain almost unchanged. The corporatist character of wage bargaining survived, and its importance is increasing with the acceleration of inflation and no indexation. No government, communist or otherwise, could liberalize wage formation in the immediate future, to open the way for meaningful wage negotiations. (Recently, wages were strictly controlled by prohibitive taxes on the increment of the firm's wage fund, and any local concession to the workers requires governmental exemption.) The importance of the second economy as a source of individual gains further increased, and may further reduce expectations connected with collective action. It is highly improbable that 'classical' collective bargaining over wages will become a central issue in a new regime. Informal struggles, individual strategies, corporatist features and government-set constraints will probably remain important dimensions of capital–labour relations in Poland and Hungary, whatever the future will bring in the political arena.

The future of industrial relations can be considerably influenced by the expansion of the legal private sector.[58] Between 1975 and 1986 the output of the non-agricultural private sector increased by 10–19 per cent annually in Poland while the output of the socialist sector in 1986 was below the 1978 level. In Hungary at least 35 per cent of the GDP increment in 1986 came from the legal private sector (Laky, 1987). The further expansion of private business was encouraged by abolishing financial discrimination and loosening the employment limit in both countries. In Poland the limit was first increased to 50 employees per shift and then was abolished; in Hungary the recent limit is 500 employees in private firms and there is no limitation in cases of joint ventures of private and state-owned firms. (It should be mentioned, however, that legal uncertainty has always exerted more important influence on the expansion of the private sector; the employment limit has not been effective. Only a stable, calculable policy in the long run can result in spectacular growth.)

The expansion of the private sector may have a remarkable impact on capital–labour relations in three ways. First, small private firms (as well as joint ventures with Western participation) can accelerate structural change and contribute to a better 'infrastructure' for post-Fordian modernization. Second, the spread of private firms may have an implicit deregulation effect. Unlike state-owned firms, private firms tend to be rather unstable. In Hungary 17 per cent of private societies, 18 per cent of private manufacturers, 18 per cent of private tradesmen and approximately 2.5 per cent of private enterprises crash annually (Laky, 1987, pp. 161, 141; Kovács, 1988, pp. 10, 15). The expected partial shift from predominantly part-time and secondary employment to full-time jobs in the private sector would predictably reduce the crash rate, but growing competition may have the opposite effect. Despite these uncertainties it is reasonable to conclude that job stability in the private sector will hardly ever match the level achieved in the state sector. Existing private firms are characterized also by a more flexible and unregulated use of work time. Here again the expansion can bring about the erosion of classical full-time employment. Selection criteria may also become increasingly informal and personality-oriented instead of being based on skill rules characteristic of large state-owned firms. Last but not least a growing part of the private sector can put an end to wage stability for an increasing part of the population.

The third aspect is collective bargaining within the private sector, which is not unionized for the moment. Considering that the typical private firm is very small, dominated by highly skilled workers or professionals who are equal partners rather than employees of a boss, the problem is currently marginal. But with the spread of private enterprises, including some foreign firms which may be reluctant to hire unionized workers, as was, for example, Levi's in Hungary in January 1989,[59] the representation of workers could become a new problem, even if union independence were not curtailed by the authorities.

IV CONCLUDING REMARKS

For the majority of EE workers the 1980s failed to bring about radical qualitative changes *vis-à-vis* the state or their managers. The main experience was quantitative and disappointing: stagnating or declining real wages, accelerating inflation and/or growing shortages, lengthy work time and the strong awareness of a widening gap in the wealth, lifestyles and economic prospects between East and West.

EE is still before (or in the very beginning of) the age of post-Fordian modernization. A common heritage among all EE countries is the industrial mass production, the dominance of Taylorian organizations and technologies, uniform capital–labour relations with only small informal, individual freedoms, great masses of traditional factory workers and office employees etc. If these countries are to enter a new phase of development and flexibilization they will have to abandon this heritage, which is closely associated with the Stalinist political system and the logic of central planning.

The best thing one can do in these days of political collapse, violent revolts and general uncertainty is to end with questions. Is it possible to modernize the economy without sacrificing full employment, job stability, state ownership and party hegemony? – as is suggested by the endeavours of the Bulgarian, Czechoslovak and East German rulers – is a question of historical importance. Can a socialist political system be changed by reforms? – as is the aim of Soviet, Polish and Hungarian efforts – might be another one?. Is the Roumanian collapse just a tragic accident? – this seems to be a question better not asked.

NOTES

1. Bulgaria, Czechoslovakia, East Germany, Hungary, Poland, Roumania and the Soviet Union. Although sporadic references to Yugoslavia do occur in this paper we exclude this country from the analysis. Despite crucial similarities in its political and economic system, Yugoslavia has a different history of capital–labour relations. The inclusion of the Yugoslav case would require frequent digression from the main line of this chapter.
2. The phases of negotiation and implementation are obviously logical stages rather than distinct time periods.
3. On shop-floor bargaining in post-reform Hungary see Haraszti (1978); Kemény (1978); or several empirical studies in Révész (1984).
4. Remember Mills (1959) on human relations.

5. See, e.g. Dubois (1976) and Scott (1985). The quotation is from Scott (1985), p. xvi.
6. On early Soviet labour shortages see Schwarz (1954); Manievitch (1985); Barber (1986). On Eastern Europe see Adam (1982) including a chapter by Schroeder on the USSR.
7. Munkaero kereslet es kinalat 1989. I. negyedev, ABMH-MIK, Budapest, 1989.
8. Ibid., note 7 and Johanesson (1985) p. 15.
9. 'Skill shortages in British Industry', *DE Gazette*, May 1979, p. 433; Fallenbuchl (1982), p. 33.
10. *Munkaugyi Statisztikai Zsebkonyv*, Budapest 1985, pp. 169–70.
11. *Heti Vilaggazdasag*, 26 May, 1984 on an article of *Hospodarske Noviny* (Prague).
12. Verbal information. Institut für Wirtschaftswissenschaft, Berlin (East), 1983.
13. The access to voluntary changing of employer in these high-mobility countries can also be characterized by the modest role of labour offices. Placements through offices amounted to 15–22 per cent in Hungary in 1964–80, 1985–88 (Fazekas and Köllö, 1989) 3–4 per cent in Poland in 1954–80 (Fallenbuchl, 1982, pp. 33, 40) and 17.2 per cent in the USSR in 1976 (Schroeder, 1982, p. 11).
14. Redor (1988), p. 214; see a comparison between two firms in Révész (1984), vol. 24, pp. 25–6.
15. The distinction has been introduced by Grossmann (1977).
16. The main sources we use here are Ofer and Vinokur (1980), O'Hearn (1980, 1981), Grossmann (1977) on the USSR; Wisniewski (1986) on Poland; Brezinski (1987) on East Germany; Galasi and Gábor (1983), Révész (1986), Petschnigg (1987) and Tímár (1988) on Hungary; Vassiliev (1983) on Bulgaria; Sampson (1986) on Roumania; Katunarič (1982), Bičanič (1985), and Prpič for Yugoslavia.
17. Own calculation based on Révész (1985) and Petschnigg (1987). This is not to say that the illegal redistribution of income is insignificant. According to CSO estimations and Petschnigg 10–12 per cent of the population's income was spent on tips, bribery, under-the-counter sales, trading with council flats, paying 'black' interest, etc. Purchasing current consumer goods on the black market accounted for only 1–2 billion forint (Ft), or less than 0.5 per cent of the total expenditure, however.
18. See reports on middlemen – 'tolkachi' – in the USSR, East Germany or Yugoslavia. See Feldbrugge (1983), p.15 on the USSR; Brezinski (1987), pp. 90–91 on East Germany, Bičanič (1985), p. 15 on Yugoslavia.
19. See examples in Kemény (1978); Fazekas and Köllö (1989); Kalász and Köllö (1984); Makó (1985); Ladó and Tóth (1985).
20. I studied the rolling mill with Istvan Kalasz. See a detailed description in Révész (1984), vol. 23, pp. 89–113.
21. See Makó (1985) on 'quasi-Taylorism'.
22. See a documented case for Hungary in Fazekas and Köllö (1989), pp. 385, 482.
23. The notion is from Lowitt (1979).
24. *A munkaeropiac keresleti es kinalati jellemzoi a munkaerokozvetites informacioi alapjan*, State Office of Employment and Wages, Budapest, 1987.
25. See a comparison of shop-floor bargaining along these criteria in Köllö (1981).
26. *Economically active population 1950–2020*, ILO, Geneva, 1986.
27. See Teague (1986), p. 244 or Moskoff (1984), p. 75 on Soviet experience, a report on women workers' strike in Kisvarda, Hungary because of compulsory and partly unpaid overtime in *Beszelo*, no. 2, 1981, pp. 49–51. It should also be remembered that work time was a central issue of debates between Solidarity and the state in spring 1981 (see Fratellini, 1988, pp. 173–5). A bus-drivers' strike in Prague–Dejvice, 1968, because of overtime has been mentioned by Kusin (1972), p. 15.
28. See Katunarič (1982) on Yugoslavia; Sampson (1986) on Roumania; Sík (1988) on Hungary.
29. 'Grey and exhausted as we are' was the refrain of a popular poem known as the 22th Claim of the Gdansk strikers in August 1980.
30. Interview with Sándor Rácz, president of the Great-Budapest Worker's Council in 1956, *Beszelo*, no. 7, 1983, pp. 343–58. About more radical but marginal views during the Prague Spring see Harman (1974), p. 236.

314 *Capital, the state and labour*

31. A two-thirds majority was needed to decide about bonuses, premia, managers' nomination and removal or mergers, but directly elected members formed a simple majority. See Kusin (1972), pp. 29–30.
32. *Tygodnik Solidarnosc*, 17 April 1981. Staniszkis (1982a), p. 13, mentioned a network of radical workers' councils of approximately 50 firms.
33. The acceptance of branch-level negotiations was a matter of sharp debate within the ranks of Solidarity (Acherson, 1982, p. 175) but finally, according to Fratellini (1988, pp. 188–95), the typical negotiating body was one or other national committee of coordination of an industry on the part of the union, and one or other branch ministry. This indicated a great and pragmatic transformation of the original, strictly territorial, structure. J. Staniszkis followed a similar pattern when she proposed organization of self-managing bodies along product lines, that would also mean that the union structure was approaching the logic of a shortage economy.
34. The only exception was Poland in 1958, when the workers' councils were transformed into corporative bodies in a peaceful way. See Lane and Kolankiewicz (1973), pp. 118–20.
35. It should be added that the following reflects my understanding (and knowledge) of the problem in mid-1989. The fate of EE can be crucially influenced by unpredictable political developments. I shall, therefore, try to concentrate on the main evolutionary trends instead of commenting on political change or making some kind of prophecy.
36. WIWW Report for 'Die Erste Österreichische Spar-Casse Bank', Vienna, 1987.
37. *Overall economic perspective for the year 2000*, UNO ECE, New York, 1988, pp. 70–72.
38. Ibid., p. 121.
39. As above, note 35.
40. Life expectancy at one year of age decreased by one month (in East Germany) up to 14 months (Poland) in 1970–80, a period when the countries of WE experienced 12–23 months' increase of the same indicator. See Sauvy (1984), p. 232.
41. Such vertically integrated systems are, e.g. AutoVAZ for the FIAT–Lada cooperation or KamAZ for the special treatment of truck production with modern Western technologies. The history of three Soviet automobile factories is analysed by Hardt and Holliday (1977), pp. 192–212.
42. Nagy and Simonyi (1983), p. 105. In the same volume see Bogdán (1983) and Szurkos (1983) about the introduction of such techniques in Hungary.
43. See a still valid analysis by Burks (1970).
44. Op. cit., note 37, pp. 144–6.
45. In Poland the president of the State Commission of Planning announced the closing of 200–300 unprofitable firms within nine months on 28 March 1982 and forecasted 700–800,000 unemployed workers (*Lengyel dokumentumok*, Beszelo, 8 July 1982, p. 36). In Czechoslovakia the state plan of 1980 included a list of factories to be closed (Csaba, 1982). In Hungary plans to regroup hundreds of thousands of workers were elaborated (*Ez azonban nem munkanelkuliseg*, Beszelo 1988). None of these plans became a reality.
46. On the allocation of high-school graduates see *Hungarian Press of Transylvania*, 15 June 1983.
47. It might be interesting to note that the initiators of the remarkable Brasov demonstration in winter 1987 were tractor factory workers just leaving an irregular night shift.
48. *Neue Zürcher Zeitung*, 20 November 1985.
49. *Hungarian Press of Transylvania*, September 1984.
50. *Neue Zürcher Zeitung*, 29 November 1985.
51. *Pravda*, 28 October 1988.
52. 'Ministries as well as the authorities of the USSR and the governments of federal republics should more actively perform the role of organizers of co-ordination between suppliers and buyers' [instead of the Gosplan and Gosamt] (ibid.).
53. See the Ministry of the Finance's report on the 1989 budget in *Pravda*, 28 October 1988.
54. On their early history see Teague (1986).
55. 'Goskomstat SSSR soobshaiet o razvitii progressivnih form organizaczii truda', *Sozialisticheskii Trud*, no. 10, 1988, p.61.
56. See Sillaste and Rääkk (1988), pp. 18–21; Popov (1988), pp. 11–12 and *Moskovskie Novosti*, December 1988, p. 8, respectively.

57. An article that raised the problem of 'efficient employment' as against general job stability, for the first time, provoked sharp debate in the journal *Kommunist*, despite its very circumspect formulation. See Kostakov (1987) and responses in the following issues.
58. The non-agricultural private sector's share in the GDP was 6.4 per cent in Poland and 12 per cent in Hungary (including societies, cooperatives and firms founded by private persons that are classified as part of the 'socialist sector' in Hungary) in 1986. The shares in employment were 5.8 and 8.6 per cent respectively. See *Rocznik Statistyczny*, Warsaw, 1987, p. 406; Kovács (1988).
59. The case was reported by the MTV-1 News, Budapest, 5 February 1989.

REFERENCES

Acherson, N. (1982) *The Polish August*, New York.

Adam, J. (ed.) (1982) *Employment Policies in the Soviet Union and Eastern Europe*, Macmillan.

Aitov, N. (1985) 'Социално – экономическая эфек тивносгь гехнического прогресса', *Социалистический Труг*, vol. 10.

Barber, J. (1986) 'The development of employment and labour policy 1930–41' in Lane (ed.).

Bauer, T. (1987) 'Ciklusok helyett válság?', *Közgazdasági Szemle*, vol. 34, no. 12, pp. 1409–34.

Berliner, J. (1957) *Factory and manager in the USSR*, Cambridge, Mass.

Bičanič, I (1985) *The Influence of the Unofficial Economy on Income Inequality in Yugoslavia*, University of Zagreb, mimeo.

Boda, B. and B. Falussy (1984) 'Az egységnyi szabadidöre jutó összmunkaidö és a gazdasági fejlödés', *Statisztikai Szemle*, vol. 4.

Bogdán, J. (1983) 'Teljesitménynövelés és a munkaszervezeti viszonyok' in Simonyi (ed.)

Bogdán, J. and A. Páll (1987) *A technikai fejlödés és az ipari munka a kelet-európai szocialista országokban*, Budapest, mimeo.

Brezinski, H. (1987) 'The second economy in the GDR – Pragmatism is gaining ground', *Studies in Comparative Communism*, vol. 20, no. 1, Spring, pp. 85–101.

Burks, R.V. (1970) 'Technology and political change in EE', in C. Johnson (ed.) *Change in Communist Systems*, Stanford.

Csaba, L. (1982) 'A csehszlovák gazdaságirányitás új vonásai', *Bankszemle*, vol. 1.

Dascalescu, C. (1984) 'Fordulat a törvényes úton', *Béke és szocializmus*, vol. 10.

Dubois, P. (1976) *Le sabotage dans l'industrie*, Paris.

Ellmann, M.J. (1979) *Full employment – Lessons from state socialism*, Leiden-Antwerpen: H.E. Stenfert-Kroese B.V.

Fallenbuchl, Z. (1982) 'Employment policies in Poland', in Adam (ed.), pp. 26–48.

Farkas, J., I. Harcsa and A. Vajda (1988) 'Csehszlovákia és Magyarország társadalmi jelzöszámainak összehasonlitása', *Statisztikai Szemle*, vol. 12, pp. 1108–21.

Farkas, J., I. Harcsa and A. Vajda (1985) 'Fluctuations of labour shortage and state intervention in the seventies' in P. Galasi and G. Sziráczky (eds) *Labour Market and Second Economy in Hungary*, Frankfurt–New York.

Fazekas, K. and Köllö, J. (1989) *Munkaeröpiac tökepiac nélkül*, PhD thesis, Budapest.

Feldbrugge, F.J.M. (1983) 'Government and shadow economy in the Soviet Union, paper presented at the Bielefeld Conference: 'The Economics of the shadow economy', 10–14 Oct.

Fink, G. *et al* (1989) *Die Wirtschaft der RGE-Länder und Jugoslawien 1988–9*, WIWW Reprint-Serie 119, Vienna.

Fratellini, N. (1988) *La syndicat Solidarité*, Paris, mimeo,

Frey, M. (1988) *Kötöttöl a rugalmas munkaidörendszerek felé*, PhD. thesis, Budapest.

Galasi, P. and R.I. Gábor (1983) *A második gasdaság*, Budapest.

Granick, D. (1987) *Job Rights in the Soviet Union: Their Consequences*, New York, Cambridge Univ. Press, 1987.

Gregory, P. and I.L. Collier (1988) 'Unemployment in the Soviet Union: evidence from the Soviet interview survey', *American Economic Review*, Sept., pp. 613–632.

Grossman, G. (1977) 'The second economy in the Soviet Union', *Problems of Communism*, vol. 26, no. 5, pp. 25–40.

Gyekiczky T. (1988) *A fegyelem csapdájában*, Budapest: MTA Szociológiai Intézete.

Haraszti M. (1978) *A Worker in a Workers State*, New York.

Hardt, J.P. and G.D. Holliday (1977) 'Technology transfer and change in the Soviet economic system', in F.J. Fleron (ed.) *Technology and Communist Culture*, Praeger, pp. 183–221.

Harman, C. (1974) *Bureaucracy and Revolution* in EE, Pluto.

Johanesson, J. (1985) *Labour market policy in Sweden*, thesis, Canberra.

Kalász, I. and J. Köllö (1984) 'Work, power and wages at a plastic rolling mill' in Révész (ed.).

Katunarič, V. (1982) Ethnic society – the social framework of the hidden economy, Frascati Conference: 'The Hidden economy, social conflicts and the future of industrial societies', 25–28 Nov.

Kemény, I. (1967) 'A gazdasági növekedés és a munkaerö szerepe', *Közgazdasági Szemle*, vol. 5.

Kemény, I. (1978) 'La chaine dans une usine Hongroise', *Actes de la Recherche en Science Social*, November.

Köllö, J. (1981) 'Teljesitménytaktikásás az ipari üzemben', *Közgazdasági Szemle*, nos. 7–8.

Köllö, J. (1984) 'Labour shortage, manpower allocation and wage payment in a cotton weaving mill' in Révész (ed.).

Kornai, J. (1980) *A hiány*, Budapest.

Kostakov, V. (1987) 'Полная занятость. Коммунист ' *Kommunist*, vol. 14.

Kostin, L. (1968) 'Ноьый эман развишии коонераишьоб и ингубугуално – шругобой геяшелносши', *Социалистический Труд*, vol. 7, pp. 3–12.

Kovács, G.J. (1988) *A kisszervezetek munkahelyteremtése 1987-ben*, Budapest: ABMH-MÜKI.

Kusin, V.V. (1972) *Political grouping in the Czechoslovak Reform Movement*, Macmillan.

Ladó, M. and F. Tóth (1985) 'A hivatalos szabályok árnyékában', *Mozgo Vilag*, vol. 11, pp. 4–9.

Laky, T. (ed.) (1987) *Az új típusú kisszervezetek 1986-ban*, Budapest: ABMH-MÜKI.

Lampert, N. (1986) 'Job security and law in the USSR', in Lane (ed.).

Lane, D. (ed.) (1986) *Labour and employment in the USSR*, Wheatsheaf/Harvester.

Lane, D. and G. Kolankiewicz (eds) (1973) *Social Groups in Polish Society*, Macmillan.

Lowit, T. (1979) 'Le Parti polimorphe en Europe de l'Est', *Revue francaise de science politique*, vols 4–5, pp. 812–46.

Makela, V. (1986) *The regional differences in the excess demand for labour and its effect on the aggregate inflation rate*, University of Tampere Dept. of Economics, Series E.

Makó, C (1983) *A társadalmi viszonyok erötere: a munkafolyamat*, Budapest: KJK.

Manievitch, E. (1985) *Labour in the USSR*, Moscow: Progress.

Marglin, S. (1988) *Losing Touch: The Cultural Conditions of Worker Accommodation and Resistance.*

Mills, C.W. (1959) *The Sociological Imagination*, Oxford University Press.

Mishchenko, V.T. (1982) 'Курс за лушее исползование', *Eko*, vol. 3 pp. 106–16.

Moskoff, W. (1984) *Labour and Leisure in the Soviet Union*, Macmillan.

Nagy, K. and A. Simonyi (1983) 'A szervezés határai, az ösztönzés korlátai, in Simonyi (ed.).

Ofer, G. and J. Vinokur (1980) 'Private sources of income of the Soviet Urban Household', *Studies in Comparative Communism*, vol. 13, pp. 283–309.

O'Hearn, D. (1980) 'The second economy. Size and effects', *Soviet Studies*, vol. 32, pp. 218–24.

O'Hearn, D. (1981) 'The second economy in consumer goods and services', *Critique*, vol. 15, pp. 93–110.

Olivera, J.H.G. (1960) 'Cyclical growth under collectivism', *Kyklos*, vol. 2.

Petschnig, M.Z. (1987) 'Adalékok a második és harmadik gazdaság terjedelmének felméréséhez', manuscript, Budapest.

Pietsch, A.J. and H. Vogel (1982) 'Displacement by technological progress in the USSR', in Adam (ed.)

Popov, G. (1988) 'Kmo npomub?' *Ogoniok*, vol. 18, pp. 4–6.

Prpič, K. 'The scope and structure of the employment of the population: Results of research of a sample of households in Yugoslavia', manuscript, University of Zagreb.

Redor, D. (1988) 'Les inegalités de salaires a l'est et a l'ouest', *Economica*, Paris.

Révész, G. (ed.) (1984) *Wage Bargaining in Hungarian Firms*, Budapest: Studies.

Révész, G. (1986) 'On the expansion and functioning of the direct market sector of the Hungarian economy', *Acta Oeconomica*, vol. 36, no. 1–2, pp. 105–21.

Sampson, S. (1986) 'Society without the state in Romania', paper presented at Conference on After the Fall, Universitz of Nebraska, 25–28 Oct.

Sauvy, A. (1984) *Le travail noir et l'economie de demain*, Paris: Calmann-Lévy.

Schroeder, G. (1982) 'Managing labour shortages in the USSR', in Adam (ed.), pp. 3–25.

Schwarz S. (1954) *Labour in the Soviet Union*, London.

Scott, J. (1985) *Weapons of the Weak*, New Haven: Yale University Press.

Sík, E. (1988) *Az örök kaláka*, Budapest: Gondolat.

Sillaste, J. and Rääkk, V. (1988) '*Опыт и продлеты развитии кооператиbob b народном хозяйстве*, Tallin.

Simonyi, A. (ed.) (1983) *A teljesitménynövelés feltételei a munkaszervezetben*, Budapest: ABMH-MÜKI.

Skurkhok S. and A., Meshchorkin (1987) 'Széleskörü gazdasági kisérlet a résztvevök szemével', *Közgazdasági Szemle*, vol. 11, pp. 1381–95.

Staniszkis, J. (1982a) 'Lengyelország útban a katonai államcsiny felé', *Önkorlátozó forradalom,* Budapest: AB.

Staniszkis, J. (1982b) *A Szolidaritás veszélyeztetettsége*, Budapest: AB.

Sziráczki, G. (1984) 'Stratification of drivers and their earnings in a transport company', in Révész (ed.)

Szurkos, M. (1983) 'A munkaszervesési módszer bevezetése és átalakulása', in Simonyi (ed.), pp. 43–64.

Teague, E. (1986) 'The USSR law on the Work Collectives', in Lane (ed.), pp. 239–55.

Tímár, J. (1988) Idö és munkaidö, Budapest: KJK.

Vassiliev, V. (1983) 'Politique des revenues et dinamique de l'economie paralelle en Bulgarie', *Le Courier des Pays de l'Est*, vol. 279, Dec., pp. 23–36.

Wiles, P. (1982) 'A note on Soviet Unemployment by US definitions', *Soviet Studies*, April, vol. 23, pp. 619–28.
Wisniewski, M. (1986) 'The sources of the second economy in Poland', *Acta Polonii*, vol. 2, pp. 247–76.

9. Reform and system change in China[1]

Carl Riskin

I INTRODUCTION

China in the 1960s and early 1970s under Mao was engaged in trying to eliminate remaining distinctions of class and status, including those within enterprises. By the late 1980s, not only had such distinctions become legitimate again, but 'many of the woes of 19th century laissez-faire capitalism and of feudal China, have re-emerged ... child labour, prostitution, gambling, income inequalities, criminal gangs and unregulated production of goods that are useless or even dangerous.'[2] Moreover, such phenomena as child labour and excessively long work weeks were not limited to plants organized and run by Taiwanese or Hong Kong capital; they could also be found in state-run establishments, especially those under local jurisdiction. Between these two periods, then, there had clearly been a change in relations between labour, capital and the state.

An agrarian, largely pre-industrial, pre-capitalist country when the Chinese Communist Party (CCP) took power in 1949, China was not an obvious candidate for any of the particular social and production systems that marked industrialization in other parts of the world. The revolutionary leaders had spent decades in the countryside and knew next to nothing about modern industry. They needed help, and sought it first from their own small business class and its international contacts.

After a historical detour of over three decades they have returned to a similar posture. What has changed during this time is clear:

1. The Soviet central planning system was tried and found alien to Chinese conditions and needs.
2. A Maoist radical alternative to this system was tried and, besides proving incomplete conceptually, gave rise to unacceptable levels of social conflict.
3. These twin failures created a new and critical attitude, especially among the educated, toward Marxism and socialism, particularly as late modernizing ideologies.[3]

4. The Soviet command economy proved subject to decelerating growth and unable to cope with the new technologies of the 1970s and 1980s, and was abandoned in principle in its own home base.
5. Rapid economic growth by East Asian capitalist countries with cultural backgrounds similar to China's held out a promise of a more successful route to 'modernization'.
6. The international climate changed and became amenable to China's reintegration into the world market, and the travel of tens of thousands of educated young Chinese to developed capitalist countries strengthened the perception of a still wide gap that required fundamental change to bridge.
7. Finally, China's own considerable accomplishments over 40 years of development in industry, science and social welfare created conditions that favoured change: a substantial industrial base, a large, educated workforce and an extremely egalitarian income distribution.

This chapter tries to sort out the significance of this historical detour to the present economic system in China, and to identify where it seems to be headed at present. The chapter is divided into two main sections, the first dealing with the evolution and character of the economic system of Mao Zedong's last two decades, the second discussing the effect of economic reform in the past decade.

The issue of capital–labour–state relations needs to be faced at once. In particular, what represents 'capital' in the Chinese context? In the 1980s in 'special economic zones', such as Shenzhen in Guangdong Province, or Xiamen in Fujian, where private production, much of it foreign-financed, began accounting for a major share of total output, 'capital' seemed to be taking a form familiar in the capitalist world. But even here the embracing presence of the state cannot (yet) be ignored. Elsewhere the answer is anything but obvious; indeed, China's formal verbiage – public ownership being called 'whole people ownership' – obfuscates the continued class or stratum differentiation. Private ownership all but disappeared by the mid-1950s, leaving a mix of various kinds of state and collective ownership. During much of the post-1949 years collective ownership (outside agriculture) entailed little if any true independence from the local government. Larger collective enterprises were treated virtually as state-owned, while smaller ones enjoyed somewhat more autonomy.

State enterprises also were operated by different levels of the government, from the centre to the county, which often had different and opposing interests. Local governments wanted rapid expansion, especially of enterprises in industries with high profit margins, even if these duplicated more efficient enterprises elsewhere. Local industrialization created jobs, revenues and prestige. Both Maoist policies and those of the reform years after 1978 – policies totally different in other respects – encouraged administrative decentralization, i.e., a shift in control of resources and investment from the centre to the regions and localities. In both cases the results were an 'overheated' economy, excessive rates of capital accumulation, widespread waste from duplication and local protectionism.

In contrast, during periods of greater centralization of state control, such as the First Five Year Plan period (1953–57) and the early 1960s, the emphasis was on technocratic management of the economy through national ministries or vertically integrated industrial companies.

This suggests that as the proportions in which the central, regional and local state apparatuses played the role of 'capital' shifted over time, the main objectives and interests of 'capital' also shifted. With the exception of the highest élite there was (by international standards) little class differentiation in consumption levels in Maoist China. During the great demonstrations for democracy in the spring of 1989 workers carried huge portraits of Mao and Zhou Enlai, whom they looked back to as past epitomes of the ethic of plain living that had disappeared from the contemporary scene. Managers and party heads of enterprises often earned no more than skilled workers.

It is tempting to say that the main objective of 'capital' was maximization of industrial growth, and thus of surplus for reinvestment. After all, a bureaucracy, which is what the holders of positions in the state apparatus surely were, benefits by expansion of the resources under its control. Moreover, China's leaders were patriots who wanted to ensure their country's military security, a goal which also required rapid industrialization. Many aspects of the record are consistent with the objective of maximizing industrial growth: the almost indecent emphasis on producer goods industries, the extraordinarily high rates of investment, the virtual stagnation of wages for two decades after the mid-1950s, the neglect of state investment in agriculture, etc.

But such a view overlooks other aspects of China's political economy: the payment of a social wage to full-status state sector workers that was well above the marginal product of labour in China's surplus labour economy; the provision of resources to sanitation, health care and education that gave China an enviable record in reducing mortality rates and increasing basic literacy; the periodic campaigns led by Mao which, with the exception of the Great Leap Forward, cannot be interpreted as efforts to speed up growth. Indeed, to the extent that elements of the party fought against the consolidation of power by the bureaucracy and tried to establish means of popular supervision over it, the bureaucracy's interest in maximum industrial growth was tempered. Moreover, sections of the party–state apparatus, as in other centrally planned countries, have resisted restructuring policies designed to promote growth but detrimental to the bureaucracy's own role in the economy. In the end, 'capital', with respect to both its identity and its interests, remains somewhat ambiguous and ill-defined in the Chinese context.

II   MAOISM AND THE CENTRAL PLANNING REGIME

Early CCP Policy

There was a distinct pro-capitalist development component to early People's Republic of China (PRC) policy. Mao sought to develop relations with the US as early as 1945; early PRC strategy of the 'New Democracy' was aimed at protecting and fostering 'national capitalism', i.e., private firms free of ties to foreign corporations and to the former Guomindang government. The same was true of the land reform, which preserved substantial inequalities in land ownership and sought to protect the industrial assets of landlords and wealthier farmers. Early policy toward industrial labour was also mild; the party, with roots in the countryside, had only limited dependence on the urban working class and was able to exert discipline on it.

It is possible that the New Democracy would have disappeared in any case, but a good argument can be made that its replacement by a more radical strategy was substantially due to China's international isolation, especially after China entered the Korean War. It was during the war that the land reform and policy toward private enterprise turned harsh and punitive.

What followed was total nationalization and collectivization in the mid-1950s and the establishment of Soviet-type institutions of planning, management and control which in distorted form have lasted right up to the present day. The degree of state ownership and control was extreme; through the mechanisms of collectivization and formation of 'joint state–private enterprises', virtually all production and service enterprises in the towns and cities became *de facto* state-owned. Handicraft production was wounded badly. Private enterprise was not tolerated even in the myriad small services and retail trade establishments. All initiative was left with the state budget (and its local components, China's being a consolidated system in which each unit's budget is included in that of the unit above), which, inevitably, short-changed low-priority sectors such as trade and services.

In agriculture, similarly, total collectivization had been carried out by 1956. Here the chief impetus came from the inadequate growth of farm production in the early part of the First Five Year Plan (1953–57) and the consequent threat to the rapid industrialization programme. In addition, however, Mao (who overrode internal party dissent and pushed through the collectivization despite previous promises of gradualism and voluntarism) was motivated by the apparent contradictions in the gradual cooperativization process, under which better-off farmers were loath to invest in land they knew would ultimately be taken from them; and by pressure from land-poor farmers who favoured the redistribution of income that rent abolition entailed.

Despite their longevity, however, the Soviet-type institutions and approach to economic planning and organization put in place in the mid-1950s have never gone unquestioned either in Chinese Communist ideology or in practice. They were challenged almost immediately after their installation by a faction of the leadership, led by Mao, which objected to the overcentralized, hierarchical socioeconomic system required for these institutions to work. The challenge was maintained at varying levels of intensity until Mao's death in 1976 and resulted in a crippled, distorted and sometimes inoperative system of central planning with its own peculiar production relations. After his death, equally strong objections came from another direction, that of a liberal, pro-market contingent of reformers, who had a similar critique of the central command economy but a different solution.[4]

Early Conflicts

The approach to factory organization adopted after Liberation in 1949 was known as the 'East China' system: it featured collective management by a committee under the leadership of the factory director and it sought to bring rank and file workers into the management process. Under the influence of guerrilla practice during the Civil War, payment to cadres was egalitarian, largely in kind and based on need. Economic and social distinctions within the work unit were minimal.[5]

At the same time, however, the Soviet Union was helping China construct several hundred large-scale industrial and mining projects under aid agreements reached in the early post-Liberation days. With these projects came Soviet organizational and management methods to run them. At the plant level this meant hierarchical organization with clearly defined responsibilities and unambiguous authority relations leading up to the supremacy of the enterprise director. Under the influence of the Soviet example, China tried to put into effect a system based on 'scientific management,' articulated material incentives and centralized leadership. Piece rates were favoured wherever feasible. This effort reached its apogee in 1956 with the implementation of a wage reform that considerably increased the wage spread in comparison with the pre-reform practice.

The 'one man management system' and its accoutrements were pretty much confined to the large, heavy industrial establishments (most of them in the Northeast) set up by the Soviets. They did not penetrate the great majority of small and medium-scale enterprises. Nor did piece rates, which at their peak in 1956 covered 42 per cent of industrial workers, spread to anything like the extent they had in the USSR (74 per cent).[6] This was due in part to criticism from workers and others (including Mao) who felt that the high degree of centralization and the rigidity of work organization entailed did not fit Chinese conditions and violated Marxian principles; workers also complained about the effects of piece wages on group morale, as well as on accident rates (Howe, 1973, pp. 120, 131–2). The situation that existed in the mid-1950s, before the Great Leap Forward changed everything, was ambiguous with respect to capital–labour relations. By 1956 the great majority of the population that remained in agriculture had been organized into collectives and no longer privately owned the land they farmed. The ultimate authorities in the collectives were state-appointed cadres. Payment was based on accumulated earnings of work points, which were often, like piece rates, based on elaborate lists of task values; or sometimes based on evaluation of the individual's strength, skill and attitude, and then automatically awarded for a day's work. The first system suffered from inordinate complexity and the impossibility of rationally fixing task rates in agriculture (where the importance of particular tasks varies by season and weather). The second system, on the other hand, failed to provide much work incentive to individual farmers. Both systems shared out risk among all members, since the value of the work point, however earned, depended on the size of the harvest. The tendency over time was for payments to become rather equal as a means of avoiding disputes, but this also had a disincentive effect. Low-level cadres were paid by work point like everyone else, while collective-level leaders drew a state wage. Farmers had to agree to the amount of collective revenue that could be assigned to paying local cadres.

In the towns and cities, state sector workers, still a small minority of the labour force, were undoubtedly a favoured class, enjoying higher than average incomes, permanent job security, retirement pensions and other welfare benefits that were very generous for a low-income country. Ideologically they were a favoured group, as well, and were told they were the 'true masters' of their enterprises. On the other hand, their union organizations were not independent but controlled by the party, which depended on them to be a 'transmission belt' between party and workers – explaining and implementing party policy in the enterprise while reflecting worker sentiment back to the party. Their dilemma was how to serve their worker constituency (in the main by organizing and supervising welfare benefits and activities, but also by handling grievances) well enough to avoid entirely losing legitimacy because of their basic fealty to the party–state. There were also workers' representative congresses, nominally to give workers power of supervision over management, but in fact these were coopted by the enterprise bureaucracy and degenerated into *pro forma* exercises in ratifying management plans. Workers were essentially disenfranchised in return for economic benefits and security.

Management and supervisory personnel were not rewarded disproportionately to workers. Their authority was limited by workers' job security and by their own subservience to the enterprise party committee (of which, of course, they might be members). Together with the unions, they had power to allocate valued goods and services to workers (housing, leave for visits home, etc.) but also depended on workers for their ability to establish a successful record of their own. Facing the state, they had a common interest in obtaining low targets and high investment, and exercised what Köllö in his contribution to this volume (Chapter 8) calls 'everyday power'. The links that grew up among workers and management therefore resembled patron–client relations.[7]

Thus China was led by an ascetic modernizing group which contained within it (we were to discover only later) what we might think of as centralist, populist and Bukharinist elements. The centralists wanted to maintain and perfect the system inherited from the Russians; the populists, periodically led by Mao, wanted to decentralize planning and management authority and rule through ideological conformity rather than centralized command mechanisms; the Bukharinists wanted to relax the pace of industrialization and allow greater latitude for market forces and private ownership.[8] In terms of outcomes, the record of the 1950s was one of rapid industrial growth, lagging agricultural growth, generally rising incomes in both cities and countryside (with some exceptions), and increased equality of income distribution.

Despite the successful industrial growth of this 'Stalinist' period, there were problems not so far under the surface that called into question the continuation of that strategy. Agriculture was growing too slowly to sustain continued rapid industrialization, very few new jobs were being created for China's surplus masses by the capital-intensive heavy industries being established, and authority over resources was increasingly concentrated in a narrow group of planners and technocrats at the centre – a group which lacked the information (and the means for obtaining it) required to make rational plans and decisions. Mao, whose writings of the mid- to late 1950s increasingly reflected these problems, acted to thrust aside the strategy of the First Plan.

Maoism as Rejection of Central Planning[9]

Current consideration of Mao's impact on Chinese society from the mid- to late 1950s until his death understandably tends to concentrate upon the political and economic results, especially the negative ones. Political results include the violent factionalism and persecutions of the Cultural Revolution period, and the mindless dogmatism and sloganeering that characterized its political atmosphere. Negative economic results include first and foremost the famine that ended the Great Leap Forward and that is now believed to have been largely due to the policies of that movement; and the stagnation of food consumption and real wages for two decades and the failure to improve the living standards of between 100 and 200 million people living below the official poverty line.

Less attention is given to understanding the reasons for the intervention of Mao and his colleagues. This question is answered by the assumption that Mao was an aging megalomaniac with utopian goals and the power and prestige to implement them. But, despite Mao's undoubted prestige and authority, his policies appealed to many Chinese and triggered the response they did because they spoke to some real conditions and problems: the urban bias, overcentralization, and authoritarianism of the First Plan period, its reduction of most people to a relatively passive role of carrying out orders from above, and its creation of a fledgling ruling stratum of urban bureaucrats who threatened to monopolize the few channels of upward mobility.

The Maoist programme in China was thus, in general, a response to – and a rejection of – the Soviet-type capital–labour relations in process of being consolidated in the 1950s. Central administrative planning, which tended to require a narrow control over capital and its allocation by the top leadership, a stratified chain of command from this leadership to the enterprise, and a rigid division of labour within the enterprise, struck the Maoists as ineffective in China's conditions as well as offensive to Marxist values.

Maoist policies delegitimized and then dispersed to 'May 7 cadre schools' and common labour the experts at information gathering, processing and dissemination, without whom central planning could not function. Statistics at times actually ceased to be collected. For a brief period at the height of the Cultural Revolution, workers' committees of one faction or another took over control of the enterprises, until the violence and chaos brought the People's Liberation Army (PLA) in, eventually to restore management to its position. 'Three-in-one' management and technical innovation teams consisting of workers, technicians and cadres were thought of as a means of overcoming the class stratification of the First Plan approach and thrusting workers into positions of technical and administrative leadership. An attack on all individual material incentives, and especially on the use of bonuses and piece rates in industry, and the *de facto* levelling of wages and salaries that occurred as a result of failure to give (pay) rises for an extended period of time, embodied not only an ethic of egalitarianism, *per se*, but also a rejection of the advantages of the nascent élite favoured by the earlier strategy.

Not only the institutions of capital – enterprise management, central planning bodies, statistical bureaus, party committees – were attacked, but also those representing workers. The labour unions disappeared, having been attacked as tools of the authorities. The factory was promoted as a social institution, not merely a place of production. It was a 'university', in Mao's term, where workers studied politics and learned thereby how to push the relations of production in a socialist direction. Factories were to link up with scientific institutions to promote technological change, seek to learn the needs of their customers and earnestly strive to meet them. This conception of the enterprise clearly rendered Taylorism and 'scientific management' a dead letter. The ideal worker was a generalist, interested in and good at many things, ready to volunteer to go where needed.

Even the principle of 'payment according to work' was difficult to implement when 'work' was so broadly defined.

The Maoist revolution in the relations of production was primarily a micro-economic revolution. It concerned production relations in the workplace, the unit of production. The macroeconomic component of Maoism was a rebellion rather than a revolution: it overthrew without having a genuine replacement in mind. In Mao's hierarchy of evils, the bureaucratism of centralized command planning came second only to the market, because the market thoroughly and continuously trains its participants in bourgeois rather than socialist values. Mao thus gave no thought to encouraging the development of market institutions as a substitute for administrative planning, and was left virtually without any glue to hold the economy together.

Self-Reliance

Making a virtue of this lacuna, the Maoist vision extolled 'self-reliance', whose functional meaning in this context was: if there is no principled way for the parts to hang together, let them hang separately. The economy would resemble a beehive of individual cells, each relatively self-sufficient, rather than a highly articu-lated 'single chessboard', as the leadership had urged during the recovery from the Leap. Already present in the faltering, overcentralized regime of the 1950s and early, post-Leap 1960s, was the strong tendency of administrative units, whether vertical (sectoral, ministerial) or horizontal (territorial), to lock up within their own gates production capacity for inputs needed to meet their targets. By such localist integration they insulated themselves against the capricious, undependable material supply system and also promoted their own material interests.

With the crippling of the central planning system, first during the Great Leap and then in the Cultural Revolution years, the ability of the centre to direct and control economic activity throughout China melted away. Except for the 'third-line' industries – controlled directly by the centre – which were established in the interior of the country against the threat of war (Naughton, 1988), production everywhere tended to lapse by default into the hands of the locality or admin-istrative bureau under whose jurisdiction it fell. These units of necessity became more 'self-reliant' than ever, dealing as much as possible only with their own network.[10] Even individual enterprises sought protection by establishing general-purpose machine shops to repair and produce needed parts. The point was to minimize the need for distant (and non-existent) coordinative bureaucracies.

The most dynamic part of the Maoist economy, i.e., that of the Great Leap and of much of the 'Cultural Revolution decade' (1966–76), was local industry. Run by the counties and communes, this industry began – first in 1958, then in 1969–72 – the chapter now being written by the local authorities of Jiangsu,

Zhejiang and Guangdong provinces, whose economies have run away from the rest of China during the 1980s (see below).

In the Maoist economy, in principle, 'capital' was represented by the local party–state bureaucracy. Technology was generally and necessarily conventional, albeit with labour-intensive adaptations in ancillary processes. Wages were low, but significantly above local farm incomes; working conditions were sometimes primitive; management and administrative salaries were also low and there was little or no obvious material sign of class stratification. Surplus obtained from profitable light industries was expected to be ploughed back into further development of less (or un-)profitable heavy industries, especially those producing farm inputs such as chemical fertilizer, and into social consumption such as schools and clinics. Such a local economy was known as a 'comprehensive local industrial system' (Riskin, 1978a, b). The centre's role was to provide the occasional piece of sophisticated equipment beyond the capacity of the locality to produce. In practice, higher authorities (e.g., at the municipality or province level, or even the centre) often intervened to supply necessary inputs (relatively few localities have their own coal, for instance) and thus lay claim to part of local output. The centre also guided the overall direction of local development through the use of ideology.[11]

Problems and Evaluation of Self-Reliance

In a beehive the individual cells are waxed together in a coherent pattern. In the Maoist economy, the adhesive wax was to be ideology. The extreme politicization that marked periods of high Maoism was, from this perspective, an attempt to give coherence to a potentially anarchic situation by ensuring that the quasi-independent local economies would march in step with the tune played at the top. The leaders tried to use ideology to govern the product mix (e.g., by condemning conspicuous consumption and luxury goods), the balance of industrial structure (e.g., by insisting that rural industry 'serve agriculture'), and the choice of techniques (e.g., by glorifying 'local methods' [*tufa*] and censuring the use of materials needed by centrally controlled industries). The use of simple slogans to convey desired resource allocation principles to semi-independent and self-reliant localities was a novel chapter in the history of decentralized planning and deserves more attention than it has received. Of course, slogans were not enough – there also had to be a threat of penalty to prevent the centre's wisdom from being ignored in favour of decisions governed by local self-interest. Hence, the moral–political content given to the slogans: to violate them was to adopt a bourgeois standpoint, to oppose the revolution and Chairman Mao's thought. Whatever the mix of causes that gave rise to the extraordinary factionalism of the Cultural Revolution period, the politicization of ordinary economic decision making, in order to make the writ of the centre run beyond its direct reach, inevitably bred such factionalism.

There were other obvious problems with the cellular solution. Localities inevitably used resources the centre wanted and needed and thus interfered with national priorities; primitive technologies wasted scarce resources; the confinement of planning to the local political jurisdiction sacrificed the advantages of specialization and exchange and led to widespread duplication of production on a small and inefficient scale; localities with better conditions for industrial development grew much faster than poorer localities, with the result that the regional inequalities sharpened over the Maoist period; and the quality of local planning and management skills varied widely but was generally low.

In agriculture, where the great majority of the labour force still worked, the degree of ideological and administrative control of the nominally collective rural communes turned them into virtual state farms. Everything from sowing plans to income distribution was subject to state dictation. The result was that, despite substantial investment and spread of new technology in agriculture, and despite an enormous increase in nominal labour inputs between the 1950s and 1970s, farm output only kept pace with population growth and farm incomes failed to grow. The potential increases in output and income unrealized because of irrational resource allocation and poor work incentives are suggested by the unprecedented spurt in farm output that followed the agricultural reforms of the late 1970s and early 1980s.

In addition, administrative control of the rural population was rigid. Rural people were not permitted to migrate to towns and cities, a policy that helped sustain and widen the urban–rural gap during the late Mao period. In return for this protection, urban workers had to sacrifice job mobility and accept a permanent state of 'war communism' in which they were assigned work, usually for life.

On the other hand, the era of collectivized agriculture saw some remarkable achievements in provision of basic needs to the rural population, chief among them longer expected life. During the collective period, mortality rates declined and life expectancy at birth reached into the mid-to-high sixties, a laudable achievement at such low income levels. The spread of basic health care, sanitation and education must get the credit, rather than any significant increase in income or in the quantity and quality of the diet. Thus, while the extraction of surplus by the state from the countryside, mostly in the form of price differentials between farm and industrial goods (the 'price scissors'), continued throughout the period, some surplus was left in the countryside where it was devoted almost entirely to social investment and collective consumption, with significant results.

Income distribution during the late Mao period was shaped in a peculiar profile, combining extraordinary equality along social dimensions with substantial inequality among regions and localities. The overall urban income distribution was remarkably even; not only was this true of money income, but class could also not be deduced from one's neighbourhood or housing. Distribution within work units was also very even, with a relatively small gap between high and low wage, and between administrative salaries and ordinary wages (Riskin, 1975). The same held true in the countryside, where the use of work points evolved as described above towards producing closely similar evaluations of each person's contribution. There was a remarkable degree of equality among occupations in the possession of housing and durable consumer goods: 'statistics on consumption among those just below the top elite suggest that administrative position does not add measurably to consumption level' (Parish, 1981). Only in a tendency for cadre children to get disproportionate access to favoured occupations was this picture of social equality tempered somewhat (ibid.).

Thus, along dimensions with potential political significance – between classes and occupations, within neighbourhood and village – relatively equal distribution obtained. Wider inequalities were found along dimensions farther from the social purview of most Chinese, especially among regions and localities, and between town and countryside generally.

The party–state in China, in resisting (under Mao's influence) the urban, bureaucratic pull of the central planning system, thus achieved a mixed record. On the one hand, it contributed to producing the worst famine on the historical record, a result that surely must weigh heavily in any evaluation. On the other, it then went on to produce a good record of provision of basic needs, especially mortality reduction, increase in life expectancy, and spread of literacy and primary education, and a considerable degree of social and economic equality. But the political and social costs of this achievement were high: periodic violent social conflict, and alienation of the bureaucracy and intelligentsia. Economic costs were high as well: great waste of resources in production not geared towards demand, and stagnant living standards in much of the country. Mao's strategy of brooking neither plan nor market was not a viable one in the long run.

III REFORM

Objectives vs Achievements

With the retreat of the US from Vietnam, the faltering of Soviet economic growth and the rise of a multipolar world, China's options changed and widened. Mao himself initiated the Chinese response with his invitations to Nixon and Kissinger. To an increasingly protectionist world the unexploited China market seemed an irresistible bait, while to some Chinese, informed about the rest of the world, the East Asian model, implemented by people of a similar cultural background, seemed a more promising path to 'modernization' than the Soviet road. To move towards a market-regulated export-oriented system from the Maoist political economy was to make a long leap indeed. Yet elements of the strategy of transition and some unanticipated interim results of it have masked the full nature of the intended change. Furthermore, the transition has not been based upon a pre-drawn blueprint; in this respect, ironically, the reformers are acting like China's central planners before, who, to a far greater extent than in the USSR, treated central planning as a process of 'groping for stones to cross the river'. Now, too, the reformers hope to learn by doing, devising new policies and approaches as they go along. Thus the idea of selling off state enterprises to shareholders is not a pre-planned idea carefully hidden until recently, but an evolving response to the perceived difficulty of 'marketizing' state-owned enterprises (see below).

The reformers' strategy was quite brilliant at first: decollectivization neutralized and won over much of the rural population and also bought a decade of booming agriculture to soften the impact of mistakes in urban reform. Longer-term goals, when they existed at all (and it is difficult to know this), have been kept well hidden to avoid provoking opposition. In the public sector, while the state planned to lower the social wage by hiring only temporary and contract workers in the future, the relatively privileged, full-status workers already employed were frozen in place, and their jobs were made inheritable by their offspring. In return, however, they were demoted in political and ideological terms to become the object of change, not its maker. This bargain, however, began to seem less attractive to full-status workers in state enterprises as rapid inflation eroded their real incomes while they watched entrepreneurs in the new private sector leap ahead of them in earnings.

Early changes also masked the long-term potential of the reform environment to produce greatly increased inequality of distribution. Before the reform period, as we have seen, the urban–rural gap in average per capita income widened despite Maoist egalitarian principles. The basis for this result was the ever widening gap in labour productivity between industry, on the one hand, and agriculture, on the other, where per worker output had stagnated due to the enormous increase in nominal labour intensity of cultivation during the Mao years. Industry's share of total product had continuously increased, though its share of the labour force had advanced only very slowly; agriculture's share of total product had declined rapidly, while it kept the bulk of the labour force.

Between 1978 and 1986, this process was reversed. Industry's share in total output now remained almost unchanged for eight years,[12] while agriculture's share also remained stable. On the other hand, the labour force, which had shifted so reluctantly before, now quickly and substantially reallocated itself: the share of primary production (agriculture) fell from 74 per cent to 61 per cent, that of secondary production (industry) rose by almost a half (from 15 to 22 per cent), and that of services rose even faster (from 11 to 17 per cent) (Riskin, 1988).

The structural basis of urban–rural inequality thus retreated, as the productivity gap, expressed in terms of GNP per worker, between industry and agriculture declined from 8.2 in 1978 to 4.4 in 1986.[13] Whatever conscious policy might have been doing to the urban–rural gap, differential growth in productivity was tending to diminish it.

Policy and ideology in fact now openly encouraged greater inequality and, in respects other than the urban–rural gap, produced it. Inequality increased most noticeably at the edges of the income distribution, in the fortunes being made in the small but growing private sector and the failures experienced by individual farmers ill equipped to exploit the new market conditions and now without a social safety network to fall back on. Approximately 1.2 million private-sector people were said to be getting yearly incomes of over 10,000 yuan (or US $2702 at the official exchange rate; the average per capita income for urban China in 1987 was only 1119 yuan [US $302]; for rural 545 yuan[US $147]). A small number of these (100,000–200,000 people) were getting hundreds of thousands or even millions (*Beijing Review*, 15–21 August 1988, p. 7).[14]

Although the state has sometimes victimized private business people by levying all sorts of extraordinary fees and taxes on them, a symbiotic relationship exists between these two components of capital. It is widely believed in China that personal connections with influential officials is the surest route to financial success. More systematically, a conscious state policy of 'betting on the strong' has quickly widened class gaps. In Yunnan province, for instance, wealthy and well connected families have been given credit originally earmarked as aid for the poor, and in a development that brings to mind the 'enclosures' of eighteenth century England, previously common grazing land, ponds and orchards have been fenced in and turned over to better-off farmers:

> What is occurring, in almost all aspects of the rural economy, is that some advantaged families, often with government assistance, are gaining near-permanent control over local assets ... in one fell swoop a new economic/social structure in the village had been erected upon unequal access to property. (Unger and Xiong, 1990)

Inequality between regions and localities has also increased markedly, as certain regions with favourable commercial conditions in places like Jiangsu, Zhejiang and Guangzhou have sprouted industry and trade 'like mushrooms after a spring rain' while less commercialized and poorer interior areas are left far behind. Taking ten provinces and municipalities of eastern China as one group and eleven provinces of the west as another, the absolute gap between the two groups in rural average per capita net income has increased by almost five times between 1981 and 1987: from 72 yuan to 332 yuan (Lu Yun, 1989).[15]

China publishes lists of counties with average per capita incomes over 500 yuan and of those whose average incomes are under 150 yuan (see Table 9.1).

From the 1982 national census we can obtain some of the other characteristics of these counties, such as their population densities, illiteracy rates, degrees of commercialization and industrialization rates.[16] As can be seen, the average income of the richer group is five times that of the poorer. Among the socio-economic characteristics listed, population density and illiteracy rates are red herrings of a sort. Historically, Chinese have migrated towards the richer regions of the south and east, so income explains density, not vice versa. There is a similar factor at work with respect to illiteracy. In the long run, education is certainly a prerequisite for economic growth, but in the short run many Chinese have pulled their children out of school to make money. I would focus on the rates of industrial and agricultural employment as the most significant factors listed. Not only do industrial workers, whether employed by state or private firms, earn more than farmers, but industrial employment here serves as a proxy for 'the extent of the market'. Where non-agricultural sectors have been able to develop, farming itself is more prosperous.

Table 9.1   Comparison of characteristics of counties with per capita incomes of less than 150 yuan and more than 500 yuan

	Income per capita	Pop. density pop./km^2	Illitcy rate	% Agricl employmt	% Indl employmt
Below 150 yuan group (563 counties)	126.7	146.6	48.5	90.9	3.1
Above 500 yuan group (81 counties)	645.0	407.6	28.2	68.9	18.6

Sources: For per capita income: *Zhongguo Nongye Nianjian* (1987), pp. 356–60. All other data: *Zhongguo Renkou Ditu Ji* (1987), pp. 162–213.

The changing income distribution has affected women in particular. The impact begins at birth with the resurgence of female infanticide and differential care for female infants. In the countryside it remains essential to have male offspring for a number of reasons, most essentially for security in one's old age (girls marry out of the village and become responsible for their husbands' parents). The dismantling of the collective health and welfare infrastructure and promotion of an ideology of individual enrichment have thrown the rural population back even more on its own resources and thus strengthened the incentives to have boys, while the periodically vigorous campaigns to limit births have created new incentives for gender differences in the treatment of infants. The 1987 1 per cent sample population census reported a sex ratio at birth of 110 males to 100 females for 1986 and 1987 births – far higher than the expected ratio of 106:100. The difference implies a total of half a million missing girls in 1986 (Hull, 1988). This in turn suggests either a very sharp rise in female infant mortality rates, or, to the extent that the missing girls are merely being hidden to circumvent family planning quotas, the denial to the unregistered girls of the education and other services to which they should be entitled.

This is but one of a number of ways in which women are at a disadvantage in the new distribution of real income. For example, women are being fired in substantial numbers by newly profit-conscious enterprises that do not want to be burdened by the maternity and child care subsidies which are still an enterprise responsibility.[17] Moreover, of China's estimated 7 million school drop-outs more than 80 per cent are girls, and most of the 220 million illiterate adults are women. Finally, in an empirical study carried out in the major industrial city of Tianjin, Walder (1989) found a growing wage gap between men and women in state enterprises. Indeed this was the only dimension for which he found inequality widening; contrary to expectations, it was narrowing in all other respects (party membership, education, seniority, etc.).

Reform Alternatives

Unlike in the USSR, central administrative planning had a possible future in China at the beginning of the reform years, because earlier it had not been given a chance to develop normally. One early response to the changed political environment after Mao's death and the purge of the 'Gang of Four' was to reinstate the institutions and personnel of central planning and gather up in the hands of the central government the reins of authority over production and investment allocation decisions. There are still those who favour such an approach and who, if the current reform efforts produce unacceptable chaos, might possibly still get their way.[18]

There are several reasons why that approach did not immediately gain ascendancy, however. First, the continuous two-decade-long attack on rigid centralization by Mao had seriously delegitimized the transplantation of the Soviet system in China. Second, the truncated and ineffective form in which central planning had always been resurrected after periods of chaotic decentralization had further weakened its reputation as well as the position of its proponents. Third, the economic difficulties being experienced in Eastern Europe and the Soviet Union, and their own critique of command planning, reinforced home-grown doubts. Fourth, the widespread distrust of the political leadership following the debacle of the 'Cultural Revolution decade' certainly tarnished a model of economic organization that would be dominated by central political leaders. Fifth, travel abroad by increasing numbers of Chinese, including many younger and better educated ones, brought contact with alternative models, especially those of other quickly growing Asian countries.

The alternative has not been a robust move towards 'market socialism', however, but rather an unstable combination of administrative decentralization and marketization. Markets have indeed grown up around the edges of the Chinese economy, progressively impinging on its core. Forty per cent of industrial output now comes from collective and private enterprises (*Zhongguo Tongji Nianjian*, 1988, p. 311) that operate outside the plan. But at the same time provinces and localities now control the bulk of China's investment, often ignoring central policies and acting to constrain and restrict markets (Naughton, 1986).

Private Enterprise

Highly visible and growing quickly, the private sector in early 1989 was still a relatively minor part of the economy as a whole.[19] There were about 600,000 'individually owned establishments' in urban and rural China and some 200,000 'private enterprises', which, in Chinese parlance, means an individually owned enterprise with more than eight employees. The private sector in city and countryside employed over 22 million people (*Beijing Review*, 27 February–5 March 1989). Private enterprises were spread widely throughout the economy, especially in trade and services, but also in industry. The most famous model of burgeoning private enterprise is that of Wenzhou prefecture in Zhejiang province, where private production accounted for 60 per cent of rural output. Private enterprises have come under criticism for creating wide income disparities (managers getting as much as 30 times the wages of their employees) and other 'contradictions between employer and employed, particularly in realizing the theory that workers should be the masters of their enterprises' (Feng and Wu, 1989, p. 18) – a theory that does indeed seem somewhat hard to realize in a private firm.

Local Government as Entrepreneur

The other source of dynamism in recent years has been 'township industry' (*xiangban gongye*), which is technically collective in ownership. This sector started originally in the Great Leap Forward and was rejuvenated in the Cultural Revolution period (see above). The 'collective' sector in 1987 accounted for 80 per cent of the number of industrial enterprises in the country and about one-third of total output by gross value (and a significantly larger fraction by net value). The latter figure has grown from only 19 per cent in 1978. Township industry alone accounts for above half of all industrial enterprises and perhaps

12 per cent of gross output value (*Zhongguo Tongji Nianjian*, 1988, pp. 222, 257, 259). The collective sector operates largely outside the central plan.

Most larger collective enterprises are in fact controlled by local state author-ities – cities, towns, counties – which benefit economically and politically from the revenues generated by their industries and from the employment these provide. In this respect township industries are similar to local state-operated enterprises. Together these sectors are largely responsible for China's 'overheated economy' of recent years and for the accelerating inflation rate that has threatened social stability. Operating outside the framework of central administrative controls, they have continued to invest freely even when the centre has called for scaling down capital construction.

A wide range of conditions can be found in local enterprises, depending on level, location and less tangible factors. In more prosperous areas revenues generated by local enterprises are used to build up local welfare programmes. In others conditions reminiscent of the early industrial revolution can be found. Profit-oriented local state entrepreneurs in one carpet factory in very poor Gansu Province, for example, make extremely young women weavers work a seven-day 70-hour work week. The women are said by their bosses to prefer more money to more leisure; they accept these conditions because the pay, in that dry region, is at least ten times what they could earn by staying in the village and scratching the dirt as their ancestors did. Health and safety conditions vary widely within the local industrial sector, as well.

A feature of the recent erosion of central authority and legitimacy has been the tendency of provinces and localities to ignore central directives and go their own way. This includes establishing administrative and/or economic barriers to trade with other parts of China as a means of protecting local enterprises. The national market is thus threatened with a return to the kind of fragmenta-tion that characterized it in pre-communist days.

Core State Industry

It is in the 96,000 state-run enterprises, and especially the large-scale units run by central government ministries, that the problems of reform are most intractable. State industry continues to produce over two-thirds of total gross industrial output.

Early reforms include the restoration of the authority of the director and the removal of the enterprise party committee from running its daily affairs; the substitution of a taxation system for the previous practice of state appropria-tion of virtually all profits; the switch from financing investment via budget grants to the use of bank loans bearing interest; the revival of a 'scientific management' approach to organizing, disciplining and compensating labour, and the consequent adoption of various incentive schemes. More recently, the emphasis has shifted to contracting out management responsibility on bids to individuals who seek to earn high incomes by meeting their contracted promises; and to leasing out smaller state enterprises to individuals or collectives to run. Opinions vary as to whether these reforms have produced any noticeable improvement in overall economic performance, but such improvement, if any, has been modest at best. The problem of the 'soft budget constraint', in particular, remains about as severe as ever. And, in the absence of price reform, even if state enterprises accepted and responded to market signals, the allocative results would be quite irrational.

The continued responsibility of state enterprises for a range of expensive social welfare services is another impediment to their marketization. Providing housing, health care, child care, pensions and a variety of other services to their workers, state enterprises are hardly in a position to maximize the bottom line. This is but one example of the 'duties without rights' phenomenon much complained about by enterprise managers: a proliferation of obligations and targets that management remains responsible for fulfilling, but a minimum of autonomous powers that it may use to do so. If enterprises become more independent and profit-oriented, they will seek to reduce their liability, especially for such 'peripheral' welfare costs. As we have seen, this has already happened with respect to women, who are now exposed to the threat of differentially high unemployment because enterprises are responsible for maternity pay and the medical costs of childbirth, and thus prefer to hire men.

A younger, more educated group of administrators and intellectuals has been the guiding force behind the reform programme. While there may be some Marxists among them, my impression is that most are closer to a Chicago School view of the world. Burned and disillusioned by the politics of the past, they are now impressed by what they think works in the world. Their perspective has been only partly shaped by experiences in US and other Western universities and business schools (and by visits to the new luxury joint venture hotels in China's cities), and by the monied aroma of the arriving ideology. They are nationalists (with a small 'n'), who worry about China's development.

Many of these have concluded that reform is being obstructed by lack of resolution of that fundamental issue in the relations of production – ownership. They argue that state-owned enterprises cannot after all be made subject to market discipline; therefore, they must be privatized. Basically, their view attaches immediate value only to economic growth and technological modernization; social welfare gains of the past are undervalued or considered barriers to development. Socialism has been redefined instrumentally to mean anything that develops production, and modern capitalism looks to many of these reformers to be partly socialist and capable of 'peaceful transition'.

State enterprises, in the opinion of three economists who recently caused a stir in government and intellectual circles, are driven to maximize costs and resources under their control, rather than profits, and to distribute surplus based on status and rank (the similarity to the US military industrial complex is striking). The solution they call for is 'the wholesale conversion of state-owned enterprises into what would essentially be privately owned firms'. The bureaucracy would be won over by converting their present status and privileges into property, somewhat the way the samurai were treated in Meiji Japan. Neither price reform nor the formation of joint stock companies, another much discussed idea, would lead to fundamental change in enterprise behaviour under current conditions, according to this viewpoint.[20]

Labour

The reformers would clearly like to change the existing social contract with urban workers. The attack on relatively egalitarian pay ('everyone eating from the same big pot') and job security ('the iron rice bowl') are the clearest indications of this. In return, workers are to be given a more genuine labour market, and thus the right to change jobs and locations, which they have not been able to do in the past. One would expect that in a surplus labour market the real wage, including fringe benefits which would be greatly reduced for contract workers, would come down markedly. In theory, a switch from permanent employment to temporary contract employment is to take place by attrition, with the newly hired workers coming under the latter system. But in fact most state labour continues to be allocated bureaucratically as in the past, and under the same conditions, although there is some indication that people with poor connections or inferior records are being frozen out of the system to become an urban underclass that will 'function as a labour reserve' (Davis, 1988).

The subject of labour protection leads to consideration of the labour unions, which underwent rebirth after the Cultural Revolution. Born again with them was their former role as broker between the state and the workers. (The title of a recent *Beijing Review* article on the unions – 'Unions of Management and Workforce' – richly suggests their intended role.) But the unions might well become a factor in the struggle over reform, as they are inherently a 'conservative' institution. Indeed, it was the All-China Federation of Trade Unions (ACFTU) which led the criticism of the new draft enterprise law as being 'a law for directors only' and as ignoring 'the workers' position as owners'. And it is an executive member of the ACFTU who has pointed out that at present 'workers can be exploited without the possibility of legal redress'. It seems that one of the benefits to the state of contracting enterprises out to independent managements is that such managements are not bound by existing labour laws and 'can arbitrarily increase overtime or dismiss workers in pursuit of short-term profits. With no law to back it up, a union cannot step in and support its members'.[21]

Bureaucratic Capitalism and Other Problems

Reform has brought China to the point at which the interests of some large constituencies must be threatened. The question is, which ones? A case in point is the dilemma the government faces with respect to farm policy. Grain production has faltered for several years, in part because of unfavourable terms of trade with industry faced by grain farmers. If the state moves vigorously to redress the urban–rural terms of trade in agriculture's favour while investing substantially in the farm infrastructure, it will then have to choose between burgeoning deficits (already a problem) and sharply rising urban food prices with the attendant danger of social instability. If on the other hand it leaves the terms of trade essentially unchanged the likely result will be a continuing slowdown by farmers and lagging farm output, which in turn will exacerbate urban shortages, retard economic growth and complicate reform.[22] In a dilemma of this kind, political and social factors come to the fore; the farm population's reaction to unfavourable prices is passive, whereas, in the prescient words of one analyst, sharply rising urban prices could 'easily trigger widespread discontent' and 'lead to social unrest' (Chen Xiwen, 1987). In mid-May 1988, the prices of eggs, vegetables, sugar and pork were raised by 30 to 60 per cent in state stores in China's cities, occasioning anxiety and angry protests in the urban population (*New York Times*, 19 May 1988). A ten-yuan subsidy was added to monthly wages to help offset the increase, but many urban residents felt that their living standards were declining. Indeed, the urban population as a whole appears to have suffered a decline in real income after 1986,[23] a factor which undoubtedly contributed to the support the students in Tiananmen and other urban centres received from the general population in April and May 1989.

Because the structure of prices is closely related to the distribution of income, changing it is difficult and risky. But price control has its own dangers in addition to the irrational allocation of resources it encourages now that a market of sorts is functioning (e.g., the underpricing of urban grain stimulates the development of luxury uses, such as alcohol, while restricting supply). In such a constrained market those in possession of underpriced goods and services find illegal ways to extract their full scarcity value from the public. When the state remains in control of most economic institutions, those who find themselves in such a position are public officials. The spread of this kind of corruption in China has been very rapid, and the giving of expensive gifts and other under-the-table transactions have become commonplace. This is just one means by which political position is used to achieve economic gain. Most notoriously, the offspring of high officials have obtained sinecures in some of the country's most privileged and profitable companies, including those licensed to import and sell luxury consumer goods at great profit. Perhaps more than anything else, this shadowy reprise of Guomindang 'bureaucratic capitalism' has contributed to the political alienation of ordinary people.

Inflation, bribery and corruption are serious problems, but they can be put in perspective as common derivatives of systemic flux. But the rapid and thorough erosion of the former belief system, at least among the urban educated, is possibly more serious still. In part because of cynicism engendered by past abuses by the state and party, and in part because of the virtual about-face of the latter in its ideological stance, there is no longer a system of values widely shared by the public and its leaders.

Older socialist values of equality, cooperation and community, which are still adhered to by many ordinary people, have been consciously attacked broadside by the state, whose mass media have also routinely dangled luxury consumer goods before a population with US $450 average per capita income, and filled the air with tales of the emerging wealthy. 'Ordinary farmers' have been treated with contempt in official publications,[24] and economic growth has been viewed as the only valid criterion for choosing among social policies. The leadership and media have disseminated a simplistic market ideology that is a mirror image of the extreme anti-market ideology of the Mao period. Since thorough and detailed discussion of the ultimate objectives of reform – what sort of society the leadership would like China to be in ten or twenty years – has conspicuously not occurred, one turns to such ideological leading indicators for enlightenment on this point, and the results are troubling. As one observer put it, 'The reforms are secularising the party and gutting its core belief structure. There is nothing comparable to put in its place.'[25]

To the incessant harping on material incentive and the need for greater wage differentials or inequality, full-status state-sector workers have shown remarkable indifference. The state has continued year after year to criticize egalitarianism in the handling of wages. In many state industries, bonuses are routinely handed out in equal amounts to all workers, and, as they have come to represent an increasing share of total compensation, the distribution of the latter may have become even more equal than before (see Walder, 1989).

The still ubiquitous bureaucracy, which personifies 'socialism' for many people, has responded in its own way. It must operate by the old rules, with little room for material incentive or profitability. The official celebration of material incentive as the universal human virtue appears to legitimize and thus magnifies the famous indifference of government organs in their treatment of people. Not only do they thus reveal their attitudes towards the new policies, but in doing so they drive another nail into the socialist coffin.

IV   CONCLUSION

Most observers (e.g., World Bank, 1983) agree that at the start of the reforms material poverty and inequality in China were markedly less severe than in most other developing countries of similar income level. Some things China had done right, as is indicated by a functioning rural relief programme, an impressive level of public health care and sanitation, a very large gain in adult literacy and spread of primary education generally, and the extraordinarily high life expectancy that had been attained. Although all segments of Chinese society, including the poorest, seem to have benefited from the burst of economic energy that attended the inauguration of rural reform after 1978, the long-run sustainability under current conditions of improvement across the board is now in doubt. Regional, urban–rural and inter-household inequalities have grown rapidly, open unemployment is swelling despite unsustainable fast growth, environmental problems are of mounting urgency, and continuing difficulties in agriculture are cause for apprehension in a country with China's conditions and history.

Yet the political economy of the reform remains murky. A realignment of interests of considerable magnitude is occurring. Farmers have obtained some independence and openly resist attempts to reimpose controls; in suburban areas with city markets at hand many of them have realized great gains in income. Workers are threatened by a distinct demotion in their economic and social status and resist with the aid of the official union movement, which has its own reasons for being less than enthusiastic about change. A small and insecure new class of entrepreneurs in town and countryside flexes its wings and looks for political allies.[26] The bureaucracy splits as some groups resist reforms that threaten their current social position while others seek to turn their political strength to economic advantage. Young urban intellectuals scorn the entire older generation of leaders and float their own radical ideas for change, ideas born out of an amalgam of learning, attitudes and ideologies picked up at Oxford, Chicago or Harvard. And none of this includes the influence of Hong Kong, which is colonizing much of South China, and of the foreign firms that, through investment and trade ties, have increasingly coloured Chinese views of the way business is done.

The shift in political wind that occurred in June 1989 has not clarified the direction, but only the fact, of change in China's political economy. The crushed democracy movement sought liberalization of the political system; as to the basic question, what kind of system China should have, the movement attracted people with many views. Yet it seems clear from the make-up of the emigrés and victims of the repression that the trend towards a free-wheeling and liberal market system in China has been temporarily stalled by those who favour a more controlled, autocratic, state-dominated market. Either way, the state that once extolled workers and peasants has embarked on a new road.

NOTES

1. I am indebted to Terry Sicular, as well as to the editors of this volume, for comments on an earlier draft of this paper.
2. Nicholas D. Kristof, in the *New York Times*, 6 August 1989.

3. Centrally planned socialism was effective at initiating industrialization and bringing about initial improvements in living standards. What is in question is its capacity for 'intensive' growth based on continuous improvements in technology, once an industrial base has been laid.
4. See Riskin (1987) for a full discussion of the Maoist and reformist positions.
5. A good discussion of early PRC industrial management practices can be found in Andors (1977).
6. See Richman (1969), p. 314; Howe (1973), p. 119.
7. See Walder (1986) for an illuminating discussion of this syndrome.
8. Later, in the 1980s, the third group seemed further to split, throwing off a segment that advocated full-fledged marketization and took a thoroughly minimalist position on the prerequisites of a socialist system.
9. This section summarizes an argument made more fully in Riskin (1987).
10. Travellers in China even today find their schedules subject to unnecessary ancillary trips and travel at odd hours in order to fit the organizational resources of their particular host 'unit'.
11. For a good discussion of the central and local roles in industrialization, see Wong (1985).
12. This remains true whether we use gross values in constant prices or GNP (net values gross of depreciation) in current prices.
13. The main reason industry's 1978–79 productivity advantage in GNP terms is less than in gross output value terms (eight-fold compared to fourteen-fold) is that the double counting that swells industry's gross output is eliminated from its contribution to GNP.
14. Although a personal income tax with progressive rates from 20 to 60 per cent technically applies to those with monthly incomes above 400 yuan, China still lacks a reliable income reporting system and high private incomes are not difficult to conceal.
15. Lu Yun, 'Expediting Development in Minority Areas', *Beijing Review*, 27 March 1989.
16. I am indebted to Wang Jianye for helping me collect and tabulate these data.
17. See *Beijing Review*, 31 October–6 November 1988 for an official view of the problems of women in the labour force under the reforms.
18. These lines were written before the suppression of the democracy movement and the purge of Zhao Ziyang in spring 1989. While the new leadership group seems to favour greater administrative control than did Zhao, it is too early to gauge the full extent of the change.
19. The actual role of private enterprise was greater than its nominal size suggests, since a significant but unspecifiable part of the so-called 'collective' sector was made up of private firms masquerading as collectives to get favourable tax treatment.
20. The purge of Zhao Ziyang brought the arrest or flight of some of the boldest members of this group, including the director of the Institute for Reform of the Economic System, a think tank relied on by Zhao. At this writing it is too early to know what will ultimately happen to the ideas and policies advanced by this group.
21. 'Unions of Management and Workforce', *Beijing Review*, 13–16 February 1989. For a discussion of the role of unions in pre-Cultural Revolution days, see Harper (1969).
22. This dilemma is suggested by Chinese economists themselves in a running debate over the causes and solutions of the farm problem. For a summary, see FBIS 143, FBIS Trends, 8 April 1988 – China, 'China's Agricultural Policy Debate'.
23. The average monthly disposable income per capita of urban households rose by 10.6 per cent in 1987 compared to 1986, while the official 'cost of living' index in January 1988 was 11.2 per cent above that of the previous January (*China Statistics Monthly*, April 1988, pp. 70, 111). Taken together, these figures imply a decline in real per capita income. Many observers believe that the official price indexes understate the rate of inflation, some putting it as high as 50 per cent per annum in major cities in mid-1988. See *New York Times*, 19 September 1988.
24. The quoted phrase is from a remarkable article in *Nongye Jingji Congkan* (*Journal of Agricultural Economics*), no. 6, 1987, excerpted in *Beijing Review*, 21 March 1988, p. 31. This piece seeks to define the 'social structure of rural China' by 'taking social position as the main factor and combining it with psychological factors, professional status and personal income'. The result is to write off 'the great majority of ordinary farmers' as not having 'change[d] and remould[ed] their ways of thinking'; to celebrate craftspeople, small business

people and rural enterprise owners and managers as 'full of vigour and vitality ... receptive to innovations ... hav[ing] a strong desire to get rich' ... 'well-informed, experienced and knowledgeable', 'dar[ing] to take risks'. As for rural workers, although their income makes them 'the envy of ordinary farmers', 'their role is far inferior to that of rural tradesmen and enterprise owners and managers'.

25. Robert Delfs, *Far Eastern Economic Review*, 27 October 1988, p. 37.
26. Private business people were prominent supporters of the student democracy movement in spring 1989. One of the most famous entrepreneurs, Wang Yannan, head of the Stone Corporation, a remarkably successful computer company in Beijing, is now an exile, having fled the repression.

REFERENCES

Andors, Stephen (1977) *China's Industrial Revolution: Planning and Management, 1949 to the Present*, New York: Pantheon Books.

Chen Xiwen (1987) in *Jingji Yanjiu*, 20 Dec 1987, excerpted in FBIS 143 (see note 22).

Davis, Deborah (1988) 'Occupational Immobility in Contemporary Urban China', in Deborah Davis and Ezra F. Vogel (eds) *Social Consequences of Chinese Economic Reforms*, forthcoming.

Feng Tiyun and Wu Honglin (1989) 'The Rural Private Economy', *Beijing Review*, 27 February–5 March.

Harper, Paul (1969) 'The Party and the Unions in Communist China', *The China Quarterly*, vol. 37, January–March.

Howe, Christopher (1973) *Wage Patterns and Wage Policy in Modern China, 1919–1972*, Cambridge and London: Cambridge University Press.

Hull, Terence H. (1988) 'Implications of Rising Sex Ratios in China', Research Note no. 97, International Population Dynamics Program, Department of Demography, Research School of Social Sciences, The Australian National University, 15 December.

Lu Yun (1989) 'Expediting Development in Minority Areas', *Beijing Review*, vol. 32, no. 13, 27 March.

Naughton, Barry (1986) 'Finance and Planning Reforms in Industry', in US Congress, Joint Economic Committee, *China Looks Toward the Year 2000*, Washington, DC: US Government Printing Office.

Naughton, Barry (1988) 'The Third Front: Defence Industrialization in the Chinese Interior', *The China Quarterly*, September.

Parish, William (1981) 'Egalitarianism', *Problems of Communism*, January–February.

Richman, Barry M. (1969) *Industrial Society in Communist China*, New York: Random House.

Riskin, Carl (1975) 'Workers' Incentives in Chinese Industry', in US Congress, Joint Economic Committee, *China: A Reassessment of the Economy*, Washington, DC: US Government Printing Office, pp. 199–224.

Riskin, Carl (1978a) 'Political Conflict and Rural Industrialization in China', *World Development*, Winter 1977–78, pp. 681–92.

Riskin, Carl (1978b) 'China's Rural Industries: Self Reliant Systems or Independent Kingdoms', *The China Quarterly*, March, pp. 77–98.

Riskin, Carl (1987) *China's Political Economy: The Quest for Development since 1949*, New York and London, Oxford University Press.

Riskin, Carl (1988) 'Reform: Where is China Going?', in Peter Nolan and Dong Fureng (eds) *The Chinese Economy and its Future*, Oxford: Polity Press (1990).

Unger, Jonathan and Jean Xiong (1990) 'Life in the Chinese Hinterland under the Rural Economic Reforms', *Bulletin of Concerned Asian Scholars*, April–June, p. 8.

Walder, Andrew G. (1986) *Communist Neo-Traditionalism: Work and Authority in Chinese Industry*, Berkeley: University of California Press.

Walder, Andrew G. (1989) 'Economic Reform and Income Inequality in Tianjin, 1976–1986', in Deborah Davis and Ezra F. Vogel (eds) *Social Consequences of Chinese Economic Reforms*, forthcoming.

Wong, Christine (1985) 'Ownership and Control in Chinese Industry: The Maoist Legacy and Prospects for the 1980s', in US Congress, Joint Economic Committee, *China Looks Toward the Year 2000*, vol. 1, Washington, DC: US Government Printing Office.

World Bank (1983) *China: Socialist Economic Development*, vol. 1, Washington DC: The World Bank.

Zhongguo Tongji Nianjian (Statistical Yearbook of China) (1988), Beijing: Chinese Statistical Publishing House.

Zhongguo Renkou Ditu Ji (Demographic Atlas of China) (1987) Beijing: Statistical Publishers.

10. Capital–labour relations at the dawn of the twenty-first century

Alain Lipietz

I METHODOLOGICAL INTRODUCTION

Forecasting the future of capital–labour relations is far from an easy matter. As this volume has shown, there already exists a large variety of industrial relations, even within advanced capitalist countries. Moreover, in these very countries, the divergences are increasing by comparison to the 1950s and 1960s, when a rather unified pattern has prevailed: Fordism. This may be a transitory situation: the crisis of the old entails a period of random search for new industrial paradigms and new rules of the game.[1] A possibility remains for the emergence of a new paradigmatic order. But it may also be argued that the march of Fordism to hegemony was a unique success story in capitalist history. The future may be a more fuzzy situation, with a coexistence of many types of capital–labour relations, even in a single country: a configuration of complementary patterns of industrial relations. Moreover, a paradigmatic order may be just a creation of the theorist, a simplification of an unshaped reality, a subjective stylization of the chaos. Neither 'Fordism' nor 'Taylorism' ever existed as a pure reflection of their ideal models.

With all these caveats, it seems that prospective analysis in capital–labour relations (or any prospective analysis of social forms) is useless. Yet there are some reasons to believe that social relations obey an order and tend to adapt to typical forms. The best argument is that all the agents who participate in the shaping of social forms are subjects pursuing their goals in similar situations: optimization of efficiency, or at least 'sufficing' efficiency, in order to survive through conflicting interests within competition. In this process, they tend to imitate other experiences; management books and business magazine columnists are read; fashions are followed. People learn. Prospective analysis is about the possibilities of convergence within this learning process.

Yet there is no reason to believe that there is only one solution to the question of shaping social forms. In the field of industrial relations, this idea is often related to the assumption of an objective progress of productive forces to which social relations would adapt themselves through the learning process. This idea, common to some old Marxist texts and to many writings about the 'necessities of the current information revolution', is discarded by the empirical observations evoked in the present volume. In fact, between technological evolution and the stabilization of typical professional relations lies a wide field of conflicting interests, mitigated by the national (or even local) traditions of former agreements. An industrial paradigm is a social compromise, more or less reluctantly accepted by managers and workers. Moreover, this paradigm contributes to frame the forms and direction of the technological evolution itself. Prospective analysis is not a pure speculative issue: it should be rooted in the examination of actual evolutions.

Fortunately (for the forecaster, at least), the year 1989 has dramatically simplified the situation. Within a few months, with the huge and tragic (but probably temporary) exception of the People's Republic of China, and the anecdotal exceptions of North Korea, Vietnam, Cuba and Albania, the 'socialist countries' have swung back to the explicit acceptance of the superiority of 'normal' capital–labour relations – based on commodity-producing firms organized by managers hiring a labour force. Nowadays, it is certain that the dawn of the twenty-first century will be capitalist. But *what* capitalism? That remains the question. If the complex East European professional relations analysed by Köllö (Chapter 8, this volume) are likely soon to become a curiosity of the past, the future of the former socialist countries is far less definite. Their learning and imitative process may try to converge towards a British, Swedish or any original new type of compromise. For, as Boyer (Chapter 2, this volume) reminds us, there is no agreement in the OECD about what is today the 'normal form' for capitalist professional relations.

Moreover, with the breakdown of the 'eastern way to socialism', all the 'national ways to socialism' in the Third World, from India to Algeria, have lost any appeal. There, capital–labour relations will certainly present an incredible mix of forms stretching from small-scale production to quasi-Japanese methods (see the Indian example in Mohan Rao, Chapter 7, this volume). Will the main changes lead to a 'Brazilian type' as put forward by Amadeo and Camargo (Chapter 5, this volume) or to 'Korean type' (You, Chapter 4, this volume)? And are we to expect a new world hierarchy according to the choices of nations for a particular form of professional relations?

Once again the future appears very indeterminate. Yet there are limitations. Professional relations should be consistent. First, they should be consistent in themselves, that is between their different aspects: wage contracts, labour organization, social reproduction of appropriately skilled labour forces. Second, they should be consistent with the broader complex of social life in concrete ways: general goals and accepted rules for life in a common society. Third, they should be consistent with the macroeconomics of some regime or social structure of accumulation, both at the national and international level. Last, and not the least, the global ecological situation is now imposing strong constraints on the generalization of most models. This does not mean that at the dawn of the twenty-first century these constraints will be accepted. If they are not, the middle of the century may be out of control. All these social and logical constraints will limit the possibility of stabilization of new professional relations. Many things may happen, but not just anything. Unbalanced situations may develop for a while (such as Brazilian growth of the 1970s or US growth of the 1980s), but they are not stabilized regimes, with which prospective analysis should be concerned.

From what has been said so far the following points emerge:

- Technology provides possibilities; it does not determine the future.
- Social agents are trying to emerge from a crisis of outdated agreements. In doing this, they will struggle against each other in search of new agreements. The directions of research are influenced by the challenge posed by erosion of old compromises. Social agents are looking for not-yet-existing answers to existing questions. The answers proposed by social forces in any particular country depend on local traditions and experiences. Hence these answers are more likely to emerge in some countries rather than others. Yet some answers may become hegemonic worldwide by a process of imitation of the best experiments.
- However, partial answers cannot be chosen *à la carte*. Only some 'menus' are consistent. Not all the menus are mutually consistent.

These considerations lead us to the following procedure. Section II starts with an analysis of the shortcomings of the old paradigm, which was dominant in the advanced capitalist countries: Fordism. The available answers to these shortcomings will provide some internally consistent menus (we shall select two of them). Some typical countries will be seen to direct themselves towards one of these menus. But this is not a proof of their future stability. In Section III, we extend the analysis to Eastern and Southern countries. In Section IV, we look at the external constraints on the menus of professional relations: ecological, social and macroeconomic. This will not so much reduce the scope of consistent menus, but will outline the difficulties and opportunities stemming from their generalization. In the conclusion (Section V), we shall examine three scenarios based on the progressive generalization of some of the menus or a mix of them.

II TWO WAYS OUT OF FORDISM

Throughout the period after the Second World War, two paradigmatic models of development were proposed to developing countries: the Western one and the socialist one. The latter has now acknowledged its complete failure. Meanwhile, capitalism in the Northwest of the world experienced its Golden Age. The model of development of this Golden Age (here labelled Fordism) went through a major crisis in the 1970s–1980s, but nobody believes that it was the 'final crisis'. On the contrary, several reforms were proposed to this model, and at this writing (the end of the 1980s) all these reforms seem to combine into more or less promising results. We may infer from this that the fate of Fordism and the ways out of its crisis will once again be influential for the worldwide future of capital–labour relations. Hence our choice to start with Fordism, its crisis and the ways out of it, then extend these considerations to the South and the East.

The Rise and Fall of the Golden Age[2]

First let us recall briefly what Fordism was. As any model of development, it could be analysed three ways:

1. As a general principle of organization of labour, Fordism is nothing more than Taylorism plus mechanization. Taylorism implies a strict separation between the conception of the labour process, which is the task of organization and methods (O&M) on the one hand, and the execution of standardized and formally prescribed tasks on the shop floor on the other hand. Mechanization is the way in which collective knowledge of O&M is embedded into the material apparatus (both hardware and software). As a result, workers' involvement is supposed not to be needed for the implementation of the prescriptions of O&M.

2. As a macroeconomic pattern (or regime or social structure of accumulation), Fordism implied that the gains in productivity arising from these principles of production were matched, on the one hand, by an increase of investments financed by profits and, on the other hand, by an increase in purchasing power of the waged workers. As a result, both the share of wages in value-added and the capital–output ratio were roughly constant; hence the rate of profit was roughly stable and the outlets for production and consumption goods were growing in pace with productivity.

3. As a system of rules of the game (or as a model of regulation), Fordism implied long-term contracting of the wage relation, with rigid limitation of redundancies; and a programme of wage increases indexed on prices (cost-of-living adjustments) and general productivity (annual improvement factor). Moreover, a large socialization of revenues through the welfare state and social security ensured a permanent income to wage-earners. The counterpart was the acknowledgement by unions of the privileges of

management. As a result, both the principles of labour process organization and the macroeconomic pattern were respected.[3]

This model of development was the result of 'chance discoveries' and of a
process of learning through imitation. The Taylorist principles reached hegemony
throughout the first half of the century. Henry Ford and J.M. Keynes popular-
ized the idea that demand mattered and that demand from wage-earners was
the most stable basis for social demand. Workers' struggles and political changes
in the 1930s, under Roosevelt's presidency or in social democratic Europe,
imposed new rules on the game. The social compromises of the Roosevelt period
were spread in liberated Europe and defeated Japan after the Second World War,
both by the administration of the Marshall plan and by the US unions' support
for 'reformist' European unions.[4] This crusade for the 'American Way of Life'
was matched by the indigenous push of the European labour movement resulting
in important improvements of the model (e.g. the European elaboration of the
welfare state along the lines of the Beveridge report).

The success of the Golden Age model was thus based on the wage-led
increase of internal markets in each advanced capitalist country. The foreign
constraint was limited by the coincidence of growth in all these countries, the
reduced importance of growth in international trade by comparison to the
growth in internal markets, and by the hegemony of the US economy.

Yet, in the late 1960s, the stability of the Golden Age growth path began to
crumble. The first and most obvious reason appeared on the demand side.
Competitivity equalized between the US, Europe and Japan. The search for
economies of scale induced internationalization of productive processes and
markets. The increase in the price of raw materials imported from the South
(notably oil) stirred up the competition for exports in the early 1970s. The
regulation of the growth of internal markets through wage policy was now
challenged by the necessity to balance external trade.

In front of this demand-side crisis, the reaction of international élites was clearly
Keynesian. The idea was to coordinate (through the OECD, the IMF, Trilateral
Commission, etc.) the upholding of world demand. That was clearly the line
of the First Economic Summit at Rambouillet in 1975. It has been argued that
the actual policies were sub-optimal in respect of demand.[5] But at least concern
with demand remained common knowledge. In fact, real wage increases were
dramatically slowed down and more and more firms shifted their plants to non-
unionized areas, or outsourced to Third World countries, but the basic rules of
the game were maintained in advanced capitalist countries.

Yet at the end of the 1970s, the mood changed in international élites of the
capitalist world. The demand-side management of the crisis had certainly
avoided a great depression. But a significant limit appeared: the fall in profitability. This was due to several causes on the supply side: slowdown in

productivity with an increase in total labour price (including welfare payments), increase in the capital–output ratio, and an increase in the relative price of raw materials. In those conditions, Keynesian devices such as an increase in the real wage (however limited it was) and monetary laxity could only induce inflation and erosion of the reserve value of monies, especially the international one: the dollar (Lipietz, 1983). Hence the shift to supply-side policies, that is, to industrial relations, a field which encompasses aspects of the industrial paradigm and the rules of the game.

Even within the present theoretical frame work, the supply-side problem with Fordism is subject to two interpretations. First, according to Kaleckian tradition, the rise in the relative price of labour and raw materials was the result of the long boom of the Golden Age. The profit squeeze (Itoh, 1980; Armstrong, Glyn and Harrison, 1984) was the result of the previous expansion and of a full-employment situation. Moreover, the welfare state had dramatically weakened the cost of job loss (Bowles, 1985), and that could also account for the slowdown in productivity.

We shall come back to a complementary explanation, but the fact is that the profit-squeeze analysis became the official explanation by the end of the 1970s. Profits were too low because workers (and raw materials suppliers) were too strong and the rules of the game were too rigid, which led to difficulties in restructuring the productive apparatus, thus missing the opportunities of the technological revolution. This analysis was heralded at the Economic Summit in Venice, 1980, after the second oil shock. Fighting inflation (instead of unemployment) was proclaimed the 'first priority', through a commitment to increase productivity and to redistribute capital from declining sectors to sunrise sectors, from public sector to private, from consumption to investment. There was a clear commitment to 'avoid measures protecting particular interests from the harshness of adjustment'. In other words, the rigid rules of the game were to be overthrown.

That 'liberal-flexibility' policy was fostered by the UK, then the US, and was eventually implemented in many countries of the OECD, including the socialist–communist French government (Lipietz, 1984). The repudiation of the former rules of the game reached different levels on different fronts: from the annual improvement factor + cost of living adjustment rules to the scope and depth of social security protection, from the liberalization of redundancy procedures to the proliferation of precarious jobs. This process was carried on in an authoritarian manner (governments and management seizing the opportunity of defeating unions or reinforcing conservative policies) or through concession bargaining between capital and labour in the context of increased job losses.

After an experience with recession in the early 1980s, the recovery developed after 1983. Yet, that recovery was largely fostered by a renewal of Keynesian budget policies (Lipietz, 1985; 1989) and it is difficult to conclude that it was merely the result of liberal-flexibility policies. Moreover, the experience of the 1980s did not turn out to favour the most significant experiments in flexibilization in the US, the UK and France. On the contrary, these countries exhibited both de-industrialization and trade deficit. The winners in competition (Japan, Germany, the European Free Trade Agreement) seem to be characterized by *another* solution to the supply-side crisis.

Let us return to the theoretical explanation of this supply-side crisis of Fordism. An alternative or, more aptly, a complementary explanation to the Kaleckian 'full-employment profit-squeeze' theory insists on the unravelling of the efficiency of the Taylorist principles. Full employment may account for the decline in productivity growth and the rise in capital–output ratio in the late 1960s and early 1970s. However, the increase in unemployment since that time failed to bring about a recovery in productivity growth. In fact, the elimination of shop-floor workers from any initiative in relation to the labour process is of limited rationality. It is a good device to secure management's direct control of the intensity of work. But more responsible autonomy on the shop floor may appear as a better principle, especially as the implementation of new technologies, or the shift to just-in-time management, requires the involvement of direct operators and their willing cooperation with the managers and the designers.[6] And that was precisely the alternative way selected by many important firms in Japan, Germany, Austria, Switzerland and Scandinavia. There, the pressure of unions and other organizational traditions fostered the choice of a 'negotiated involvement' solution to the crisis of Fordism (Mahon, 1987).

At the end of the 1980s, the superiority of this policy is increasingly acknowledged, not only in that second group of countries, but also in management books and by writers in the first group. Certainly, the competitive success of the second group weighs a lot in this evolution, but the difficult experiments in implementing high technologies in a liberal-flexibility context also fostered a change in management fashions.[7] Yet, at this moment, liberal flexibility and negotiated involvement seem to be mere devices that could be combined *à la carte*. We now examine their mutual consistency.

After Fordism, What?

The previous survey of recent economic history may be summarized as follows:

• Acceptance, then rejection, of 'demand-side' concern, as if it had become irrelevant, because internationalization had made it unmanageable, or because the boom of the second part of the 1980s had made it useless.
• Development of two tenets about direct industrial relations: liberal flexibility versus negotiated involvement.

We shall come back to the first issue when dealing with the macroeconomic consistency of professional relations, and we focus here on the supply side. We shall not follow the complex and rich taxonomy proposed by Boyer (Chapter 2, this volume), but a quite simplified version first proposed in Lipietz (1984). The reason for this is that this prospective is only a loose exercise. Our only aim is to consider alternative paradigms after the demise of Fordism. Too much precision would eliminate the difference between conflicting paradigms and variations inside *the same* paradigm. Moreover, the two tenets represent two different possible paradigms (or menus), even when it seems that they could be mixed in a dynamic manner.

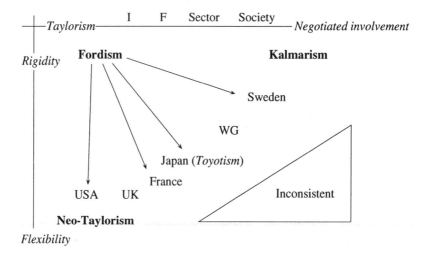

Figure 10.1   After-Fordist professional relations

In fact, the two tenets may be thought of as two axes of Fordist professional relations: Taylorism as direct control by the management of the activity of workers, rigidity of the wage contract (see Figure 10.1). The first tenet fosters move from 'rigidity' towards 'flexibility', the second from 'direct control' towards 'responsible autonomy'. In other words, the first axis refers to the external labour market, to the bond between the firms and the manpower to be hired and rewarded. The second axis refers to the internal labour market, the forms of organization of cooperation/hierarchy inside the firm.[8]

On the first, 'external' axis, there are several aspects to do with rigidity and flexibility, as we have already noticed. The rules of the game could include rules on setting of direct wage, rules on hiring and firing, rules on allocation of the indirect wage: the external market is a more or less organized one. The axis represents the synthetic solution. Moreover, the rules may be set at the level of individuals, professions, firms, sectors and society. We shall consider this when dealing with the other axis.

On the second, 'internal' axis, there are also different aspects: involvement means skilling, horizontal cooperation, participation in the definition and monitoring of tasks, and so on.[9] Once again it is a synthetic axis, but here, for obvious reasons, we must note the *level* of the negotiation of the involvement of workers. This involvement may be implemented in the following ways:

1. It may be *individually* negotiated and fulfilled by bonus, career, and so on. This is limited by the *collective* character of the required involvement in most processes of cooperative production. So the 'individually negotiated involvement' (I in Figure 10.1) may be extended to a team or a shop. This is not far from incentive practices, and thus quite compatible with a flexible labour contract.[10]
2. It may be negotiated firm by firm, between management and unions (F in Figure 10.1). Here the firm and the workforce share the rewards of the specific skills accumulated in the learning process. This implies an 'external rigidity' of the wage contract, but does not involve outsiders.[11]
3. It may be negotiated at the sector level, thus limiting firms' risks of competition through 'social dumping', and inducing them to share skilling institutions and so on. The external labour market is likely to be more organized, that is, broadly speaking, more rigid with greater socialization of labour revenues.[12]
4. It may be negotiated at the level of the whole society, unions of workers and business negotiating at the regional or national level[13] the social orientation of production, with unions seeing that 'their' people do their best on the shop floor. Here, the external labour market is likely to be at least as well organized as in the most advanced Fordist-corporatist cases.

However, collective involvement of the workers is unlikely to emerge if there is no solidarity about goals between the firms and the workforce, that is in a context of external flexibility, at any level. So, the limit of consistency between flexibility and involvement appears as an arc of a circle between our two axes, with a triangle of inconsistency and two most plausible lines of evolution, that is two real paradigms (Figure 10.1):

1. External flexibility associated with hierarchical direct control. We are back to some form of Taylorist organization of the labour process, without the social counterparts of the Golden Age Fordism. Let us call this paradigm *neo-Taylorism*.
2. External rigidity (organization) of the labour market associated with negotiated involvement of the operators. Let us call this paradigm *Kalmarian*,

in honour of the first car factory reorganized according to the involvement principle in a social democratic country: Sweden.

Looking back to the recent experience of the OECD countries, the industrial relations in these countries seem to range along the arc of the circle, with the US and the UK favouring flexibility and ignoring involvement, or introducing individually rewarded involvement (as in France); Japan practising negotiated involvement at the large-firm level; Germany at the sector level, and Sweden being closer to the Kalmarian model.

What about the attractive power of the axes? The experience of the US shows that it is difficult to negotiate involvement at the shop or even plant level in a broader flexible–liberal context, yet individually negotiated involvement may be developed.[14] On the other hand, Germany appears as a less socially advanced form of the Kalmarian paradigm. Only Japan seems to occupy an intermediate position, with a strong duality (rigid/flexible) in its external labour market. This is possible because the scope of the capital–labour agreement is the firm level. But this is not done randomly. As Lazonick (Chapter 3, this volume) points out, the Japanese model forms a system, with the major firms negotiating the involvement of their core workers, and the small subcontractors sticking to flexible Taylorized industrial relations. Moreover, Lazonick (Chapter 3, this volume) implies some forms of continuity between these two extreme situations. Let us call this pattern 'Toyotism'.

'Toyotism' is not the pattern of capital–labour relations existing in Toyota.[15] It captures the idea that the national model allows for differences between firms along the diagonal 'Kalmarism to neo-Taylorism'. How is it socially acceptable? We shall come back to this when studying the broader consistency of our paradigms. But first we consider non-OECD countries.

III   SOUTH AND EAST: TOWARDS WHICH POST-FORDISM?

While the East developed a completely original form of professional relations (self-labelled, doubtfully, 'socialist'), the South may be precisely defined as the countries which did *not* succeed in imitating either the Western or the Eastern models.

In the 1950s and 1960s there was a common idea that the fastest way to develop industrialization was the Eastern way. This idea stemmed from two considerations:

1. The East had already a model of accelerated growth, at the time faster than Fordism. The Stalinist Soviet Union could thus be considered as a former underdeveloped country which was succeeding because of the superiority of its 'rules of coordination'.
2. The West was presenting itself as opposed to the industrialization of the South. Not only had colonial rule been based explicitly on an 'international division of labour', reserving for the South primary production, but the automatic dynamics of free trade were reproducing the same division within post-Independence neocolonial relations. This fact had been realized since David Ricardo's theory of comparative advantage, and now it was negatively theorized under the heading of 'dependency theory'.[16] Thus, unorthodox models (that is including some Eastern devices) appeared as a way to catch up with the West, even in non-socialist Southern countries.

There were, however, counter-examples, such as Finland, a former part of the Russian Empire, nowadays under social democratic post-Fordism. But only the success of the newly industrializing countries, coexisting with the failures of peripheral and even central socialism, would change the general idea, more convincingly than Rostowian rhetoric. Thus we start our analysis with Eastern Europe.

The Rise and Fall of the Iron Age

The Stalinist Soviet Union adopted a peculiar model of development which could be called an 'Iron model' by comparison to the Fordist 'Golden' one (Lipietz, 1979):

*   The Taylorist industrial paradigm was explicitly imported by Lenin into revolutionary Russia.
*   The regime of accumulation was based on extensive accumulation of productive forces, through import substitution, without an important increase in mass consumption.
*   The rules of coordination (or mode of regulation) were based on central planning. This is the socialist content. The idea was that what was wrong with capitalism was its 'market' aspect. With more 'organization' – and hierarchy – the 'rationality of Taylorism' would spread to the whole society.

To be sure, that was a very efficient model in a 'Lewisian' situation (i.e. with a huge reserve army in the peasantry). Taylorism was supposed to be suited to set to work unskilled workers.[17] Extensive accumulation does not require great flexibility, and it increases the average productivity of the economy as and when industrialized and mechanized forms of production are substituted for pre-industrialized ones.[18] With a slowly growing real wage, huge surpluses could be accumulated. And the central organization of demand replaces the demand constraint with the risk of supply constraints (Kornai, 1979). As for the professional relations, their initial harshness was progressively stabilized in an acceptable compromise (by the 1950s' standards): in exchange for its Taylorist subordination, the industrial and tertiary workforce was granted quasi-tenure. Such a menu (Taylorism + tenure) was 'cousin' to Fordism; hence their similarity and competition in the 1950s.[19]

Now, problems arise when the Lewisian reserve army of labour is exhausted or never existed (as in Czechoslovakia and East Germany). As Köllö (Chapter 8, this volume) and Sapir (1990) show, the impossibility of organizing interfirm relations at the same degree as intrafirm relations is manifested through bottlenecks and wasting. In turn, anarchy in social planning is reflected within the organization of the firms. The involvement of workers is discouraged by the unravelling of revolutionary ideals, by the anarchy in industrial organization, and by the lack of any incentive, either negative (cost of job loss) or positive (access to higher consumption). The compromise of 'tenure with low wage' appears then as completely stagnationist.

Although it is different from Fordism, the Iron Age socialist paradigm is thus experiencing a similar supply-side crisis. The great differences are:

- There is no demand-side crisis.
- Socialist tenure is much more rigid than Fordism.
- Rigidity also concerns the other aspects of industrial organization.
- Even the non-involvement of workers seems to result more from insufficiency of management than from an excess of scientific management *à la* Taylor.

Clearly, the Eastern mode of coordination and regulation needs more flexibility in its industrial organization. Hence the general wish of Eastern reformists in favour of autonomy in firm management. But the first degree of freedom required by firms is the liberty to adjust their workforce to their needs, according to potential productivity of existing assets and to social demand. Thus, very quickly, liberal flexibility in professional relations – that is, external flexibility and the end of socialist tenure – appears as a panacea. Ten years after the West, some former socialist countries (typically Hungary and Poland) are rushing towards this new panacea, forgetting the other side of the problem: the inner organization of labour processes.

How could we see the situation in terms of our two axes? On the vertical axes, 'tenure' can obviously be represented as an 'excess of rigidity'. But on the inner axis (organization) the situation is less clear. The trade-off is less between 'direct control' and 'responsible autonomy' than between 'inefficient control' and 'irresponsible autonomy'. Despite Lenin's choice for Taylorism in the

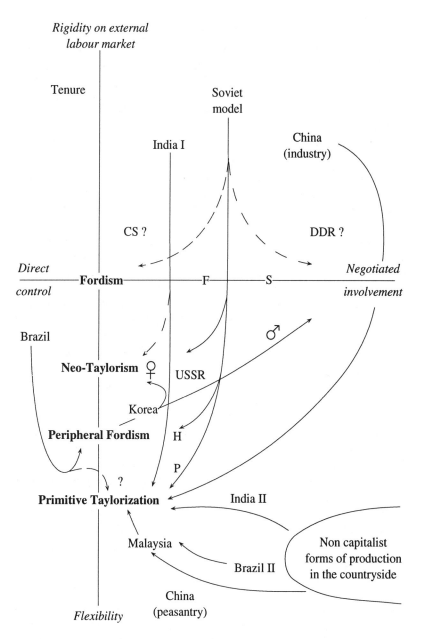

Figure 10.2   Around Fordism

industrial mobilization of former peasantry, and despite Stalin's slogan 'the management decides everything', there exists an autonomy of the direct workers, due to a revolutionary tradition[20] or an industrial tradition (East Germany, Czechoslovakia) or at any rate due to the incapacity of management to organize scientifically direct control. On our synthetic axis, this position could be placed between 'firm' and 'sector-negotiated involvement', since, as Köllö shows, the negotiation of compromises takes place between the sector ministry and the firms' directors acting as representatives of their workers.[21]

From this starting point on Figure 10.2, the movement is certainly downwards, that is to more flexibility in wage contracts. But, giving up the 'tenure' compromise, will the workers try to stick to some social-democratic compromise of the Fordist type, or will they be obliged or induced to accept the panacea of 'liberal flexibilization'? That is an open question, at this level of our analysis, and in the objective social–political process.

The situation on the horizontal axis is also open. The main tendency for 'autonomous' firm managers will certainly be to implement fully Taylorist principles, especially in less advanced countries (Poland, Hungary, Roumania, most of the Soviet Union). But they will meet severe resistance from skilled workers, especially in areas attracted by West German and Scandinavian examples of the Kalmarian paradigm: ex-East Germany, Czechoslovakia, and the Baltic countries.

We may now summarize the first part of our discussion. Facing the challenge of the crisis of their industrial paradigm from the supply side, Eastern countries will tend to answer by correcting the most obvious shortcoming: rigidity. As far as professional relations are concerned, that will mean the end of the tenure system. And since Taylorist principles have not met their limits because they were never fully implemented, the main attraction will be the menu 'Taylorism + liberal flexibility', that is, the neo-Taylorist paradigm that seems to these countries to be the basis of the West's success. Yet, between tenure and total flexibility of wage contract, they may also adopt a wiser middle way, either towards the old Fordist menu (with its possibilities in the East) or towards some 'involvement' menu of Kalmarian type. Between the tendency and these two possibilities, history will decide, according to some overriding constraints we shall discuss later.

Two Rural Giants with Industrial Islands

In the present volume, China and India have been the Southern countries which adopted most closely the model of development of the Soviet Union. The great difference from Eastern European countries is the size of their peasantry: around one-third of the world's population. The great difference between China and India is the dramatic rural revolution of China.

China enjoyed an agrarian reform and a strict organization of its rural economy. As a result, it did not experience until recently a massive exodus towards towns. Thus the situation is a 'hidden Lewisian' one, with an artificial shortage of industrial workers dedicated to a Soviet-type strategy of extensive accumulation by import substitution. This strategy was extended by Maoism to a quasi-autarchy. Moreover, the Great Leap Forward and the Cultural Revolution may be understood as the first attempts to criticize capitalist industrial relations (in fact, Taylorism) from the supply side: as a hierarchical direct control system. Attempts were also made towards decentralized forms of planning of social demand through popular communes. China thus experienced a kind of 'micro-economic revolution within the revolution' (Riskin, Chapter 9, this volume).

The success of this microeconomic and managerial revolution is doubtful, yet its failure is less obvious than the winner of the 1975 counter-revolution, Deng Xiaoping, has pretended. After a first attempt to realign to stricter Stalinist principles, the Deng regime was the first in the socialist world (with the Hungarian) to acknowledge its organizational shortcomings and reintroduce flexibility, not only in factories, but in the countryside. The Maoist attempts to involve workers in the management of firms and local communities were destroyed. All that remained was a culture of local leadership initiative. The liberal reforms revealed the Lewisian situation of the workforce as very flexible, extremely poorly paid, with a considerable cost of job loss, and a very authoritarian regime. These are the conditions of what we call 'primitive Taylorization', a model experimented with in the 1970s by the newly industrializing countries of Southeastern Asia.

In the middle of the 1980s, China, especially its coastal provinces, was clearly converging towards this model. Yet the unsuccessful revolt of Tienanmen (1989) blocked that revolution, revealing the strength of the old organizational principles, and calling the necessarily repressive character of 'primitive Taylorism'. The trend remains the same, but the participation of the working class in the next political movements could introduce some surprises.

In Figure 10.2, the trajectory of China could be represented in the following way. Starting from the Soviet model, and after a bend towards the right on the involvement axis, industrial China rushes downwards to 'primitive Taylorism' below neo-Taylorism (because the workers' rights will be worse than the most extremist dreams of liberal supply siders). Moreover, the peasantry will be set to waged work directly through the primitive Taylorization paradigm.

In India, there was practically no land reform, the country was never a 'state socialism', and it did not experience real centralized planning. Yet many features of the Soviet model are visible in its post-Independence industrial history. The state-led import-substitution policy fostered the development of an important inward-oriented industrial and tertiary structure whose workers enjoyed the 'tenure principle' (Rao, Chapter 7, this volume). These workers were less involved than in socialist countries yet they were not exactly Taylorized.

The great difference with China is the permanent flow of primitive Taylorization of workers excluded from pre-capitalist relations, or integrated into capitalist relations through some form of subcontracting system: Rao thus found a second archipelago of industrial wage relations in the ocean of rural India. For cultural and historical reasons,[22] Taylorization did not reach the degree of absolute control by (hardly existing) O&M. In Figure 10.2, this process is represented by an arrow entering the K/L diagram from the bottom right.

The stream of economic liberalization in the 1980s is likely to shift professional relations in India towards classical forms of primitive Taylorization. With the opening to international competition, the informal sector will be induced to deeper forms of direct control without improving notably real wages and social legislation. Tenure practices will have to be given up in the formal sector, yet a possibility remains that the privileged fraction of the workforce could negotiate a limited liberal flexibility, and Fordist-type social counterparts to the rationalization of the labour process.

The NICs: How Will They Continue?

Two classical examples of NICs are examined in this volume: Brazil and South Korea. At present they are important industrializing countries. Aspects of their regimes of accumulation have been examined elsewhere under two headings: primitive Taylorization and peripheral Fordism (Lipietz, 1985).

1. Primitive (or 'bloody') Taylorization is a case of the delocalization of precise and limited segments of industrial sectors in social formations with very strong rates of exploitation (in wages, duration and intensity of labour etc.), the products being mainly re-exported to more advanced economies. In the 1960s, the export free zones and the workshop states of Asia were the best illustration of this strategy, which is widespread today, and illustrated by the case of Malaysia in this volume (Chapter 6). Two characteristics of this strategy may be noted. First, the activities are mainly Taylorized but relatively non-mechanized. The technical composition of capital in these firms is particularly low. Hence, this pattern of industrialization avoids the disadvantage of import substitution: the cost of importing capital goods. On the other hand, since it mobilizes a largely female workforce, it incorporates all the know-how acquired through domestic patriarchal exploitation. Second, it is 'bloody' in Marx's sense when he speaks of 'bloody legislation' at the dawn of central capitalism. To the ancestral oppression of women it adds all the modern arms of anti-worker oppression (managed unionization, lack of social rights, imprisonment and torture of opposition). Jomo (Chapter 6, this volume) on Malaysia is a good example of what 'bloody legislation' could mean at the dawn of the twenty-first century.

2. Peripheral Fordism. Like Fordism, it is based on the coupling of intensive accumulation and the growth of markets. But it remains peripheral in the sense that, in the global circuits of productive sectors, skilled employment positions (above all in engineering) remain largely external to these countries. Further, its markets correspond to a specific combination of local middle-class consumption, along with increasing workers' consumption of domestic durables, and cheap exports towards the centre.

Brazil started its industrialization as a kind of earlier and more successful India. The agrarian reform was as limited as in India, the Lewisian labour reserve army was supplied, and, as early as in the Vargas period (during the Second World War), state-led import-substitution strategy was implemented in the urban sector by national capital, with a corporatist type of social legislation (not so far from Fordist principles). Yet, two major shifts made the difference. First, the developmentalist state, while protecting its internal market from imports, did not hesitate, under Jocelino Kubitschek, to open the doors to Northwest capital and technology. Second, the military coup of 1964 suppressed *de facto* the social advantages of Vargas legislation (precisely out of the fear of 'union power' under the presidency of Goulart). As a result, scientific management developed without other limitations than technological dependency, and a bloody repression of unions supplied capital with a quite 'flexible' workforce. In the late 1960s and early 1970s Brazil developed a very competitive industry, achieving its import substitution, and developing industrial exports.

This paved the way for primitive Taylorization. Yet Brazil did not engage clearly in an export-substitution strategy. Capital goods were mainly paid by primary goods exports and indebtedness. The benefits of primitive Taylorization were reinvested in the development of a dualistic peripheral Fordism, in which economic gains accrued only to a fraction of the population (the new middle class stabilized in a Fordist way of life, the wage-earners benefiting in the second half of the 1970s from the growth in productivity stemming from mechanization and rationalization). This fraction included a part of the formal sector (Amadeo and Camargo, Chapter 5, this volume) and also a part of the working class which, at the end of the 1970s, regained some advantages warranted by the Vargas legislation. On the other hand, a huge fraction of the workforce remained excluded from the benefits of the Brazilian miracle: 'Lewisian' ex-peasants, informal workers and low-paid formal workers in small firms.

In the 1980s, the debt crisis broke out and then democracy came. The resulting evolution is rather complex. On the one hand, democratization increased the bargaining power of workers and their legal guarantees. On the other hand, super-inflation hindered their capacity to control the evolution of their real wage. Distributional conflicts took front place in industrial debates. Professional relations cannot stabilize in this permanent tempest involving the Lewisian marginalized reserve army, the informal sector, and the different degrees of the formal sector. In this chaotic situation, Brazil remains open to three possible futures: a return to primitive Taylorization, a consolidation of peripheral Fordism, or even an evolution towards Fordism with local evolutions towards Kalmarian aspects.

By comparison, the 1985–87 revolution in South Korea is heir to a much better situation. The root of everything is the original land reform of the 1950s and the continuing support of peasants' revenues. Primitive Taylorization in Korea was not under the pressure of a Lewisian reserve army. All the workforce was hired under a flexible wage contract, but hired formally. Moreover, the state managed to plan carefully the export capacities in order to pay for the external debt. The situation of women was of terrible exploitation, especially in the export sector, but the revenues of average families increased throughout the 1970s and accelerated in the 1980s. As a result, Korea went through a transition from primitive Taylorization to peripheral Fordism. Moreover, in the male fraction of the working class, corporate patriotism was developed in a way preparing the imitation of some aspects of Japanese firm-level negotiated involvement (You, Chapter 4, this volume).

Democratization is likely to foster these tendencies, since there is no more debt constraint. Korea could evolve towards a less and less peripheral form of Toyotism. It would be a dualistic one, professional relations differing according to genders: firm-negotiated involvement for males and neo-Taylorism for women. On this example, conditions of consistency external to professional relations appear very clearly. We now consider these points.

IV   CONSISTENCY PROBLEMS OF POST-FORDISM

Professional relations are but a part of feasible model of development. Capital–labour relations are thus subject to other constraints than the ones developed within the direct wage relation. Macroeconomists commonly acknowledge demand constraint and international constraint. Political scientists emphasize the necessity to legitimate the social order. More recently, ecological constraints have appeared of paramount importance.

The Dangers of Productivism

Capitalist development not only 'degraded work' until the climax of Taylorism (Braverman, 1974). We now perceive how much it exhausted the Earth, according to Marx's prophecy (and this is also true in the state-owned capitalism of the East). In fact, capital–labour compromises have been settled until now at the expense of nature, hence at the expense of the next generations. The hole in the ozone layer and the greenhouse effect are the consequences of the great industrial boom of the Golden Age. The recovery of the 1980s has increased the frequency of industrial disasters, and is worsening the global ecological crisis. Now the limits of any productivist model are fully perceived, at the local or global level, and the necessity for future models of development to be sustainable, that is ecologically consistent, is more and more acknowledged.[23]

Yet the strength of this perception is different according to each case, so ecological limits are not equally perceived as limits to future models of development. Local dangers are more and perceived and refused by, among others, workers whose jobs are the causes of the danger. Unecological practices are perceived and refused when concentrated in a definite territory, such as Los Angeles, Netherlands, and even in an NIC like Taiwan. But global effects resulting from a model of human consumption inherited from Fordist compromises may be ignored for a while. Ecological limits are thus both absolute and loose. Humankind may select unsustainable models until the first third of the twenty-first century. The local or regional concentration of environmental damage will foster social movements opposing these models, but in many cases, the local victims will be blamed from more accountable regions.[24]

If we assume a development of ecological movements all round the world (and this is the case in the West, in the East, but less in the South), sustainability will become a factor of legitimation of the next social capital–labour compromises. From this we may infer that, if they are negotiated, the counterparts of gains in productivity will be granted in the form of an increase of free time, rather than in the form of an increase in real wage (as it used to be in Fordism). That solution will prevail in the most socialized form of Kalmarian compromises.[25] Another solution, consisting in halting the damage to the environment through ecologically-sound industries would be favoured by overconsuming upper classes attached to neo-Taylorism, thus increasing the price of consumption goods to the detriment of lower tiers of society. In Eastern and Southern countries, there is a risk that ecological sustainability remains ignored, especially if the more immediate debt constraints weigh heavily on these countries.[26]

We may conclude that when ecological constraints are taken into account – and that could be the case in fairly developed countries, without major financial constraint, especially where a regional ecological crisis is already developing – capital–labour compromises based on the increase of free time and social (public) forms of consumption will be favoured, hence Kalmarian industrial relations. This conclusion does not hold (unfortunately) in less developed countries, or in advanced countries where individualistic ideologies are too strong.

The Problem of Social Cohesion

Obviously, models of development based on Kalmarian professional relations imply general knowledge, education and culture common to all citizens, hence a rather egalitarian distribution of revenues and powers with a well organized and skilled sector of public services (Lipietz, 1989; Mahon, 1989; Mathews, 1989). On the contrary, neo-Taylorist professional relations imply a polarization of skills, revenues, ownership, and access to wealth and education. Models of development based on such professional relations are thus more conflictual than the former. In the extreme case of 'primitive Taylorization', this may be solved by 'bloody legislation' (see the Malay case). Within a liberal democratic order, serious problems of cohesion appear, that can only be solved through political and cultural specificities of places where these industrial relations are to be implemented.

The neo-Taylorian paradigm is thus more likely to develop where individualistic ideologies prevail and where the waged population is divided. This conclusion also holds when workers' involvement is negotiated firm by firm. This is what Aoki et al. (1990), writing about Japan, have labelled 'the paradox of workers' democracy'. In that case, the surpluses of productivity are specific to the firm, and the resulting quasi-rents of the firm hold as long as a differential productivity is maintained in the face of other competitors. The negotiated compensations (in terms of higher wages, reduction of labour time or lifetime career) are limited to this quasi-rent. In that condition, insiders and management are allied against newcomers and competitors. This tends to consolidate a 'workers' aristocracy' (or a 'yeomen democracy' in Piore and Sabel's – 1984 – vision) at the top of a generalized meritocratic hierarchy in the whole society, which may be a part of national culture.[27] This hierarchy may develop into a completely dualistic structure (negotiated involvement/neo-Taylorism), especially when gender differences come into play, as in Japan and Korea, or ethnic differences as in West Germany (see Walraff, 1986).

As a conclusion, the Kalmarian paradigm can prevail when the labour movement is strong, takes into account the interests of the whole waged population, accepts being involved in a dialectic of struggles and agreements with management, including on organizational and productive issues, and when feminism is strong. When labour is divided by aristocratic traditions, gender and ethnic exclusions, and when (like in France, the US and UK) management and unions have a strong conflictual tradition, neo-Taylorism, or some dualistic configuration, is more likely to develop.[28]

Now, in the South, the second group of conditions pertains generally and neo-Taylorism will largely prevail for a while. In more advanced countries (Brazil and Korea), much will depend on the capacities of labour movements to overcome intersectional, racial and gender divisions.

In Eastern Europe, the situation is still more complex, because an official labour movement has existed, in favour of equality in skills, revenues, and preaching for collective labour involvement in management. But in the mind of the waged population, this official labour movement is associated with hypocrisy and oppression! There, the ideological and political struggle will be of paramount relevance. The swing towards liberty may lead to individualistic liberalism and, as far as professional relations are concerned, towards neo-Taylorism. This seems to be the case in Poland and Hungary, and the indebted situation of these countries, with the associated IMF medicine, will foster this evolution. Or deeper traditions, sometimes rooted in religion or in the memories of the pre-Stalinist labour movement, will hinder these tendencies. Then, an alternative may develop towards a more solidaristic and ecological model, based on Kalmarian professional relations. Some chances remain for this evolution in East Germany, Czechoslovakia and the Baltic countries.

Macroeconomic Constraints

Macroeconomic constraints should be well known to economists; moreover they represent a logical aspect of prospective analysis. First, any model of capital–labour relations must be profitable. Second, it should be competitive. Third, demand should match supply.

From the first constraint it results that, when a great part of the surplus has to be reserved for debt servicing, there is little room for 'negotiating involvement' because the wage has to be as low as possible. The existing debt constraint thus induces neo-Taylorism. Second, countries which are already engaged in neo-Taylorism, and are less productive than 'involving' ones, are also handicapped in the search for a better capital–labour truce. As a result, in our sample, the US, the UK, France, Brazil, Eastern Europe and Malaysia will have a great deal of difficulty shifting towards a Kalmarian paradigm. On the other hand, Scandinavia, West Germany, Japan and Korea may be considered as marching towards the twenty-first century in a good position.

As far as demand is concerned, the Kalmarian paradigm offers much more possibility of regulating internal markets than neo-Taylorism. The latter will be associated with a cycle of exhilarating periods of boom (with an increase of profits and the revenues of the upper tier of society) and periods of depression (due to overinvestment or 'cooling-off' policies): the return of business cycles, as opposed to the more regular pattern of Fordism.

The great and open question is the combination of the two models within the same free-trade space, such as the EEC. We may assume that in labour-intensive sectors, neo-Taylorism could dominate negotiated involvement at a sufficiently low wage. Then, by transposition of Ricardo's theory of comparative advantage, countries (or regions) will tend to specialize in sectors using more intensively the factor with which they are comparatively better endowed: either flexibility – and low wages – or involvement. In that case, the total amount of demand will be limited by the competition on wages due to the coexistence of regions of 'low wage and low involvement' and regions of 'higher wage and higher involvement'. The greater the possibility of practising 'social dumping' in neo-Taylorist regions, the smaller will be the islands of 'workers' democracy'.[29]

Of course, a very simple way to limit social dumping (of competitors!) is protectionism, either through a low rate of exchange, or through explicit or implicit import limitations. Japan and Korea have been using both these devices for a while. The EEC is not fully open to the competition of the NICs, especially of the Malaysian type; the US becoming less so. Once admitted that it is unfair to be protectionist against a group of countries and at the same time insist on paying off their debt, reasonable protectionism appears as a way to open the way for better social compromises than pure free trade. But it only opens the way!

PROSPECTIVE CONCLUSIONS

The post-Second World War ruling paradigm in industrial relations, Fordism, is exhausted. It was so powerful that for twenty years it marginalized Southern and Eastern countries from world industrial trade. It used to combine a rigid organization of the external labour market with collective bargaining, the welfare state, social legislation, and direct control of the management of a semi-skilled workforce in the labour process.

Challenged by the decline of the rate of growth in productivity, management reacted in the 1970s in two ways: relax the rigidity of Fordism, or shift from direct control to negotiated worker involvement. These two ways appear mutually inconsistent when applied to the same workforce. Thus two major paradigms emerged in the 1980s. On the one hand, neo-Taylorism may be defined as a return to pre-Fordist flexibility of the labour force, with lower wages and increased risks of job loss, with direct control by management in the implementation of more or less modernized technologies. On the other hand, collectively negotiated involvement may be defined as the commitment of the workforce in the battle for quality, productivity, and improved new technologies, in exchange for social guarantees and sharing out of gains in productivity. The two paradigms may coexist in the same society when the involvement is negotiated firm by firm, but the greatest social achievements are obtained when the involvement is negotiated at the level of the whole society: then we called it 'Kalmarian'. The US, the UK and France are shifting towards the first direction, Scandinavia and West Germany towards the second; and Japan represents a clear dualistic example.

At the end of the 1980s, the second paradigm seems to have outclassed the first one in the Northwest. Yet, Soviet-type management–labour relations, characterized by very high rigidity in the external labour market, are also exhausted. The Eastern countries are hesitating between the two Western paradigms, but the neo-Taylorist seems to be the most attractive. This is also true in the South, with the exception of the most successful NICs, notably Korea.

What have been, and what will be the main causal factors of these national evolutions? Debt and short-term competitivity constraints, division of the labour movement, traditions of individualism or hierarchy, and gender or ethnic divisions in society will foster the first paradigm or the dualistic combination. Social concern for ecology, egalitarianism, solidarity, equal rights between genders and races, preference for macroeconomic stability, existence of strong and universalistic unions, will foster the Kalmarian paradigm where the competitivity of the economy is already secured.

At the international level, several scenarios are thinkable. The dominance of the neo-Taylorist paradigm no doubt was the dream of Anglo-Saxon management, the administration of Ronald Reagan and Margaret Thatcher. But the Kalmarian paradigm proved its superiority in the implementation of new technologies. On the other hand, it seems unlikely that the latter could marginalize neo-Taylorism at the global level just as Fordism did to any other industrial relations in the 1960s. The most credible scenario is the formation of a new hierarchical world economy. It will not oppose an industrial Fordist core to a primary-goods-producing periphery, but will present itself as a *de facto* new industrial division of labour. The core economies will be those which have adopted a Kalmarian compromise in a great part of production, with a possibility of internal dualism (Kalmarism/neo-Taylorism), for instance, according to gender. They will dedicate themselves to high-tech and less labour-intensive production. The periphery will be composed of economies organized according to the neo-Taylorist paradigm, and dedicated to routinized and labour-intensive activities.

In this new world industrial hierarchy, some former core economies may become semi-peripheral, including the UK, France, and even many states of the US. Conversely, Japan and West Germany will consolidate their place in the core, with some other former core economies like Sweden, and some former peripheral ones catching up, such as Korea, renewing the trajectory of Finland. A part of Eastern Europe could be involved in this process, while the rest would be integrated as a periphery in the unified world economy.

The proportion of core to periphery is an open question. The more important the neo-Taylorian share of the world, the more unstable its macroeconomics, the less advantageous the social compensations for worker involvement even in Kalmarian countries, and the greater the ecological threat. Faced with this conclusion, not surprisingly, the author would favour the choice of a progressive generalization of Kalmarian professional relations. This requires not only national social struggles, but also the setting up of an international economic order preventing social and ecological dumping (Lipietz, 1989).

Humankind has given up, for the time being, the dream of non-capitalist development. At the dawn of the twenty-first century, it has yet to make the choice between several forms of capitalism, based on different capital–labour relations. The consequences of these choices will include social, international, democratie and ecological effects. Professional relations are not a matter restricted to unions and management specialists. They concern all the social movements that work towards shaping our common future.

NOTES

1. This term will be made more precise later. Equivalent terms are used in the US 'social structure of accumulation theory' (e.g. Bowles, Gordon and Weisskopf, 1986), or French 'regulation theory' (e.g. Boyer, 1986; Lipietz, 1985) or in previous works of the WIDER project (e.g. Marglin and Schor, 1990). The word 'paradigm' should be understood both in its original greek meaning ('example') and its modern linguistic and epistemological meaning (set of terms unified by a common notion, like the branches of a tree).
2. The following subsection is a summary of Glyn et al. (1990); Lipietz (1985; 1989).
3. Here we see that Fordism was a 'menu'. The coexistence of Taylorism and pre-Fordism 'rules of the game' for the determination of wages led to the Great Depression.
4. On the support of US unions to this 'politics of productivity' and their role in its spread through Western Europe and Japan, see Carew (1987).
5. This is the well known position of Ajit Singh: see Glyn et al (1990). The position of Lipietz (1985) emphasizes credit-based overtrading in the 1970s.
6. See Aoki (1987; 1990). Long ago, Andrew Friedman (1977) had opposed 'responsible autonomy' to 'direct control' as two *permanent* conflicting tendencies in capitalist organization of labour. In Aoki's writings (e.g. 1987), the opposition of '(semi-)horizontal' and 'vertical' structures is connected to broader considerations of industrial organization. Significantly, he first demonstrates the superiority of the former on the latter in the case of just-in-time (*kanban*) management of 'river-like' production process (car assembly lines). Then he admits the superiority of responsible autonomy in most kinds of labour process. Here we notice the relative independence of industrial relations, not only *vis-à-vis* technology, but also *vis-à-vis* other aspects of intrafirm management and of industrial organization. This independence is only relative: my bet is that new technologies emphasize the superiority of responsible autonomy (without determining it, *à la* Piore and Sabel, 1984). Moreover, responsible autonomy may fit peculiarly well with sophisticated forms of industrial organizations (just-in-time, 'network-corporation', and so on). This is outside the scope of the present paper. On the possible menus crossing professional and industrial relations, with spatial consequences, see Leborgne and Lipietz (1987; 1990).
7. See quotations from the US business press in Messine (1987), Lorino (1989), and the French Report to the Prime Minister by Riboud (1987).
8. See Doeringer and Piore (1971). The term 'market' may be confusing: even the (external) labour market is not a real market, and the internal market is certainly not a market at all. Yet the opposition internal/external (or 'hierarchy vs market' *à la* Williamson, 1985 is rooted in a long tradition established by Marx (1865), Ch. XIV) as technical vs social division of labour. As shown in Lipietz (1979) (in the Marxist line) and Favereau (1989) (in a 'conventional economics' line), there are strong tendencies to project the 'organized' character of intrafirm relations towards outside market relations, and vice versa.
9. As may be seen here, 'involvement' in wage relations may imply external aspects of professional relations, such as general schooling, participation in planning commissions in corporatist states, and so on.
10. The fact that incentive practices could be dealt with in the frame of extended microeconomic theory is an index of the liberal-market character of these industrial relations (see for instance Laffont and Maskin, 1982).

11. In the mainstream heterodox framework, this situation is captured through 'contract theory' (for instance McLeod and Malcomson, 1988).

12. Here we see the complexity of the synthetic 'external' axis flexibility/rigidity. The best example is the Italian *Casa Integrazione*, a collective fund which facilitates the flexibility of redundancies. Another example is the US practice according to which redundant workers still belong to the scope of major firms and are re-hired as a priority.

13. If not at the international level! The problem of the adequate geographical scope of paradigms is one of the most difficult and unexplored (however see Lipietz, 1985b; Leborgne and Lipietz 1989). We come back to this point later.

14. In a previous attempt at taxonomy Leborgne and Lipietz (1987), following Messine (1987), had labelled *Californian* the menu: flexibility + individually negotiated involvement. In fact the Californian model appears to be a form of incentive practice within the neo-Taylorian context each time the involvement of the wage-earner is required, such as high skills or high-profile office jobs. Messine (1987) had proposed 'Saturnine' for the menu: rigid labour contract + collective involvement, but the limitation of the General Motors Saturn project has proved the difficulty of its implementation in a *single* firm. Thus, according to a suggestion by Rianne Mahon, we moved to the Kalmarian label. In another text (Leborgne and Lipietz, 1990), we made a clearcut distinction between the two labels frequently met in the Anglo-Saxon literature on this topic: neo-Fordism and post-Fordism, and we associated them respectively with the neo-Taylorian and the Kalmarian axes.

15. Otherwise, it would be a decentralized form of Kalmarism, which Kenney and Florida (1988) label 'Fujitsuism'. This would ignore the precarious condition of subcontractors. But it would be just as unfair to emphasize only the dark side of capital–labour relations in Japan. As some commentators have emphasized, the industrial paradigms in major Japanese firms are a real breakthrough. This debate was presented in the Japanese review *Mado* throughout 1990.

16. For a critique of dependency theory, see Lipietz (1985).

17. It is not exactly true. Taylorism implies the pre-existence of industrial social knowledge by the management, and a culture of industrial discipline among operators. So implementation of Taylorism was as deceptive in the Soviet Union as in developing countries. Any process of industrialization requires a process of primitive accumulation of industrial social knowledge. Yet Taylorism may appear as an accelerated form of systematization of this process.

18. On the contrary, intensive accumulation of the Fordist type allows for a regular increase in productivity of existing plants.

19. On the common origins of Stalinism, Fordism and corporatism in the 1920s–1930s debates, see Lipietz (1979).

20. This raises the difficult point of a worker-aristocracy's support of Sovietism. Stakhanovism should not be reduced to a mere alienation, even in countries where socialism was imported by the Soviet Army as in Poland (see the great movie by A. Wajda, *Iron Man*).

21. Here, a double principal–agent representation could be useful.

22. The classical transition from precapitalist forms of production to capital–labour relations goes through subcontracting system, then simple integration in a single plant, then division of labour within factories, to Taylorism. In Marxist terms, formal subordination of labour to capital precedes its real subordination. Moreover, Marglin (1990) argues that the resistance of Indian workers to Taylorism reflects a cultural resistance to the Western separation between intellectual and operative aspects of labour (*techne* versus *episteme*). In Figure 10.2, this is expressed by the shape of the arrow from non-capitalist forms of production to primitive Taylorization, which moves horizontally to the left, through non-Taylorized organizational forms (e.g., craftwork). A more vertical transition (directly to Taylorism) is also allowed for the NICs and China.

23. 'Sustainable' is the term adopted for 'long-term ecologically consistent' in the report of the United Nations Commission on Environment coordinated by Brundtland (1987).

24. Northern writers have recently criticized the Brazilian people for the burning of Amazonia. Yet the gross yearly contribution of France (40 per cent of Brazilian population) to the global greenhouse effect is 120 per cent of the total Brazilian contribution. More generally, this is a basis for a new opposition between North and South, which is fully expressed in the

process of negotiation at the United Nations Conference on Environment and Development (Rio, 1992). See the polemics between the World Resources Institute (1990) and Agarwal and Narain (1991).

25. When strong unions take into account the 'outsiders', they include reduction of work time in their objective in order to fight unemployment *and* to improve the quality of life. See the German I.G. Metall strategy.
26. In a statement at the Pacific Forum (March 1991), Mahathir Mohamad, Prime Minister of Malaysia, rejected ecological constraints, democracy, labour legislation and human rights altogether.
27. This may be the case with Confucianism in Japan and Korea.
28. As an extended consequence of the 'paradox of workers' democracy', a feedback effect may be expected from the superiority of an industrial paradigm adopted in a single country to the 'aristocratic' attitude of the unions of this country. The British labour movement developed this attitude, then the AFL–CIO in the Fordist US, despite the origins of the CIO (see Davis, 1986), and now it could be the case in Japan.
29. This is a new consequence of Aoki's paradox. For the example of the EEC, see Leborgne and Lipietz (1989).

REFERENCES

Agarwal, A. and S. Narain (1991) *Global Warming in an Unequal World: A Case of Environmental Colonialism*, New Delhi: Center for Science and Environment.

Armstrong, P., A. Glyn and J. Harrison (1984), *Capitalism since World War II*, London: Fontana.

Aoki, M. (1987) 'Horizontal vs Vertical Structures of the Firm', *American Economic Review*, December.

Aoki, M. (1988) 'A New Paradigm of Work Organization and Coordination: Lessons from Japanese Experiences', UNU/WIDER Working Papers, to be published in Marglin (1990).

Aoki, M., B. Gustafsson and O.E. Williamson (1990) *The Firm as a Nexus of Treaties*, London and Newbury Park: Sage Publications.

Boyer, R. (ed.) (l986) *Capitalismes, fin de siècle*, Paris: PUF.

Bowles, S. (1985) 'The Production Process in a Competitive Economy: Walrasian, Marxian and Neohobbesian Models', *American Economic Review*, vol. 75, no. 1 (March), pp. 16–36.

Bowles, S., D. Gordon and T. Weisskopf (1986) 'Power and Profits: The Social Structure of Accumulation and the Profitability of the Postwar US Economy', *Review of Radical Political Economics*, vol. 18 (Spring and Summer), pp. 132–67.

Braverman, H. (1974) *Labor and Monopoly Capital. The Degradation of Work in the XXth Century*, New York: Monthly Review Press.

Brundland, G. (1987) *Our Common Future*, Oxford: Oxford University Press.

Carew, A. (1987) *Labour under the Marshall Plan: The Politics of Productivity and the Marketing of Management Science*, Manchester: Manchester University Press.

Davis, M. (1986) *Prisoners of the American Dream: politics and economy in the history of the U.S. working class*, London: Verso.

Doeringer, P.B. and M.J. Piore (1971) *International Labor Markets and Manpower Analysis*, New York: Sharpe (revised 1985).

Favereau, O. (1989) 'Marchés internes, marchés externes', *Revue Economique*, vol. 40, no. 2 (March), pp. 273–328.

Friedman, A. (1987) *Industry and Labour*, London: Macmillan.

Glyn, A., A. Hugues, A. Lipietz and A. Singh (1988) 'The Rise and Fall of the Golden Age', UNU/WIDER Working Papers, to be published in Marglin (1990).

Itoh, M. (1980) *Value and Crisis*, London: Pluto Press.

Kenney, M. and R. Florida (1988) 'Beyond mass production: production and the labor process in Japan', *Politics and Society*, vol. 16, no. 1 (March), pp. 121–58.

Kornai, J. (1979) 'Ressource-constrained versus demand-constrained systems', *Econometrica*, vol. 47, July.

Laffont, J.J. and E. Maskin (1982) 'The theory of incentives: an overview' in W. Hildebrand (ed.) *Advances in Economic Theory*, Cambridge: Cambridge University Press.

Leborgne, D. and A. Lipietz (1987) 'New Technologies, New Modes of Regulation: Some Spatial Implications', International Seminar 'Changing Labour Processes and New Forms of Urbanization', Samos, September. Published in *Space and Society*, vol. 6, no. 3, 1988.

Leborgne, D. and A. Lipietz (1989) 'Avoiding Two-Tiers Europe', paper presented at the European Association of Labor Economists' First Congress, Torino, September. Forthcoming in *Labour and Society*.

Lipietz, A. (1979) *Crise et inflation: pourquoi?*, Paris: F. Maspéro.

Lipietz, A. (1983) *The Enchanted World: Inflation, Credit and the World Crisis,* London: Verso.

Lipietz, A. (1984) *L'audace ou l'enlisement. Sur les politiques économiques de la gauche*, Paris: La Découverte.

Lipietz, A. (1985a) *Mirages et miracles. Problèmes de l'industrialisation dans le Tiers-Monde.* English edition London: Verso (1987).

Lipietz, A. (1985b) 'Le National et le Régional: quelle autonomie face à la crise mondiale du capital?', CEPREMAP Working Paper no. 8521.

Lipietz, A. (1989a) 'The Debt Problem, European Integration, and the New Phase of the World Crisis', *New Left Review,* no. 176.

Lipietz, A. (1989b) *Choisir l'Audace. Une alternative pour le XXIème siècle*, Paris: La Découverte.

Lorino, P. (1989) *L'économiste et le manager*, Paris: La Decouverte.

MacLeod, W.B. and J.M. Malcomson (1988) 'Reputation and Hierarchy in Dynamic models of Employment', *Journal of Political Economy*, vol. 96, no. 4 (August), pp. 832–54.

Mahon, R. (1987) 'From Fordism to ? New Technologies, Labor Market and Unions' *Economic and Industrial Democracy,* vol. 8, pp. 5–60.

Mahon, R. (1989) 'Towards a Highly Qualified Workforce: Improving the Terms of the Equity-Efficiency Trade-Off', *The Colleges and the Changing Economy*, Toronto, forthcoming.

Marglin, F.A. and S.A. Marglin (1990) *Dominating Knowledge: Development, Culture and Resistance*, Oxford: Clarendon Press.

Marglin, S. (ed.) (1990) *The Golden Age of Capitalism: Lesson for the 1990s*, Oxford: Oxford University Press.

Marx, K. (1865) *Das Kapital*, Book One.

Mathews, J. (1989) *Age of democracy. The politics of post-fordism,* Melbourne–Oxford: Oxford University Press.

Messine, P. (1987) *Les Saturniens*, Paris: La Découverte.

Piore, M.J. and C.F. Sabel (1984) *The Second Industrial Divide: Possibilities for Prosperity*, New York: Basic Books.

Riboud, A. (1987) *Modernisation, mode d'emploi*, Paris: Union Générale d'Edition.

Sapir, J. (1990) *L'economie Mobilisse: Essai sur les Economies de Type Sovietique*, Paris: La Découverte.

Walraff, G. (1986) *Ganz Unten*, Köln: Tiepenhauser & Witsh.

Williamson, O.E. (l985)*The Economic Institutions of Capitalism: Firms, Markets, Relational Contracting*, New York: The Free Press – Macmillan.

World Resources Institute (1990) *World Resources 1990–91: A Guide to the Global Environment*, Oxford: Oxford University Press.

Index

Abegglen, J.C. 71, 81
Abernathy, W.J. 95, 96
Abramo, L. 163, 165, 166, 168
ACC *see* advanced capitalist countries
Adam, J. 287
Adler, P. 58
advanced capitalist countries 71–3, 75, 98
Africa 19
Aglietta, M. 21, 22
Ahluwalia, I. 260
Aitov, N. 302
Akerlof, G.A. 88
Albania 346
Algeria 346
Altshuler, A. 95
Amadeo, E.J. 9, 11, 148, 152–83, 346, 361
Amsden, A.H. 122, 124, 128
Andersson, J.A. 28
André, C. 21
Anubhai, P. 271
Aoki, M. 30, 32, 59, 79, 101, 364
Argentina 121
Armstrong, P. 350
Arthur, B. 59
Asanuma, B. 75
Asia 85, 335
Asian Development Bank 227, 233
Atkinson, P. 45
Austria
    average day of year composition
        (adult men) 295
    and Eastern Europe 294, 295
    Fordist capital–labour relation 24, 36, 45
    Fordist compromise variants 30
    Golden Age 351
    labour contract and worker categories 52
    nominal formation, changing 41
    nominal wage and consumer price 39
    Organization for Economic
        Cooperation and Development
        19, 27, 28, 29, 32, 40, 43, 48
    Social Democratic 61
    unemployment and wages 42
    workers' bargaining power 49
Ayres, R.U. 58

Badham, R.J. 58
Bai, M.K. 115, 116
Bakshi, R. 265
Ballon, R.J. 86
Baltic countries 358, 365
Banerjee, N. 273
Bangladesh 77
Barone, C.A. 117
Barre, R. 33
Basle, M. 26
Bauer, T. 303
Bello, W. 118, 138, 146
Benassy, J.P. 25
Berliner, J. 283
Bernstein, M. 21
Berthet-Bondet, C. 45
Bertrand, H. 22, 52
Beveridge state 21, 27, 34, 38, 349
Bičanič, I. 294
Blades, D. 45
Boda, B. 295
Bogdán, J. 300, 301
Bonelli, R. 167
Bosworth, B. 32
Bowles, S.D. 32, 43, 46, 48, 104, 112, 350
Boyer, R. 6–8, 14, 17, 18–64, 105, 112, 142, 143, 164, 346, 352
Brahmananda, P.R. 241
Braverman, H. 88, 362
Brazil 152–83, 346–7
    automotive industry labour turnover 163
    Brazilian Constitution 170

Catholic Church 170
CEDEC 169, 171
Central Unica dos Trabalhadores (CUT) 153, 169, 170, 173, 182
centralization 169
Chrysler 163
Confederaçao Geral dos Trabalhadores (CGT) 153, 169
conflict, indexation and wage dispersion 171–81
Consolidação das Leis do Trabalho (CLT) 152, 158, 169
Consolidation of the Labour Laws *see* Consolidação das Leis do Trabalho
Cruzado Plan 181
decentralization 169
'dissídio' 159
'economic miracle' 165
employed workers distribution by occupation in non-agricultural activities 156
Fiat 162, 163
FNM 163
Ford 163, 164
Fordism 357
General Motors 163
Guarulhos 168
income, personal distribution of 167
and India 263
industrial sector
  output growth rates 161
  productivity, real wage, product wage 175, 177
  wages share and real wage/productivity 176, 177
inflation rate, monthly 174
labour force 155, 156
Labour Justice 159, 181
labour market, structural heterogeneity of 154–7
Law 1330 160
macroeconomic constraints 365
Mercedes Benz 163
Ministry of Labour 153, 158, 159, 160, 181
National Accounts 167
'new unionism' of 1980s 169–71
newly industrializing countries 360, 361, 362

on-the-job accidents 165
Organization for Economic Cooperation and Development 164
Osacsco 168
production structure and labour process 160–64
production system 157–64
  coordination rules 158–60
relative prices, CPI components and WPI base 180
research and development 162
Santo André 168
São Bernardo 168
São Caetano 168
São Paulo 155, 163, 168
  'new unionism' of 1980s 169, 170–71
  1980's crisis 173, 175, 176, 177, 179, 180, 181
Scania 163
social cohesion problems 364
social security and health expenditures 167
social security institute (INPS) 165, 166
and South Korea 143
strikes 172
Taylorism 162
  without 'Fordist compromise' 164–9
Tribuna Metalurgica 168
Unicamp 172
Volkswagen 163
wages 178, 179, 180
Workers' Party (PT) 153, 170, 182
Brenner, R. 21
Bretton-Woods system 5
Brezinski, H. 288
BRIE 27
Broclawski, J.P. 52
Brunetta, R. 38, 63
Brunhes, B. 60
Bruno, M. 48
Bulgaria 287, 288, 299, 300, 302, 312
  'associations' or 'kombinats' 301
  selected indicators 303
  work time, paid holidays and overtime rates 293

Californian capital labour relation 54, 55
Calmfors, L. 32, 48, 63
Camargo, J.M. 9, 11, 143, 152–83, 346, 361
Campinos-Dubernet, M.J.M. 30, 56
Canada 60, 135
Cannings, K. 83
Castro, M. 159, 169, 170, 171
Ceausescu, N. 304
central economic management 301
Cha, H. 124, 125
Chalmers, N. 75, 81
Chan-Lee, J.H. 29, 36, 45
Chandler, A.D. 40, 51, 55, 80, 90, 97
Chandra, M. 186–7
Chandra, N.K. 258
Chang, Y.T. 185
Chatterjee, P. 258
Chee, P.L. 185
Chen Xiwen 339
Chia, E. 187
Chile 135
China 319–43
    All-China Federation of Trade Unions 338
    and Asia 335
    Bukharinist elements 325
    'bureaucratic capitalism' 339
    Chinese Communist Party 319
    Civil War 323
    Communist ideology 323
    Cultural Revolution 325, 326, 327, 328, 334, 335, 338, 359
    and East Asia 320, 330
    'East China' system 323
    and Eastern Europe 334
    'everyone eating from the same big pot' 338
    First Five Year Plan 321, 322
    First Plan 325, 326
    Fordism 357
    Fujian province 320
    'Gang of Four' 334
    Gansu province 336
    Great Leap Forward 321, 324, 325, 335, 359
    Guangdong province 320, 328
    Guangzhou province 332
    and Hong Kong 319
    and India 263
    'iron rice bowl' 338
    and Japan 338
    Jiangsu province 327, 332
    and Korean War 322
    Liberation 323
    and Malaysia 189–90, 191, 193, 208
    Maoism and central planning regime 322–30
        CCP policy, early 322–3
        conflicts, early 323–5
        Maoism as rejection of central planning 325–7
        self-reliance 327–30
    'market socialism' 335
    'May 7 cadre schools' 326
    'New Democracy' 322
    Northeast 323
    'ordinary farmers' 340
    Party dissent 322
    People's Liberation Army 326
    People's Republic of China (PRC) 322, 346
    per capita income 333
    post-Fordism 358, 359
    'price scissors' 329
    reform 330–40
        alternatives 334–5
        bureaucratic capitalism 339–40
        core state industry 336–8
        labour 338
        local government as entrepreneur 335–6
        objectives versus achievements 330–34
        private enterprise 335
    and Soviet Union 319–20, 323, 325, 326, 330, 331, 334
    and Taiwan 319
    Tianammen 339, 359
    Tianjin 334
    'township industry' (*xiangan gongye*) 335
    'Unions of Management and Workforce' 338
    and United Kingdom 332
    and United States 330, 332, 337, 340
    and Vietnam 330
    'war communism' 329
    World Bank 340
    Yunnan province 332

Zhejiang province 328, 332, 335
see also Chinese *under* Malaysia
Chirac, J.R. 33
Choi, J. 118, 122, 131
Choudhury, U. 257
Chouraqui, J.C. 45
Chun Government (South Korea
    1980–87) 118, 119, 133, 134, 138,
    139, 140
Clark, K.B. 96
CMEA (Comecon) 298
Cold War xii
Cole, R.E. 95, 96
Collier, I.L. 285
consumer price 39
cooperatist 54
cooperative employment relations *see*
    Japan
Coriat, B. 25, 56
Cornell, J.B. 78
Cuba 346
Cummings, B. 130
Cusumano, M. 94, 96, 97, 98, 99, 100
Czechoslovakia 287, 288, 299, 300, 310,
    312
    average day of year composition
        (adult men) 295
    Federation of Engine Crews 297
    Great-Budapest Workers' Council 296
    Iron Age 356, 358
    Ministry of Heavy Industry 296
    post-Fordism 356
    selected indicators 303
    social cohesion problems 365
    State Commission for Management
        and Organization 296
    VHJ 301
    work time, paid holidays and overtime
        rates 293

Daito, E. 91
Dascalescu, C. 305
Davis, D. 338
Dell'Aringa, C. 36, 38, 63
Delorme, R. 21
Deng Xiaoping 359
Dertouzos, M.L.R.K. 59
Deshpande, L.K. 241
Deyo, F.C. 117, 119, 123, 126, 133, 138,
    141

d'Iribarne, P. 55, 58
Doeringer, P. 26
Dore, R. 75, 76, 93
Driffill, J. 32, 48, 63
Dumenil, G. 60
Dutch East Indies 190, 208

East Asia 185, 189, 226, 234, 236, 320,
    330
East Germany 287, 288, 289, 299, 300,
    302, 312
    Iron Age 356, 358
    post-Fordism 356
    selected indicators 303
    social cohesion problems 365
    VVB 301
    work time, paid holidays and overtime
        rates 293
Eastern Europe 282–315, 346
    and Austria 294, 295
    average day of year composition
        (adult men) 295
    and Central Asia 285
    and China 334
    CIB 301
    CMEA (Comecon) 298
    command economy 282
    communism 287
    computer-aided design (CAD) 300,
        301
    corporatist view 282
    Csongrad region 286
    and Finland 286, 294, 295
    future capital–labour relations 367
    Great Leap Back 299
    International Monetary Fund 304
    Komarom region 286
    legal deprivation and 'everyday
        power' 285–97
        collective autonomy, attempts to
            regain 296–7
        inequality 292–3
        labour market 285–7
        open crises 291
        price to pay 293–7
        rights versus chances 291–2
        second economy 287–9
        work process under input shortages
            289–90
    macroeconomic constraints 365

and Malaysia 231, 284
member enterprises 301
1980's crisis and modernization
    challenge 298–303
Organization for Economic
    Cooperation and Development
    51, 63
Pest region 286
polymorphous power 292
post-Fordism 355, 358
reforms 303–12
research and development 302
selected indicators 303
social cohesion problems 364
and Sweden 286
'Third Italy' 300
and Third World 285, 298, 299
'trusts' 301
and United Kingdom 286
and Western Europe 284, 293, 298
Western management techniques 283,
    301
Western statistics 286
Western-like unemployment benefits
    285–6
work time, paid holidays and overtime
    rates 293
see also in particular Bulgaria;
    Czechoslovakia; East Germany;
    Hungary; Poland; Roumania;
    Soviet Union; Yugoslavia
Economic Summit in Venice (1980) 350
Edgren, G. 268
Edwards Deming, W. 99
Edwards, L.N. 82
Edwards, R. 123
Ellmann, M.J. 289
Emerson, M. 63
Epstein, G. 44
Europe
    Golden Age 349
    and Japan 85, 95
    and Malaysia 208
    Organization for Economic
        Cooperation and Development
        19, 34, 48, 50, 62, 64
    see also Eastern; European Economic
        Community; Western
European Economic Community 19
    macroeconomic constraints 365, 366

Organization for Economic
    Cooperation and Development
    20, 27, 51, 62, 63
European Free Trade Agreement 351
Evans, R. Jr 91, 93

Falussy, B. 295
Farkas, J. 288
Fazekas, K. 291
Federal Reserve Board 33
Feigenbaum, A.V. 99–100
Feng Tiyun 335
Fields, G.S. 111, 126
Fink, G. 303
Finland
    average day of year composition
        (adult men) 295
    and Eastern Europe 286, 294, 295
    future capital–labour relations 367
    post-Fordism 355
First Economic Summit at Rambouillet
    (1975) 349
Flanagan, R.J. 60
flexible manufacturing systems 96, 97,
    100, 101, 300
flexible specialization 54, 57
Florida, R. 85, 98
Ford, A. 51
Ford, H. 51, 349
    see also Fordist/Fordism
Ford, T. 51
Fordist 'A' 54, 55
Fordist capital–labour relation 24
    changes in components 38–44
    economic trends affecting 45
    Organization for Economic
        Cooperation and Development
        countries 22–7, 32–4, 36, 38–46,
        48, 50
Fordist 'T' 54, 55
Fordist/Fordism xii
    agreements 50
    Brazil 164–9, 181
    collective agreements 59
    compromise 20–22, 30, 45
    corporate-led 57, 63
    corporatist 54
    democratic 31
    division of labour 33
    Eastern Europe 300, 308, 311, 312

flawed 29, 31
flex 31, 32, 37
future capital–labour relations 345,
   347–54, 366, 367
genuine 31
Golden Age 18–64, 353
growth regime 43
hybrid 32
hypothesis 23
industrial relations 33
inertia 63
institutions and compromises 34
labour regime 38
Malaysia 189, 236
market-led 63
mismatched 29
national virtuous circle 46
Organization for Economic
   Cooperation and Development
   countries 32, 34–6, 38, 40, 43,
   44, 51, 53, 55–7
peripheral 357, 360, 361, 362
post-Golden Age 3–7, 9–12, 15, 16
regime 33
Social Democratic 32, 54, 55, 57
South Korea 123, 126, 129, 142
typical 29
see also Fordist capital–labour
   relation; post
France
   Fordist capital–labour relation 24, 36,
      45
   Fordist compromise variants 30
   future capital–labour relations 366,
      367
   Golden Age 350, 351
   hybrid 61
   and Japan 71
   labour contract and worker categories
      52
   macroeconomic constraints 365
   nominal formation, changing 41
   nominal wage and consumer price 39
   Organization for Economic
      Cooperation and Development
      19–20, 25, 27, 33, 34, 40, 43, 46,
      58
   post-Fordism 354
   post-Fordist professional relations 352
   social cohesion problems 364

unemployment and wages 42
wage share stability 26
workers' bargaining power 49
Freeman, R.B. 49, 63, 80
Frey, M. 293, 302
Friedman, D. 73
Fucini, J.J. 98
Fucini, S. 98
Fukasaku, Y. 93
future capital–labour relations 345–70
   Fordism 357
   Fordism, ways out 347–54
      Golden Age, rise and fall of
         348–51
      post-Fordism 351–4
   newly industrialized countries 360–62
   post-Fordism 351–62
      Iron Age, rise and fall of 355–8
   post-Fordism consistency problems
      362–6
      macroeconomic constraints 365–6
      productivism 362–3
      social cohesion problems 363–5

Gandhi, M. 249
Garon, S. 91, 93
Gelpi, R.M. 25
General Agreement on Tariffs and Trade
   (GATT) 231
General Motors 51, 53, 54, 55
Germany 302
   Fordist capital–labour relation 24, 37,
      45
   Fordist compromise variants 31
   future capital–labour relations 366,
      367
   Golden Age 351
   Iron Age 358
   and Japan 71, 72, 75, 92
   labour contract and worker categories
      52
   macroeconomic constraints 365
   and Malaysia 226
   nominal formation, changing 41
   nominal wage and consumer price 39
   Organization for Economic
      Cooperation and Development
      19–20, 25, 27, 28, 32, 34, 38, 40,
      58, 63
   post-Fordism 354

social cohesion problems 364
Social Democratic 61
stoppage incidence 135
unemployment and wages 42
wage share stability 26
workers' bargaining power 49
see also East Germany
Ghosh, A. 260, 273
Gintis, H. 104
Glyn, A. 24, 25, 44, 350
Golden Age xii
China 326
India 238
Malaysia 224, 233
Organization for Economic
Cooperation and Development
countries 25, 30
productivism 363
in retrospect 20–32
see also Fordist/Fordism; post
'Golden model' 355
Gomper, S. 93
Gorbachev, M. 299, 306, 307
Gordon, A. 91, 92, 93, 94
Goulart, J. 361
Gould, W.B. IV 80, 95
Grace, E. 188, 227
Grando, J.M. 30, 56
Granick, D. 285
Great Depression 92, 102
Gregory, P. 285
Guomindang government 322, 339
Gupta, L.C. 272
Gyekiczky, T. 286, 291

Haggard, S. 118
Halberstam, M. 94
Harris, H.J. 94
Harrison, B. 51
Harrison, J. 350
Hayashi, M. 99
Hayek, F.A. von 63
Helper, S. 75
Hillkirk, J. 96
Hirschmeier, J. 91
Hirshman, A. 172
Hodgson, G. 111
Holmstrom, M. 248
Hong Kong
and China 319

and Malaysia 231
stoppage incidence 135
work week and accident rate 121
Hounshell, D.A. 51, 55
Howe, C. 324
Hull, T.H. 334
Humphrey, J. 163
Hungary
average day of year composition
(adult men) 295
Bacs–Kiskun region 292
Budapest 286, 290
collective autonomy 296, 297
Communist Youth Organization 291
flexible manufacturing systems 300
Gyor 293, 294
inequality 293
Iron Age 356, 358
just-in-time 300, 301
labour market 285, 286, 287
1980s crisis and modernization 299,
300, 301, 302
Party 291
Party Congress (13th) 299
price to pay 294
reforms 304
rights versus chances 291
second economy 288, 289
selected indicators 303
social cohesion problems 365
Szabolcs–Szatmar region 292
worktime, paid holidays and overtime
rates 293
see also Hungary and Poland
Hungary and Poland 308–12
Levi's 312
Nowa Hut 310
Party 309
Solidarity 310
TUC 310
VAT 309
Western participation 311
Hunter, J. 77
Husain, S. 273

Iacocca, L. 86
Imaoka, H. 128
India 238–78, 346
Ahmedabad textile industry 240, 245,
248, 252, 267, 272

Ahmedabad Textile Labour
   Association 249
Arogya Mills 240, 244, 245, 246, 248,
   252, 267, 268, 271
ASI data 258
badlis (temporary substitutes) 244
Bangalore 240
Bata lockout 267
Bombay 243, 244, 249, 265, 267, 272,
   273
and Brazil 263
Bureau of Public Enterprises 247
Calcutta 272
and China 263
Coimbatore 248
Communist Party 249
computer-numerically controlled tools
   (CNC) 268
conflict and stalemate 255–61
Congress 262
Congress Party 250
Delhi 273
Dunlop strike 267
economic structure and production
   relations 241–9
   segmented markets and labour
      supplies 241–3
   small versus large firms 247–9
   work processes in large firms 243–7
Emergency 261–2
emergent production relations 266–74
   large-firm sector, changes in
      266–70
   small-firm sector 270–74
Factories Act 252
Fordism 357
Golden Age 238
growth regime changes 262–4
Gujarat 256
HMT Limited 240, 245, 246, 247,
   252, 261, 268, 269
Independence 238, 244, 250
and Indonesia 263
Industrial Disputes Act 250, 251
Industrial Relations Act 250
Indian National Trade Union
   Congress (INTUC) 250
Jamshedpur 272
and Japan 244
Jupiter Mills 240, 246, 271

Kerala 255, 256
labour movement domination by state
   249–55
labour politics in flux 264–6
Maharashtra 256
Majoor Mahajan 260, 267, 268
and Malaysia 189–90, 191, 208
manufacturing
   employment growth 256
   employment, non-household 242
   product wage 259
Naveen Mills 240, 244, 246, 250, 251,
   260, 267, 269, 274
newly industrializing countries 361
ownership structure of factories 243
and Pakistan 263
PH processing 240, 271, 273
PL weaving 240, 247–8, 252, 253,
   273
post-Fordism 358, 359
Rashtriya Mill Mazdoor Sangh
   (RMMS) 250
and Singapore 263
and South Korea 263
and Sweden 255
Tamil Nadu 256
Tiruppur knitwear industry 248, 271
Trade Unions Act 249, 250
tripartism 265
wages, salaries and workforce
   composition 257
West Bengal 255, 256, 267
see also Indians *under* Malaysia
Indonesia
and India 263
and Malaysia 189, 191, 204, 207, 208,
   217, 230
International Labour Organization 121,
   188, 233
International Monetary Fund 349, 365
   Eastern Europe 304
   Malaysia 227, 233
'Iron model' 355
Ishak Shari 202, 224
Ishikawa, K. 100
Italy
   Fordist capital–labour relation 24, 36,
      45
   Fordist compromise variants 30
   hybrid 61

labour contract and worker categories 52
nominal formation, changing 41
nominal wage and consumer price 39
Organization for Economic
    Cooperation and Development
    19, 20, 27, 28, 29, 33, 40, 44
unemployment and wages 42
workers' bargaining power 49
Ito, T. 120, 122, 130
Itoh, M. 350

Jacobson, G. 96
Jacot, J.H. 32, 51
Japan xii, 70–105, 346
    Burakumin 78
    Canon 70
    and China 338
    Chinese 77
    cooperation and economic growth
        102–5
    economic trends affecting
        capital–labour relation 45
    employment environment 71–81
        classifications 78–9
        enterprise unions 80–81
        hours, earnings and income
            distribution 71–4
        labour force segmentation 77–8
        labour management relations 75–6
        labour shortages, responses to 83–6
        opportunities 74–5
        permanent 79–80
        standards of living 76–7
        women in labour force 81–2
    employment relations evolution 90–95
        post-Second World War
            developments 94–5
        pre-Second World Origins 90–94
    employment relations and
        technological change 87–90
        effort-saving technology 87–8
        shop-floor skills and industrial
            leadership 88–90
    Equal Employment Opportunity Law
        (EEOL) 83–4
    export-led industrialization 129–31
    Filipinos 77
    flexible manufacturing systems 96,
        97, 100, 101

Fordist capital–labour relation 24, 37
Fordist compromise variants 31
Fujitsu 70
future capital–labour relations 366,
    367
Golden Age 349, 351
Hitachi 70
and India 244
just-in-time inventory systems 96, 97,
    98, 99, 100
Kimitsu works 85
Koreans 77
labour contract and worker categories
    52
macroeconomic constraints 365, 366
and Malaysia 185, 186, 187, 189, 190,
    208, 209, 226, 228
manufacturing capital–output ratio
    and capital–labour ratio 131
Matsushita 70
micro-corporatism 61
NEC 70
newly industrializing countries 362
Nippon Steel Corporation 85
Nissan 70, 74
nominal formation, changing 41
nominal wage and consumer price 39
Organization for Economic
    Cooperation and Development
    19, 20, 78
    convergence theory 63
    Golden Age in retrospect 25, 27,
        28, 29, 32
    1970s breakdown 34, 38
    1990s configurations 53, 58, 60
oyakata skilled workers 92, 93
post-Fordism 354
post-Fordist professional relations 352
quality control 96, 99, 100
Red Purge 94
Rules of Employment (under Labour
    Standards Law) 80
shop floor organization and
    technology 95–102
social cohesion problems 364
Sony 70
and South Korea 122, 125, 126
Spring Offensive 76
stoppage incidence 135
Toyota 70, 74, 97, 98

unemployment and wages 42
wage share stability 26
work week and accident rate 121
workers' bargaining power 49
see also Japanese Occupation *under*
  Malaysia
Jean Xiong 332
Jomo, K.S. 9, 12, 186–236, 360
Jones, L.P. 118, 119
Juillard, M. 43
Juran, J.M. 99
just-in-time
  Hungary 300, 301
  Japan 96, 97, 98, 99, 100
  Malaysia 189, 227

Kalecki, M. 350, 351
Kalmarian 8, 14, 54–6, 352–4, 358, 362
  future capital–labour relations 363–7
Kamata, S. 79
Kang, K. 120, 122, 130
Kantrow, A.M. 96
Katz, L. 88
Kelkar, V.L. 263
Kemény, I. 284
Kenney, M. 85, 98
Keynes, J.M. 349
  see also Keynesianism
Keynesianism 63
  future capital–labour relations 350
  Organization for Economic
    Cooperation and Development
    countries 21, 27, 33, 34, 36, 43,
    44, 50
  post-Golden Age 1, 4, 5, 7, 16
  see also neo
Khong How Ling 189
Kidd, Y.A. 77
Kim, H. 116, 124, 125
Kim, L. 125
Kissinger, H. 330
Klau, F. 36
Kobrin, C. 60
Koike, K. 28, 72, 91, 95
Köllö, J. 12, 13, 14, 15, 282–315, 325,
  346, 356, 358
Kondratieff depression 46
Koo, S. 125
Korea
  Fordism 357

future capital–labour relations 367
Korean War 209, 322
macroeconomic constraints 365, 366
social cohesion problems 364
see also North; South
Kornai, J. 282, 285, 295, 356
Koshiro, K. 72, 76, 77, 80
Kostin, L. 308
Kovács, G.J. 311
Kremp, E. 36, 40
Kreye, O. 126
Krishnaswami, C. 248
Krueger, A. 111
Krugman, P. 40
Kubitschek, J. 361
Kumar, R. 263
Kurien, C.T. 275
Kuznets, S.S. 274

Laffer curve 34
Laky, T. 311
Lamounier, B. 160
Lampert, N. 291
Latin America 19
Lawrence, R.Z. 60
Lazonick, B. 8, 14, 27, 28
Lazonick, W. xii, 70–105, 186, 354
Le Dem, J. 24, 29
Le Ven, M. 162, 163, 166
Leborgne, D. 35
Lee, J.W. 122, 142
Lee, K.B. 138
Lee, K.U. 139
Leibenstein, H. 112
Lenin, V.I. 355, 356
Levine, S. 91
Lew, D. 60
Lewisian 355, 356, 359, 361, 362
Lim, T.G. 190
Lipietz, A. 8, 14, 15, 17, 21, 35, 53, 123,
  189, 345–70
Locovici, S. 36
Loveman, G. 52, 53
Lu Yun 332
Luedde-Neurath, R. 127
Lutz, B. 32

McCraw, T.K. 74, 85
macroeconomics policy project 1–3
Maddison, A. 22, 72

Mahathir Mohamad government 12, 185,
  186, 187, 188, 230, 234
Mahon, R. 351, 364
Makela, V. 286
Malaysia 185–236
  Alliance period 193
  Asian Development Bank 227, 233
  Axis threat 191, 208
  and China 189–90, 193, 208
  Chinese 197, 200–201, 202–3
    employment status 194, 196, 198
    political factors 231
    trade union membership 210, 211
  Communist Party of Malaya (CPM)
    191, 208
  Congress of Unions of Employees in
    Public and Allied Civil Services
    (CUEPACS) 188
  Consumer Price Index (CPI) 207
  Dravidians 190
  and Dutch East Indies 190, 208
  and East Asia 226, 234, 236
  and Eastern Europe 231, 284
  economic crisis 227–8
  Electrical Industry Workers' Union
    (EIWU) 187
  Emergency 192, 204
  employment by sector and ethnicity
    198
  Employment Ordinance (1955) 204
  employment status 194–5, 196, 197,
    198
  and Europe 208
  Federal Industrial Development
    Authority 229
  Federated Malay States 191, 192
  First World War 192
  Fordism 357
  General Agreement on Tariffs and
    Trade (GATT) 231
  General Labour Unions (GLU) 230
  General System of Preferences (GSP)
    187
  and Germany 208, 226
  Golden Age 224, 233
  Great Crash of 1929 190
  Great Depression 190, 191, 208
  Harris Solid State 188
  Highland Highway 234
  Hindu Tamils 190
  historical perspective of
    capital–labour relations 189–204
  and Hong Kong 231
  Independence 192, 193, 207, 209,
    211, 217, 224, 234
  and India 189–90, 191, 208
  Indians 195–8, 200–203, 210, 211, 245
  and Indonesia 189, 191, 204, 207,
    208, 217, 230
  industrial disputes 215–24
  Industrial Incentives Act 229
  Industrial Relations Act (1967) 204
  internal developments 224–7
  Internal Security Act 187
  international division of labour,
    changing 229–31
  International Labour Organization
    188, 233
  International Monetary Fund 227, 233
  International Tin Agreement 227
  and Japan 85, 185, 186, 187, 189, 208,
    209, 226, 228
  Japanese Occupation 190, 191, 192
  just-in-time 189, 227
  KL Telecommunications Tower 234
  and Korean War 209
  labour force *see* Peninsular
  labour law and policy, post-war 204–8
  Labour Minister 188
  Labour Party of Malaya 209
  'Look East' policy 185, 186, 187,
    233, 234
  macroeconomic constraints 365, 366
  and Malacca 192
  Malayan People's Anti-Japanese
    Army (MPAJA) 209
  Malayan Trade Unions Council
    (MTUC) 209
  Malays 194, 198, 200–201, 202–3,
    210
  Malaysian Airlines System (MAS)
    187, 205–6
  Malaysian Business Council 188
  Malaysian (formerly Federal)
    Industrial Development
    Authority 205
  'Malaysian Incorporated' policy 185,
    186
  Malaysian Labour Organization
    (MLO) 188

Malaysian Trade Unions' Congress (MTUC) 187, 188
mass production to flexible specialization 232
and Middle East 207, 225, 228
Ministry of Labour 210, 211, 213, 215, 216, 218, 220, 222
Mitsubishi 230
National Union of Bank Employees (NUBE) 188
National Union of Plantation Workers (NUPW) 187, 217, 229, 230
New Economic Policy 192, 212
New International Economic Order (NIEO) 231
newly industrializing countries 206, 360
1947 Census 196, 197
1957 Census 192, 193, 194, 196, 197, 200
1970 Census 192, 193, 194, 196, 197
Organization for Economic Cooperation and Development 228
Pacific War 208
Penang 187, 192
Peninsular 192, 199, 207, 208, 228
    employment status 196, 197, 198
    labour force 200–201, 202–3
    strikes 216, 218–19, 220–21, 222–3
    trade union membership 210, 211, 213, 214, 215
and Philippines 189, 207
Pioneer Industries Ordinance (1950s) 229
Plaza II agreements 226
political factors, exogenous 231–2
Proton 230
quality control circles 186, 187
RCA *see* Harris Solid State
research and development 232
Second Industrial Revolution 187
and Singapore 207, 225, 226, 231
Sino–Malaysian business community 185
social cohesion problems 364
Social Security Organization (SOCSO) 205–6
and South Korea 185, 186, 228

and Southeast Asia 231
Sri Jaya bus company 187
stoppage incidence 135
Straits Settlements 190, 192
strikes *see under* Peninsular
and Taiwan 226, 231
and Thailand 189, 207
Third World standards 231–2
Trade Disputes Ordinance (1949) 204
trade union membership 208–15
Trade Union Ordinance 204
Transport Equipment Industry Employees' Union 187, 230
Transport Workers' Union (TWU) 187
'tripartism' 229, 234
Unfederated Malay States 192
and United Kingdom 185, 186, 191, 192, 208, 209, 210, 229, 230
United Malayan Estate Workers' Union (UMEWU) 217
United Motor Works (UMW) 206
and United States 187, 226, 231
and Uruguay 231
Volcker-triggered interest rate increase 225
West Coast Land Reclamation Scheme 234
World Bank 227, 233
Malthus, T./Malthusianism 21
Mao Zedong 13, 319, 320, 323, 325, 326, 330, 334, 340
    see also Maoism/Maoist
Maoism/Maoist 320, 321, 322–30, 331, 359
Marglin, S.A. 18, 103, 112, 124, 284
Marsden, D. 27
Marshall plan 349
Maruani, M. 29
Marx, K./Marxism 63
    China 319, 323, 326, 337
    future capital–labour relations 346, 360, 362
    Japan 88, 89
    post-Golden Age 1
    see also neo
Mathews, J. 364
Mathur, A.N. 269
Mathur, D.C. 251
Mazier, J. 26
Mazumdar, D. 243

Meshchorkin, A. 307
Mexico 121, 135
Meyer-Zu Schlochtern, F.J.M. 45
Middle East 207, 225, 228
Mincer, J. 72
Ministry of Finance 40
Ministry of Labour 33
    Brazil 153, 158, 159, 160, 181
    Malaysia 210, 211, 213, 215, 216,
        218, 220, 222
    South Korea 116, 124, 130, 132, 134,
        137, 140
Mishchenko, V.T. 293
Mistral, J. 21, 36, 40
Mittelstadt, A. 36
Mjoset, L. 28
Mohan, R. 256
Monappa, A. 249
Moon, C. 118
Moore, J. 94
Morikawa, H. 91
Moskoff, W. 294, 302
Mut, I. 186

Nagaraj, R. 244, 261, 263, 272
Naughton, B. 327, 335
Nehru, J. 254
neo-Fordist/Fordism 57, 58, 60
neo-Keynesianism 70
neo-Marxism 70
neo-Schumpeterian 34
neo-Taylorism
    future capital–labour relations 352–3,
        357–9, 362–7
    Organization for Economic
        Cooperation and Development
        countries 54, 55
    post-Golden Age 14, 15
    rejuvenated 54
    Social-Democratic 54
Netherlands 363
'New Industrial Divide' 50
New International Economic Order
    (NIEO) 231
'new unionism' *see* Brazil
newly industrializing countries 360–62
    future capital–labour relations 367
    macroeconomic constraints 366
    Malaysia 206
    productivism 363

South Korea 125
Nixon, R. 33, 330
Noble, D. 27, 58, 101
nominal wage deindexing 39
North America 50
    see also Canada; United States
North, D. 111
North Korea 346

O'Brien, P. 74, 85
Odaka, K. 73, 75
Ohno, K. 122, 128
Ohno, T. 96
Okayama, R. 91, 93
Okuda, K. 193
Oliver, N. 85, 98
Olivera, J.H.G. 295
Organization for Economic Cooperation
    and Development (OEDD) 18–64,
    346
    Brazil 164
    breakdown in 1970s 32–53
        adverse and converging pressures
            44–6
        corporatisms 46–60
        historical outline 33–8
        structural changes 50–53
    capital–labour compromise 53
    capital–labour restructuring 47
    connective bargaining 35
    convergence theory 63–4
    defensive strategies 35
    Fordism to alternative capital–labour
        relations 57
    Fordist capital–labour relation,
        economic trends 45
    Fordist capital–labour relations
        changes in components 38–44
        changing pattern 36–7
    Fordist compromise 30–31
    Fordist hypothesis 23
    Golden Age 349, 350
    Golden Age in retrospect 20–32
        Fordist capital–labour relation 22–7
        Fordist compromise 20–22
        national brands 27–32
    Japan 78
    Kondratieff depression 46
    labour contract changes and worker
        categories 52

Malaysia 228
market mechanisms 59
'New Industrial Divide' 50
1990s configurations and issues
    18–20, 53–63
    alternative capital–labour relations
        53–6
    national trajectories 60–63
    strategic choices 56–9
    training organization 56
nominal formation, changing 41
nominal wage and consumer price 39
offensive strategies 38
post-Fordism 354
scientific management 53
Social Democratic 48, 50, 59, 62
South Korea 142–3
strategies for adapting capital–labour
    relation 35
unemployment impact on wages 42
wage formations 35
wage share, stability of 26
welfare and Keynesian state 35
work organization 35
workers' bargaining power 49
Organization of Petroleum Exporting
    Countries (OPEC) 33
organization and methods 348
Orléan, A. 28
Orwell, G. 291

Paguman, S. 206, 236
Pakistan 263
Páll, A. 300, 301
Papola, T.S. 242, 272
Parish, W. 330
Park, K.-K. 120
Park, S.-I. 120, 122, 130, 135
Park, C.-H. 118, 119, 133, 134
Parmer, J. 191
Pastore, J.H. 171
Peitchinis, S.G. 55
Petit, P. 40
Philippines 77, 135, 189, 207
Phillips curves 28
Pietsch, A.J. 302
Piore, M.J. 25, 26, 40, 43, 50, 364
Poh, P.P. 185
Poland 286–8, 296, 298, 299, 302, 304,
    312

'associations' or 'kombinats' 301
average day of year composition
    (adult men) 295
Iron Age 356, 358
KOR 291
selected indicators 303
social cohesion problems 365
Solidarity 291, 297
work time, paid holidays and overtime
    rates 293
see also with Hungary
Popov, G. 307
Poret, P. 30
Porter, M. 40
post-Fordism 351–4, 354–62
China and India 358–60
consistency problems 362–6
Iron Age, rise and fall of 355–8
newly industrializing countries
    360–62
post-Fordist professional relations 352
post-Golden Age 1–17
current environment 14–15
macroeconomics policy project 1–3
recent developments 15–17
turmoil in capital–labour relations 3–6
Pura, R. 185
Pyo, H. 116, 131

quality control
Japan 96, 99, 100
Malaysia 186, 187
South Korea 122, 125

Rääkk, V. 308
Racz, S. 296
Ralle, P. 40
Ramaswamy, E.A. 246, 248, 250, 251,
    260, 265, 268
Ramaswamy, U. 246, 250
Ranis, G. 125
Rao, J.M. 13, 14, 238–78, 346, 359, 360
Reagan, R. 367
reform and system change *see* China
Rehmus, C. 48, 50
Reich, M.R. 72, 73
Rema Devi 189
research and development 162
Eastern Europe 302
Malaysia 232

South Korea 125, 144
Révész, G. 288, 294
Rhee, S. 117, 118
Ricardo, D. 355, 365
Riskin, C. 13, 14, 319–43, 359
Rivlin, A. 32
Robinson, A. 241
Rodan, G. 187
Rodrigues, L.M. 159
Romer, P. 59
Roos, D. 58
Roosevelt, T. 349
Rosenberg, S. 48
Rostow, W.W. 355
Roumania 287, 288, 292, 298, 299, 302,
    304–6, 312
  CMEA countries 303
  Iron Age 358
  selected indicators 303
  Self-Management Act 305
  work time, paid holidays and overtime
      rates 293
Rowthorn, R. 24, 27, 32, 38, 43, 48
Rudolph, L. 247, 255, 265
Rudolph, S. 247, 255, 265
Ryder, W.J. 187

Sabel, C.F. 40, 50, 364
Sabóia, J. 155, 156
Sachs, J. 25, 48
SaKong, I. 118, 119
Samant, D. 265
Sampson, S. 306
Sanger, D.E. 76
Sapir, J. 356
Sarfati, H. 60
Saturnian 54, 55, 56
Sawada, S. 72
Saxonhouse, G.R. 77
Scandinavia 28, 351
  future capital–labour relations 366
  Iron Age 358
  macroeconomic constraints 365
  Organization for Economic
      Cooperation and Development
      32
  see also Finland; Sweden
SCAP *see* Supreme Commander of the
    Allied Powers
Schmidt, H. 34

Schmitter, P. 60
Schor, J.B. xii, 1–17, 18, 25, 44, 112
Schroeder, G. 292
Schultze, C. 60
Schumpeter, J. 63
  see also neo-Schumpeterian
Schwarz, S. 286
Sedlacek, G.L. 167
Sen, A. 258
Sengenberger, W. 52, 53
Sethi, R. 247, 252
Shaiken, H. 58, 101
Sheard, P. 75
Sherlock, S. 268
Shewhart, W.A. 99
Shimada, H. 76
Shimokawa, K. 75
Shirai, T. 71, 75
Sillaste, J. 308
Simon, R. 86
Simonsen, M.H. 166
Singapore 192
  and India 263
  and Malaysia 207, 225, 226, 231
  work week and accident rate 121
Siti Rohani Yahya 189
Skurkhok, S. 307
Smith, A. 22
Smitka, M. 75
Social Democratic 61, 62
  compromise 48, 59
  model 50
  see also Fordist/Fordism; Taylor,
      F.W./Taylorism
Sonyism 54, 55
South Asia 19
South Korea 111–46
  agricultural terms of trade 139
  authoritarian capital–labour relations
      111, 112, 117–25
    intra-firm control of labour:
        authoritarian paternalism
        121–4
    labour-market institutions and
        wage formation 119–21
    state and labour repression 117–19
    system of production and
        Taylorism 124–5
  authoritarian capital–labour relations
      breakdown 131–8, 138–45

democratization, politics of 138–40
labour protests 1970s 132–3
labour protests 1980s and
    economic crisis 133–4
new independent unionism
    characteristics 135–8
Organization for Economic
    Cooperation and Develop-
    ment experience 142–3
working class, increase in strength
    in 140–42
authoritarian capital–labour relations
    and export-led industrialization
    125–31
Japan model, comparison with
    129–31
macroeconomic structure 126–9
Bank of Korea 113
'Big Push' 114
BOK 127, 139, 144
capital intensity and labour-market
    characteristics 116
capital–output ratio and capital–labour
    ratio in manufacturing 131
chaebols 118, 134, 136, 138, 139, 145
Chemical Workers' Union 136
Chun-no-hyup 135
Chunpyong 117
Daewoo Apparel Textile Company 134
Daewoo Motor Company (DMC)
    133–4, 137
Economic Planning Board 113–16,
    127, 132, 137, 140, 141
employment
    adjustment 130
    share of formal sector 116
    structure 114, 115
export-led growth indicators 113
Factory Saemaul Movement (FSM)
    122, 125, 133
Federation of Korean Trade Unions
    117, 118, 119, 122, 130, 132,
    133, 135
Financial Workers' Union 136
General Motors 134, 137
Grand Conservative Coalition 146
gross domestic product 113, 144
gross national product 113
Hyundai Heavy Industries Company
    123

Hyundai Motor Company 124
Hyundai shipyard strike 137
and India 263
industrialization and wage labour
    113–16
    export-led 113–15
    labour-market segmentation
        115–16
and Japan 85, 125, 126
Korea Employers' Association (KEA)
    122, 130
Korea Labour Institute (KLI) 132, 144
Korean Alliance of Genuine Trade
    Unions (KAGTU) 135
Korean Central Intelligence Agency
    (KCIA) 118–19, 121
labour disputes 134
Labour Management Council 122
labour rights 111
and Malaysia 185, 186, 228
management rights 111
manufacturing 128, 137, 139, 141
Metal Workers' Union 136
Ministry of Labour 116, 124, 130,
    132, 134, 137, 140
Ministry of Science and Technology
    144
National Employers' Association 137
National Security Commission 119
newly industrializing countries 125,
    360, 362
POSCO 125
productivity and wages in
    manufacturing 127
quality control 122, 125
remuneration system of production
    workers 122
research and development 125, 144
Seoul 123, 141
social expenditure in central
    government expenditure 120
Spring Wage Offensive 120
stoppage incidence 135
system of production 112
system of rights 112
Taylorism 124
technology of production 112
Textile Workers' Union 136
unemployment and underemployment
    rates 140

union membership 132, 136
and United States 130
United Workers' Union 136
wage bargaining settlements by size
    of employer 144
wage determination 111
wages and profits 112
work week and accident rate 121
World Bank 120
Young Chang Musical Instrument
    Company 137
Southeast Asia 144, 359
Souza, A. 160
Soviet Union 298, 306–8, 312
    'associations' or 'kombinats' 301
    brigadnii podrjad system 307
    and China 319–20, 323, 325, 326,
        330, 331, 334
    'everyday power' and legal
        deprivation 285, 286, 287, 288,
        289, 291, 294
    Fordism 357
    future capital–labour relations 366
    glasnost 306
    goszakaz state orders 306, 308
    hozraschet system 306
    Iron Age 358
    Kirghizia 292
    Latvia 292
    Leningrad 308
    Ministry of Finance 306
    1980s crisis and modernization 299,
        301, 302
    perestroika 306
    post-Fordism 355, 359
    reforms 304
    selected indicators 303
    Tallin 308
    work time, paid holidays and overtime
        rates 293
Stalin, J./Stalinism 312, 325, 355, 358,
    359, 365
Stalk, G. Jr 105
Standing, G. 28, 188, 230, 233
Staniszkis, J. 297
Steinberg, B. 43
Strah, B. 28, 30
Streeck, W. 32, 56, 59, 60
Sugeno, K. 84
Sundaram, K. 243

Sundrum, R.M. 242, 246, 258
Supreme Commander of the Allied
    Powers (SCAP) 94
Suzuki, Y. 86
Sweden 346
    and Eastern Europe 286
    Fordist capital–labour relation 24, 37,
        45
    Fordist compromise variants 31
    future capital–labour relations 367
    and India 255
    and Japan 75
    labour contract and worker categories
        52
    nominal formation, changing 41
    nominal wage and consumer price 39
    Organization for Economic
        Cooperation and Development
        19, 26–9, 32, 38, 43, 46, 48, 58,
        63
    post-Fordism 354
    post-Fordist professional relations 352
    Social Democratic 61
    unemployment and wages 42
    wildcat strikes 50
    workers' bargaining power 49
Switzerland 351
Sziráczki, G. 289

Taira, K. 243
Taiwan 226, 231, 319, 363
Tanzer, A. 86
Tavares de Almeida, M.H. 172
Taylor, F.W. 2, 100
    see also Taylorism
Taylorism xii
    Brazil 153, 162, 164–9
    Eastern Europe 290, 291, 299, 300, 312
    future capital–labour relations 359
        Golden Age 348, 349, 351
        Iron Age 355, 356, 358
        newly industrializing countries 361
        post-Fordism 352, 353, 354
    India 239, 244, 245, 246, 248, 260,
        269–70, 275
    Malaysia 227, 232, 235, 236
    Organization for Economic
        Cooperation and Development
        countries 28, 30–31, 53, 54, 55,
        56

post-Golden Age 1–13 *passim*, 15
primitive 357, 359, 360, 362, 364
South Korea 123, 124, 125, 129
Tendulkar, S.D. 243
Thailand 85, 135, 189, 207
Thatcher, M. 367
Therborn, G. 48
Third World 285, 298, 299, 346, 349
Thouluc, H. 28
Tímár, J. 288, 293, 294, 302
Tokugawa 77
Tomita, I. 86
Toyotism 51, 54–8, 62, 63, 352, 354, 362
Trilateral Commission 349
Tsuchiya, K. 72
Tsuru, T. 36, 40
Tsurumi, E. 77

Uddevallist 8, 54, 55, 56, 57, 62, 63
Unger, J. 343
United Kingdom 346
    and China 332
    and Eastern Europe 286
    economic trends affecting capital–
        labour relations 45
    Fordist capital–labour relation 24, 37
    Fordist compromise variants 31
    future capital–labour relations 366,
        367
    Golden Age 350, 351
    hybrid 61
    and Japan 71, 72, 89, 90, 98, 99
    labour contract and worker categories
        52
    macroeconomic constraints 365
    and Malaysia 185, 186, 191, 192, 208,
        209, 210, 229, 230
    nominal formation, changing 41
    nominal wage and consumer price 39
    Organization for Economic
        Cooperation and Development
        19, 20
        capital–labour nexus 22, 25, 28, 29
        1970s breakdown 34, 38, 40, 43,
            44, 51
        1990s configurations 59
    post-Fordism 354
    post-Fordist professional relations 352
    social cohesion problems 364
    stoppage incidence 135

unemployment and wages 42
wage share stability 26
workers' bargaining power 49
United States 347
    Amalgamated Association of Iron and
        Steel Workers 91
    American Federation of Labour 91,
        93, 94
    American Federation of
        Labour–Congress of Industrial
        Organization (AFL–CIO) 187, 188
    Bureau of Labor Statistics 126
    Carnegie Steel 91
    and China 330, 332, 337, 340
    Congress 187
    decentralized and adversarial 61
    Fordist capital–labour relation 24, 37,
        45
    Fordist compromise variants 31
    future capital–labour relations 367
    General Electric 99
    Golden Age 349, 350, 351
    IBM 80
    and Japan 102–4
        employment environment 72, 73,
            74, 79–80, 81–2, 85, 86
        employment relations and
            technological change 89, 90,
            91–4, 95
        shop floor organization and
            technology 96–8, 99,
            100–101
    Kodak 80
    labour contract and worker categories
        52
    macroeconomic constraints 365, 366
    and Malaysia 187, 226, 231
    nominal formation, changing 41
    nominal wage and consumer price 39
    Organization for Economic
        Cooperation and Development
        19, 64
        Golden Age 20, 22, 25, 27, 28, 29
        1970s breakdown 34, 38, 40, 43,
            46, 48, 50, 51
        1990s configurations 55, 58, 59,
            60, 62, 63
    post-Fordism 354
    post-Fordist professional relations 352
    productivism 363

Public Peace Act (1900) 93
social cohesion problems 364
and South Korea 117, 130
stoppage incidence 135
unemployment and wages 42
wage share stability 26
work week and accident rate 121
workers' bargaining power 49
UNU/WIDER xii
Upham, F. 78
Uruguay 231

Vargas, G. 9, 152, 158, 361
Vermeulen, B. 247, 252
Vidal, J.F. 26
Vietnam 330, 346
Vogel, E. 72
Vogel, H. 302
Volcker, P. 5
Volvo plant 55
Vos, G.A. de 78

Wagatsuma, H. 78
Walder, A.G. 334, 340
Walentinowicz, A. 291
Walesa, L. 296

Walraff, G. 364
Walton, R.E. 103
Wan, H. Jr 111
Watanabe, S. 75
Western Europe 92, 298
Wiles, P. 285
Wilkinson, B. 85, 98
Wolleb, E. 29, 44
World Bank
China 340
Malaysia 227, 233
South Korea 111, 120
Woronoff, J. 77
Wu Honglin 335

Yakushiji, T. 95, 96
Yellen, J.L. 88
Yonekawa, S. 91
You, J.-I 1–17, 111–46, 346, 362
Yugoslavia 288, 292, 294
Yui, T. 91

Zhongguo Renkou Ditu Ji 333
Zhongguo Tongji Nianjian 333, 335, 336
Zhou Enlai 321
Zylberstagn, H. 171